ARCHITECTURE AND LANDSCAPE

The Design Experiment of the Great European Gardens and Landscapes

Clemens Steenbergen • Wouter Reh
with the co-operation of Gerrit Smienk

Prestel

This publication has been made possible by the financial support of the Dutch Foundation of Architecture.

First published in the Netherlands by THOTH Publishers, Prins Hendriklaan 13, 1404 AS Bussum, the Netherlands.
Tel. 035:6944144 Fax 035:6943266

Cover illustration Villa Cetinale (photograph by Hans Krüse), Villa Giulia (drawing by Bert van den Heuvel); back cover Vaux-le-Vicomte (drawing by Bastiaan Kwast)
Cover design and layout Hans Lemmens
Printing Mart.Spruijt bv, Amsterdam
Production editor Wim Platvoet

Library of Congress Cataloging-in-Publication Data

Steenbergen, Clemens
      Architecture and Landscape: The Design Experiment of the Great European
Gardens and Landscapes / Clemens Steenbergen, Wouter Reh
            p.   cm.
      Includes bibliographical references and indexes.
      ISBN 3-7913-1720-2 (alk. paper)
        1. Landscape architecture – Europe, Western – History.
2. Landscape design – Europe – History.   3. Urban landscape design – Europe – History.
4. Gardens – Europe – Design – History.   5. Europe – Western – Surveys. I. Steenbergen,
Clemens M.   II. Title.
SB470.55.E85R44   1996   96-38386
712'.094'0903 – dc20

Distributed outside the Netherlands and Belgium by:
Prestel-Verlag • Mandlstraße 26 • D-80802 Munich, Germany
Tel. (89) 38 17 09-0; Fax (89) 38 17 09-35
and 16 West 22nd Street, New York, NY 10010, USA
Tel. (212) 6 27 81 99; Fax (212) 6 27 98 66

Prestel books are available worldwide.
Please contact your nearest bookseller or write to either of the
above addresses for information concerning your local distributor.

ISBN 3-7913-1720-2

Printed on acid-free paper

CLEMENS M. STEENBERGEN (1946) is a landscape architect and since 1993 professor at the Faculty of Architecture at the Delft University of Technology. He has written various books and articles on architecture, landscape and urban design, including, in 1992, *Italian Villas and Gardens*, the first of this series. His dissertation *De stap over de horizon* (The Step over the Horizon, 1990) examines the technique and the architecture of the rational and formal scenic staging of the Italian Renaissance villa and the classic French garden, respectively.

WOUTER REH (1938) is a landscape architect and assistant professor at the Faculty of Architecture at the Delft University of Technology, as well as a one of Professor Steenbergen's colleagues. He runs his own design bureau and has several publications and design studies to his credit. His dissertation *Arcadia en Metropolis* deals with the theory and technique of pictorial landscape architecture in the 18th-century English landscape garden and 19th-century urban design.

Photographs
Unless otherwise credited, photographs are by Paul van der Ree, Wouter Reh, Gerrit Smienk, Clemens Steenbergen and Hans Krüse

Drawings
Ellen Bestebreurtje, Bert van den Heuvel, Christ Hochstenbach-Vanderheyden, Paul van der Ree, Sascha Schramm, Petrouschka Thumann, Tom Voorsluys, Henriëtte van der Werff, Daniëlle Wijnen

Digital 3D models
Produced under the direction of the Landscape Design Department of the Faculty of Architecture of Delft University of Technology (Wouter Reh, Clemens Steenbergen) and made by Wim Haan (New River landscape, Castle Howard), Bastiaan Kwast (Castle Howard, Stowe, Vaux-le-Vicomte, Thames Valley, London) and Hans van der Horst (Villa Medici, Tiber Valley, Rome, Seine Valley, Paris)

Measurements
Site measurements, in cooperation with the Dutch embassies in Rome and Paris as well as the respective villa owners, were carried out by Wim Kempen, Gerrit Smienk, Clemens Steenbergen, Tom Voorsluys and Freek Vos in collaboration with the Hogere Bosbouw en Cultuurtechnische School in Velp and the Faculty of Mathematics and Physical Geodesy of Delft University of Technology.

ACKNOWLEDGEMENTS

The idea of analysing and comparing the architectural principles underlying villa and landscape design as a continuity of change was born within the Landscape Design Department of the Faculty of Architecture and Urban Design at the Delft University of Technology. The idea for this book dates from 1984 and was supported by the then head of the department, Frans Maas. The first version was conceived and written by Clemens Steenbergen in collaboration with Rudi Kegel, Wouter Reh and Gerrit Smienk and was published in 1985. In this earlier phase, Wilfried van Winden and Willem Heesen also made important contributions. Since then, this book has been a work in progress for over a decade and the end is not yet in sight. On the contrary, there are various new plans in the pipeline.

The analytical tools for such a study have gradually become more detailed and precise; the overview more broad-based. The book's basic concept, however, of examining the techniques of rational, formal and pictorial scenic staging of the landscape remains the same. These are placed within a theoretical framework whereby, it is hoped, the conceptual development of landscape architecture and its relevance for contemporary design clearly come to the fore.

Major influences on the book's maturation were *De stap over de horizon* (1990), a dissertation by Clemens Steenbergen, the book *Italian Villas and Gardens* by Paul van der Ree, Gerrit Smienk and Clemens Steenbergen (1992) and *Arcadia en Metropolis* (1996), a dissertation by Wouter Reh. These influences are reflected in the authorship of the book's three major chapters. Steenbergen wrote chapters one and two, whereby the first chapter makes use of material written, in an earlier phase, with the assistance of Gerrit Smienk and Paul van der Ree. Wouter Reh wrote chapter 3.

We are indebted to the many people who, directly or indirectly, assisted in bringing this book to fruition. It would be impossible to mention by name all those who stimulated discussions and provided inspiration to make such an investigation possible – in the first instance our colleagues at the university of course. Their influence is difficult to trace precisely.

Many students were also involved with the research. Together with the authors they drew a number of the plans and axonometric projections included here. Our thanks to Enno Ebels, Jan Frederik Groos, Bert van den Heuvel, Christ Hochstenbach-Vanderheyden, Tom Voorsluys (chapters one and two), Ellen Bestebreurtje, Sascha Schramm, Petrouschka Thumann, Henriëtte van der Werff and Daniëlle Wijnen (chapter three), who made the analyse-drawings, which were often tiny wonders of economy, ingenuity and concentration. Wim Haan made the digital model of the New River landscape at Castle Howard, while Bastiaan Kwast and Hans van de Horst made colour digital models of the most important prototypes.

Lynn George translated the original Dutch text and edited several earlier translations by Marja Kramp and Paul Willcox that originally appeared in *Italian Villas and Gardens*. The final text was edited by Prestel Verlag and the authors.

For wordprocessing and other administrative tasks we were ably supported by Astrid Roos and the secretariat of the Urban Planning Study Group of the Faculty.

Hans Krüse of the Delft University of Technology was responsible for some of the photographs of Italian Villas reproduced in this book.

We owe a special debt to the many villa and garden owners who extended their hospitality to us during our visits, in particular to Signora Anna Mazzini (Villa Medici, Fiesole) and comte Patrice de Vogüe (Vaux-le-Vicomte). Carla van Vlaanderen and Pia 't Lam, both of the Istituto Olandese in Rome, A. Frangioni, the mayor of Fiesole, jonkheer Vegelin van Claerbergen, the Dutch ambassador to Paris and his secretary H.A. Barfoed were helpful in providing us with introductions to several villa and garden owners.

Wim Kempen and Freek Vos of the Hogere Bosbouw en Cultuurtechnische School in Velp, together with Gerrit Smienk and Clemens Steenbergen surveyed the Villa Medici in Fiesole, while the architect E. Baldari provided us with useful geographical information on Rome. The main axis at Vaux-le-Vicomte was surveyed by Tom Voorsluys and Clemens Steenbergen.

We are indebted to Kees van den Hoek of THOTH Publishers for his unshakable faith in this project. The Faculty of Architecture of Delft University of Technology provided us with many facilities. The extensive research underpinning this book forms part of various long-term study programmes, among others, of the Landscape Design and Urban Design study groups as well as the Research School for Design and Computation. We also wish to thank the Dutch Ministry of Education, Culture and Science whose sensible policy made the publication financially possible. Finally, a special thanks to Gerrit Smienk, director of the Amsterdam Academy of Architecture, who as co-author was involved from the very beginning with a systematic and critical analysis of the landscape design. It is partly thanks to him that this now belongs to the fine Dutch tradition of landscape architecture.

PREFACE

It was at the end of the seventies when a few students of the Faculty of Architecture at the Delft University of Technology made it known they would like 'to do something' on Italian villas. Nobody could have realized at the time that such a simple intention would have formed the starting point for an ongoing investigation into the fundamentals, vocabulary and cultural aspects of landscape architecture. At that moment there was no tradition of research into this field and it was almost an act of rebellion to expressly take villa architecture – described by several writers as *Herrschaftsarchitektur* – as a subject of study. However, the students' interest could be explained by the fact that they had just returned from Italy and were fascinated by the way in which art historians and other culturally minded described gardens according to a plan in which both the villa and the surrounding landscape were defined within an architectonic framework.

In retrospect – and certainly in the light of the presence of landscape architecture lecturers within the group of visiting architectural students, one can question whether the interest was purely coincidental. Within the architectonic and urban planning disciplines of the faculty, a design/analytical tradition had already evolved, while typological and morphological research, mainly developed by the Venetian School, provided starting points for a redefining of the architecture of the garden and the landscape. It is ultimately credit to the still small group of landscape architecture theorists that they took up the gaunlet and laid bare not only the roots of the discipline but also provided a framework within which the importance of current developments could be assessed.

It all began with the Italian villa, the opening of the medieval enclosed garden towards the landscape and the architectonic and cultural treatments of the topography within the scenic staging of casino, garden and landscape. The fact that Rome's urban landscape was able to be approached from this architectonic standpoint formed a logical second step in the first phase of the study. It is mainly the figure of Palladio, however, who, within the tradition of the still undivided discipline, played an important role. Both 17th-century French landscaping and 18th-century English landscape art can be traced back to the scenic staging of his agricultural villas in the Veneto landscape. Little imagination is needed to observe how his control over a large-scale perspective must have influenced the almost relentness number of masterly compositions by Le Nôtre, the 17th-century French landscape architect. The *Grande Axe* of Paris along the Seine is evidence of the force of the well-ordered mind in that after three centuries it still influences the development of the metropolis. As with the Palladio villa, English landscape art was born out of the concept of the garden as an autonomous space 'dissolving' into the surrounding landscape. In the English garden, movement through the landscape itself is an affirmation of the modern-day man's zest for life. The classical symbols in the landscape also make this an exercise for the mind, in keeping with 18th-century cultural thinking.

It has taken almost 15 years to compile this extensive account on the development of the vocabulary describing the three most important periods in western landscape architecture, which took place on the eve of our modern age. This field of study was always intended to benefit design teaching but there was also a gradual awareness that never before had such a thorough and complete study of the foundations and experimental developments within the discipline been undertaken. This body of knowledge is now available to architects, urban planners, landscape architects and to anyone else who is interested in the richness of the landscape. The laying bare of the architectonic roots of landscape design contributes in no small measure to the new enthusiasm for landscape architecture as a design discipline.

Gerrit Smienk

CONTENTS

Chapter Three **THE GEOMETRY OF THE PICTURESQUE** THE 18TH-CENTURY
ENGLISH LANDSCAPE GARDEN

THE GARDEN AS AN ARCHITECTONIC LABORATORY

'See Lipsius', Langius said to his pupil, 'this is the true meaning of the garden: peace, seclusion, thinking, reading and writing'.
Justus Lipsius, *De constantia in publicis malis*, 1584

Between history and experiment

In antiquity the tomb-strewn 'holy way', just outside the city limits, indicated the route through the landscape to the Elysium, the dwelling place of the gods. In Christian tradition the garden was the ultimate symbol of paradise, the 'origin' of the human world. A theme of landscape architecture that has been used consistently throughout the years is the story of Creation. At the same time, however, it represents an experimental tradition in which the *horror vacui* is overcome and the public domain is conquered. What has 300 years of western landscape architecture produced?

THE DISCOVERY OF THE LANDSCAPE

At the beginning of the Renaissance, between 1458 and 1462, Cosimo de' Medici had a villa built for his son, Giovanni, at Fiesole in Florence. The local, steeply curved slope of the Arno valley was made habitable by an imposing construction of terraces, some 100 metres long, and by retaining walls, roughly 10 metres high. Given the site conditions and the available financial resources, these terraces were made as large as possible. The surfaces conformed to a geometric system of squares. Within this geometric grid the interplay of the natural measurements and alignments of the terrain with the size of the construction could be controlled. By using perspective, the rational grid was projected over the space. From the interior the horizon was shifted, by means of terraces, loggias, arcades and flights of steps, towards the spatial depth of the panoramas. Natural elements like rocks, undergrowth and water had a double role. Their material presence represented the physicalness of nature while their form alluded to the natural archetypes of the mythical world.

In this example the rational matrix is laid over the natural landscape. The relationship between humankind and nature is treated within this system of measurements and proportions. The landscape elements that fall within this matrix are ordered and transformed. The structure of the landscape architecture was a sort of theatrical production; the villa walls were broken through, while the horizon formed the visual boundary.

CONQUERING SPACE

Two hundred years later, between 1656 and 1661, Nicolas Fouquet, Louis XIV's finance minister, commissioned André le Nôtre to landscape some 1,500 hectares of land from scratch. This was to be his new residence at Vaux-le-Vicomte in Paris. Villages were removed, hills levelled and rivers shifted. The projected one-kilometre-long formal garden, a broad and straight strip with large level parterres in an undulating terrain, necessitated large-scale excavations. Yet by shrewdly positioning the central axis diagonally through the morphology of the river valley, the shifting of earth was minimalized. By correcting the composition, this asymmetry was then brought into balance with the garden's formal bilateral symmetry. The natural, basin shaped landscape and the flow of water through the terrain were optimally exploited by the diagonal positioning of the principle axis. The resulting effect of spatial depth was artificially accentuated by a perspectively manipulated sequence of surfaces and screens. This gave the optical illusion of undistorted spatial depth and completely controlled geometric order. Seeping, spraying, tumbling and reflecting, the water – programmed by a painstakingly created natural hydraulic system – moved through this mysterious setting.

This second example illustrates the scope of the rational construction of the landscape architecture. One line of the geometric grid was highlighted, extended and became functional as a telescope, as it were, aimed at the horizon. By it being meticulously sited within the context, this looking device became an autonomous work of art.

THE 'ESCAPE' FROM THE ARCHITECTONIC SYSTEM

A century later in 1772 Horace Walpole, one of the 18th century's eminent landscape design critics, invited his readers to loose themselves in the 'great scenic creation' of Castle Howard, the 'masterpiece of the Heroic Age of English landscape architecture'. He continued: 'I never was so agreeably astonished in my days, as with the first vision of the whole place [...] nobody [...] had told me that I should at one view see a palace, a town, a fortified city, temples on high places, woods worthy of being each a metropolis of the Druids, vales connected to hills by other woods, the noblest lawn in the world fenced by half the horizon, and a mausoleum that would tempt one to be buried alive. In short I have seen gigantic places before but never a sublime one.' The pivot of this composition was an Arcadian landscape in which architectonic monuments were scenically positioned in each other's line of sight. The Temple of the Four Winds, the Mausoleum and the Howard Pyramid, which, in size and shape, were in keeping with the site's morphology, formed a natural amphitheatre. The works of art are observed as a series of open-air stage sets in which a woodland, running water and bridges all play a role.

The composition of this third example eluded from the logic of the rational and formal schemes, which were only obvious in fragments of the plan. The garden plan as a whole dissolves into the physical and geographical lines of force of the natural landscape.

This example brings us back to the beginning of our tour of classical influences, which also impinge upon the landscape architecture of our own time. Rational architecture orders the landscape but the reverse also seems to be the case. Landscape never allows itself to be entirely captured in formal abstractions.

HISTORICAL AND EXPERIMENTAL RESEARCH

The architect, Bernard Tschumi, once said in an interview: 'In the second half of the seventies there was a huge gap in architecture. There were two diverging movements. Some sought refuge in the history of architecture. In order to redefine the discipline they began emphasizing the memory, the typology and the morphology of the cities. In this way they returned to the centre. But I felt – perhaps because of inclination or instinct – that you have to go as far as you can. In the centre I would never find anything new. I can break new ground on the edge, in the margin. And what is the margin of architecture? It is the point where it comes into contact with other areas (rather than disciplines) [...]. Because I operate on the boundaries, I believe I can ask the *real* questions. But if I had operated from the centre, from history, then I could only dig more deeply into that same centre.'

Does this indicate a dilemma in the development of a theory? Is there any point in returning to the past, to the core of professional practice, or should the margins be explored? Can a designer actually *learn* anything from history? Here one needs to distinguish between the dynamics of designing and the substance of the profession, the professional tradition. Designers – and this is revealed in the interview – are not driven by their knowledge, but by curiosity. On the other hand, knowledge of the profession is, in a broader sense, a prerequisite for properly understanding the issues of our own time and to interpret these within the terms of the profession. Perhaps studying history does not teach one how to design, but without a knowledge of history one cannot design.

The need to have an entire overview of the structure of landscape architecture also arises from a need to update the view on the basic premises of the profession. Here historical research and modern experimentation merge. Excursions are necessary, not only into the gardens, but especially into the mind itself – an exploring of the conceptual possibilities of landscape architecture, of one possible landscape architecture.

TYPOLOGY AND INVENTION

Regarding the question of how knowledge of the landscape garden tradition can be employed in contemporary design, the concept of 'type' plays a role. In several respects the form of one garden is like that of another; there is a 'typological' similarity amongst gardens. A 'type' can be perceived as a scheme, derived from a historic sequence of designs having a clear formal and functional resemblance. Until now the concept of 'type' was linked theoretically to the way the garden was constructed (a 'type' can be practically reproduced), but nowadays it is also associated with the technique of the design.

The architecture theorist Gulio Argan attempts to establish the role of typologies in the development of architectonic thinking. He sees them as abstract and reduced forms in which powers of understanding and imagination converge. According to Argan, a typology embodies a specific relationship to historical experience. By accepting a type, the designer takes existing general notions of imagery and by so doing acknowledges the ideological significance and content as a starting point for creating a new work. During the design process Argan presupposes continuity between the typological moment (tradition or convention) and the inventive moment (a break with tradition).

Anthony Vidler distinguishes three typologies, which assume different theoretical architectural meanings. The first is the construction taken from its origin in nature, distinguished by an ideal geometric order like Marc-Antoine Laugier's simple 'peasant hut'. The second appeared during the industrial revolution and coupled constructions with mechanized production, and considers architecture to be a simple question of technology, subject to the laws of mechanization and efficiency. This typology, like the first, is a logical outcome of development ideology of the Enlightenment. The typology of the Italian architects Aldo Rossi, Giorgio Grassi and Carlo

Aymonino regard Vidler as a 'third typology'. This one also turns to the past, albeit in another manner. Its aim is to encourage the use of structural analyses of urban building forms when designing, the premise that architectural rules can only be found and applied in architecture itself.

This study is an extension of the third typology, but there is one important difference. The gardens shown in this book are, first and foremost, 'prototypical' examples. In certain ways they are unique: each garden is a work of art which, to some extent, resists paraphrasing. For an explanation of the form, one needs to look within the garden itself. By comparing these prototypes conclusions can be drawn regarding the development of the formal idiom of landscape architecture, which can be seen as a series of interconnected 'formal' transformations. This enables the design tools to be isolated from their historical context and – disregarding typological categorization for the time being – to be understood as 'links' between the myriad forms of landscape architecture of the past and experimental design of today. The study of various gardens reveals the types of design tools utilized in landscape architecture and clarifies the various theoretical and technical steps of the design approach.

A 'CORSO DI DISEGNO'

Thomas Schumacher, a lecturer in architecture at the University of Maryland, says: 'I don't see anything in schools that have the pretension of training the avant-garde; a school must teach straightforward architectonic logic'. To illustrate his point he tells the story, borrowed from his dean, about two Wild West sharpshooters, one the teacher, the other the pupil. The latter challenges his teacher to a duel, with the words, 'I think I'm faster than you; you have taught me everything I know'. 'Yes', replies the mentor, 'but I haven't taught you everything *I* know'. Schumacher continues: 'The first generation of important fashionable names such as Le Corbusier, Wright and Aalto has been taught classicism in one form or another. They have learnt about it, they've gone on further but haven't taught it to us anymore.'

All things considered, Tschumi is wrong if he only focuses on the experimental and the exceptional. However, his argument is useful in that just focusing on typology has a numbing effect. Whether a study of historical examples contributes anything to design knowledge depends on the way in which one looks at the material. We can come to understand the dynamics of the designs and the thinking behind them by rediscovering the originality of historical garden concepts. The study, as it is understood here, brings about a 'decomposition' of the historical material, making it possible for us to recognize the design tools as original inventions, which can be transformed and employed again, once the dust of centuries has been wiped away. One can come to discover the mastery with which the landscape architects worked, by means of imaginary reenactment. In the world of chess, reenactment is quite common and is known as 'learning from the grandmasters'. Herein lies the deeper meaning and the actual purpose of research on landscape architecture. It implies departing from the romanticized preconception of historic examples in favour of 'unearthing' the dynamic and creative thinking process that lay behind them.

One could therefore read this book in an entirely different way. The aim of the study is to penetrate the dynamics of creative and experimental thought in landscape architecture. Of course, the original design process cannot be precisely reconstructed, as it is forever lost in history. But it can be brought to life by inviting the reader to 'redesign' in his own mind the gardens and the landscapes of this book. This will require of the reader a certain imagination to relate to the problems faced by the original designers. As a reward the reader might experience the beauty of the experiment and the landscape in a new way.

The landscape

The term 'landscape' has been interpreted in various ways throughout the ages, depending on the cultural, scientific and social context of a given time. Hidden behind this lies the development of the understanding of nature, time and space.

TOPOS AND LOCUS

The Italian poet Petrarch wrote that his *villetta* in France had two gardens, one dedicated to Apollo, who exemplified control and reason, and the other dedicated to Bacchus, who symbolized sensuality and instinct. This duality is fundamental to landscape architecture and can be related to various ideas on time and place.

The origins of the word *topos* are rooted in Greek mythology and refer to the natural landscape as the dwelling place of the gods. *Topos* is therefore a magical, or mythological, concept defined in the mythical landscape. It is labyrinthian and without scale: it has no geometric determinates. The Greek temple is the oldest, best-known architectonic form in which the *topos*, or site in the natural landscape, is linked to the *ieros odos*, or holy route.

The concept of rational space represented an entirely new modality that left the labyrinthian concept still intact. What is more, the one presupposed the other. In the villa design, labyrinthian space was consciously positioned next to the rational space. At Villa Lante, from around 1560, the *bosco* and the ceremonial garden were roughly the same size and were of equal importance. In the 17th century the labyrinth was elbowed out of the garden by the Baroque explosion in the main bilateral axis, but lived on in the magical tradition of the hydraulics and the playful games of the surrounding plantings. The early 18th-century English landscape garden revived the labyrinthian space and the *topos*.

The origin of the term *locus* is rooted in the *templum*, the mythical cross of the founding of a town and the design matrix of Roman cultivation. The *locus* is geometrically determined: it is the point in the rationally ordered agricultural landscape from which distance is measured and to which time is related. When the Romans founded a new city, a priest was present to mark out the terrain. He drew two orthogonal lines with his staff, one towards the Pole Star and the other parallel to the sun's path. This ritual stamped the city as a holy place, which represented nature's order. In Paris such an axis stretches across the River Seine where it intersects the strategic north to south route. The junction creates a town plan facing in a westerly direction along the Seine, and includes the Louvre, the Tuileries and the Champs-Élysées, respectively. The city grew rapidly; its boundaries were continually being extended, which prompted the question of how it should be kept under control. At the behest of the Sun King the landscape architect Le Nôtre assembled the various urban fragments along the Seine into a geometric spatial axis measuring some kilometres long. Its positioning was such that the axis eliminated the route along the banks of the Seine and took over its function as a main formal component of the urban morphology.

THE VILLA URBANA AND THE VILLA RUSTICA

In his *Quattro libri* Palladio drew perfectly organized agricultural villas which were to function simultaneously as ideal dwellings. They were used as working farms in the fertile Po Plains and were strategically sited at the junctions of roads and flowing water. This was practical, since during the reclamation of the Veneto in the 16th century the land was completely parcelled out, creating many such junctions. Positioned in the centre of the farmlands, the villa was easily accessible to the landowner, enabling efficient management of his estate. Nevertheless, capital investment was really only transferred from Venice to the countryside because of the cultural and architectonic dimension Palladio was able to contribute to the process of reclamation.

In keeping with the flatness of the terrain and the Roman parcelling out of land, Palladio advised laying out the villa roads according to military road-building principles – broad, paved and straight so that it was possible to survey great distances. He also advised lining the roads with trees and building them slightly higher than the fields to allow for a view. The importance Palladio attached to having unrestricted views is largely evident in the way he sited the agricultural villas on the intersection of these straight avenues. The avenue formed the axis of symmetry of the estate with the raised villa at the centre and the administrative offices and servants' quarters in the basement and side wings. While the avenue was a formal expression of the agricultural landscape, Palladio used the flight of steps, loggia, arcade and tympanum to present the *villa rustica* as also a *villa urbana*. He extracted classical architectonic elements from their military and sacramental context and placed them in a new environment. In this way a formal composition was fashioned, using selected functional elements of the farmland. By employing a Roman scheme, Palladio was able to lend a theatrical expression to the agricultural programme.

THE FORMAL LAYERING OF THE LANDSCAPE

It is possible to analyze the landscape as a 'build-up' of various systems or types of cultivation, the one laid out over the other and interacting with each other over time, as the result of a series of functional and morphological transformations. Agricultural landscape is a result of cultivation processes carried out on the natural landscape. Likewise, the urban landscape is a result of civil engineering processes on both the natural and farming landscape. The historical layering and the merging of nature's (geo)morphogenic system, agriculture's farming techniques and a city's civil engineering system comprise the structure of the urban landscape.

Besides this structure, upon closer examination the landscape reveals layering in its form, which is shaped by the endemic flora and fauna, cultivation, water supplies, road networks, land enclosure, buildings and garden architecture. The form of the natural landscape reflects its geological history but does not have any formal determination. The form of the agricultural landscape is the result of colonizing the natural landscape via a cultivation grid. That layer, in which the form has been most consciously determined, can be termed the architectonic landscape. This is evident in the implied formal components of the cultivation grid or is made specific as an architectonic definition of lines, points and surfaces within this. The landscape form can be explained in terms of three imaginary layers: the 'natural' landscape, the 'agricultural' landscape and the 'architectonic' landscape, respectively.

This stratification is not harmonious. The 'substructure' is not endlessly mirrored in the surface nor is the substratum always reflected in the form. Instead it is linked to a change in the nature of the formal transformation. Generally, a distinction can be made between direct adaption of the natural topography, architectonic transformations and visual references. Topographical adaption is of a technical nature and, in a landscape architectonic sense, is one or two dimensional, while architectonic transformations assume a three-dimensional, architectonically controlled form. Visual references are associative and they relate to the age or the history of the site.

Design and analysis

The German architecture theorist Paul Frankl (1914) assumed that designs are always a combination of traditional forms and new responses. He defined the architectonic spatial design as comprising four elements: the aim, the spatial form, plasticity and appearance. According to Frankl the 'aim' (*Zweckgesinnung*) indicates how the programme is dealt with and determines whether it takes on its own expressive features and contributes to the form. The 'spatial form' reveals how the programme is spatially accommodated, and whether it takes the form of an agglomeration of limited spaces or is comprised of subdivided unbounded space. 'Plasticity', or the 'shell', of the space reveals the extent to which a 'central force' binds the design together, or whether the construction's lines of force assume an autonomous position in the design. The 'appearance' (colour, texture, light) can be unequivocal or ambiguous, one image or several that say something about the design's meaning: whether it is monumental or can be understood in various contexts. Frankl's four elements are general concepts that systematically indicate the relationship between the various aspects of the architectonic design and one's perception thereof. Together they provide insight into the design's spatiality.

ASPECTS OF LANDSCAPE ARCHITECTONIC FORM

The design of the landscape architecture is arranged into various treatments in which specific design themes are utilized. The landscape design can be 'read' according to these themes and is generally identified by its 'basic form', or layout, resulting from the geometric rationalization of the topography, its 'spatial form', or the architectonic treatment of the landscape's three-dimensional space, its 'visual structure' in which the landscape's visual features are incorporated and its 'programme form', the spatial organization and interpretation of the programme. With the help of this interplay between the architectonic design and the landscape pattern can be studied further.

THE BASIC FORM

Every landscape architectonic design has its roots in the morphologic characteristics of the natural landscape, for instance, a site close to the sea, on a hilltop, in a vale or by a river. The topography of the medieval agricultural landscape was very much in keeping with the natural site conditions.

During the Renaissance Leonardo da Vinci experimented with a rationalization of the topography. He studied for instance the link between a geometric grid plan and a river's natural course. In this way the idea evolved that an ideal proportional system, a rational scheme of dimensions and proportions, could be derived in which the relationship between humankind and nature could be enhanced. In the Renaissance villa both the surrounding landscape and the positioning of the garden were determined by this architectonic design matrix. The interaction of the design matrix on the topography was established within the garden layout. In the French formal garden this design matrix was perspectively manipulated in order to create a three-dimensional landscape theatre along the garden's central axis. These design rules were imposed on the natural morphology; the topography of the agricultural landscape remained outside this formal system. The early 18th-century English landscape gardens were, without exception, based on rational and formal systems, which later on were often retained in the form of a 'hidden order'. The development of the subsequent landscape garden, however, witnessed a steady, yet progressive, move away from the geometric layout. The formal ordering of the matrix was transformed into a linking of rational and formal compositional fragments which were held together by the contours of the natural morphology.

THE SPATIAL DESIGN

The design of the 15th and 16th-century Italian villa demonstrates the architectonic unification of the villa, the city, the landscape and nature, in which the medieval concept of preserving separate realms was transcended. This *integrazione scenica* came about by framing the scenic and urban panoramas. In 17th-century French design the magic of three-dimensional space prevailed. Every aspect of the three-dimensional Grand Ensemble of house and garden was brought under one absolute system of design principles. The horizon was artificially brought within the garden boundary as in a stage set. In the 18th-century English landscape design the link with antiquity was restored and at the same time reconsidered. The agricultural landscape outside the garden was incorporated as an Arcadian landscape within the plan's horizon.

THE VISUAL STRUCTURE

While the concept of a secluded garden was preserved in the *giardino segreto* of the Renaissance garden, the villa garden reflects a fundamental change in attitude towards nature compared to that prevalent in the Middle Ages. Unspoilt nature became an essential component of the villa programme, a set for the nobility when sojourning in the countryside. Humanist poets, such as Petrarch, referred to Arcadia and the mythical garden of the gods in which natural elements, such as earth, water, plants and animals, were a fixed and expressive form of reality. Depictions of the Christian concept of paradise, such as Hercules in the garden of Hesperides, were linked to classical mythology. The transformation and architectonic treatment of such classical references in the villa's plan enhanced one's enjoyment of nature to the required intellectual and cultural level.

In the French formal garden, nature was depicted in contrasting features, like the parterre, the *tapis vert* and the forest, in a hierarchical sequence of increasing naturalness. Water was presented in a sequence that depicted an ever-diminishing rush of movement, ending as a reflecting pool on the horizon. In this manner nature was represented in the garden as a scientific classification system. The natural landscape was developed from 'spring to ocean' and symbolized the life cycle (birth, life, death) within the perimeters of the estate.

In the 18th-century English landscape garden, nature in all its physicality and growing power is set against 'culture'. Culture was represented in the iconography of classicistic structures: nature as a living organism, determined by the shape of the terrain, the various arrangements of plantings and running water.

THE PROGRAMME FORM

During the Italian Renaissance the delight taken in the Arcadian landscape was part of the urban culture. The classical stoa, previously part of the cultural centre, was shifted to the villa outside the town. Urban pursuits and agrarian production came together in the *villa rustica*. In the 17th-century French garden the agrarian landscape was banished from the line of sight: wide-ranging forests with avenues and radial road networks formed the ceremonial decor for hunting and urban outdoor amusements. The garden's axial zone was the stage on which the official ceremonies took place, while recreation was incorporated into the surrounding *bosquets*. In the English landscape garden, forestry, often for speculative reasons, was the most important, economically speaking, followed by hunting and fishing. During the 18th century a scientific approach evolved with regard to horticulture and agriculture, which was propagated by the owners of the country estates and contributed to their economy.

The garden as a mirroring of art

The Dutch writer Gerrit Komrij refers to the link between the concept of the garden and the history of ideas and discusses how the controversy between these ideas is reflected in the gardens of the 16th, 17th and 18th centuries. 'In the conflict between English and French gardens, which both aimed at creating a world from the garden, and in the emergence of the pastoral idyll, which wished to make one garden from the world, is reflected, with regional and political nuances – nuances of national character and power – the conflicts, triumph and misfortune of classicism and baroque, of Enlightenment and romanticism [...]. The *concordia discors*, the sublime, the picturesque, the Chinoiserie, the asymmetrical, the sentimental – all are key words that turn up in painting and poetry, and play an important role in the way gardens were realized or idealized in the imagination.'

In landscape architecture the spatial categories of house, garden, landscape and town became increasingly interrelated. The scenic staging of the 15th and 16th-century Italian villa marked a new phase in the development of garden design. Due to a new attitude towards nature the surrounding landscape began to play a crucial role in the garden's design. In this sense the villa garden was an extension of the traditional medieval secluded garden. On the other hand, the development of the Italian villa garden as it evolved in England from the 18th century onwards revealed several harbingers of French garden design and of landscape art.

The relationship of the French Baroque garden to the villa is obvious. French garden art made use of architectonic devices developed in Italian villa design, though this should not be thought of in terms of a continuous development. To the Renaissance architect, the design matrix, the coherent system of dimensions and proportions, formed a design model in which the landscape, by co-ordinating the elements, could be incorporated into the architectonic composition of the villa. In the Renaissance villa the axis, even when it became autonomous to a degree, remained only one of the elements used in ordering the plan.

In keeping with the Renaissance villa, in French garden design the relationship between buildings, gardens and landscape is formalized using geometry and proportional theory, and resolved within a perspective spatial concept. In the French Baroque garden, however, the plan was subordinate to the central axis so that a new perspective reality was conceived and controlled. Unlike the Renaissance villa, the French Baroque garden was not part of a panoramic landscape: Vaux-le-Vicomte, for instance, is situated in a valley. Here the unordered agricultural landscape is shut out, while the nature within the garden is once again organized by means of a system.

The link between the villa garden and the development of English landscape gardens is of a different nature. The break with the classical design scheme can chiefly be explained by the emergence of new attitudes towards nature and the influence of romantic literature and painting. If, however, we imagine the garden as a natural tableau in which the building is one of the physical elements, like for instance the layout of the landscape at Castle Howard, then the similarity to Italian villa architecture becomes evident.

The most important change in English landscape art in relation to the villa and the French garden was the departure from the unity of the architectonic composition so that the shared architectural references and landscape elements were no longer treated within one formal model, but were brought to the level of autonomy. In the French garden the perception of the landscape was certainly made objective in a formal model but this perception remained the prerogative of the king who 'mediated' between the individual and the landscape. In the English landscape garden the perception was individualized and made subjective: everyone looked with their own eyes and experienced their own responses.

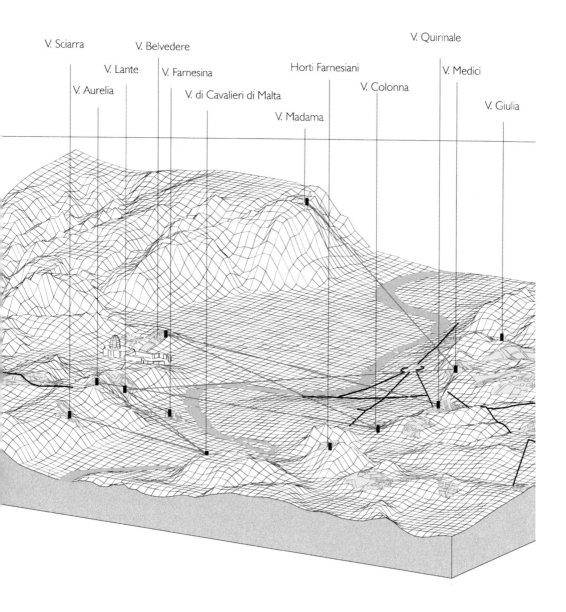

V. Sciarra

V. Belvedere

V. Quirinale

V. Lante

V. Farnesina

Horti Farnesiani

V. Medici

V. Aurelia

V. di Cavalieri di Malta

V. Colonna

V. Giulia

V. Madama

I ROME The theatrical arrangement of the Renaissance villas on the Tiber valley

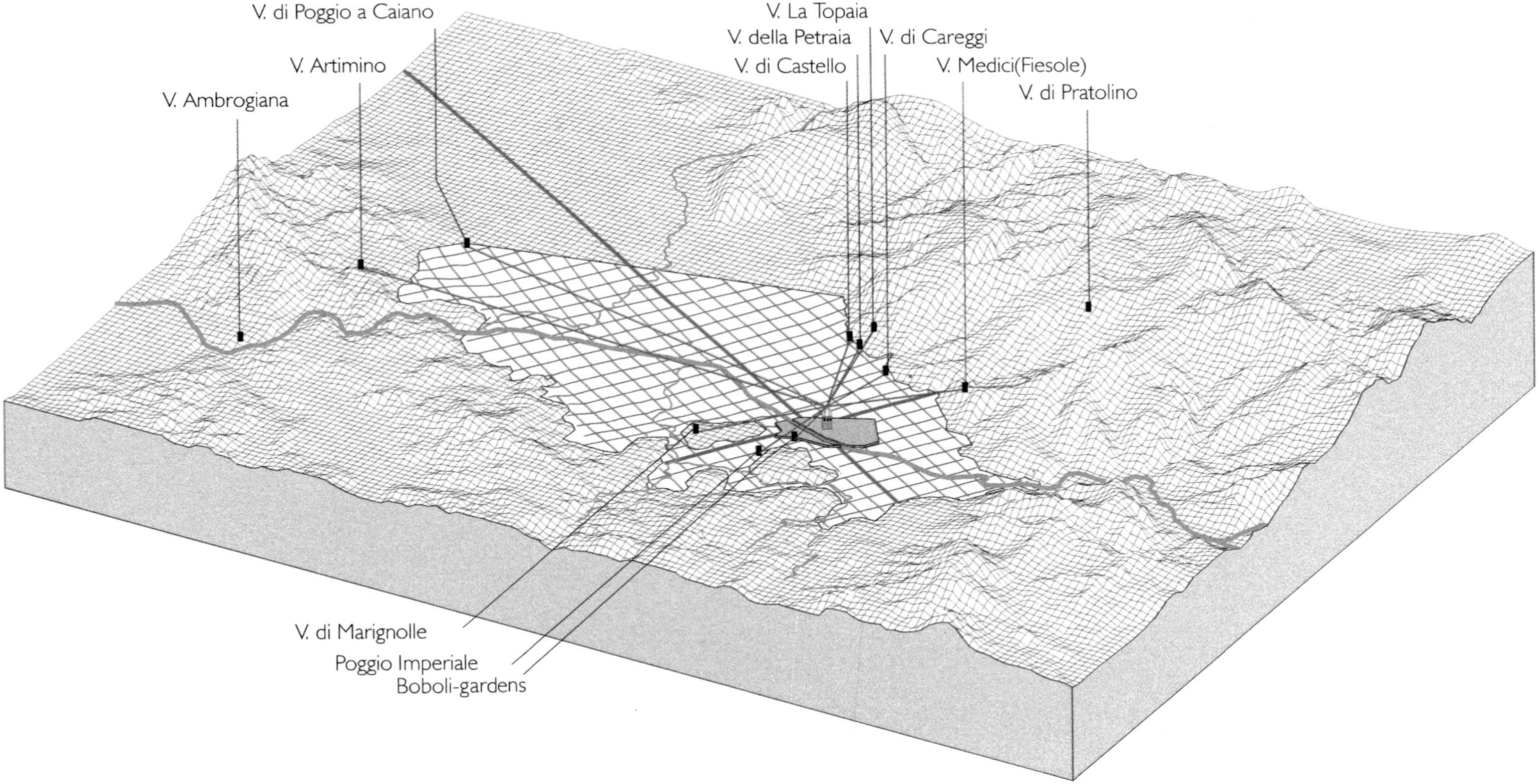

V. La Topaia
V. della Petraia
V. di Castello
V. di Careggi
V. Medici(Fiesole)
V. di Pratolino

V. di Poggio a Caiano
V. Artimino
V. Ambrogiana

V. di Marignolle
Poggio Imperiale
Boboli-gardens

11 FLORENCE The territorial arrangement of Medici villas along the Arno valley

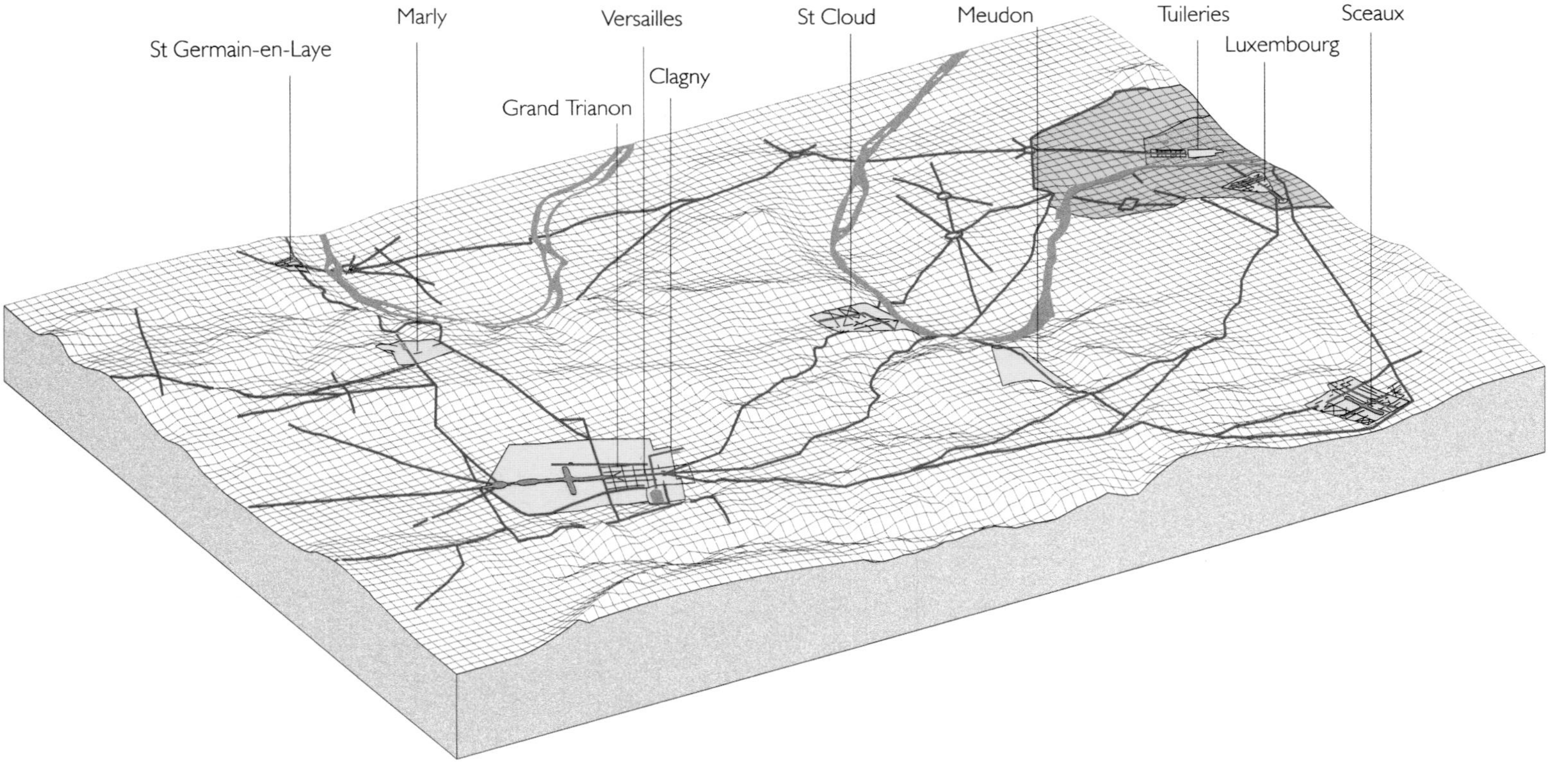

St Germain-en-Laye

Marly

Grand Trianon

Versailles

Clagny

St Cloud

Meudon

Tuileries

Luxembourg

Sceaux

IV PARIS The regional arrangement of the 17th-century residences in the Seine landscape (south-west of Paris)

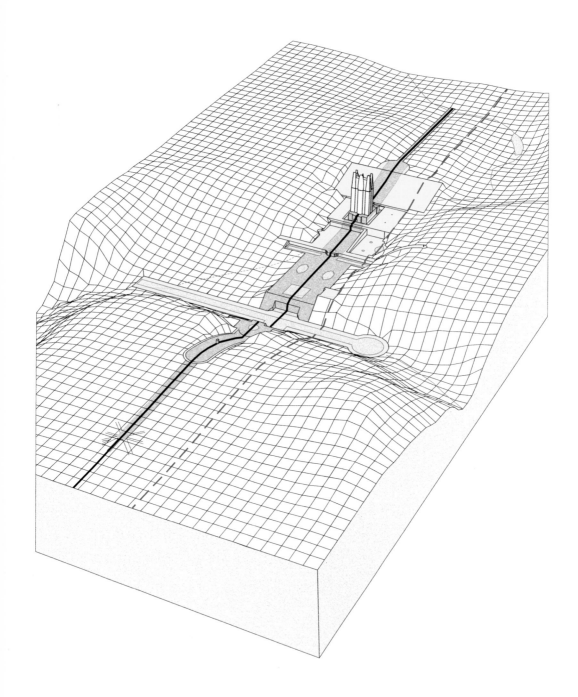

VI VAUX-LE-VICOMTE The balance between the geomorphology of the site and the symmetry of the design

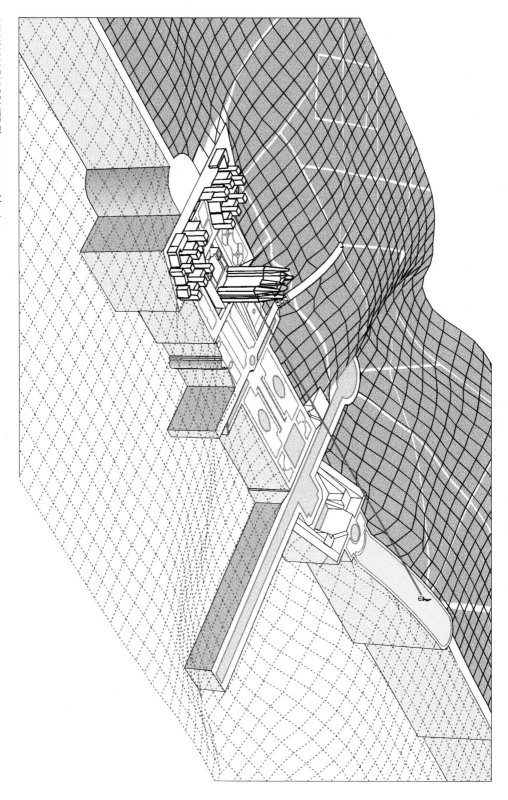

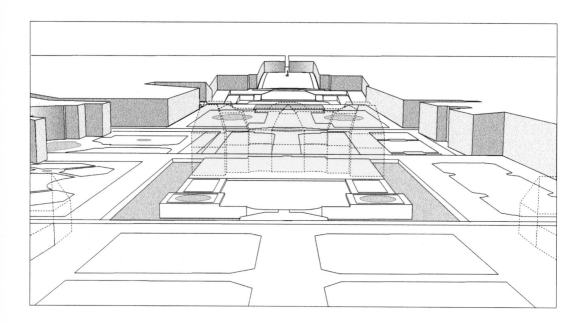

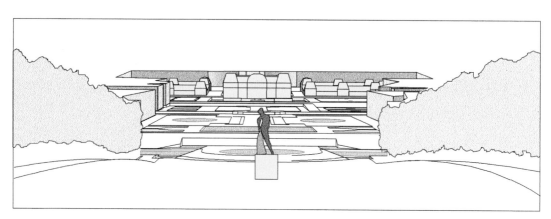

VIII VAUX-LE-VICOMTE The illusion of a perfect harmony

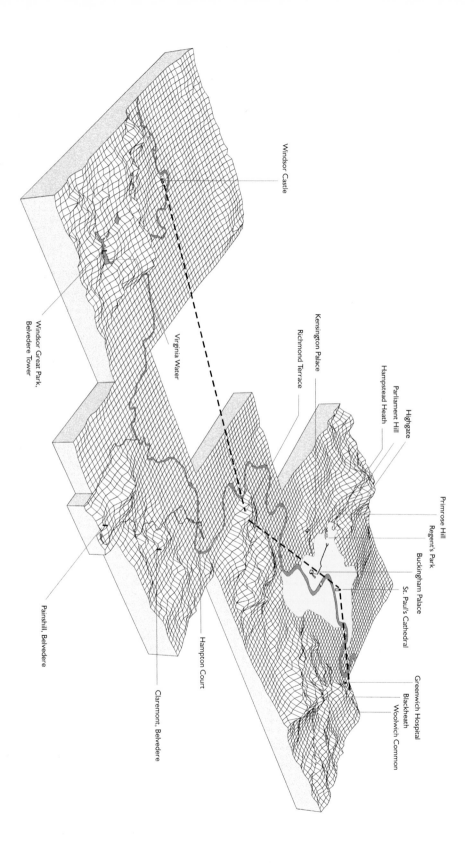

IX LONDON The visual control over the continuity of space along the Thames valley

Windsor Castle

Windsor Great Park, Belvedere Tower

Virginia Water

Kensington Palace

Richmond Terrace

Highgate
Parliament Hill
Hampstead Heath

Primrose Hill
Regent's Park

Buckingham Palace
St. Paul's Cathedral

Greenwich Hospital
Blackheath
Woolwich Common

Painshill, Belvedere

Hampton Court

Claremont, Belvedere

Legenda

A. Coneysthorpe
B. Great lake
C. Dairy Pond
D. Rolling Spring
E. Wray Wood
F. South Lake
G. New River
H. Mount Sion Wood
I. Lowdy Hill Wood
J. Ready Wood
K. Pretty Wood
L. East Moor Banks
M. St Anne's Spring
N. Welburn
O. Bulmer Hag
P. Brandrith Wood
Q. Brickkiln Wood
R. Sata Pond
S. Park Quarry
T. Slingsby Bank

1. The Great House
2. Temple of the Four Winds
3. Temple of Venus
4. New River Bridge
5. Mausoleum
6. Low Gaterley
7. Pyramid
8. Tumulus
9. Howard Pyramid
10. Obelisk
11. Pyramid Gate
12. Towers
13. Carmire Gate
14. Monument

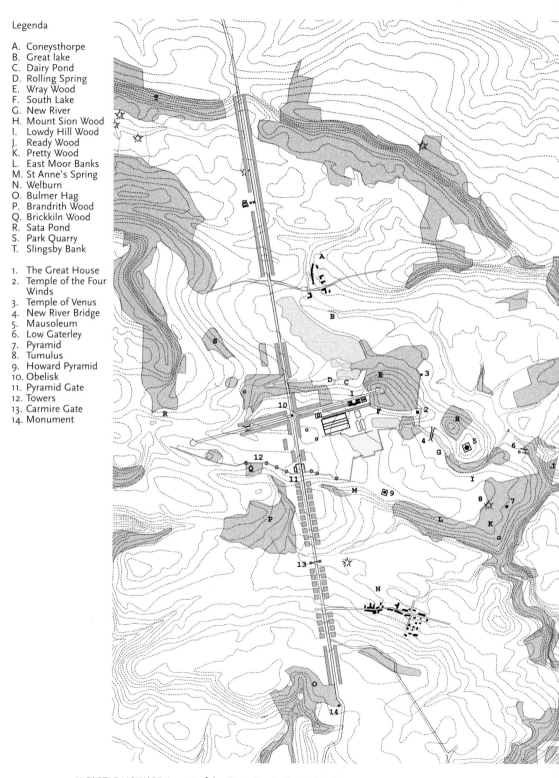

X CASTLE HOWARD Layout of the Great Scenic Creation

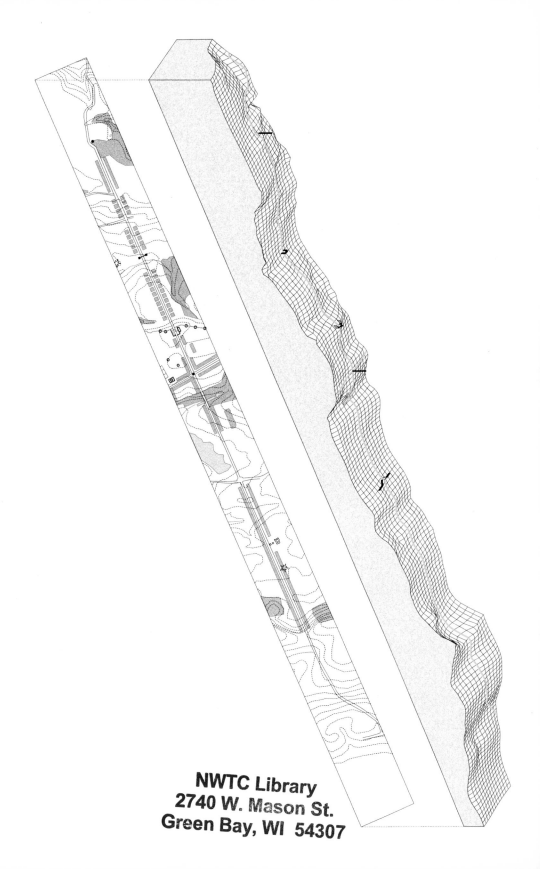

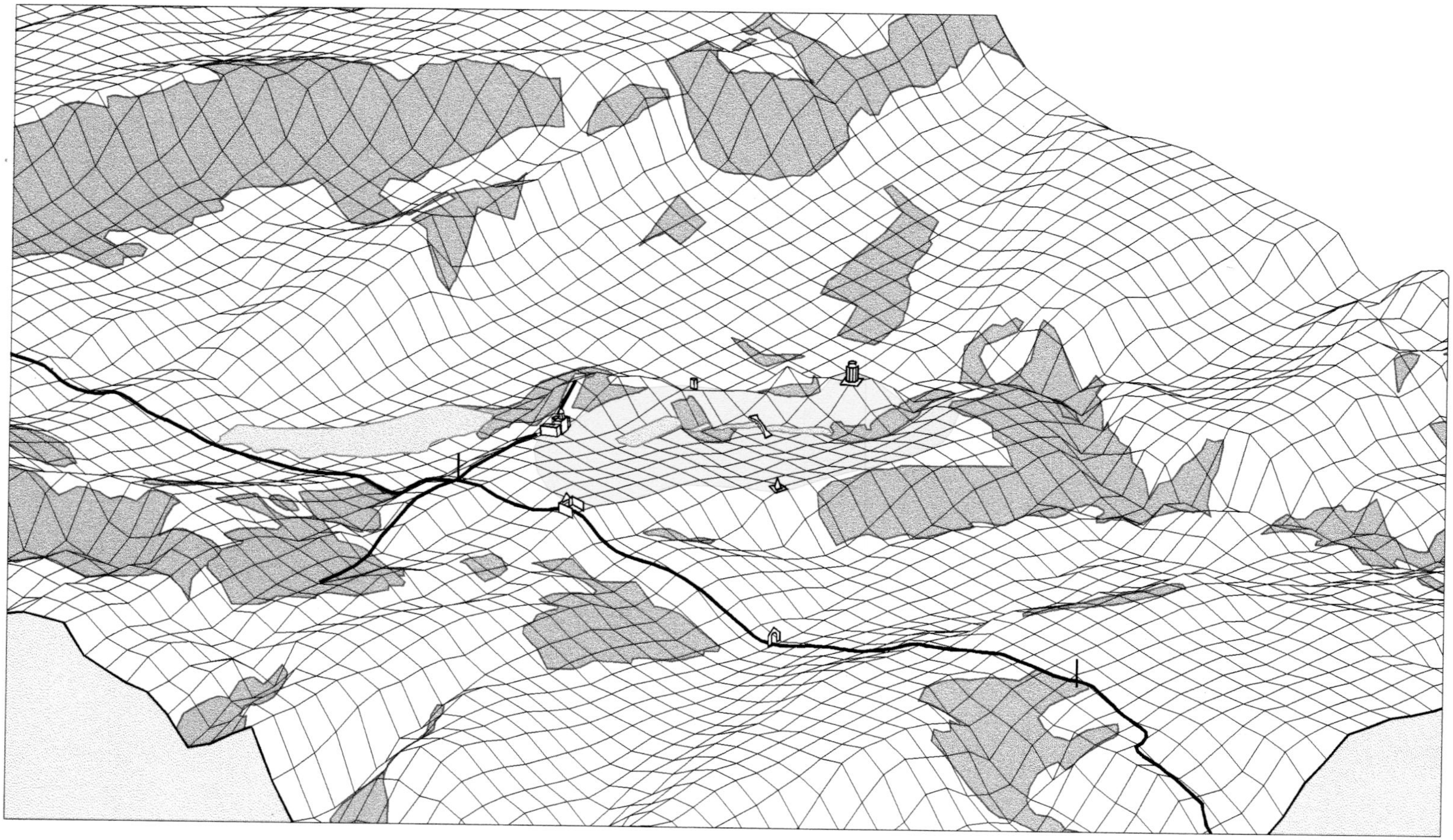

XII CASTLE HOWARD The Arcadian landscape

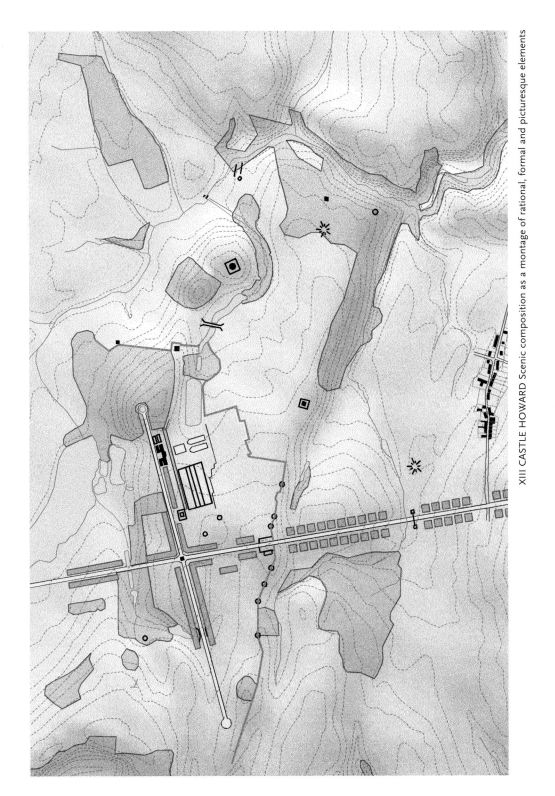

XIII CASTLE HOWARD Scenic composition as a montage of rational, formal and picturesque elements

Legenda

1. Stowe Church
2. House
3. Lake Pavilions
4. Stowe Castle
5. Boycott Pavilions
6. Keeper's Lodge / Bourbon Tower
7. Cobham Monument
8. Oxford Avenue
9. Wolfe's Obelisk
10. Oxford Bridge and Water
11. Oxford/Boycott Lodges
12. Corinthian Arch
13. Grand Avenue
14. Buckingham Lodges
15. Stowe Ridings
16. Equestrian Statue
17. Column (?)
18. Buckingham Church

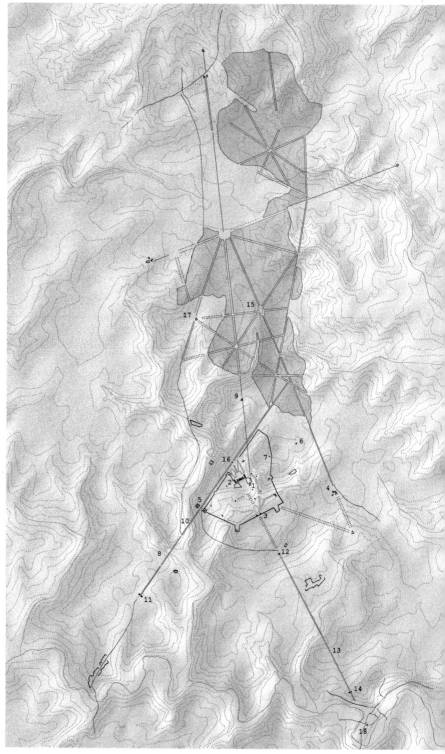

XIV STOWE LANDSCAPE The integration of forest plantations, agricultural and natural elements in a large-scale composition

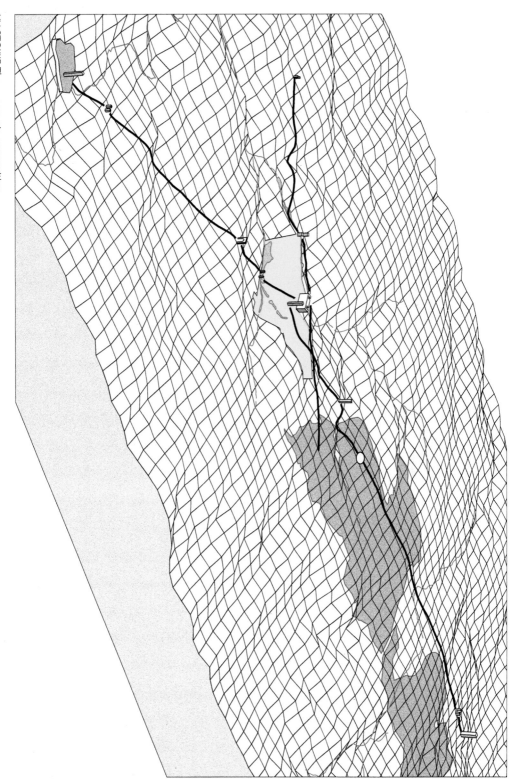

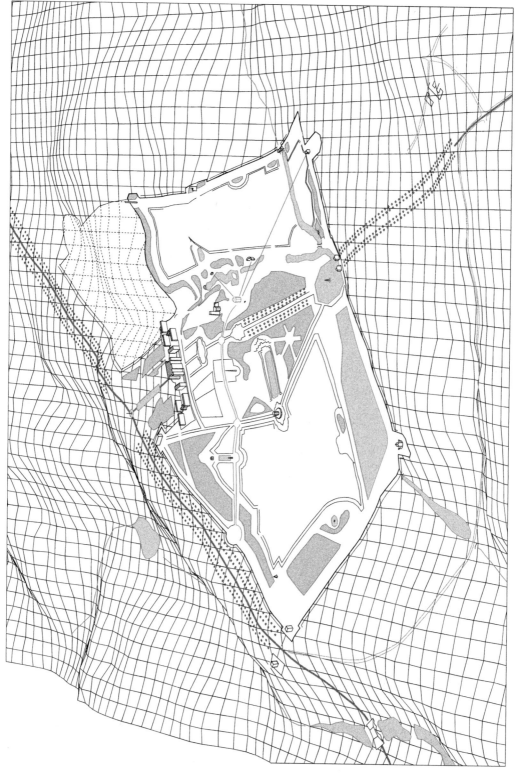

XVI STOWE The garden as a design laboratory

THE POETICS OF
THE RATIONAL

THE ITALIAN RENAISSANCE VILLA

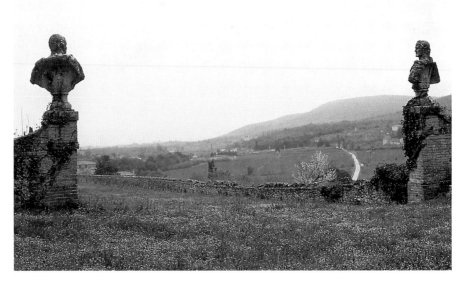

Villa Cetinale, Sovicille, Siena

The discovery of landscape as an architectural object

ARCADIA AS THE URBAN IDEAL

The possibility of building villas arose at a time when control of the hinterland by the cities rendered fortified rural settlements unnecessary. Existing country houses belonging to the large landowning town nobility could be converted, and newly-built villas, built solely for enjoying rural life, did not need to be defensible. Both types represent the cultural ideal of rural life, the so-called *villeggiatura*.

The beginning of this development, the transformation of *castello* and *podere* into villas, can be observed in 15th century Tuscan villas. In the *villeggiatura*, as it matured in Italy from the quattrocento onwards, a humanist elite breathed new life into the classical ideal of *otium* as opposed to *negotium*, while remaining within the

framework of Christian culture. In the villa one could recover from the fatigue and the obligations associated with a high social or ecclesiastical position.

One withdrew from the town, but not to turn one's back on it, and even less as a form of criticism. When the architect and theorist Leone Battista Alberti (1404-72) recounts in his treatises the ideal location of a villa, he recommends sites from which there is, apart from a view of hills and plains, also a view of the town. The villa embodied the enjoyment of rural life, which was undertaken in an urban manner: its construction, for instance, complemented the concept of the town and urban palazzo. The artificial arrangement of nature was determined by rules dictated by the cultural world of a ruling class. Alberti determined the degree to which the villa remained essentially utilitarian by the social and economic status of its owner.

During the 15th century the villa increasingly became a place for contemplation and sensuous pleasure. The Romans already distinguished between the villa *rustica* as a farm and the villa *urbana* as a spacious country house, to which, in the warm season, the owner would retreat from his urban *domus*. The letters of Pliny the Younger, with their extensive descriptions of his own villas and the landscapes in which they were situated, were among the most important classical sources to have had a direct influence on garden architecture in the Renaissance.

In classical times Cicero and Seneca associated a peaceful stay in the countryside with the urban culture of study and philosophy. In 1462 Cosimo de' Medici wrote to his humanist friend Marsilio Ficino: 'Yesterday I went to my villa in Careggi, not to cultivate my land but my soul'. He also made his villa at Careggi the seat of the Academia Platonica, where Ancient Greek literature and philosophy were studied.

Here the humanists tried, in fact, to combine two traditions: monastic contemplation and pastoral seclusion. In Ficino's concept of contemplation, nature takes a central position. The ideal place for contemplation was the garden, where geometry

The secrets of classical architecture. From Colonna's *Hypnerotomachia poliphili*, 1499

was a reflection of cosmic order and, therefore, of divine order. Since, according to Ficino and his associates, virtue is nothing other than nature transformed into perfection, the garden, in which nature was sublimated, was also the place in which virtue was nurtured. In Careggi, Ficino thought, young men could learn moral laws without any effort. Poetry and intellectual discipline were as established here as the sensuous enjoyment of nature. It was therefore in a villa, L'Albergaccio, that Machiavelli completed his *Il principe* (1513).

One of the books which had a great influence on garden architecture and it being accepted by the cultural elite was Frater Francesco Colonna's *Hypnerotomachia poliphili* (1499) in which insight into Poliphilus' nature is identified with insight into the secrets of classical culture, especially classical architecture. The development of the *villeggiatura* and the contrast between *vita contemplativa* and *vita activa* went hand in hand with a cultural reorientation towards classical literature. Humanist poets, Petrarch in particular, referred to Arcadia (Virgil) and the mythical gardens of the gods.

In association with specific topoi of classical literature, nature 'in the wild' was also introduced into the villa, especially through such elements as the *bosco*, the grotto and the nymphaeum. Ovid's *Metamorphoses* (AD 8) became an important source for revealing the hidden meaning of such elements to the initiated.

THE TRANSFORMATION OF THE HORTUS CONCLUSUS

The Renaissance villa substitutes the sensuous pleasure of tangible nature for the symbolic medieval representation of worldly paradise. In medieval thought the distinction between celestial and worldly spheres was discernible in the Creation. The cyclical movement of the celestial bodies attested to the perfection of the original creation, while in the terrestrial domain the consequences of the Fall had an appreciable effect on the unpredictable and chaotic movements of nature.

The attitude of humankind towards nature was influenced by the awareness that the latter had been perverted by the sin of Adam and Eve. In art and architecture there was no question of the sensuous enjoyment of nature, but rather of it representing the lost perfection as symbolized in the portrayal of the Garden of Eden. The archetypical paradisiac garden consists of a square plan with a centrally placed tree or spring. From there four streams flow towards each of the four points of the compass. They can be regarded as an iconographic representation of the four Evangelists, with Christ in the middle. The individual elements have a mystical significance (the Tree of Knowledge, the *fons salutis*, for example) and are linked in a symbolic-anecdotal manner. Since the garden is a miniature representation of God's Creation in a *hortus conclusus* (enclosed space), it follows that the portrayal of nature in art and architecture is distinct and separate from real nature.

One of the most important written sources on garden architecture in the late Middle Ages is the *Liber ruralium commodorum* (1305), by Pietro de Crescenzi. Although he does not refer, either directly or indirectly, to the environment or the landscape, his depiction of a farmyard and, just beyond it, a dovecote and an orchard, distinctly evokes a harmonious, closed life cycle. Although the idea of the *hortus conclusus* was preserved in a specific place in the Renaissance garden, the so-called *giardino segreto*, the villa concept nevertheless reflects a fundamental change in attitude towards nature. The landscape itself is given meaning in relation to the ideal of the *vita rustica*. Unspoilt nature was an essential part of the villa programme as a setting for the sojourn of the aristocracy in the countryside. At the same time, the significance of the elements of the garden changed.

Persian and Arab influences manifested themselves in the 13th and 14th cen-

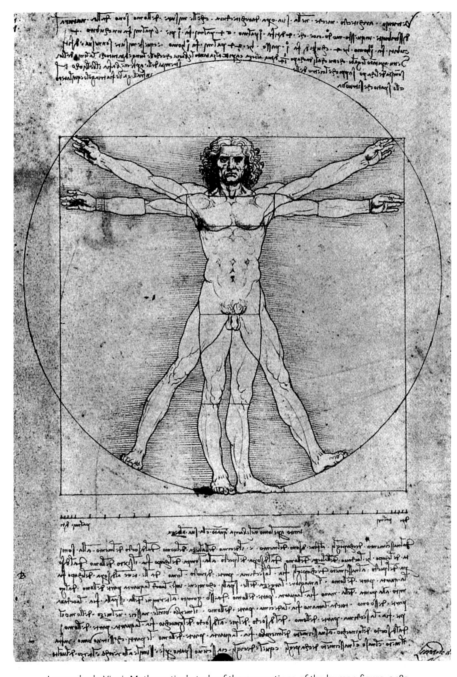

Leonardo da Vinci. Mathematical study of the proportions of the human figure, 1485

turies as a result of Islamic expansion and the Crusades. The Islamic garden, like the European medieval garden, is arranged geometrically, but is, in its layout, more orientated towards sensual enjoyment, expressed especially in the water features. The medieval *fons salutis*, for instance, became the centre of sensuous enjoyment in pastoral poetry (in Boccaccio's *Decameron* (1353), for example). It became a fountain representing the forces and pleasures of nature. The classical topos of the sleeping nymph beside a spring or grotto (nymphaeum) was associated with the Muses, the patrons of art and poetry. It was, after all, to a grotto dedicated to the Muses that Plato summoned his students for profound conversation.

Another important image in which the Christian concept of paradise is coupled with classical culture is the figure of Hercules in the mythical garden of the Hesperides. The architectural interpretation of similar classical literary references in the villa's plan heightened one's enjoyment of nature to the desired intellectual and cultural level.

THE HIDDEN GEOMETRY WITHIN NATURE

Although in the Renaissance the relationship between art and science remained undivided, a profound change in the way nature was understood and represented took place in the 14th century. In the Middle Ages the depiction of nature took on a metaphysical, symbolic meaning. The medieval garden represented both nature and the supernatural. To Gothic architects, the scientific basis of art was the science of geometry. Together with Pythagoras, Plato, and the neo-Platonists, a long succession of theologians from St Augustine onwards were convinced that 'all is number'. Divine numbers (such as 3, 4, 7, 12, 40), divine proportions (golden section) and divine forms (the equilateral triangle, the square, the circle) were partly derived from Holy Scripture as a secret canon, preserved by the guilds and used by the masters in works of art.

In the doctrine of nature corrupted by the Fall, the accent shifted from corruption to the view that God's order is present in nature, although concealed in an apparent chaos. This order could be exposed by keen observation: Leonardo da Vinci's minute investigations of natural shapes and phenomena are examples of this. 'I learn more from the anatomy of an ant or a blade of grass than from all the books written since the Creation,' wrote Bernardo Telesio in the first part of the 16th century.

According to the philosophy of Marsilio Ficino and his pupil Giovanni Pico della Mirandola, the two most important protagonists of Lorenzo de' Medici's, 'the Magnificent's', Florentine academy, in this way terrestrial nature became a means of coming closer to God rather than an obstacle. As art was directly connected with science for the *uomo universale*, the old platonic concept of art as imitation of nature was revived in 14th-century Italy, as expressed in the maxim '*Natura artis magistra est*'.

Although Cicero had already rejected the theory of literal artistic imitation, it was the neo-Platonist Plotinus (*c.* 205-270), in particular, who laid the foundations of a new abstract theory of art: what the artist 'sees' is a reality hidden under the outward visible appearance of the material world but ascertainable through human reason and intuition. By moulding this observation into comprehensive, visible shapes, he reveals the harmony concealed in nature. In 15th-century Florence, the cradle of political, scientific and artistic experiment, the neo-Platonist idea of the imitation of nature was stated mathematically. It was Alberti who, in his *Della pittura e della statua* (1436), and especially in his *De re aedificatoria* (*c.* 1450), concluded that the mathematical interpretation of nature is an artistic concept. The study of proportion, based on the scientific measurement of the human figure, created a framework for a renaissance of classical orders and proportions.

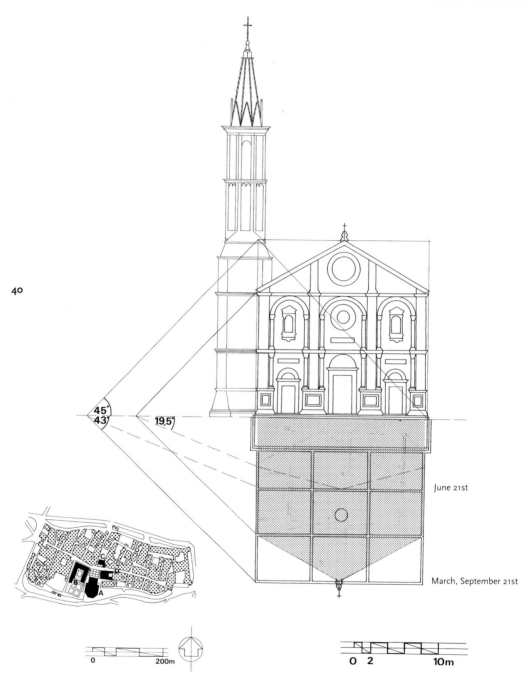

45°
43'

19,5'

June 21st

March, September 21st

0   200m

O 2   10m

An interesting example of science 'embodied' in an architectonic form is a plan by the Florentine architect Bernardo Rossellino (1409-64). At the request of Pope Pius II Piccolomini he transformed his native village of Corsignano into a seat called Pienza (1460-64). Among other buildings a new church was built in a north-south direction rather than the traditional east-west. Its north façade casts a shadow on the square before it, which, when the sun is at its highest position during the spring or autumn equinox, corresponds with the square's geometric shape. Because Pienza is situated at a latitude of 43 degrees north and the sun's rays simultaneously fall at a 47-degree angle, the façade's measurements are foreshortened in the projection onto the square. An *ombelico*, or ring, has been placed in the square's pavement which is the same distance from the foot of the façade (horizontal) as the *occhio*, or eye, in the front of the church (vertical). From these fixed reference points the degree of foreshortening of the façade's silhouette can be determined. The complex acts as a calender and clock at the same time, with the square as the dial, the tip of the tympan shadow as the hand and the *ombelico* as the centre.

Antonio Filarete. The ideal city of Sforzinda as a geometric stamp in the landscape, *c.* 1460

In Vitruvius's *De architectura* (*c.* 25 BC) the proportions of an ideal human figure, with the navel as the centre of a defined circle and square, had already been expressed. 'If nature has formed the entire body in such a way that the limbs are in proportion to the entire body, it would seem that the ancients reasonably determined that, when executing a building, they should also take into consideration the precise measurements of the parts in relation to each other and to the entire body [...]. They derived the basic measurements, apparently essential for all buildings, from the limbs of the body, such as the palm, the foot and the yard.' For Vitruvius it was the human figure in particular that harboured the secret codes of natural order and beauty.

In the Renaissance this idea was justified by Holy Scripture, in which man is called 'the image of God'. As a reflection of the perfect Creator, the human figure could now be interpreted in a wider sense, that is to say as an embodiment of the harmonies of the universe. As such it was a microcosmic image of the macrocosmos. Thus the architectural plan, which in turn reflected *humanitas*, also attained cosmographic significance. It was a metric diagram in which the hidden order of nature was made evident.

In Alberti's architectural theory three categories were distinguished for this purpose: number (*numerus*), dimension (*finitio*), and ordering (*collocatio*). Favoured numbers were 6 and 10, being, respectively, the ratio of the length and breadth and the ratio of the length and thickness of a human being. Ten was the sum of 1, 2, 3 and 4. Six was the same as 1+2+3 as well as 1×2×3. Series such as 2:4:6, 2:3:6, 2:4:8 etc. were thus derived. In a graphic sense this preoccupation with small integers resulted in the search for square grids. Apart from Alberti, contributions were made to the early architectural theory of the Renaissance by, among others, Antonio Filarete and Francesco Colonna. Filarete, too, preferred the square as a basis for plans and elevations. Colonna used the same source in order to achieve correct proportions for plans and elevations by means of square grids.

An important consequence of this for villa architecture was not only the concept that it should be possible to devise an ideal, proportional system, but also that, above all, the relationship between villa and landscape, or, in an even broader sense, between humankind and nature, could be established within this rational scheme of dimensions and proportions. As has already been mentioned it was important for the villa architect to represent natural landscape within the domain of the villa, and, in addition, to deduce the hidden order from the chaos nature presented to him. Within the confines of the garden, which formed the link between landscape and villa, a game could be played with the representation of nature and its regulation. Natural morphology was defined geometrically in the plan of the villa.

In the Tuscan and Roman Renaissance villa this mathematical model became the new 'aesthetic', designed by the architect, which, within the domain of the villa, placed the landscape under the control of human intellect. At the same time, this determined the position of the villa with regard to the surrounding landscape. In the model of the Veneto villa, as developed by Palladio a hundred years after Alberti, this aesthetic is placed in the centre of the classical Roman trio of 'useful, beautiful and correct'. In the plans of his Veneto villas, which are efficiently organized farms, the functional (Roman) division of the farmlands themselves is represented aesthetically, thus establishing the villa and the landscape in one architectural order.

VIEWPOINT, PERSPECTIVE AND HORIZON

The geometric scheme of the Renaissance plan expresses the order revealed in nature by science as a 'divine model'. When observing spatial attributes of the geometric plan, it should be noted that its proportions presuppose a subjective point of view. It is the mathematical construction of a perspective that establishes this position and systematically determines the proportions observed.

Space emerges as an independent condition and is defined by scientific perspective. The discovery of perspective was closely related to the discovery of the horizon. Alberti spoke of visible objects whose forms were measured in the mind. Perspective was not considered to be an illusion or trick to manipulate reality, but rather a hidden order – a mathematical structure which gave space, and the objects within it, coherence. Perspective presupposes a vanishing point on the horizon, which thus becomes the limit of the composition.

In medieval art the observer was not involved in the mathematics of optical space. The ideas of the artist were subject to the evocation of a spiritual truth. According to Aristotle's philosophy, place (*topos*) was an accessory of the object. Space did exist, but not as an independent aesthetic entity. On the other hand, Bernardino Telesio (1509-88), in his *De rerum natura iuxta propria principia* (1565), proposed that space and time could be independent of matter and movement, and therefore distinguished between *locus* (the Greek *topos*) and *spatium*.

In Renaissance painting foreground and background, which were originally independent elements of the picture-plane, were placed in a spatial relationship in experiments in perspective. The optical distinction between foreground and background, between the scene of action and the landscape backcloth, was thus abolished; both were united in one spatially continuous composition. Not only did the landscape, in which the various actions took place, form a spatial unity, but it was also suggested that it was accessible. The landscape was no longer a changeable backcloth; it had become an integral part of the composition.

In 16th-century theatre design the question of a correct optical relationship between painted background and three-dimensional stage props also led to experiments with actual built space. The background, however, continued to assume the form of a painted surface, framed by columns, arches and building projections. The entire stage was organized in perspective from a viewpoint at the centre of the auditorium. Only from this point, the seat of the monarch, was the perspective illusion of spatial unity perfect.

Important theorists who tried to rationalize subjective observation by experi-

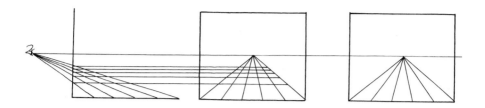

Perspective construction in which optical foreshortening is determined by the lines of vision intersecting with the vertical picture plane.

menting with perspective were Alberti (*Trattato della pittura*, 1435), Jean Pélerin, alias Viator, (1440-1524) (*De artificiali perspectiva*, 1505), and Albrecht Dürer (1471-1528) (*Unterweysung der Messung*, 1525). Leonardo da Vinci (1452-1519) experimented with it in his paintings and constructed practical perspective into a method known as *costruzione legittima*.

The experimental constructions of the first perspectivists proposed a new, speculative hypothesis. Whereas descriptive Euclidean geometry had, until then, stated that two parallel lines do not intersect, they experimented with a hypothetical intersection of such lines at infinity (the vanishing point).

Alberti assumed that a picture is nothing other than a particular section of the imaginary optical pyramid (formed by the rays of vision from the eye), depicted on a projection plane. To him, the most important technical problem was to create a construction method which systematically correlated the observer's position with the size and shape of the object depicted. Projected onto a picture plane, the size depends on the observer's distance from this particular plane and from the object itself. The shape changes according to the direction of the main line of vision. In his shortened version of the *costruzione legittima*, Alberti, for the first time, created a rational and systematic construction method by means of combining the plan with the front and side elevations.

In the villa the perspectival stage management of natural space became an architectural exercise. When the Italian poet, Francesco Petrarch (1304-74), gave his famous literary account of a completely new kind of spatial experience (1366), the dramatic occasion took place on the summit of a mountain, Mount Ventoux near Avignon. The extreme remoteness of the location had reduced conventional reference points to meaningless dots in the distance. When all reference points disappear it becomes impossible to measure space. All movement in the panorama, too, is modified by the distance and reduced to nothing. Thus the notion of time, which can only be measured by movement, disappears. Petrarch 'placed himself outside reality'. Reflecting on our world, infinite space emerges as an unknown phenomenon; the uninterrupted vistas bring about a feeling of enclosure on a cosmic scale. Moreover, to Petrarch, actual physical space was assimilated into the purely inner perspective of contemplation and poetry.

It is this experience of space which can be recognized in the villa and which was brought under control by means of architecture. The villa was always projected against the background of the landscape. This natural landscape was integrated into the panorama of the villa; it is the setting to which the villa, in the foreground, had to be linked perspectively. It was still impossible to design this background as a panoramic

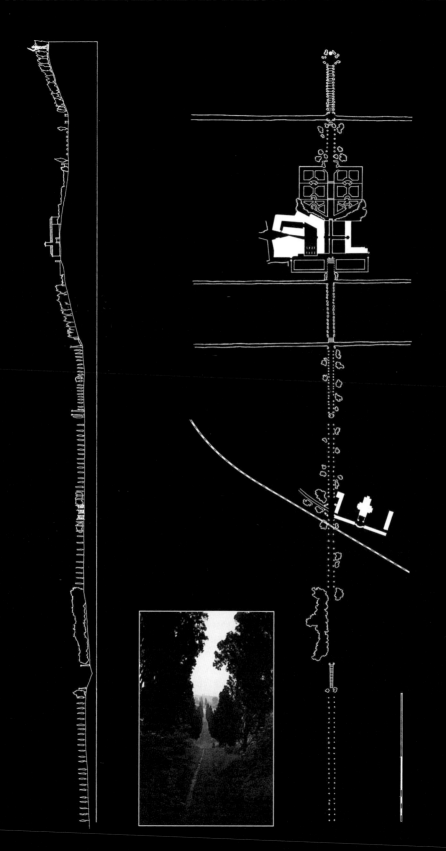

Villa Crivelli, Inverigo

landscape of great spatial depth. It was, however, possible to place it in a perspective relationship with the garden in the foreground. Framed by a loggia, an arcade or a portico, or disconnected by means of foreground terraces, the panorama became a decorative and controllable part of the villa architecture. In such a segment of the panorama the horizon, framed by the architecture, could be presented as an orderly impression of infinity. It was not the perimeter of the estate which was portrayed as the boundary of optical space, but the natural horizon far beyond it.

THE CONCEPT OF RATIONAL STAGE MANAGEMENT

In the garden the organization, conversion and perfection of the natural elements were carried out according to prescribed architectural rules, which brought about the *integrazione scenica* of the villa into the landscape. The villa plan can be seen as a rational scheme superimposed on the landscape in which those parts of the landscape covered by the scheme are ordered and intensified. Thus, at Villa Medici (Fiesole), the position of the villa in relation to the contour lines of the landscape is emphasized by the oblique garden wall in the upper garden and by the verticality of the terraces in the sloping terrain. The Villa Giulia in Rome is situated in such a way that its architectural axis coincides with the natural axis of the side valley of the Tiber in which the villa is situated. It is particularly due to the treatment of the edges of the garden that the villa is defined in the landscape. At the Villa d'Este the boundary on the Tivoli side has been treated very differently from the one opposite it, which adjoins the panorama.

Apart from the manipulation of the geometric matrix and the edges of the plan, the differences in interaction between villa and landscape are determined by number, grouping, and the specific architectural treatment of the elements in the garden. In placing the elements of the garden like objects in a grid, nature becomes ordered, the interaction with the landscape is established and the representation within the overall composition of unordered nature is determined. It is also a matter of the architect employing a codified sequence of particular parts. Such a series of elements, which recurs in all plans, is formed, for example, by the sequence casino-parterre-*bosco*. Examples of other sequential combinations are: nymphaeum-grotto-cascade-reflecting pool, house-*giardino segreto*-terrace-panorama and loggia-arcade-pergola.

The number of elements is limited if they are categorized according to formal characteristics: a half-round wall, a screen, a gate, a reflecting surface, a column, a colonnade, and so on. The separate elements only receive their various meanings through the organization of the garden.

The position of the house as an element in the plan is ambiguous. It is part of the architectural composition, but its siting in the villa complex also coincides with its symbolic significance. At Aldobrandini, for instance, the villa is represented by the façade of the house facing the valley, and its relationship to the landscape is directly determined by the incorporation of the hillside into the two intersecting tympans. The garden is situated between the slope and the house at the rear.

The significance of the garden as a link between villa and landscape did not remain constant, and in Palladio's villas, for example, a number of shifts occurred by which house and landscape became more directly involved with each other. Palladio's villas were situated in a vast, flat, fertile landscape, which did not encourage a direct reference to the Arcadian ideal of the *vita rustica*.

In Palladio's agricultural villas the garden is a ceremonial introduction to the steps and the *piano nobile* in which the status of the landowner is symbolized. The interaction between villa and landscape is defined by the way in which the landscape itself is organized.

There comes a time in the villa-building process, therefore, when one could ask whether the scenic staging is still controlled within the plan or whether its organization has been taken over by one of the elements of the plan. This is the case in the introduction of the axis, superimposed onto the landscape.

In the Renaissance villa the axis, even when it has become autonomous to a certain extent, remains one of the elements around which the plan is arranged. When special perspective effects have been used, such as those found at the Villa Giulia or the perspective distortion of the cascade at Villa Aldobrandini, they remain linked to the special development of one of the parts of the plan.

The point at which the axis became more independent and detached from the plan signified the end of the development of villa architecture as such, and at the same time marked the inception of new regulating principles in landscape architecture related to another concept of nature and its spatial representation in the landscape. Up to the mid-17th century a number of developments can be discerned which lay the foundations of French landscape architecture and the development of landscape art as it evolved in England from the 18th century onwards. In the French Baroque garden perspective was restricted to the central axis in order to dominate the plan all the way to the horizon. The *trompe-l'œil*, which is a small component of the plan in the Renaissance garden, became an essential compositional device. The ingredients supplied by villa architecture to the development of English landscape art are to be found, for example, in the way in which the landscape elements are linked along the axis. When this axis is removed from the formal structure of the plan and when the route through the landscape connects the separate pictorially determined parts, the spatial concept of the English landscape garden is born.

Domenico Ghirlandaio. Villa Medici, Fiesole, 1486-90. Fresco in the Santa Maria Novella, Florence

Villa Medici

HISTORY

In Tuscany the *villeggiatura* was to be found around towns such as Lucca, Pisa, Siena and Florence, though the latter was the most important centre. In the 15th century many prosperous citizens built numerous villas on the slopes of the hills surrounding the city of Florence. Villani says that the greater part of the nobility and the rich citizenry used to spend four months of the year in the countryside. The city dwellers and the court followed a seasonal cycle, moving from town to countryside and from one villa to another. The villas built around Florence during the Renaissance suited the already existing system of the *case coloniche*, the modest residences in the countryside.

In 15th-century Florence, it was the Medici family in particular who were historically important in initiating the building of villas outside the city. Cosimo de' Medici 'the Elder' (1389-1464) had the Careggi, Cafaggiolo and del Trebbio villas built by the architect Michelozzo di Bartolommeo (1396-1472). In the villas built by him the transition from *castello* (castle) and farm to villa is visible. Lorenzo de' Medici (1449-92) commissioned Giuliano da San Gallo (1445-1516) to build the agricultural Villa Poggio a Caiano and in 1477 he bought Villa Castello.

When, in the 16th century, a new branch of the Medici family came into power, their possessions were expanded into an imposing territorial system of villas: Cosimo I (1519-74; Villa Castello, the Boboli Gardens, Petraia, Poggio Imperiale), Francesco I (1541-87; villas Pratolino, Marignolle and Lapeggi) and Ferdinando I (1549-1609; villas Artimino and Montevettolini). The choice of new locations was determined by general economic, political and speculative considerations. Furthermore, a view of the town (the centre of their power) and a view of their other property played an important part. The villas were preferably situated in each other's field of vision. Those that were not

Villa Medici, Fiesole.
View of Brunelleschi's
dome in Florence and the
extended axis of sym-
metry of the lower terrace

48

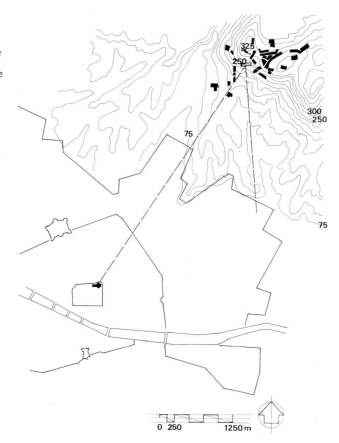

0 250   1250 m

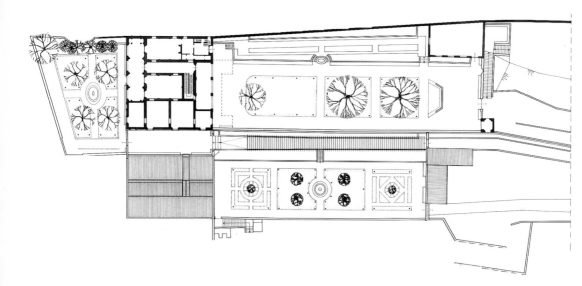

Villa Medici, Fiesole. Ground plan

actually visible could be admired in paintings in the interior.

According to Vasari the Villa Medici at Fiesole was built between 1458 and 1462. Built for Giovanni, son of Cosimo de' Medici 'the Elder', it was also designed by Michelozzo. A fresco in the Santa Maria Novella in Florence by Domenico Ghirlandaio (1449-94) depicts the villa in what was possibly its original state. The eastern loggia of the villa is shown as having four arches, while the terraces, also on the east side, are entirely bounded by retaining walls. Agnolo Poliziano (1454-94) wrote a poem, *Rusticus*, about the villa and, in a letter to Marsilio Ficino, praised its location, the local climate and the view. In 1671 the Medici family sold the villa.

Based on the evidence of the few available sources, including drawings by Zocchi of 1744 and by Buonaiuti of 1826, Bargellini, among others, surmised that between these dates the villa had undergone some changes. The villa was at the time owned by Margaret, Lady Orford (from 1772), and by Giulio Mozzi (from 1781). The part of the house located north of the corridor would have been built during this period. This assumption is supported by the fact that the southernmost loggia-arch in the east façade was bricked up in order to restore the balance of the façade. Geymuller and Patzak also assumed that this arch had been bricked up. In another drawing by Zocchi of 1744, cited by Bargellini and her followers, the western loggia still has three arches, which makes it probable that the present fourth (northern) loggia-arch was added later. It is also possible that during the same period stables and a coach house were built at the eastern entrance of the garden and connected with the Via Fiesolana by the construction of a *viale* (drive). The edges of the eastern terrace must have been reconstructed at the same time. Around 1850 William Blundell Spence became the owner of the villa and in 1860 he enlarged the *viale*. At the beginning of the 20th century, Lady Sybil Cutting-Scott-Lubbock bought the villa. She had the library on the *piano nobile* refurbished. In 1959 the villa was bought by Aldo Mazzini, whose widow still occupies it.

SITE

The villa is situated at a height of around 250 metres above the Arno valley, in which, about 5 kilometres further on, the old centre of Florence is situated. On the site of the villa the undulating foreground changes into a steeper, south-facing hilltop (325 metres), against which the southern façade stands out convincingly on its foundation of terraces. A southern exposure of the garden was recommended by the theorist Pietro de Crescenzi. The slope protects the villa against the cold north-east winds in winter. In summer the sea wind can bring cool air from the west. The building is aligned with the points of the compass and at an angle to the natural slope. This slope, therefore, closes the field of view to the east, whereas the building is orientated towards the Mugnone side valley and, across that, towards the distant line of the Arno valley. In the transverse direction the scheme is laid out like a balcony overlooking the source of the Arno valley to the south. The view is in accordance with what Alberti later recommended. Cosimo, however, was not particularly happy with it. He, more than his son, believed that the view should really be part and parcel of his country property.

PLAN

The villa consists principally of three levels. The upper level is formed by the extensive north terrace, which is now reached via the *viale*. This level is joined to the *piano nobile* and the two loggias of the house. The lowest level consists of the south terrace, which today is bounded by coach houses on the east and west sides. The total difference in height between the north and south terraces varies from 11 to 12 metres and is supported by means of a massive retaining wall with a pergola running along it.

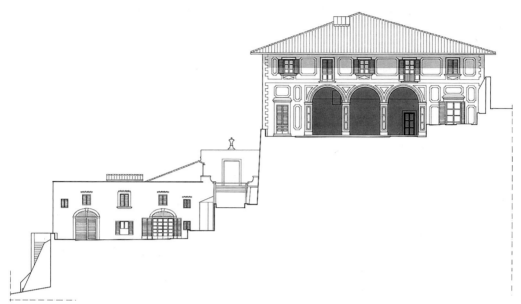

Villa Medici, Fiesole. North-south cross-section with view of the east façade

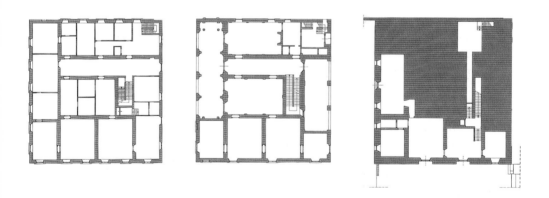

Villa Medici, Fiesole. Plan of the upper floor, *piano nobile* and basement

Inside the garden it is impossible to move from one terrace to another. Apart from an outside path that now meanders down along the *viale*, the two levels are only connected to each other inside the house. A long, single flight of stairs descends one storey from the corridor to the level of the garden rooms on the south façade. The narrow terrace in front, the west terrace and the rest of the basement comprise an intermediate level situated roughly halfway between the highest and lowest terraces. On this level there are large French windows in the south façade. In the west façade of the basement there are only small windows. It is striking that the ceremonial entrance to the villa in the west façade is not directly connected to the *piano nobile*. The north-east part of the basement is carved out of the rock and consists of storage space linked to the kitchen by a service staircase.

Beneath the east loggia on the *piano nobile* is what is now the most commonly used entrance to the house. From here a long off-centre corridor leads directly to the west loggia. The central position in the floor plan is occupied by the rectangular salon. North of the corridor are the dining room and kitchen, the latter being connected by a service staircase to an intermediate floor above and, subsequently, to the second floor of the villa. The façades of the *piano nobile* are largely determined by the loggias. The north façade is closed, apart from a few high windows and a small service entrance. The second floor of the house consists mainly of bedrooms. Above the dining room and kitchen, adjacent to the intermediary floor beneath, are separate living quarters for the servants. On this floor all the façades are defined by fairly small, identical windows. Several windows have been bricked up from the inside. Generally speaking, the present state of the façade is remarkable for its lack of any system. In the existing west façade only the ceremonial entrance is symmetric.

GEOMETRY

In the spring of 1986 the dimensions of the entire villa were surveyed and studied by Gerrit Smienk and Clemens Steenbergen in order to provide a more detailed analysis. The survey enabled a hypothesis to be made on the precise manner in which the connection between house and landscape was realized. This resulted in a hypothetical geometric model in which the villa can be explained as an architectural system. As a result of this the conclusions based on both historical research and the geometric model can be cross-checked for consistency.

In the villa plan a certain dimension, which we shall call A, appears to occur regularly. A turns out to be approximately 4.9 metres. The present plan of the entire *piano nobile* is 5A by $5^1/_3$A. Excluding the area with the dining hall north of the corridor, which was added at a later date, the floor plan measures 5A by 4A. This rectangle can be interpreted as being composed of two squares, each 4A by 4A, with an overlap of 3A, which takes up precisely the central part of the house, while the loggias with a depth of A are not included. Likewise, if a certain strip on the north side of the villa is omitted, the plan of the north and south terraces together measures 9A by 14A, from the rear wall of the east loggia to the rear of the half-round wall and hedge on the top terrace. This rectangle, too, can be explained as consisting of two squares, each 9A by 9A, now with an overlap of 4A. The north-south axis, which formally connects the two terraces, is situated centrally and symmetrically within overlap.

A, which functions in the house as a margin and which accommodates the depth of the loggias, therefore appears to have a similar role in the garden. The geometric systems of the house and of the garden overlap each other by this dimension A (the depth of the east loggia). Furthermore, A can be recognized as the margin of the half-round hedge at the end of the upper terrace. A is also the depth of the pergola along the retaining wall between the north and south terraces. Even the main dimen-

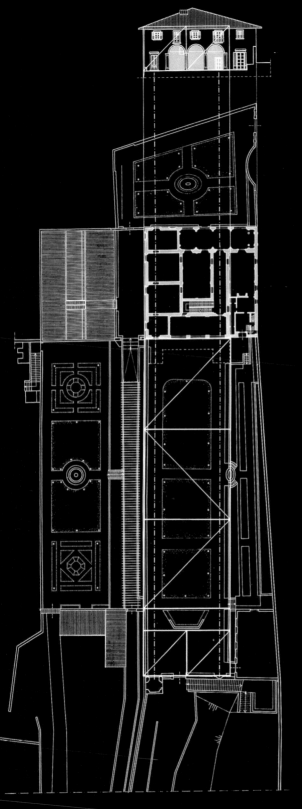

Villa Medici, Fiesole. Geometric model

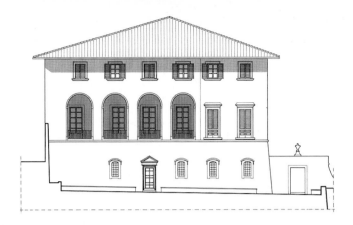

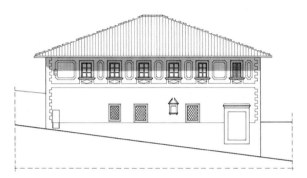

Villa Medici, Fiesole. Views of the
west, north, south and east façades

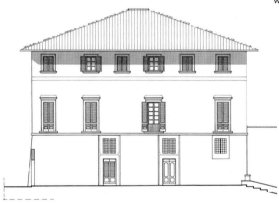

Villa Medici, Fiesole.
Reconstruction of the east façade

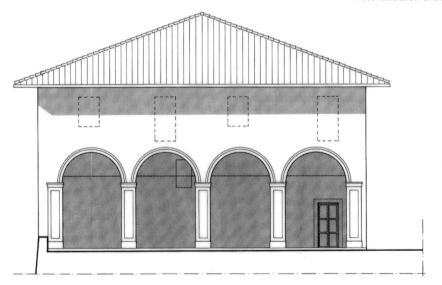

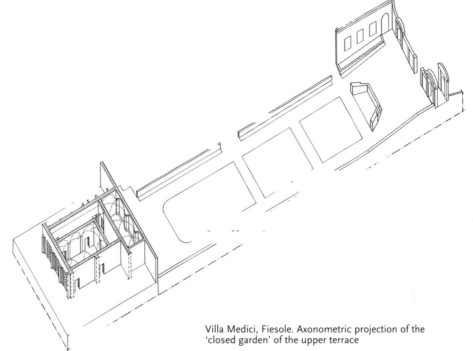

Villa Medici, Fiesole. Axonometric projection of the 'closed garden' of the upper terrace

sions of the east façade (wall height 2A and width 4A) seem to fit into the geometric system if its northern part is omitted.

It is clear that some parts of the present villa plan do not conform to the hypothetical geometric system of squares. This is especially the case with the strip on the north side of the villa. Bargellini and her followers had already assumed, on the basis of their historical research, that this northern part of the house had been added in the 18th century. This is confirmed by the geometric interpretation of the villa. It now seems safe to suppose that at the same time the changes were made in the 18th century the entire garden edge was also shifted northwards. With this a zone of varying width was created which enabled the irregularities of the hillside to be accommodated. The levelling operations associated with the construction of the *viale* also led to modifications to the edge of the east terrace. Except for the north-south axis, the patterning of the upper terrace does not comply with the geometric system and is probably also of a later date.

In short, the original ground-floor plan of the villa can be seen as a system of squares: two small ones in the house and two larger ones in the garden. Further refinement of the analysis shows that the large squares in the garden appear to be constructed from the basic square (module) found in the casino (4A by 4A). The salon and the north-south axis (elements of the central plan) are situated in the overlaps of the squares. Incorporated into the margin, whose width is A, are the transitional elements: the west retaining wall, the two loggias, the winter and the summer houses on the upper terrace and the pergola.

The hypothetical geometric system can be seen as a dimensional scheme in which the connection between the plan of the house, the garden and the landscape could be controlled mathematically. It is a means of rationalizing this connection. In the following section it will become clear that the elements defined by the geometry of the plan also play a leading role in the spatial *integrazione scenica* of the villa.

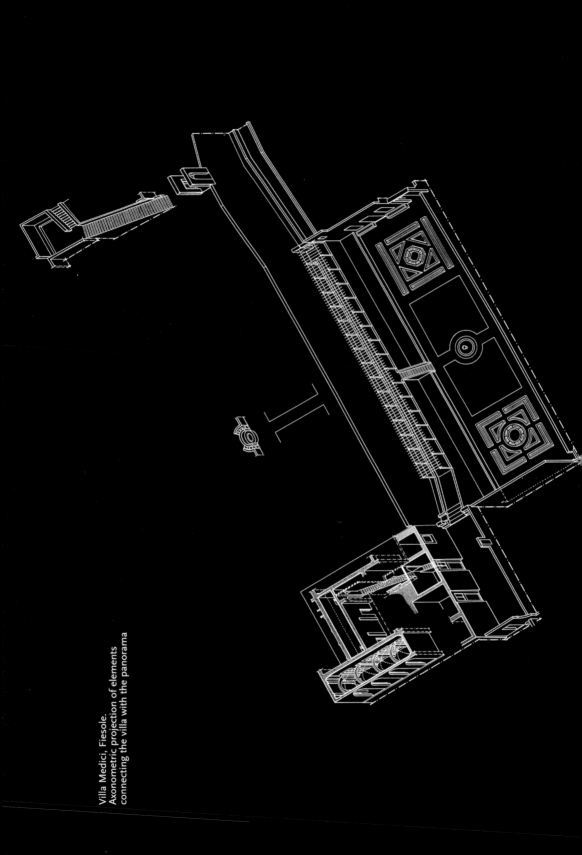

Villa Medici, Fiesole.
Axonometric projection of elements
connecting the villa with the panorama

INTEGRAZIONE SCENICA

The parts of the villa which in the previous geometric model were distinguished as essential elements must now be placed in their spatial context. In what manner do they form a coherent architectural system, and how is the particular location of the villa, with regard to the panorama, determined?

The house is the representative centre of the villa. In the salon, which has no windows in the outer façade, the *villeggiatura* is represented by paintings. The feeling of enclosure is not really overcome, however, by the landscape painted on the walls: there is still no connection between the natural perspective of the salon and the perspective of the framed paintings. The salon is directly connected to the loggias by a corridor. Because of the low situation of the west terrace the panorama from the west loggia has no foreground. The panorama itself is deep and lacks architectural features to lend scale to the space. This causes the meeting of the villa and the natural space on the west side to appear as a confrontation.

At the other end of the corridor is the east loggia. This is moved southward, downhill from the west loggia. The east loggia looks onto the north terrace, which, sloping upwards from the loggia, presents itself as an enclosed garden. It is the *giardino segreto*, which meets the *bosco* on the natural hillside at the *viale*. In the present layout the east-west direction of the terrace is accentuated by the symmetric location of a niche and belvedere at the rear of the *giardino segreto*. These correspond, respectively, to the corridor and the door in the bricked-up loggia-arch of the house. On the rear wall of the belvedere is a painting representing the actual scene behind it.

It is possible that this device was intended to suggest the view from the garden, while at the same time obstructing the actual view from the *viale* in the garden. In the middle of the north terrace the east-west direction is pierced by a transverse axis of symmetry, which begins at a spring. It is an incidental reference to the southern panorama, which, from here, only appears as an indefinite space without any scale.

To return to the corridor in the house the descending steps and garden rooms form the first links in the connection with the south terrace. However, the most important spatial link is the pergola, situated high up along the massive retaining wall, between the north and south terraces. Visually enclosed by ramps at each end, it is a shady porch facing the southern panorama. Apart from the framing effect of the columns, the view is given depth by the carpet-like foreground on the south terrace. On the terrace, topiary and terracotta pots containing small citron trees provide the panorama with a readable scale and subdivision. Brunelleschi's dome in Florence is, after all, clearly visible from here. This gives the natural space of the panorama an architectural definition. It may be said that the spatial system of the villa consists of three levels: the salon, the *giardino segreto* and the panorama. Inside the house itself these three levels are connected by the corridor, two loggias, the staircase and garden room. The panorama is of the new spatial type which had to be integrated into villa architecture. The extended terrace and stoa are the classical means which have been used to control this natural space. In Villa Medici this lateral structure is only incidentally intersected by axial elements. This serves to direct the view, which is not yet fixed by, for example, interventions in the panorama itself.

THE ARCADIAN IDYLL

The plan of the villa is determined by two main directions. In a west to east direction the most important garden elements are the west terrace lying on the lower side valley of the Arno; the west loggia; the east loggia with its large upper terrace, which has been moved southwards, and the curving mountain slope, still further to the south, with the entrance drive (*viale*). The west terrace, apart from its northern strip, com-

Villa Medici, Fiesole. Panorama (photograph by G. Smienk)

Villa Medici, Fiesole. View from the east
(photograph by G. Smienk)

prises a grass parterre with box dwarf hedges and four high column-shaped trees (*Magnolia grandiflora*). At the foot of the east front, on the elevated northern terrace that slopes upwards in an easterly direction, is natural stone paving and, further up, a grass parterre. This is terminated by a small wall with a holly hedge running along it at the now eastern entrance to the garden. The parterre is divided into three sections, each one smaller than the other. In the section by the east front of the house is a *Magnolia grandiflora*, while in each of the other two there is an old *Paulownia tomentosa* that provides shade in summer.

Grass parterres with (fruit) trees were mentioned, among others, by Colonna in his *Hypnerotomachia poliphili*. At Villa Medici these trees are integrated into the natural vegetation of olive trees and cypresses (the *bosco*) of the mountainside outside the garden. In their mutual cohesion and as a visual, west-east series, the parterre, hedge and *bosco* can be seen as pictorial gradations of naturalness. The most important elements of the garden in a north-south direction are symmetrically placed on the axis, which links both large terraces geometrically to each other. The northern garden wall is covered in ivy, while roses have been planted in the border running along it. The transverse axis begins on the northern terrace at a small natural spring in the middle of the northern garden wall. It ends at a round reflecting pond in the centre of the south terrace. Halfway along are steps linking the level of the pergola along the retaining wall with the lower situated south terrace, which is also divided symmetrically into four parterres. The centre two consist of grass bordered by box, while the two outer ones are filled in with various clipped box patterns. *Calendula officinalis* have been planted between the low box hedges. Box parterres are mentioned by Alberti when quoting from the descriptions of Pliny the Younger. Colonna also refers to them in his *Hypnerotomachia poliphili*. Such parterres were planted, among others, with aromatic herbs, such as basil, thyme, myrtle and marjoram as well as violets.

According to some, the patterns of the box parterres refer to the ideal plan of a city. Four clipped *Magnolia grandiflora* grow in the middle parterres, while cone-shaped *Laurus nobilis* can be found in the two outer ones. The pergola between the north and south terrace is overgrown with *Campsis radicans*, while the walls of the coach house are covered with *Wisteria floribunda* and *Bougainvillaea*. In the summer small orange trees in large terracotta pots on stone pedestals are set out along the parterres. In their mutual cohesion, the elements placed symmetrically on the axis form a (water) system (spring-steps-reflecting pond) that incorporates nature into the estate in a tangible and pictorial way.

The overgrown elements and the water series have been integrated into the geometric and spatial system of the villa, so as to form an Arcadian idyll of poetry and proportion.

OBSERVATORY AND LABYRINTH

The Villa Medici at Fiesole was one of the first villas in Tuscany in which the cultural ideal of country life was separated from the traditional context of farm and *castello* and evolved into an independent architectural form. In the house this is shown most clearly in the way Michelozzo made use of the loggia, a traditional element in Tuscan farm building, as a separate element added to the exterior of the house.

A second aspect that distinguishes Villa Medici as an independent architectural type is the scale and the shape of the terrace structure. This must have involved the usual technical and financial problems which arose when dealing with the steep, poorly accessible slope. The ground is also entirely unsuitable for agriculture. This all suggests that the choice of location must have been determined primarily by social, visual and climatic factors. The terraced construction of the villa was possibly inspired

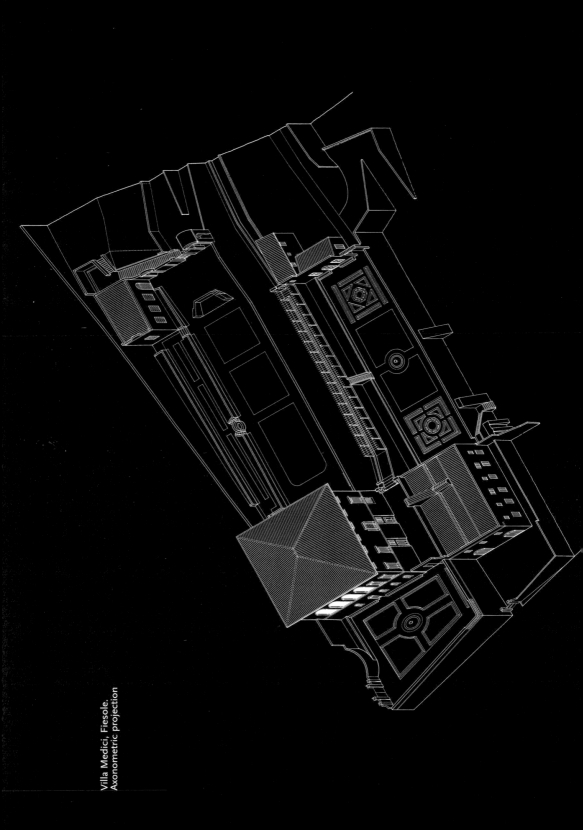

Villa Medici, Fiesole.
Axonometric projection

by Pliny the Younger's description of his terraced villa. When visiting the villa one is struck by the fact that these two elements, the loggias and the terraces, still occupy key positions in the architectural effect of the villa's interaction with the landscape. The 18th-century modifications discussed earlier do not seem to be of overriding importance as they do not really affect the original *integrazione scenica* of the villa, but in some respects actually reinforce it. The villa remains one of the first and clearest examples of the new way of thinking about nature, geometry and space in the quattrocento. It is an observatory in the complex web of nature.

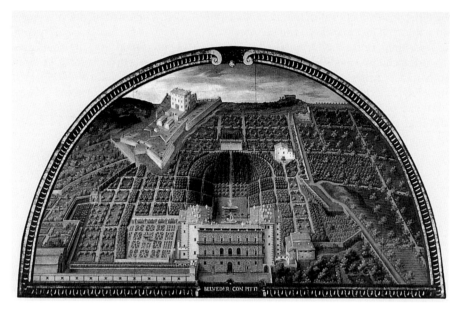

Palazzo Pitti, Boboli Gardens and Forte di Belvedere in 1599, Florence (Justus Utens)

The Boboli Gardens

Between 1450 and 1465 Lucca Pitti had a number of houses along the Via Romana in Florence demolished in order to build a palazzo with a piazza in front, designed by Brunelleschi. In 1550 Grand Duke Cosimo I de' Medici's wife, Eleonora di Toledo, bought the palazzo. Behind it, on the slopes of the hill of Boboli, a garden was laid out after a design by Niccolò Tribolo (1500-50), who, at the same time, was working on the Villa Castello.

After Tribolo's death in 1550 Bartolomeo Ammanati began extending the palazzo and, in 1558, building the *cortile* and its grotto. In 1565 the Palazzo Pitti was connected to the ancient Palazzo della Signoria in the city centre by a covered, raised walkway, which went over the Ponte Vecchio, along the Arno and through the Uffizi. The walkway was designed by Vasari to mark the wedding of Francesco de' Medici, Cosimo I's son. It forms the tailpiece to a century of developing the relationship between the city and surrounding landscape.

FLORENCE AS A RATIONAL URBAN LANDSCAPE

The original Roman centre of Florence (59BC) is rectangular and as a *templum* (holy plan) orientated in the traditional north-south manner. The city lies in the valley of the River Arno, which flows in a northwest-southeast direction. This orientation is emphasized by the layout of the Roman settlement, which is laid out across the entire valley as a framework. The *cardo maximus* (axis) of this settlement grid is at right angles to the river, while the *decumanus maximus* (transverse axis) runs parallel to it. These orthogonal axes form the basis of the landscape divisions in the valley. The landscape grid has a module size of roughly 2,400 square Roman feet (710 square metres). The north-south orientated heart of Florence appears in this grid as a rotated

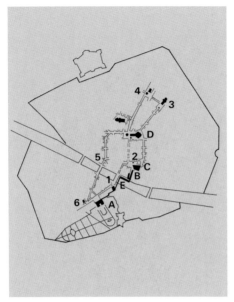

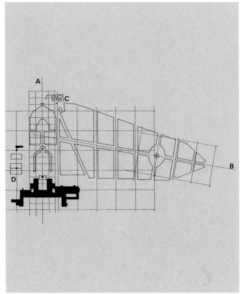

The Boboli Gardens in Florence and the 16th-century ceremonial urban circuit.
1. Ercole e il Centauro
2. Equestrian statue of Cosimo I
3. Equestrian statue of Ferdinando I
4. Column on Piazza San Marco
5. Column on Piazza Santa Trinita
6. Column on Piazza San Felice
A. Palazzo Pitti
B. Uffizi
C. Piazza della Signoria
D. Santa Maria del Fiore
E. Corridor by Giorgio Vasari

Palazzo Pitti and the Boboli Gardens, Florence.
A. Original layout
B. Viottolone and Isolotto by Alfonso Parigi (1620)
C. Giardino del Cavaliere (1670)
D. Kaffeehaus (1776)

rectangle and lies where the grid's main and transverse axes intersect. This is the strategic point where the most important tributary, the Mugnone, flows into the Arno, the valley widens and the river can still be crossed. In later city planning the landscape grid was 'translated' into streets and incorporated into the city so that the town plan lost its autonomy in relation to the landscape. From the 13th century onwards the appearance of the city changed radically. New city walls incorporated huge chunks of the settlement and the Arno into Florence. The guilds also commissioned Arnolfo di Cambio (1232-1302) to build two important new centres within the city. To the north of the old city work began on a new cathedral, the Santa Maria del Fiore on the Piazza del Duomo (started 1296). Just outside the southern boundary of the Roman city Arnolfo built the new Palazzo della Signoria (1299-1310) for the city council on the piazza of the same name. The new buildings were linked to each other by the Via dei Calzaiuoli. During a process of demolition, relocation and renovation spanning the 14th century, in which aesthetic motives played an increasingly dominant role, the Piazza della Signoria was made into a ceremonial square. The north and south sides of the square are orientated according to the grid of the city, while the west and south sides follow the direction of the landscape grid. The dialectic between both systems architectonically comes together in the walls of the piazza.

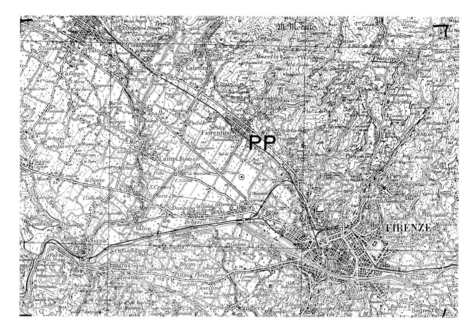

Topographic map of Florence: 1:100,000, 1956. Istituto Geografico Militare Firenze

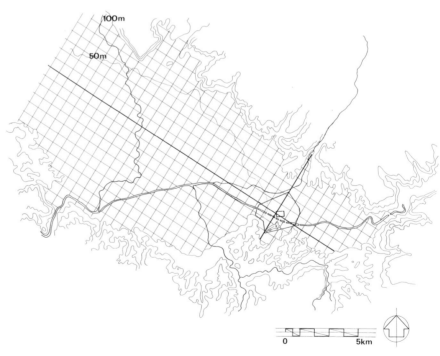

The *centuriatio* scheme, Arno valley, Florence; the *cardo* (axis) and *decumanus maximus* (transverse axis) follow the main natural axes of the valley. The old city of Florence follows the directions of the compass rose as a *templum*.

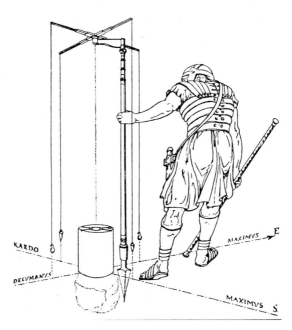

The *centuriatio* or determining the axis and transverse axis using a so-called *groma*. From Leonardo Benevolo, *The history of the city*, 1980.

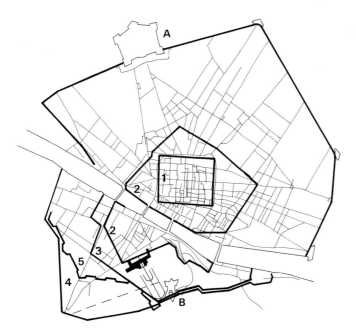

Scheme of the continuous city walls and city layout. In the angle between 1 and 2, it is clear that the layout beyond the old city follows the direction of the landscape.

1. Roman wall (100 BC)
2. *Cerchia communale* d'Oltr'Arno (1173-75)
3. *Mura* d'Oltr'Arno (1258)
4. *Cerchia communale* (1299-1333)
5. Cosimo's wall (1544)

A. Antonio da Sangallo. Fortezza di San Giovanni Battista, 1534-35
B. Bernardo Buontalenti. Fortezza di Santa Maria di Belvedere, 1590-95

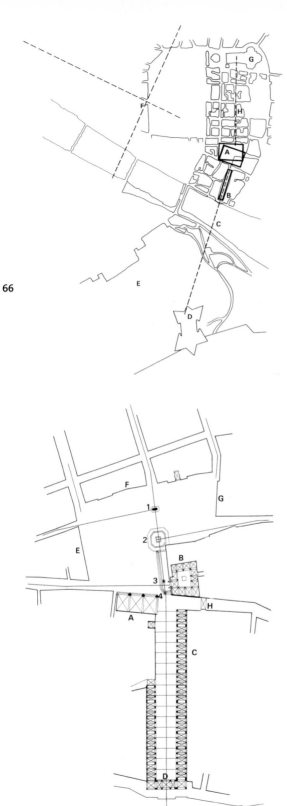

The Piazza della Signoria,
Florence, on the border of the
old city and a city plan.
Two walls are contained in the
grid of the old city, while two
other walls, and those of the
Uffizi, follow the direction of the
centuriatio.
A. Piazza della Signoria
B. Uffizi
C. Amo
D. Fortezza di Santa Maria
E. Boboli Gardens
F. *Centuriatio*
G. Santa Maria del Fiore
H. Via de' Calzaiuoli

Piazza della Signoria and the
Uffizi, Florence.
A. Loggia della Signoria
B. Original entrance of the
Palazzo della Signoria
C. Uffizi
D. Loggia of the Uffizi
E. Santa Cecilia and Loggia dei
Pisani
F. Santo Romolo
G. Tribunale della Mercanzia
H. Link between Palazzo della
Signoria and the Uffizi
1. Equestrian statue of Cosimo I
(Giambologna)
2. Neptune Fountain
(Ammanati)
3. David (Michelangelo)
4. Ercole and Caco (Bandinelli)

The Uffizi portico as a gateway between the city of Florence and the land-scape.
The buildings on the opposite bank of the Arno are from a later date (photograph by P. v.d. Ree).

In 1540, when the ruling Medici family moved their place of residence to the Palazzo della Signoria, Cosimo I had the idea to bring together the most important magistrates of the city in one complex. For this purpose he designed the so-called Uffizi (begun 1560), a 'street' of administrative buildings built where there was an opening in the Piazza della Signoria leading to the River Arno. Longitudinally, the street, with its severely arranged layout and walls, functions as a 'telescope' especially in the direction of the river, where a large open portico frames the hilly landscape with the Boboli Gardens on the opposite bank of the Arno. The landscape is thus incorporated into the town in the form of a picture. The 16th-century paintings in the Palazzo Vecchio depicting, among others, views seen through the town and panoramas across the landscape have now become reality. A reality which is physically accessible via Vasari's walkway to the Boboli Gardens.

THE BALCONY GARDEN

The Boboli garden was adorned with statues during the celebrations of the wedding of Francesco de' Medici. The *cortile* served as an open-air theatre, while the larger stone amphitheatre, linking the garden to this, is ascribed to Bernardo Buontalenti, who worked on the garden from 1583 until 1588. He also designed the *Grotto Grande* to the north-east of the palazzo. From 1620 to 1640 Giulio and Alfonso Parigi further extended the palazzo. It was then that the *bosco* – on the top of the hill at the end of the garden axis – was felled. A second, even larger amphitheatre was created, consisting of grassed terraces (this theatre is not shown on the Utens lunette of 1599), which was used for important festivities. The niche with the Medici coat of arms at the termination of the garden axis was replaced by a statue of Abundance by Giambologna.

Alfonso Parigi also extended the garden westwards. Up until then the garden had been bounded to the west by the city wall of 1544. Parigi laid out the Viottolone,

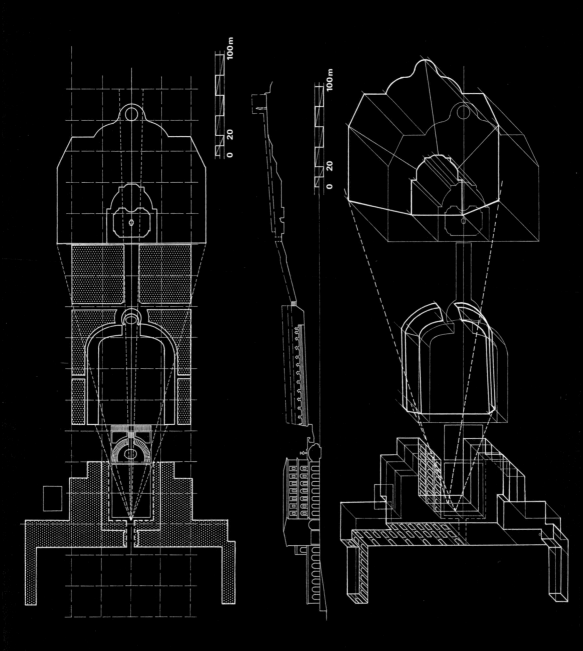

Boboli Gardens, Florence. Plan, elevation and axonometric projection illustrating the sequence piazza, *cortile*, first amphitheatre, *bosco* and second amphitheatre

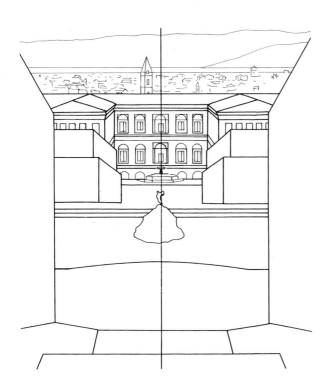

View back from the highest point of the Boboli Gardens. In the 16th century, the city could not be seen in the panorama above the palazzo.

the long avenue which descends to the Porta Romana. Originally the avenue was overgrown like a tunnel, as many of the paths still are. It was later planted with cypresses. There were also labyrinths along both sides. The *isolotto* (island), which was very similar to the one at the Villa Hadriana, was constructed at the lower end of the Viottolone.

The two non-aligned wings of the palace, called the *rondo*, were built between 1746 and 1819. In 1860 the palazzo became the property of the Crown. In 1919 Victor Emmanuel III presented it to the Italian State.

The colossal dimensions of the Palazzo Pitti, made possible by the rock foundations, were kept under control by Brunelleschi by means of the square modular structure of the façade. This dimensional system was also followed during the later extensions to the palazzo.

The building is symmetrically placed on the axis, which ascends the hill from the north-west to the south-east. On the axis are situated from below to above: the piazza on the Via Romana, the palazzo, the *cortile*, the Artichoke Fountain, the first (stone) theatre, the Neptune Fountain and the second (green) amphitheatre. The piazza was used to introduce a sense of distance from the Via Romana, and Brunelleschi's façade was placed against the background of the wooded hill. Entrance to the *cortile*, which is cut out of the rock, is via the archway at the centre of the ground floor of the palazzo. The rock base remains visible on the garden side because of the grottoes of Moses, Hercules and Antaeus which have been cut into it. From here steps lead up to the garden on the hillside, which can be surveyed from the (former) loggia of the central axis on the *piano nobile*. The *cortile* and the first and second theatres are not only placed above each other, they also become successively bigger so that they appear to be the same size and suggest a vertical plane facing the loggia. The first amphitheatre, with its elongated curved shape, seems visually to be a continuation of the

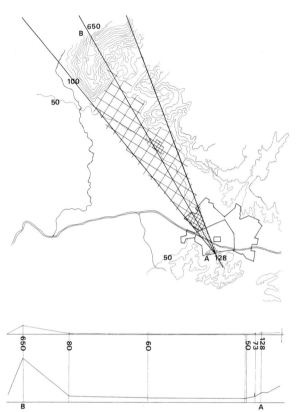

Ground plan and elevation of the Florence panorama seen from the furthest point from the city in the Boboli Gardens. The depth of the panorama is around 15 kilometres. In the elevation, the vertical scale is exaggerated.

Lines of vision between the Boboli Gardens and the city of Florence.
1. Palazzo Pitti
2. Dome of Santa Maria del Fiore
3. Campanile of Santo Spirito
4. Campanile of the Palazzo della Signoria
5. Uffizi
6. Fortezza di Belvedere

Boboli Gardens, Florence

palazzo's *piano nobile*. Its height is such that the rear façade of the palazzo acts as stage scenery and determines the view in the direction of the town. It is only along a diagonal line of vision that the sacred and political poles of the city of Florence become visible: Brunelleschi's dome and the campanile of the Palazzo della Signoria. From the large upper amphitheatre the palazzo is reduced to a neutral screen concealing the ancient city: only the campanile of Santo Spirito protrudes above its roof. The Arno valley with its hills, however, is visible above this screen.

The sequence of spaces provided by the theatres, and which seems to cumulate at the top of the hill, is given a surprising sequel. The view back over the palazzo and the city shows the garden united with the natural arena of the Arno valley. This 'periscope' effect is a way of siting the urban palazzo as a villa in the landscape. The staging of Brunelleschi's dome from the first theatre and the landscape from the second has the additional effect of separating the observer's optical experience of the landscape from that of the city. In contrast to the sequence of levels, spaces and dimensions on the axis of the palazzo, the Viottolone forms a continuous link with the Porta Romana and the Villa Poggio Imperiale outside.

Villa Gamberaia, Settignano. Loggia

Villa Gamberaia

Written sources do not reveal who designed this villa. An engraving of 1610 ascribes the creation to a certain Zanobi Lapi, whose heirs claimed the property on his death in 1627. The villa came into the hands of the Capponi in 1717; they enlarged the house, embellished the garden with fountains and statues, and laid out the bowling green, with the grotto and entrance to the orchard at right angles to the house. In all probability the villa was given its present form during this period. Towards the end of the 19th century Princess Giovanna Ghyka came into possession of the villa, after a long period during which it had been neglected. She added the reflecting pools in the parterre. The house, which was destroyed during the Second World War, has been reconstructed in its original state by the present owners, the Marchi family.

The location of Villa Gamberaia is similar to that of Villa Medici at Fiesole in that it is situated at a similar distance from Florence. Both villas are almost invisible from their access roads. The Villa Medici is separated from the road by a high wall, and the Villa Gamberaia remains concealed from the entrance road because of a difference in level; in the latter case the road even runs beneath a part of the garden. The two villas are also similar in their modest setting. Villa Gamberaia, which occupies a prominent position on top of a ridge, is nevertheless tucked away among trees. In both villas the relationship with the landscape is revealed from within the villa by the way the panorama unfolds from the terraces.

PLINY'S LANDSCAPE THEATRE
The northern and eastern slopes of the Arno valley rise to more than 700 metres. On the southern side of the valley the terrain is less accentuated. In antiquity Pliny the

The Arno valley and Brunelleschi's dome.

Younger had already described this natural space as a gigantic amphitheatre. The panorama extends to 15 kilometres from east to west and 8 kilometres from north to south. From the villas, which are situated at an ideal height of 50 to 150 metres above the valley floor, this panorama was observed from visually strategic positions. Thus the Florentine landscape was spanned by a network of lines of vision, with the town of Florence as an integral part of the panorama.

Yet the town also plays an active part in the architectural development of the natural space in which it is situated, thanks to the town-planning of Brunelleschi in Florence (1377-1446). This is most clearly expressed in his design for the dome of the Santa Maria del Fiore Cathedral in Florence (1418-46), the shape of which expresses perspective equilibrium and continuity. From whatever side it is observed the dome is identical. With this dome, Brunelleschi achieved not only a new coherence and spatial unity within the town plan, but also provided a reference point for the town from the surrounding landscape and hills. This is indicated by the numerous toponyms in the Florence area, such as L'apparità and L'apparenza, which are at points from which the city is revealed by the dome's outline. The dome also attested to the historical significance of a city with new cultural and political prestige, which controlled an extensive territory. Its 'shadow' had to 'cover' not only the Florentines but also the other inhabitants of Tuscany. The dome has the ideal shape with which to relate the town in its totality to the horizon of the surrounding hills, on which the natural dome of the sky seems to rest. In this sense Brunelleschi's dome transforms the natural landscape into an architecturally determined space.

Villas in the Arno valley.
The shading indicates in which areas of the valley
the dome by Brunelleschi is (in theory) visible.

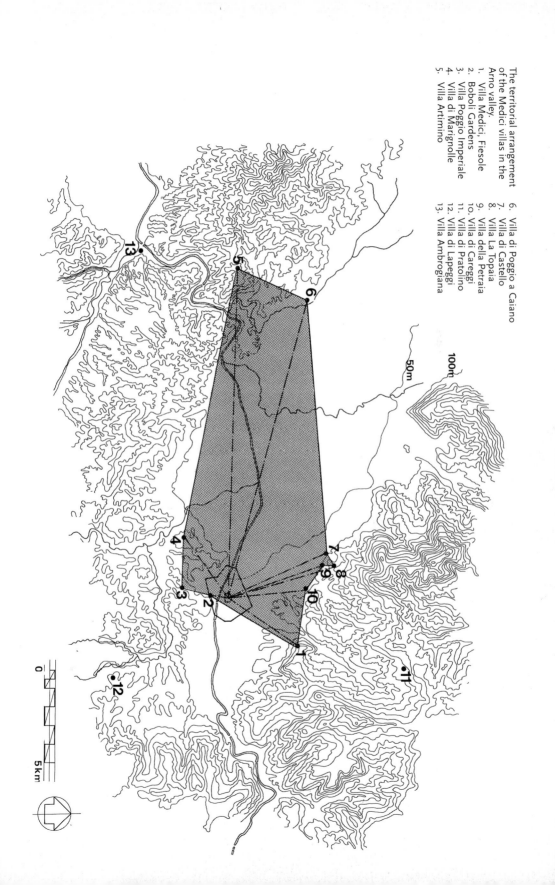

The territorial arrangement
of the Medici villas in the
Arno valley.

1. Villa Medici, Fiesole
2. Boboli Gardens
3. Villa Poggio Imperiale
4. Villa di Marignolle
5. Villa Artimino

6. Villa di Poggio a Caiano
7. Villa di Castello
8. Villa La Topaia
9. Villa della Petraia
10. Villa di Careggi
11. Villa di Pratolino
12. Villa di Lapeggi
13. Villa Ambrogiana

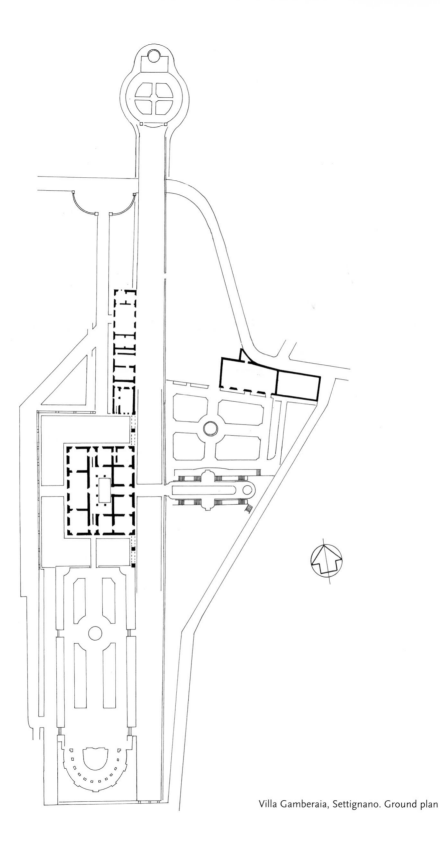

Villa Gamberaia, Settignano. Ground plan

Florentine villas, seen from the city, against the backdrop of the Arno valley

THE STANZE GARDEN

The plan of Villa Gamberaia was designed according to the stanze concept in that it comprises a number of autonomous and separately designed parts defined within the total composition. The various parts of the garden are devoted to one single motif such as the strong-smelling lemon trees, the *amora bosco* and the perfectly clipped topiary garden with its semicircular 'theatre'. The separate elements are united by the long, central lawn – the bowling green – which, on one side, connects the villa to the earth by means of a grotto cut into the hill; on the other, the statue of Diana, on the edge of the ravine, directs the view to infinity.

There are several views from the villa. On the terrace at the top of the hedge-screened entrance avenue the villa opens out, almost as if by surprise, to the panorama of Florence. The city can also be seen through the house itself from the grotto garden, which lies at right angles to the bowling green on the building's main axis. The panoramic view reoccurs like a projected image in the archways on each side of the house and is, thus, inserted into the series of themes which are connected by the long open central space of the bowling green. The house is also an element of this series.

From the side of the approach avenue the entrance to the house, which is directed towards the bowling green, is not visible; nor is there direct access from the topiary garden. In this arrangement the patio of the house is the counterpart of the enclosed space of the grotto garden. Whereas at Villa Medici at Fiesole the spatial system of the villa is finally distilled in the house itself, at this villa it is the long rectangular open space between the hillside and the statue of Diana which constitutes the focus of the stage management. According to this interpretation the patio can be seen as an internal loggia connecting the two parts of the house on the axis from the grotto garden to the panorama.

Within the matrix of the composition the references to nature and landscape

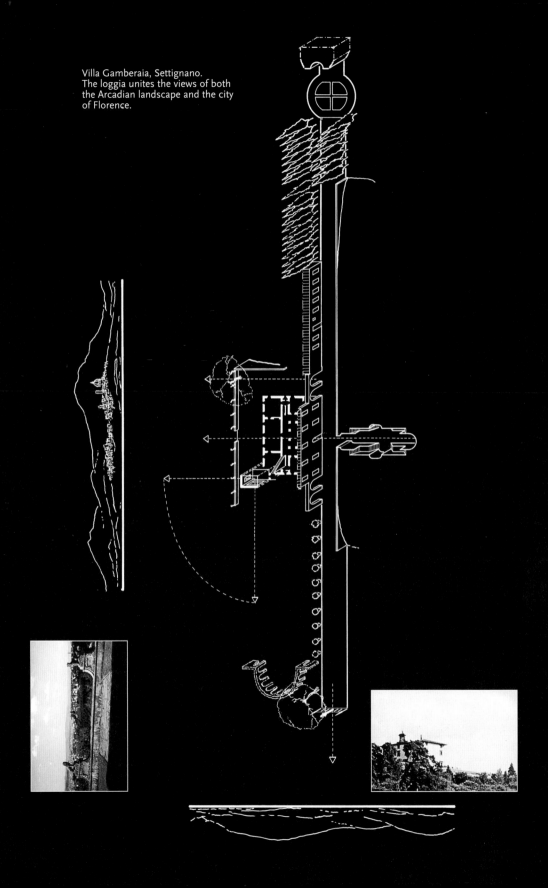

Villa Gamberaia, Settignano.
The loggia unites the views of both
the Arcadian landscape and the city
of Florence.

Villa Gamberaia, Settignano. The garden at the base of the south façade
(photograph by G. Smienk)

are expressed in different ways. The topiary garden is an extraction from nature. The secrets and patterns of nature are revealed in this geometric garden and controlled by imitation. The trees and hedges are transformed into spheres, cones and statues. The reflecting pool mirrors nature and presents its image to humankind. The edge of this garden is enclosed by a high semicircular hedge in which archways have been cut, the central one revealing 'real' nature outside the domain of the villa. The loggia of the house is not situated at the centre of the façade but at a corner of the first floor. It is detached from the geometric arrangement of the villa, and from here the view over the garden to the landscape and the town is organized into one single panorama.

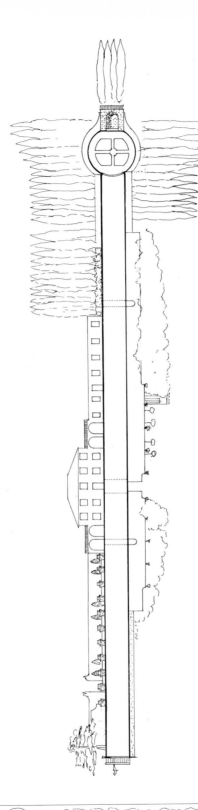

Villa Gamberaia, Settignano.
The bowling green

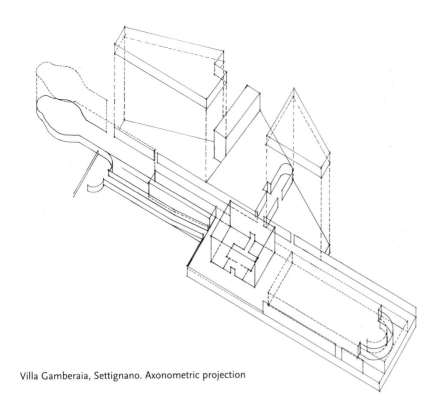

Villa Gamberaia, Settignano. Axonometric projection

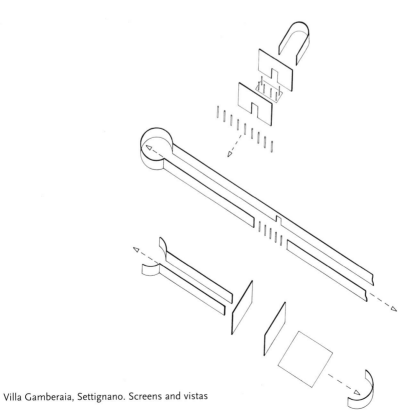

Villa Gamberaia, Settignano. Screens and vistas

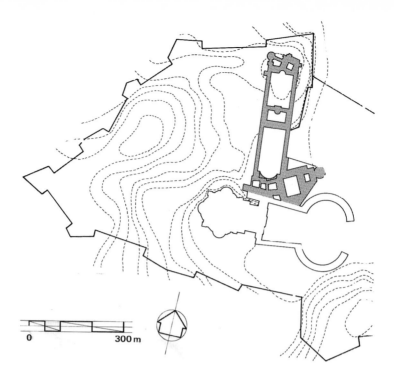

0   300 m

The Cortile del Belvedere between the Villa Belvedere to the north and the Vatican to the south, Rome

Cortile del Belvedere

The Cortile del Belvedere was part of the cultural programme undertaken by the popes, from Nicholas V onwards. Giuliano della Rovere 'Il Terribile' in particular, as Pope Julius II (1503-13), wished to make Rome the centre of civilization. He especially took it upon himself to restore the ecclesiastical state which, under his predecessor, Alexander Borgia VI, had been on the verge of collapse. This aim was furthered, among other things, by a building programme intended as the *renovatio imperii*, the revival of imperial Rome, and which was to have a great impact. The Vatican was the starting point of the *instauratio Romae*. The old Basilica of Constantine and the papal palace next to it were to be transformed into a complex that could compete with other imperial seats, such as Constantinople. Donate Bramante (1444-1514) was appointed architect to achieve this aim.

THE ROMAN VILLEGGIATURA

The Roman *villeggiatura* of the 15th and 16th century was greatly influenced by the church's bid for dominance of Renaissance culture. Popes and cardinals acted as protectors and patrons of humanists and artists, convinced that cultural leadership was the responsibility of the church. Two periods can be distinguished in the prelates' endeavours to turn Rome into the leading city of world culture. The first began during the reign of Nicholas V (1447-55) but was dramatically interrupted by the Sack of Rome (*sacco di Roma*) in 1527. The second period started with the Council of Trent (1545-63) and lasted for a hundred years. During both periods the papal *villeggiatura* was, more than ever before, concerned with cultural life. In the Middle Ages, too, the popes had fled from the oppressive heat of the city during summer to their country seats in the hill towns of the Roman Campagna. It was only during the Renaissance

Cortile del Belvedere, Rome. Engraving, *c.* 1560

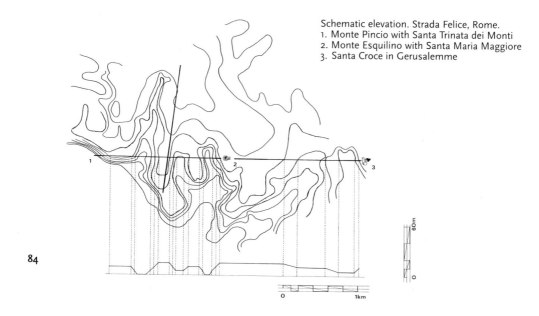

Schematic elevation. Strada Felice, Rome.
1. Monte Pincio with Santa Trinata dei Monti
2. Monte Esquilino with Santa Maria Maggiore
3. Santa Croce in Gerusalemme

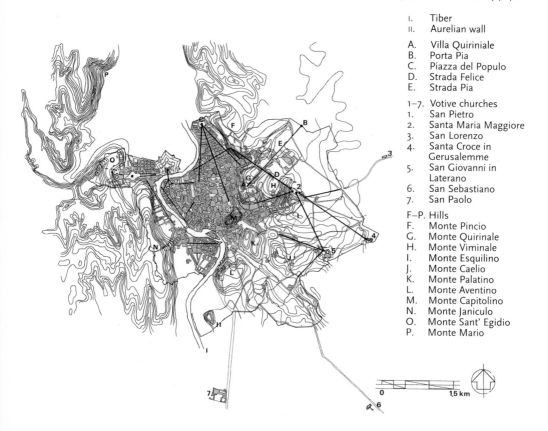

Roman streets laid out by 15th and 16th-century popes

I.	Tiber
II.	Aurelian wall

A.	Villa Quiriniale
B.	Porta Pia
C.	Piazza del Populo
D.	Strada Felice
E.	Strada Pia

1–7. Votive churches
1.	San Pietro
2.	Santa Maria Maggiore
3.	San Lorenzo
4.	Santa Croce in Gerusalemme
5.	San Giovanni in Laterano
6.	San Sebastiano
7.	San Paolo

F–P. Hills
F.	Monte Pincio
G.	Monte Quirinale
H.	Monte Viminale
I.	Monte Esquilino
J.	Monte Caelio
K.	Monte Palatino
L.	Monte Aventino
M.	Monte Capitolino
N.	Monte Janiculo
O.	Monte Sant' Egidio
P.	Monte Mario

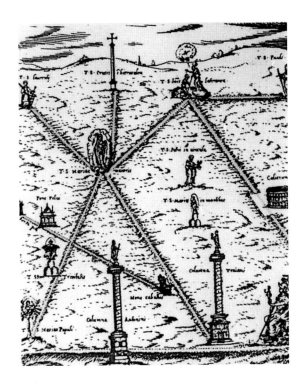

G.F. Bordino, 1588.
Map of Rome in which the streets
of Sixtus v are shown as straight
lines interlinking churches.

that villas were built in Rome itself, giving the city an important cultural and representative status. Between about 1485 and the Sack of Rome, important villas were built near the Vatican, on the west bank of the Tiber. During the period after the Council of Trent, villas were built in the hilly eastern area of the city. This took place within the framework of the urban schemes of Gregory XIII (1573-85) and Sixtus V (1586-90) in particular. They granted licences to build and provided water supplies, with the intention of systematically developing the eastern part of the city. Finally, towards the end of the 16th and at the beginning of the 17th century competing cardinals were building increasingly larger villas on the outskirts of the city. The largest of them all were the Villa Borghese (1608) and the Villa Doria Pamphili (1630) situated just outside the city wall.

ROME AS A LANDSCAPE THEATRE

In Rome the topographical conditions faced by the *villeggiatura* were determined by the structure of the Tiber valley. On its western side the north-south line of the main Tiber valley is bounded by the steep slopes of the Janiculum, which projects a strategic finger of land to the north, jutting into the Tiber valley. This is Monte S. Egidio, on which the stronghold of the Vatican lies. Beyond the deep side valley, north of this promontory, the river continues its way past the steep hills of the Monte Mario. The difference in height between the Tiber valley and the western hills is roughly 50 metres. On the east bank the relief is less pronounced, the difference in elevation being some 25 metres on average. Thus, there is no steep slope here, only hills gently rolling down to the river. Here are the proverbial seven hills on which the ancient city was built. The geographical origin of Rome was the Palatine Hill above the Forum Romanum, where, at a sharp bend in the Tiber, an island facilitated the fording of the river. The successive hills lie more or less orthogonally along the winding main Tiber

Roman villas

1. Albani
2. Borghese
3. Bosco Parrasio
4. Cavalieri di Malta
5. Chigi
6. Cortile del Belvedere
7. Colonna
8. Doria Pamphili
9. Farnesina

10. Giulia
11. Lante
12. Madama
13. Mattei
14. Medici
15. Orti Farnesiani
16. Quirinale
17. Sciarra

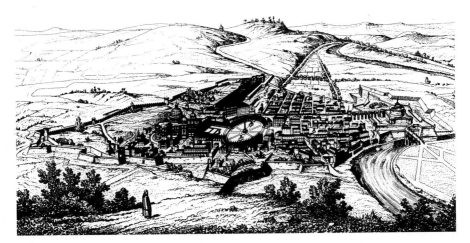

Paul Marie Letarouilly. Rome from Monte Gianiculo, 1853. Villa Belvedere is situated on a projecting north-west point of the city wall (the Vatican fortress).

valley. The outline of the old city, defined by the Aurelian wall, consists principally of the asymmetric Tiber valley and the hills surrounding it like an amphitheatre.

Three elements of the ancient city show a structural relationship with the situation of the villas. The first of these are the consular roads, the great ancient Roman arterial roads. In the hilly district it was especially along the Via Pia and Via Appia that numerous villas were constructed. In the north the Via Flaminia and, in the west, the Via Aurelia also linked a series of villas to each other. The second element is the Aurelian wall. In the Middle Ages the area enclosed by these fortifications had become too big for the decayed city and numerous villas were built in a wide green belt inside as well as outside the wall. In this way the wall was quite often breached and integrated into the villa plans (Villa Medici, Villa Belvedere). Finally, the water supply was an important factor in the siting of the villas. The deserted hilly area only became inhabitable after old aqueducts had been repaired and new ones built by the popes (including the Aqua Vergine by Sixtus IV, Aqua Felice by Sixtus V, and Aqua Paolo by Paul V). Aqueducts were an indispensable source of water for the villas (e.g. Aqua Vergine for Villa Medici and Aqua Felice for Villa Montalto).

One of the first villas to be built along the Tiber valley was Villa Belvedere, built by Pope Innocent VIII in 1485, just outside the Vatican, where the strategic north wall of the stronghold dominated the Tiber valley. Villa Belvedere radically broke with the closed character of the medieval Vatican fortress. In the north wall of the villa an open loggia has an unrestricted view of the *prati* (meadows) along the Tiber, the city, Monte Mario and the Sabine Hills. Most pilgrims and processions from the north, on their way to the Vatican, could be seen from afar and when they passed below the villa. The closed rear wall of the loggia was painted with a landscape panorama. Vasari mentions that this depicted the city of Rome as well as Milan, Genoa, Florence and Naples and showed much more than could be seen in the real panorama. As the city of Rome

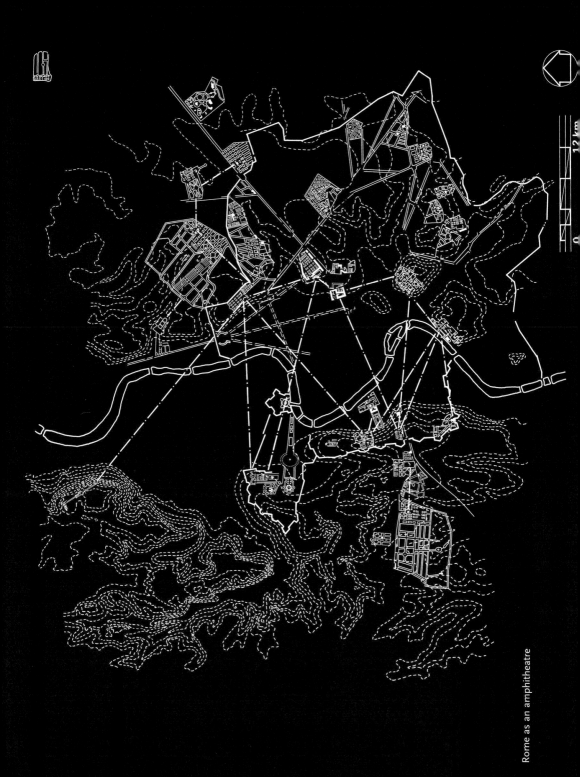

Rome as an amphitheatre

Panorama of Rome from St Peter's. Villa Borghese is to the left of the horizon, Villa Medici is to the right (photograph by P. v.d. Ree).

could not be seen from the north-facing loggia this 'defect' was thus remedied by its depiction on the rear wall. Thus the art of painting made it possible to include the entire conceivable space within the panorama.

In the early 16th century other villas were built on prominent viewpoints on the western slopes of the Tiber. Villa Sciarra (c. 1530) and Villa Lante (1518) were built on the Janiculum and Villa Madama (1517) was built outside the town on Monte Mario. Villa Farnesina on the other hand was located on the Tiber, while Villa Barberini (which no longer exists) was on the Janiculum near the Vatican.

The representative layout of villas to the east of the Tiber was established during the period of the Counter-Reformation. Villa Medici (1564), Villa Quirinale (1574), Orti Farnesiani (1570) and Villa dei Cavalieri di Malta (c. 1560) are all situated on hills along the Tiber. Towards the end of the 16th and the beginning of the 17th century, Villa Ludovisi, Villa Montalto (neither of which now exists), Villa Colonna and Villa Mattei were built.

From this it would seem that in the western and eastern areas of the town the visually strategic locations were occupied by villas. In the bowl shape (two or three kilometres in diameter) formed by the geomorphological conditions, the town is the stage for the villas nestled on the balconies of this gigantic open-air theatre. The residents of the villas could look down on the ecclesiastical and political centre of the world.

In this elevated position above the low-lying city the villas were in each other's field of vision. Just as in Florence, the villas balanced on the edge of free space, making it perceivable without creating it themselves. In Rome, however, the scale of the landscape-theatre was different. In Florence the panorama measured some 15 kilometres east to west and 8 kilometres north to south; in Rome it spanned only 2.5 kilometres by 3 kilometres respectively. Thus both vertical and horizontal dimensions

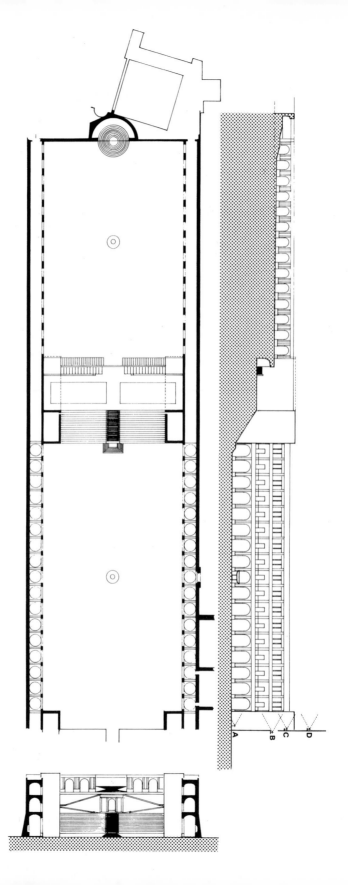

Cortile del Belvedere, Rome. Plan, elevation and cross-section

Cortile del Belvedere, Rome

were far more restricted in Rome. In Florence the villas were also situated higher (150 to 200 metres above the valley) than those in Rome (50 metres). The most important difference, however, was that in Rome the entire panorama had become urbanized. Towards the end of the 16th century control of this urban space was confirmed by the building of the 119 metre-high dome of St Peter's (1558-89). Just like Brunelleschi's dome in Florence, it was a central reference point in the panorama, precisely defining the natural space of the town landscape.

At the same time, the views in the villas changed character. The area of the villa grounds increased after 1550. This demanded adequate internal organization, which was solved by the axial organization of the villa plan. Towards the end of the 16th century the view from the terraces was channelled by visual axes (as at Villa Doria Pamphili, for example). The origin of this development can be seen at the Cortile del Belvedere (1504), in which Bramante created an axial link between the Vatican and the Villa Belvedere. Through the axial framing of views the villas were more forcefully connected with each other, like a powerful chain.

THE TERRACE GARDEN

The Cortile del Belvedere was Bramante's most important commission regarding the extension of the papal palace. In 1505 a start was made on the northern extension and the link to Innocent VIII's Villa Belvedere. Bramante's plan consisted of an elongated, enclosed courtyard between the palace and the villa. It is possible that this idea was derived from ancient villas (such as the Domus Aurea) and from fragments of imperial Rome (such as the Vatican naumachia of the first century). Internally the courtyard was divided into three terraces. The lowest served as a hippodrome or open-air theatre; the middle had seating terraces, a nymphaeum and steps; and the highest was arranged as a garden with parterres and trees. On their long sides the terraces

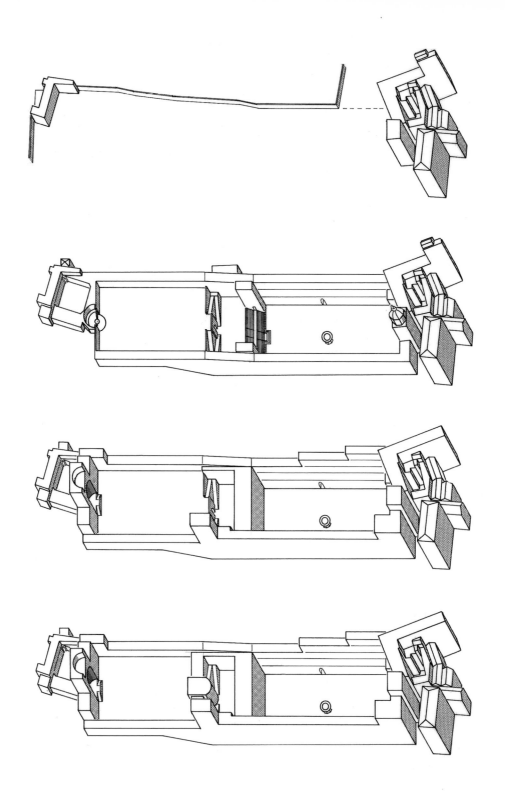

Cortile del Belvedere, Rome. Development phases

were flanked by *ambulations* (corridors) with crypto-*portici* (galleries). In Bramante's plan the latter consisted of superimposed orders (Doric, Ionic and Corinthian) in the lowest courtyard and one single order in the top one. Two small projecting towers were placed beside the seating on the central terrace. The east wall, which coincides with the city wall, was the first part to be completed. The entrance from Porta Julia was in the centre of the section bordering the lower courtyard. The north end of the *cortile* consisted of a round concave-convex flight of steps adjoining an exedra, which originally had only one storey. To the north, as a last link between the *cortile* and the Villa Belvedere, was an antiquarium in the shape of an open, square sculpture gallery. After 1505, when Bramante concentrated all his attention on the new plans for St Peter's, the construction of the *cortile* was entrusted to other architects, among whom were Antonio da Sangallo and Baldassare Peruzzi. Under Julius III (1550-55) the exedra in the rear wall was raised by one storey, as were parts of the east gallery. At the same time, the flight of steps by Bramante was replaced by a straight one. Under Pius IV (1559-65), Pirro Ligorio converted the exedra into a niche, crowned by a semicircular-shaped loggia. He was also responsible for the earlier design of the west gallery of the *cortile*. Pius V (1566-72) had all the antique pagan sculptures moved from the Belvedere and transported to cities such as Florence. Gregory XIII (1572-85) had the Torre dei Venti built roughly in the centre of the west wing.

Sixtus V (1585-90) who, together with his architect Domenico Fontana broke through the hilly part of Rome by constructing axial streets, built an impediment in the axial structure of the *cortile* in the form of the Biblioteca Sistina. This cut straight through the *cortile* at the point where the seating terraces were and destroyed the original spatial concept. Under Pius VII (1800-23) the Braccio Nuovo was also built straight across the *cortile*, this time at the point where the steps and nymphaeum were situated. In its present state, Bramante's *cortile* has disintegrated into a series of separate courtyards.

The overall size of the original Cortile del Belvedere was roughly 100 by 300 metres. From the ground floor, the *cortile superiore* and exedra were hidden from view. The visitor, entering the complex through the gate and looking north, saw a vertical accumulation of galleries, steps and a nymphaeum. The total plan could only be seen from the papal rooms situated above (the Borgia apartments and Raphael's Vatican Stanze). The best viewpoint was the window of the Stanza della Segnatura, the private study of Julius II. Seen from there, all the elements of Bramante's plan coalesced into one central perspective scene. The floor of the *cortile superiore* slants upwards in a northerly direction more than the architrave of the sidewalls. This shortened the columns of the adjacent galleries in the direction of the garden, causing an illusory increase in the depth of the space, just as in Mannerist and Baroque stage constructions. Viewed from the papal rooms, the horizon was, as it were, pulled forward. This optical lengthening was reinforced by the treatment of the walls of the *cortile*. The junction of the sidewalls of the *cortile superiore* was concealed by two small towers, placed level with the centre terrace, like the side wings of a stage. The exedra, whose depth is difficult to judge because of its semicircular shape, is wider than the opening in the back wall, making this junction invisible as well. The optical lengthening is also reinforced by the treatment of the orders. The openings in the porticoes of the *cortile inferiore* are separated by a single pilaster, whereas in the *cortile superiore* there are two, making the opening smaller.

Due to this perspective distortion, space, in Bramante's design, was manipulated by architectural means as if in a painting. Like an illustration, framed by the Stanza della Segnatura window, this scene became a part of the mural decoration of the room.

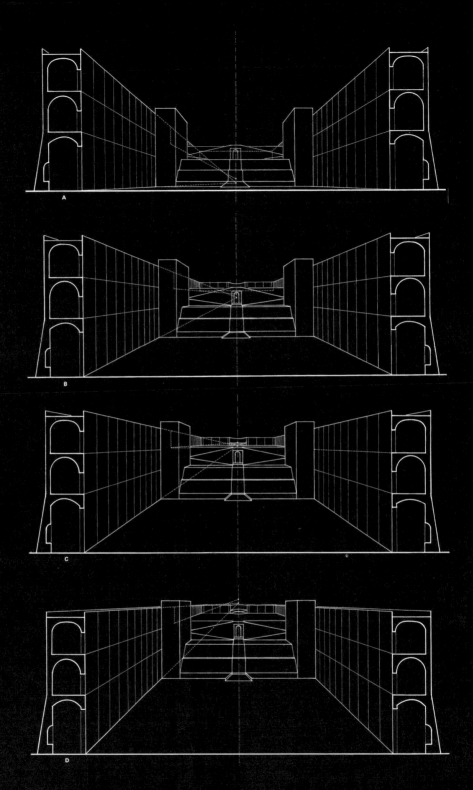

Cortile del Belvedere in Rome seen from the various Vatican floors (A: ground floor)
The vanishing point is manipulated by the upward slant of the floor of the upper court.

The *giardino segreto* on the upper terrace only became visible to the visitor moving in an axial direction through the plan. The raising of the exedra at a later date changed this. Moreover, Ligorio's loggia built above the exedra introduced a view from the opposite direction over the Vatican to St Peter's, which was then under construction. The Torri dei Venti, built even later on the west wing, offered Gregory XIII a view over the town to Villa Buoncompagni (family property of the Pope) and the Quirinale (the papal summer palace), both on the east bank of the Tiber.

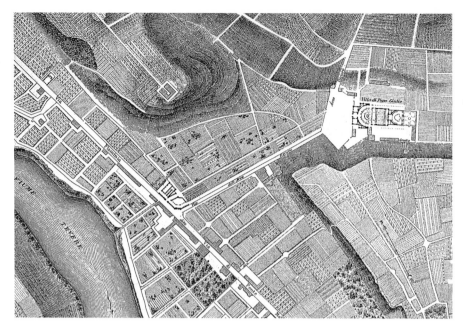

Paul Marie Letarouilly. Villa Giulia, Rome. Topographic map showing the side valley of the Tiber and the Via Flaminia, 1853

Villa Giulia

Preliminary work on the building of Villa Giulia began in 1550, immediately after the election of Cardinal Giovanni Maria Ciocchi del Monte as Pope Julius III. In accordance with his new status he ordered an extensive villa complex to be built. Before his appointment he already owned a villa and several country estates along the Via Flaminia, just outside the Porta del Populo, the city gate on the north side of Rome. From 1550 onwards, the property was rapidly extended to include the vineyards in the immediate surroundings until it incorporated all the hills between the Aurelian wall and Ponte Milvio. Within a relatively short time it could compete with the Villa Madama (1517) on the other side of the Tiber.

The villa site included a small strip of land along the River Tiber, and the building of a new harbour provided a direct link between the villa and the Vatican Palace. A covered passage connected the Vatican with Castel Sant' Angelo, from where a ceremonial boat transported the Pope and his guests to his country residence. From the mooring point a pergola led to a gate on the Via Flaminia that gave access to the garden grounds.

Some of the most famous architects of the time were engaged in the project. The original concept was probably developed by Giorgio Vasari (1511-74), while Michelangelo, who was working at St Peter's, acted as adviser. Vignola and Ammanati, both still at the beginning of their careers, worked on the central part of the villa. Vignola was responsible for the building of the casino and for engineering the waterworks of the sunken nymphaeum, while Ammanati designed the nymphaeum itself and the courtyard connecting it to the casino.

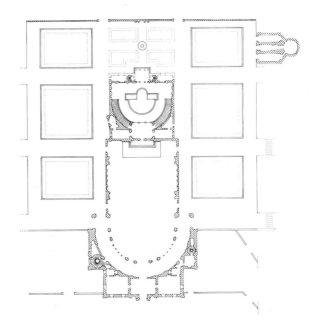

Villa Giulia, Rome. Plan

MOVEMENT AND ILLUSION

In the early 16th century an influential new approach to villa architecture emerged. This became known as Mannerism and the basic principles of Mannerist villa architecture can be traced to the design of the Cortile del Belvedere. The axial construction, the linking of a series of autonomous inner and outer spaces, and the internal manipulation of perspective, which were characteristic of the Cortile del Belvedere, were further developed in subsequent Mannerist villa architecture.

Villa Madama (1516-27), designed by Raphael and Giulio Romano, was the first villa design in which these principles were applied and in which house and garden were treated simultaneously. While still under completion the villa was almost entirely destroyed by fire during the Sack of Rome in 1527 and the second half of the villa was never finished.

Because of the instability of the period, villa building in the Roman Campagna ceased almost entirely over subsequent years and Mannerist villa architecture developed only in northern Italy. In Mantua, Giulio Romano, one of the architects who had fled Rome to take advantage of a more stable political and geographical climate, built the Palazzo del Tè and gardens (1525-35). The elaborately painted iconographic programme in the palace, with themes from classical mythology and geographical references, became one of the characteristics of Mannerist villa architecture, for which the Palazzo del Tè would serve as an example.

Yet it was in and around Rome, however, that a more mature form of Mannerism developed in the second half of the 16th century. Its most important exponents were the archaeologist and architect Pirro Ligorio (1491-1580), the Bologna educated architect, perspective designer, and theorist Giacomo Barozzi da Vignola (1507-73), and the architect Giacomo del Duca (1520-1601). Individual contributions were also made by the noblemen Niccolo and Vicino Orsini. The most important

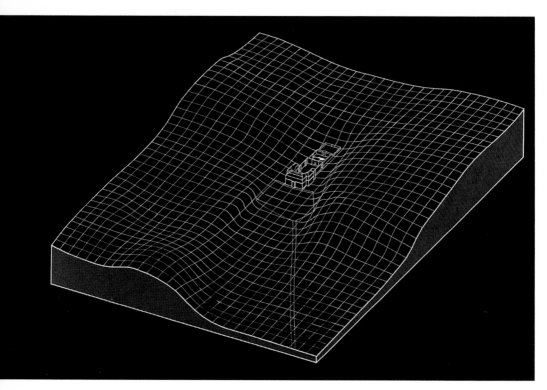

Villa Giulia, Rome. Axonometric reconstruction of the geomorphology

Paul Marie Letarouilly. Villa Giulia, Rome, 1853. View from the top of the valley

Villa Giulia, Rome. View across the axis from and to the main building

clients at that time were the Farnese and Orsini families, who owned the greater part of the northern Roman Campagna. The design which heralded the new period was that of the Villa Giulia (1550-55), which lay just outside the walls of Rome and which Vignola and Ammanati built for Pope Julius II. The main elements of this villa were arranged geometrically in a linear series of screens and views.

THE THEATRE GARDEN

The villa has a remarkable situation. The house was not erected on a hilltop, but low in a side valley of the Tiber that runs in a north-westerly direction. The two directions, arising from a bend in the valley, meet each other at the point where a long entrance drive ends at the forecourt of the villa. As the avenue is laterally defined by trees, it only becomes apparent at the last moment that it does not lie in the main axis of the villa but follows the bend of the valley. Because of this bend, it seems as though the villa, from whatever direction it is viewed, is situated in a broad enclosed valley. The villa, however, is not only an object against the background of the natural landscape but the landscape itself is integrated into the architectural treatment of the villa plan, which extends as far as the eye can see. Nothing is left to chance. The slopes were completely covered with trees by the landscape architect Jacopo Meneghini. In one of his letters Ammanati reports that 36,000 trees of various species were planted from 1550 onwards.

The architecture of the villa, with its main building and series of garden court-yards to the rear, clearly alludes to the design of Cortile del Belvedere of Julius II, while the semicircular enclosure of the first courtyard is reminiscent of Villa Madama. Following these two large designs, which were built in the same area as Villa Giulia, a spatial scheme was developed in which a synthesis occurred between architecture and landscape.

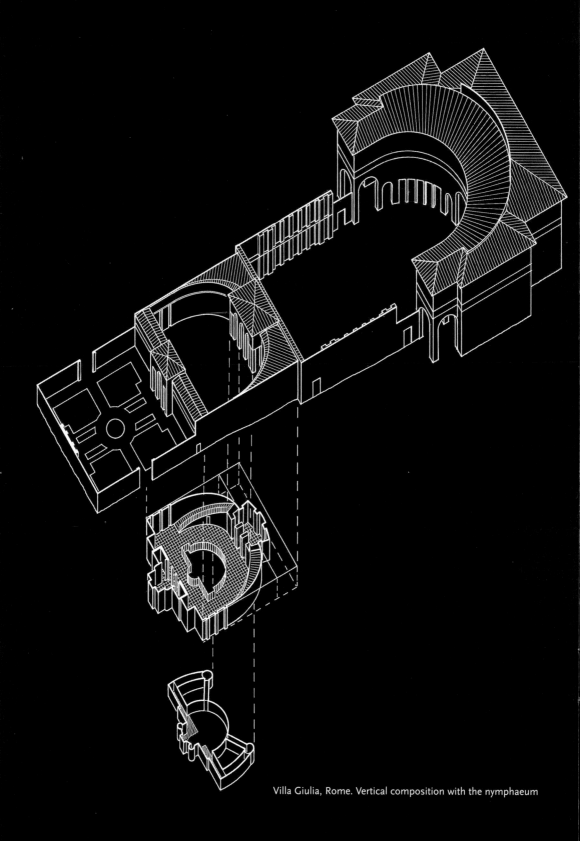

Villa Giulia, Rome. Vertical composition with the nymphaeum

Paul Marie Letarouilly. Villa Giulia, Rome, 1853. In the background the edge of the valley is framed by the portico of the main building.

Whereas the building at Villa Madama acts as a gateway to the garden, in Villa Giulia the transition from building to garden is less immediate. The courtyards, as a series of voids, are developed to such an extent that the architecture of the building becomes the framework for the garden itself.

Vignola's fondness for using the façade as *decorum* is discernable in the contrast between the front and rear elevations of the house. The openness of the villa towards the landscape is not evident at first sight; the severe, closed front elevation of the villa is directed towards the square and has a clearly representative function. The triumphal arch motif in the centre of this façade is repeated in the rear elevation and thus forms the link between the two sides. The playful rear elevation has the character of an inner façade in that the treatment of the concave shape refers directly to the interior of the Pantheon. Facing this apparent inner façade, the central section of the garden manifests itself as a series of inner spaces, and the sense of intimacy of both the building and garden behind it is intensified. The surrounding landscape is also an integral part of the composition. The interaction between the architecture of the house and the garden, as well as the surrounding landscape, are central to this design and has been treated in several different ways.

The main elements are organized geometrically on the central axis in a linear series of screens and perspectives. From the building towards the hill the openings in the screens widen while the density of the elements and the height of the walls decrease. This increasing transparency is also given material form by the gradual transition from stone to vegetation. From the hill towards the casino the density of the vegetation diminishes. It is only from the first floor of the building that there is an accurate view across all the walls, and that the view over the central axis is directed towards the surrounding landscape, although the curved loggia also offers an initial view of the adjoining hills across the side gardens before the visitor actually enters the garden.

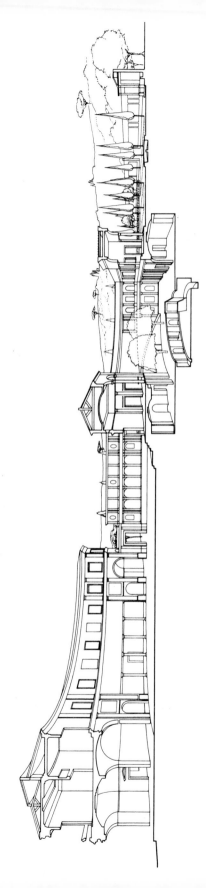

Paul van der Ree. Elevation. Villa Giulia, Rome, 1992

In one of his letters Ammanati compares the building to a theatre and the garden to a proscenium and a stage. The play is initiated by the visitor himself; he is both spectator and actor in his progress through the plan. Movement is essential for unveiling the spectacle.

Although the three middle garden courtyards are visually linked to each other on one axis, each consecutive space can only be reached by leaving the axis obliquely. Thus, a tension between axis and route is created and even heightened by the vertical construction of the nymphaeum, which consists of three layers, thereby forming a repetition of the tripartite division of the entire geometric garden layout. Opposite the semicircular colonnade in the main building, an almost closed wall originally concealed this nymphaeum from the entrance. Only a small doorway in this wall (now replaced by three open arches) gave access to a loggia, offering a view over this sunken *giardino segreto* carved out of the rocks. Two paired ramps lead to the middle level, while two small flights of steps descending to the lowest level are hidden from view.

From the intimacy of this hidden lowest level of the garden, which is decorated with grottoes, a relationship with the broad valley has been created by means of a vertical sequence which broadens and becomes increasingly transparent. The decorations, too, reinforce this sequence. The lowest floor is dominated by various water elements and by the surrounding mossy grottoes. Here the original *topos* of the villa is hidden: the low-lying marshy valley. On the edge of the middle level two enormous statues of river gods were placed in niches and four plane trees were planted around the open centre. On the highest level the inner walls were painted with landscape scenes and the screen was broken open twice above the niches towards the sky; behind these openings birdcages were placed. Eventually the vegetation of the surrounding landscape became visible above the walls. In this villa the panorama was controlled as far as the horizon, not from above but from below.

Two small staircases, again hidden from view, connect the nymphaeum and the section at the extreme rear. These finally emerged next to the birdcages and were covered by small towers, whose shapes referred to the planned (but never executed) domes above the staircases of the main building. In the rearmost section the axis is terminated by a niche in the end wall, and it was only here, that the full width of the plan was properly visible and emphasized. Movement was directed towards the sides, where there were several features along the boundary, including an ice cellar at the south side.

The ridge of hills was also accessible from here by means of various paths that were embellished with statues or specific plantings. In the wooded *barchetto* several arbours, birdcages and loggias marked the viewpoints from which one could see not only the villa itself in the valley below, but also the Vatican Palace, Castel Sant' Angelo and Villa Madama. These features were integrated into the villa's plan in order to compensate for its deficiency: that it could not afford a view of Rome.

The building of the villa was interrupted after the death of Julius III in 1555. Some years later a number of changes were carried out by Pius IV, probably under the direction of Pirro Ligorio. The casino near the fountain on the corner of the Via Flaminia is also ascribed to him. Towards the end of the 18th century, however, during the restoration work carried out for Pius VI, some changes were made that seriously affected the nymphaeum; at its rear, for example, a loggia was added and the birdcages and the small staircase towers were bricked up. The villa also suffered greatly during the 19th and 20th centuries from its constantly changing functions and from extensive changes to its urban setting: the wings added to the museum and the busy road around it now obscure the actual relationship between the villa and the landscape.

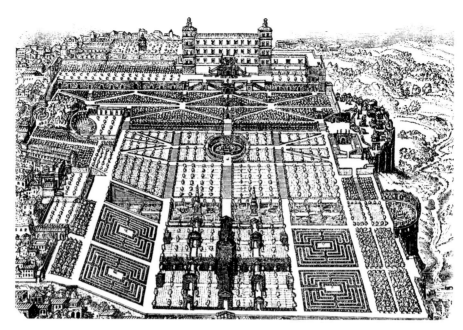

Etienne Du Pérac. Villa d'Este, Tivoli, 1573

Villa d'Este

In 1550 Ippolito d'Este II (1509-72), cardinal of Ferrara, also a patron of the arts and a keen collector of antiques, was appointed governor of Tivoli, 30 kilometres north-east of Rome, by Pope Julius II. His residence there was a 13th-century Franciscan monastery situated on a hillside. It was built on the western wall of the city, between the Porta Santa Crucis and the Porta Romana, where the terrain descends in a north-westerly direction to the Valle Gaudente. Because of its fresh air, Tivoli had been a favoured resort for well-to-do Romans since ancient times. Nearby are the ruins of villas such as Hadriana, and those of Quintilius and Varro. With these examples in mind, Cardinal d'Este bought up gardens and vineyards on the hillside, with the idea of transforming the whole area into a villa complex.

The introverted character of the original monastery complex can still be felt in the *giardino segreto*, the former cloister garden with its modest layout and restricted views of the outside world. In the developments which followed, the complex was expanded and became more extraverted. Ippolito's wish was to surpass the achievements of his rival, Cardinal Farnese at Caprarola. Just as at the Villa Farnese at Caprarola, the Villa d'Este also contained an additional element: close to the small village of Bagni di Tivoli a *barco* (hunting grounds) was laid out in which an elaborate hunting lodge was constructed. Ippolito was advised on the villa's design by the archaeologist and architect Pirro Ligorio, who had studied the ruins of Villa Hadriana and had assisted him with his archaeological purchases and excavations.

Around 1565 the sloping site was excavated and filled in to allow for terraces, with the city wall acting as a retaining wall. At the same time, an aqueduct from Monte Sant' Angelo and an underground canal from the River Anio were constructed to ensure a constant water supply of 1,200 litres a second. The terraced gardens were laid out during the next seven years. The addition of a double loggia on the garden side gave the monastery the appearance of a country residence. Several years later a dining loggia was built at the south-west point of the upper terrace.

After Ippolito's death the villa passed into the hands of his cousin Luigi. For most of the 17th century the villa remained the property of the Este family and the garden was well-maintained. During this period Bernini designed the Bicchierone (shell) Fountain and the waterfall between the water organ and fishponds. During the 18th century the villa deteriorated and was put up for sale in 1743. In 1750 the antique statues began to be sold off, which explains why, by 1803, when the male line of the Este family died out and the complex came into Habsburg hands through Maria Beatrice d'Este, archduchess of Austria, almost all of these had been removed from the building and garden. Today some of them can still be seen at the Museo Capitolino in Rome.

The villa continued to be neglected until 1850, when a German priest, Gustav Adolf von Hohenlohe, was allowed to live in the villa under the condition that he maintain it. After the death of von Hohenlohe in 1896 the House of Habsburg again became responsible for the villa. After the First World War the Villa d'Este became the property of the Italian state. Although the garden has remained for the most part intact, most of the hedges, as well as the statues, have disappeared, the pergolas have been demolished, the fountains are overgrown with moss and ferns, and the cypresses have grown tall. Nature, freed from its restraints, has given the garden a romantic 'patina'.

VILLEGGIATURA IN THE ROMAN CAMPAGNA

The 15th and 16th-century *villeggiatura* in the Roman Campagna was mainly concentrated in two areas. A great number of villas are situated in the neighbourhood of Lago Albano, south-east of Rome, and another conspicuous group of villas is found in the neighbourhood of Lago di Vico, near Viterbo, north-west of the city.

There were two distinct motives which determined the choice of these locations. The first group of villas are situated close to the ruins of classical Roman villas. From the beginning of the Christian era this rural area had been a favourite location for the *villeggiatura* of the affluent nobility. Between 118 and 138 AD Emperor Hadrian built his Villa Hadriana, some 25 kilometres east of Rome. The remains of this gigantic villa complex at Tivoli were to inspire many Renaissance architects. During the same period the small town of Frascati, close to the remains of classical Tusculum in the Alban Hills, became the most fashionable location for the summer residences of the high-ranking members of the ecclesiastical hierarchy.

The location of the second group of villas, near Viterbo, was determined by earlier medieval history. During the Middle Ages ecclesiastical dignitaries escaped the internal conflicts in Rome by taking refuge in the Roman Campagna. In many cases a complete removal of entire residences to a safer region occured: Viterbo, for example, functioned as the centre of papal power from 1266 to 1281. Moreover, during the 13th century the phenomenon of papal summer residences grew. A number of towns, including Viterbo, Orvieto and Anagni, became the regular abodes of travelling prelates. Their stay was determined by the religious calendar and the weather. As far as the accommodation itself was concerned, the existing facilities, local monasteries, episcopal palaces and castles were mostly adequate.

It was only in the second half of the 15th century, at the beginning of the Renaissance, that political stability in the Roman countryside allowed a greater degree of openness towards the landscape. Many of the country residences were decorated, enlarged and, in many cases, laid out with extensive gardens, and thus transformed into villas.

Rome and environs: villas from the 16th and 17th century.
Their heights are given in metres. From the Carta d'Italia,
Istituto Geografico Militare, Rome

K. Monte Mario
L. San Pietro
M. Frascati
N. Grottaferrata
O. Rocca di Papa
P. Lago Albano
Q. Albano
R. Castel Gandolfo
S. Lago di Nemi
T. Tivoli

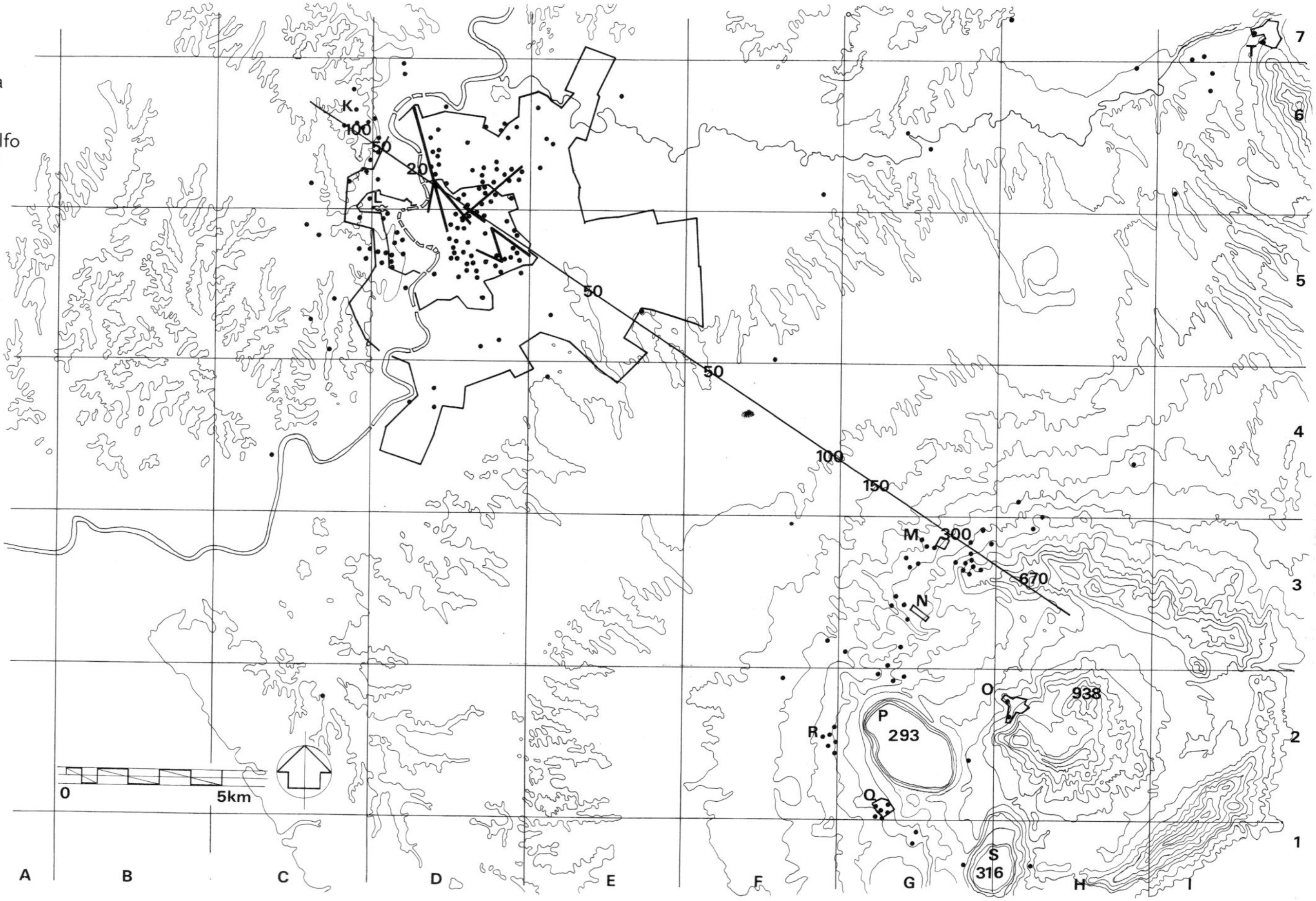

Villa Hadriana, Tivoli

BOSCO, BARCO, BARCHETTO

In Mannerist villa designs in and around Rome during the second half of the 16th century, it was not only axiality which evolved into an independent and essential part of the garden, but also the *bosco*, which served to represent untamed nature and which, in its labyrinthine organization, provided a contrast to the linearity of previous designs. The *bosco* increased in size and significance in relation to the garden. In many cases a piece of natural landscape of considerable size, frequently former hunting grounds (*barco*), was integrated into the design in a slightly formalized manner. The resulting *barchetto* was a wooded garden park which incorporated specific functions. One of these was a *casino*, a small building used for recreational purposes such as open-air banquets, which was located in the middle of the 'natural' landscape. Earliest examples include Pius IV's casino (1560) by Ligorio, next to the Cortile del Belvedere in Rome, and the Casino Farnese at Caprarola by del Duca (1586).

THE PARADISE GARDEN

The original approach to Villa d'Este was from below, from the north-west, along the street leading to the Porta Romana. In this street there was an entrance gate on the main axis of the villa. Flanked by fountains and high walls the visitor proceeded to the lower garden terrace and to a cruciform pergola from which the villa could not be seen. At the sides of the lower terrace were four labyrinths. Where the two pergolas in the centre of the terrace used to intersect, a roundel of cypresses was later planted, and from here the villa is now displayed in all its magnificence. Since the slope is now hidden behind high cypresses and pines, the building when seen from the reflecting fishponds, seems to be symmetric, with its central part composed of an impressive series of vertical porticoes. The porticoes on the series of garden terraces form, in perspective, a single unity with the double loggia of the building. It also seems as if the

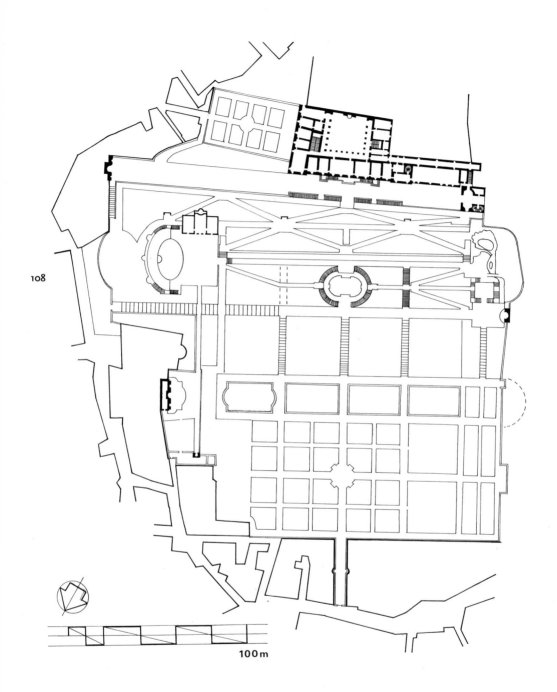

100 m

Villa d'Este, Tivoli. Ground plan

path to the house continues along the main axis. On the second terrace, at the Fountain of the Dragon, it is impossible to continue along the axis, however, and the visitor has to take the circular steps around the fountain. These lead to a third terrace, the Avenue of the Hundred Fountains. There the visitor loses sight of the building and must walk along the terrace and diagonal ramps in order to return to the main axis. The main axis is discovered, as if by accident, at the Fountain of Pandora, and you can then proceed via a flight of steps to the fourth level, the terrace in front of the house.

Due to the manipulation of visual impressions and the enforced detour in its approach, the villa, which when seen from the lowest level appeared to be a comprehensible axial scheme, is gradually revealed as a confusing and mysterious complex.

Today entrance to the garden is via the former monastery courtyard at the centre of the building on top of the hill. The plan of the house is detached from the axiality of the grounds. To reach the terrace at the foot of the building, the visitor must walk in a south-westerly direction through a succession of rooms and, at the end, descend two floors by means of a spiral staircase. This comes out at an indeterminate point on the terrace, where there is hardly any incentive to enter the main axis. The building and the central axis are linked by the loggia on the *piano nobile*, which is attached asymmetrically to the central salon.

The appearance of the garden axis from the balcony comes as a surprise. Because of the steep slope, this main axis, which seems so dominant when viewed from the garden below, is only of subordinate importance in the total concept. The garden as a whole is no more than a foreground to a much broader panorama. Moreover, the axis is not placed exactly at right angles to the garden elevation but points, at a slight angle, towards one of the Sabine hilltops on the horizon. In this way the villa is related to the enormous space of the landscape by a single wide gesture over the garden.

The natural slope in the transverse direction of the terrain is formalized throughout the whole garden. It is used to relate the garden and its constituent parts to the outer-lying landscape. On the highest terrace this relationship is architecturally defined by the portico of the dining loggia at the south-west end. This frames the panorama of the landscape near Rome, which can be seen in the distance on a clear day.

The Avenue of the Hundred Fountains forms a second important transverse axis. It is terminated on the Tivoli side by the Oval Fountain with the water theatre and grotto of Venus. On the city-wall side it is terminated by the Fountain of the Owl and the Rometta, a miniature version of Rome. A third important transverse axis is formed by the series of fishponds. Originally these were fed from the cascade of the water organ. The water would have disappeared into a lake outside the city wall by way of the Fountain of Neptune.

Within the garden visual contact with the landscape is not so much brought about via the main axis, which when seen from the garden is closed off, but by means of the transverse axes. These divert attention away from the small town of Tivoli towards Rome. Both edges of the garden are elaborately treated, forming two independent series of attractions. The playful effect was enhanced by the extremely complex use of water elements, such as a waterfall, a curtain of water with rainbows, jets, reflecting surfaces, and the use of water-driven automata and *giochi d'aqua*. The water organ produced the sound of trumpets, the Fountain of the Dragon caused gun and musket shots to ring out, while in the Fountain of the Owl bronze birds twittered until an owl suddenly appeared and began to hoot mournfully.

Thus separated from daily reality visitors could imagine themselves to be in an

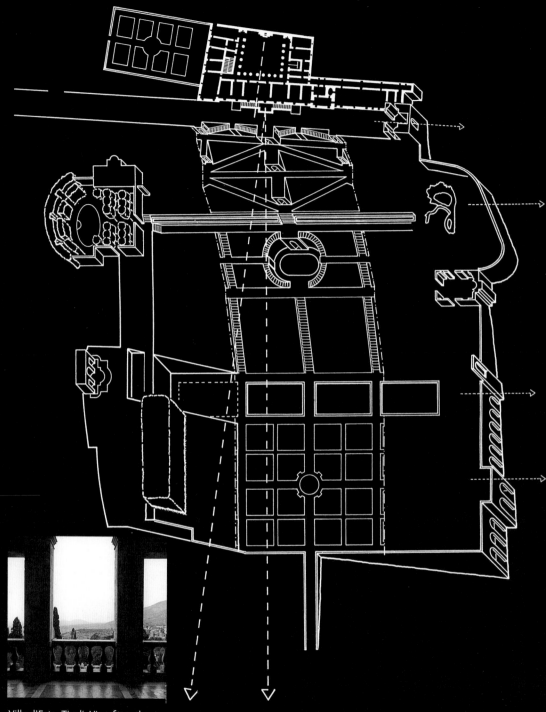

Villa d'Este, Tivoli. View from the
loggia of the house, across the
garden towards the horizon

Villa d'Este, Tivoli

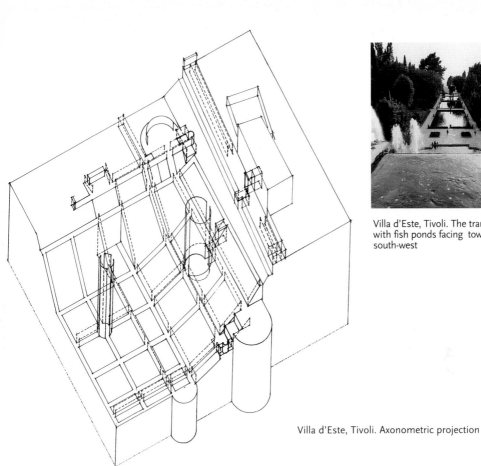

Villa d'Este, Tivoli. Axonometric projection

Villa d'Este, Tivoli. The transverse axis with fish ponds facing towards the south-west

unearthly paradise and this, in fact, was probably Cardinal d'Este's intention. His coat of arms showed a white eagle with the three golden apples of the Hesperides. The Villa d'Este is an allegorical representation of the Garden of the Hesperides, which, itself, is a mythical interpretation of earthly paradise. Hercules had to perform his heroic deed within this garden: the retrieval of the three golden apples. Visitors can experience Hercules's struggle for the three divine virtues themselves, since the cardinal also expressed moral contradiction in the transverse direction of the garden. Thus the Grotto of Venus (Voluptas) at the Oval Fountain forms the counterpart of the Grotto of Diana (Virtus) below the dining loggia. The passage from Venus to Diana and vice versa is accompanied by a hundred stucco reliefs depicting the *Metamorphoses* of Ovid in the Avenue of the Hundred Fountains. From the side, the scene of the battle is surveyed by the winged Pegasus, high over the Pegasus Fountain (above the Oval Fountain) on the hill of Tivoli, making ready to ascend Mount Parnassus.

This relationship between heathen myth and Christian philosophy completes Cardinal Ippolito d'Este's programme of ambiguously linking the exuberance of the villa ideal with the restraint of a monastery.

Villa Aldobrandini, Frascati. Front view with covered approach drive

Villa Aldobrandini

Around 1560 Pier Antonio Contugi had a small villa laid out. This was subsequently bought by Pope Clement VIII, who in 1598 gave the villa to his nephew Cardinal Pietro Aldobrandini in gratitude for his part in the recapture of Ferrara. In 1683 the villa passed into the hands of the Pamphili family and later came into the possession of the Boghese family.

After the final land purchases had been carried out, the building of the house started in 1598, in accordance with the designs of Giacomo della Porta. Papal revenues had increased so much as a result of the annexation of Ferrara that the costs of building the villa could satisfactorily be met. Della Porta died while the villa was still under construction and Carlo Maderno and Giovanni Fontana, who were also responsible for the construction of the cascade and water theatre, took over supervision of the work. Maderno designed the cascade and water theatre, while Fontana, aided by Oratio Olivieri, was responsible for the engineering. Fontana was a famous aquatic artist, having made his name at the Villa d'Este, and it was he who designed the hydraulic effects.

Villa Aldobrandini was embellished with a richness exceptional in those days. The walls of the drawing room, situated in the centre of the main block on the *piano nobile*, are covered with large tapestries and the ceiling is adorned with frescoes ascribed to Zuccari. The southernmost hall on this floor is decorated with Chinese wallpaper and the ceiling was originally painted with scenes from the Old Testament. The most important paintings, however, were in the two small buildings next to the water theatre. In one of them, a chapel dedicated to St Sebastian, the frescoes were painted by Domenico da Passignano. These were so badly damaged by damp, however, that they were removed and now hang in London's National Gallery. In the other, the Stanza dei Venti, a garden room with an artificial hill and sensational aquatic effects was created.

FRASCATI AS DECOR

Villa Aldobrandini belongs to the group of villas draped against the hills around the village of Frascati, situated about 20 kilometres south-east of Rome. Many villas were concentrated in this location, then called Tusculum, even at the time of the Roman emperors. Cato, Lucullus and Cicero all had their country seats there. The village was destroyed in the Middle Ages and its classical villas laid to ruin. After the election of Alessandro Farnese as Pope Paul III (1534-49) and the establishment of his country retreat in Frascati, there was renewed interest in the area, particularly among the Roman prelates. Between around 1548 and 1598 many cardinals built relatively modest villas there. In a second period of building between 1598 and 1650, associated with the Counter-Reformation which followed the Council of Trent, owners competed with each other in the embellishment and extension of their villas.

Initially, the main point of staying in the countryside had been to enjoy nature; now it came to be seen as a struggle to achieve the perfect Arcadia as a reconfirmation of that religious and secular power which had been questioned by the forces of reformation. The pursuit of this Arcadian ideal was practically executed in a variety of ways.

The stage management and architectural treatment were determined to a large, if not dominating, degree by the need to publicly display the restored social and cultural power of the church apparent. The early type of Tuscan villa, in which the interaction between villa and landscape took place in the garden, was thus adapted to a new function. A type of villa was created in which the situation of the complex against the hills, the position of the house on the terraces, and the design of the façades were given monumental significance. The garden at the rear was a subordinate private area, while the ceremonial aspect of the house was defined in the execution of its façades and the laying out of the front terraces.

Frascati is situated some 300 metres above the level of the River Tiber. The land slopes away to the north-west, where Rome is visible on the horizon. To the south-east the slope increases steeply, climbing over several kilometres to a height of 670 metres. From the slope the villas have a panoramic view of the sunlit Roman Campagna with the dark forest set against the hills. In general the Frascati villa embraces the difference in height between the north and south sides. The shadowed, flat north façade has a balcony or loggia. Opposite the sunlit south façade the slope of the hill is intercepted by a retaining wall with a nymphaeum. Here, opposite the entrance to the villa, the water which runs off the hills is collected. In a number of places the forestation has been cut back to give a better view. The layout of the villas, as they looked after the extensions and embellishments of the first half of the 17th century, begin to reveal the competing organizational elements: the terrace and the axis.

The terrace is a geometric surface and is used as an architectural foreground, balancing on the edge of the panorama, forming an open space and wedding it to the villa. In particular, those villas on the ridges which protrude from the slope and which have a panorama of at least half of the horizon (180 degrees) form a single terrace (e.g. the Mondragone and Aldobrandini villas). Seen from below, the striking proportions of the villa façades form a monumental unity with the terrace walls.

The improved presentation of each of the Frascati villas was augmented by an avenue leading in a totally straight line up the slope. At the end of this line the villa and terrace are arranged symmetrically. When approaching a villa, the driveway ensures a frontal, ceremonial approach to the complex. An interesting detail, supplied by Carlludwig Franck's typological study (1956), is that the avenue ends at the point where the treetops are just below the level of the terrace. Because of this, one looks over the avenue from the terrace. The actual entrance to the villa is not at the front

114

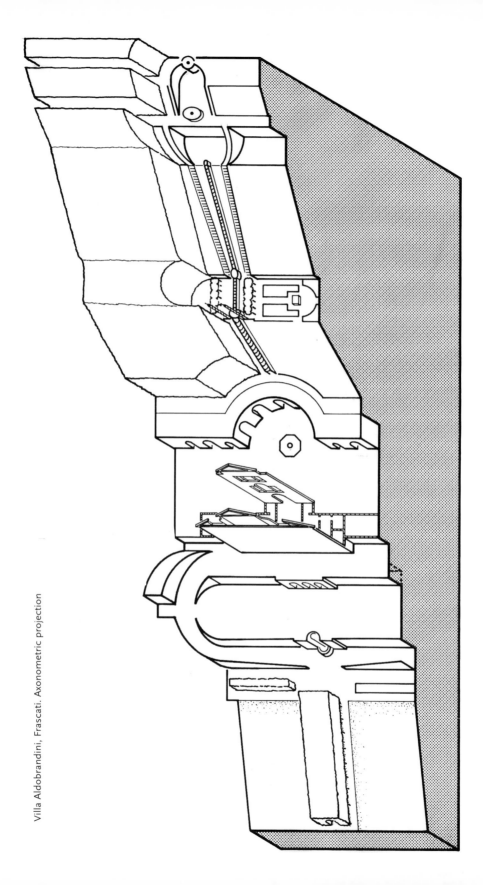

Villa Aldobrandini, Frascati. Axonometric projection

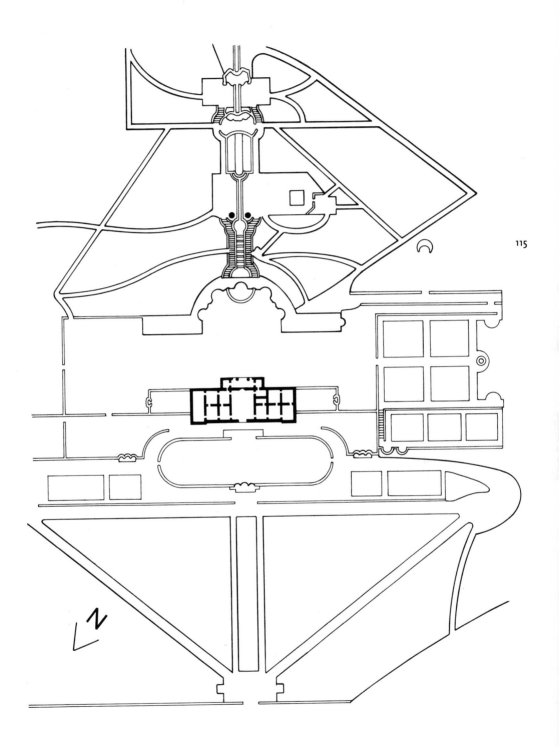

Villa Aldobrandini, Frascati

Frascati
1. Aldobrandini
2. Belpoggio
3. Borghese
4. Falconieri
5. Grazioli
6. Lancelotti
7. Mondragone
8. Muti
9. Torlonia
1o. Vecchia

however. The visitor is led around the terrace to the rear of the house and the *piano nobile*. This entrance is usually linked to a more accessible route running parallel to the slope of the hill. The longest axis, at the Villa Mondragone, is 700 metres long.

Even though the avenues remain in the foreground and one can look out over them, their layout outside the actual territory of the garden and their placement in the panorama indicate that this is no longer an open space in all directions. The panorama itself has been ordered and given visual direction. In the link between foreground and background the house appears as a set piece against the dark, forested slope. The regular spacing of the individual villas is striking. The axes of symmetry run down the slope virtually parallel to each other into the distance. This arrangement makes it clear that mutual visibility and views of the town of Frascati are of less importance here. These axes have no formal termination, but a virtual one: their reference point is the point on the horizon where the city of Rome stands.

In this orientation towards the panorama all the villas are similar and therefore no longer have different points of view. Unlike Florence or Rome there is no periphery affording changing panoramic views. There is actually only one view and one direction from which to look out over the panorama. In this monothematic concept of space the garden has lost its role as the focus of the stage management. In the Frascati villas the garden has been relegated to the rear, between the house and the slope, and is therefore much more of a component in the confrontation between the monumental and ceremonial side of the complex and the walled and private part of the garden.

Within the typology of the Frascati villa, as advanced by Franck, the axial connection of the villa's elements places the *bosco* against the slope. It unites with the hill to create a common background and binding element in the monumental stage management. Despite competing with each other in terms of the wealth they display, the separate villas hereby preserve their mutual affinity. The Frascati villa evolved within this spatial framework and Villa Aldobrandini is its most refined example.

THE FAÇADE GARDEN

In the layout of Villa Aldobrandini the forefront and the rear of the building are entirely independent of each other. The building itself acts as a screen between both; separating culture from nature. The urban forefront is controlled by means of the view and is itself dominated by the monumental façade of the house. Partly hidden behind the house is the wild overgrown *bosco*, only accessible to the owner and his guests. In engravings by Dom Barrière, Falda and Specchi it is clearly shown how the building protrudes from the hill and how the slope behind the interrupted tympan continues into the projection of the roof. To the front of the house is a bare slope with the approach avenue symmetrically situated on the axis.

This avenue, flanked by clipped trees (now grown together to form a tunnel), directs the view towards the building, giving the house its monumental backcloth-like significance with regard to the village. The entrance was originally marked by the intersection of two avenues forming two sides of a triangle and their bisector, formed by the main axis. The growth of the village and the construction of a garden wall and entrance gate, designed by Carlo Bazzicchieri, destroyed this triangular configuration.

The entrance avenue leads to a niche in the lowest retaining wall of the two-storeyed front terrace, which projects onto the slope like a bastion. Because of the interrupted tympan and the recesses in the basement, the foreground and background, the architectonic façade and the rustic decor come together. There is an unexpected combination of images at the highest point of the avenue: the niche and the upper part of the building are visually linked by perspective. This carefully constructed

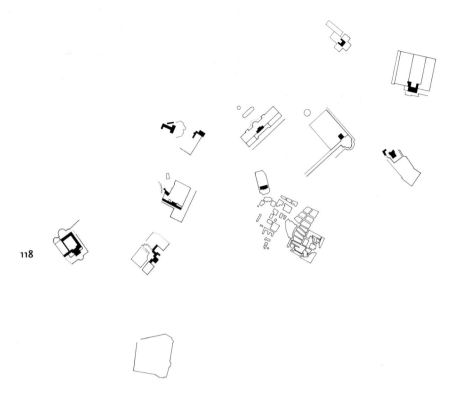

Frascati. Villas and terraces

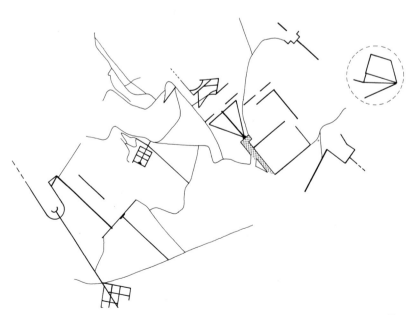

Frascati. Axes

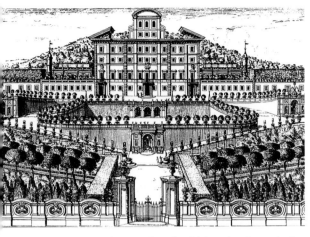

Alessandro Specchi. Villa Aldobrandini, Frascati, 1699

Villa Aldobrandini, Frascati

image disintegrates as soon as the axial approach is departed from and one moves towards the sides.

From the highest level of the front terrace there is no direct passage to the terrace at the rear, which is connected to the house one floor higher on the *piano nobile*. In spite of the pronounced axial structure, movement is interrupted for the second time. At the east side of the villa there is a domestic entrance from a narrow side road, which leads straight up the hill. Two *boschi* of plane trees lying on the transverse axes unite the front and rear in a simple manner. The west side terrace, which runs to the edge of the hillside, offers a view of the villas Torlonia, Grazioli, Muti and Belpoggio. On the rear terrace, opposite the south façade of the house, is the spectacular semi-circular water theatre. At the centre of the five niches Atlas shoulders the globe and is submerged in a curtain of water. Only a glimpse of the garden above the nymphaeum can be seen from the terrace. This *bosco*-like garden is connected by means of a ramp on the western side terrace, which again deflects movement sideways, away from the axiality of the villa. (Next to this ramp, hidden in the woods, is a giant head similar to those in the Sacro Bosco at Bomarzo.) The sequence of fountains, cascades and grottoes on the main axis and the two flanking columns are connected to the different levels of the house. The central part of the south façade, which projects slightly, consists of stacked loggias, from which a constantly changing perspective of the water attractions can be seen. Only from the highest loggia can the garden be viewed as a whole. Here, too, the visitor is on the same level as the eternal spring, from which the water flows down the slope, and is in communication with primeval nature. The upper cascade is shaped so as to counteract perspective. It seems to be projected onto a screen between the two water columns and is thus perceived from the house as a flat plane.

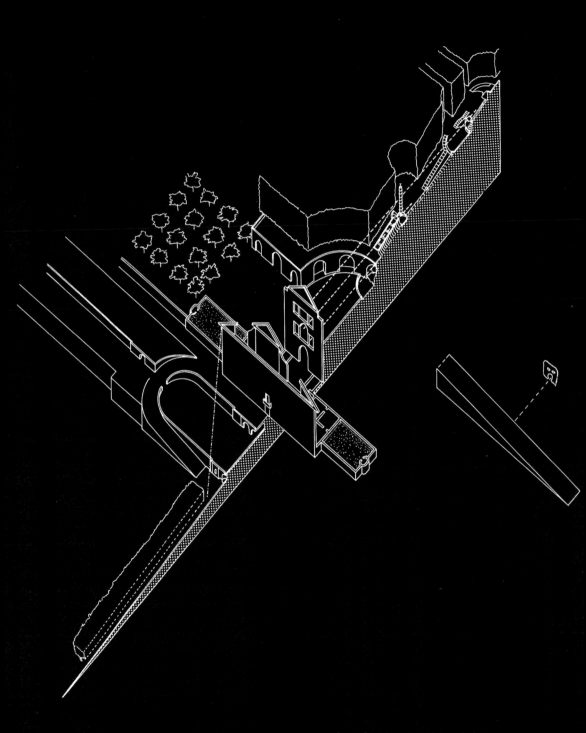

Paul van der Ree. Villa Aldobrandini, Frascati, 1992

Villa Aldobrandini, Frascati.
Cascade, water columns and rear façade with
loggias. Nymphaeum with Pan. Panorama
viewed from the front terrace

Looking in the opposite direction from the slope, the villa is seen through constantly changing frames. Only the central part with the loggias is visible, as a set piece between the two columnar fountains. The villa seems to control every part of the slope. At the level of the spring, where the horizon of the Roman landscape becomes visible above the house, the contrast between culture and nature is effaced. Even here we are being deceived. The loggias and the eaves are treated in such a way as to play tricks with perspective. Humankind is creating its own mathematical ordering of the world. Rationality is no longer confirmed but challenged in the Aldobrandini perspectives.

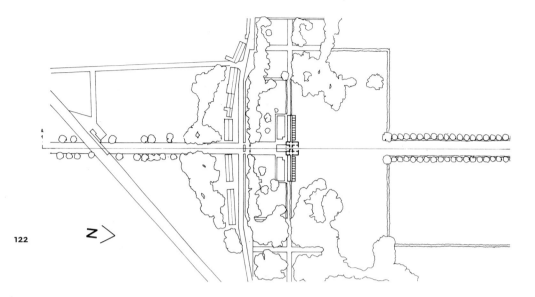

Villa Emo, Fanzolo

Villa Emo

In 1539 Leonardo Emo di Alvise inherited part of his uncle's property in Fanzolo, which had been obtained by the family as a result of their land reclamation work in the Veneto region. He was seven years old at the time. In 1559 Leonardo decided to build a residential complex at the centre of his farmland and commissioned Palladio (1508-80) to effect his plans. The frescoes in the interior of the hall, the loggia and four adjacent rooms were completed between 1560 and 1565 by Giambattista Zelotti. A mixture of heroic Roman deeds, heathen legends and scenes from Christian history were depicted between Corinthian columns painted in perspective. The restrained character of these frescoes certainly reflected the wishes of Palladio himself, who did not wish to see architecture dominated by decoration. His description of the villa in the *Quattro libri dell' architettura* (1570) is fairly concise. In contrast to his usual practice, here Palladio gives the dimensions of the rear garden. This covers a rectangle and is dissected by a small river, which lends charm to the site. Part of the garden was later remodelled as a 'natural landscape' with groups of trees.

THE VENETO VILLEGGIATURA

After the collapse of overseas trade and a series of military defeats towards the end of the quattrocento Venice had to fall back on its own region, the Veneto. The main thrust of economic policy was directed towards developing agriculture. This offered sufficient opportunity to invest capital gained through overseas trade. As part of this agricultural development the city of Venice pursued a policy aimed at opening up and reclaiming the marshy hinterland in as short a time as possible and thereby exploiting the large pool of unemployed labour in the city.

The Veneto villa differs from villas elsewhere in Italy, in part because of the

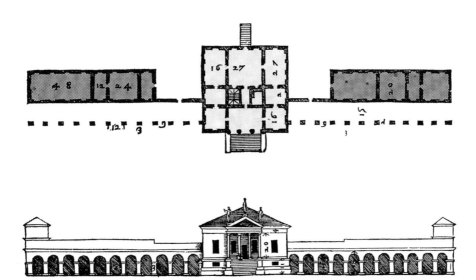

Villa Emo, Fanzolo. Plan and front view. From Andrea Palladio, *Quatrro libri*, 1570

economic circumstances which determined their function. For most of its history the Italian villa had been intended as a refuge from busy town life, a place of peace and relaxation in the midst of nature. The Veneto villa, however, was a working farm. The programme of the villa was influenced by the need to lure the Venetian aristocracy into the countryside. The renewed interest in farming coincided with the publication of a series of treatises on agriculture which extolled the virtues of country and farming life. Halfway through the 16th century the *Discorsi della vita sobria* by Alvise Cornaro, a prominent Venetian landowner, was published. Cornaro advocates the *vita sobria*, the ancient ideal of simple country life. The cultivation of the land was a divine occupation, comparable with the Creation. Agriculture equalled virtue, so it was difficult to conceive of anything more virtuous than money earned by tilling the land.

These treatises laid a sound ideological foundation for involvement in farming. With the increased status thus provided, it became worthwhile to settle down in the countryside as a landowning farmer. A number of agricultural villa designs were also described in these treatises. The *Liber ruralium commodorum*, originally dating from 1305, was republished in Venice in 1495 and included illustrations. The author, Pietro de Crescenzi, described his villa as an economically independent community consisting of the landlord, the manager of his estate and the agricultural labourers. Physically it had the form of 'an enclosed courtyard with one side pierced by the entrance road. The exit is immediately opposite. In the middle of the courtyard, along the road dividing the property and set back a little from the road, the landowner's house should be built with the façade facing the road'.

From these treatises we can conclude that the villa was a functional entity which had to meet the demands of farming, the rural idyll and aristocratic status. Initially these demands were met by a type of building that afforded status, namely the urban palazzo. It was only in the 16th century that the Veneto villa developed into

The Palladian country house

a new type of building, accommodating all aspects of the programme. Palladio's contribution was to develop an architectural scheme in which it was possible to control the agricultural programme by means of rational planning in relationship to the ideological needs of the new land policy. He designed a standard vocabulary in which the articulated components of the villa could be used to produce different combinations according to the individual wishes of the clients.

THE PALLADIAN COUNTRY HOUSE

The external appearance of the villa is sober, in accordance with the ideal of the *vita sobria*. According to Palladio the houses of antiquity were also built without decoration. He dismissed the idea of the villa as a unique object and created a series of objects instead. By so doing, his personality disappeared to a certain extent from the buildings. In this kind of architecture, without autobiographical caprices, the client had to renounce private decoration. Richness, however, showed itself primarily in the interior, with walls decorated with frescoes depicting villa life, the landowner, his possessions and his learning.

The ideal hall is square and was used for feasts, performances, weddings and receptions. Palladio termed the hall, onto which the private rooms of the house opened, a public space, analogous to the town square onto which several streets open. The hall in the villa was the centre of administration and entertainment, similar to the forum of an ancient city. The arrangement is self-evident: the villa is centrally situated in the country estate and the hall is the heart of the villa; the hall and the loggia are the crowning glories of the whole.

From the loggia the landowner looked out across the forecourt, through which the harvest was brought and in which games were held. It gave access to the living quarters and was used to beautify the house. It served many purposes: it was a place for eating, walking, and leisure activities. The loggia is related to the hall behind it, in height, width and the number of floors. The loggia and the hall are the centre of the composition. If there is only a loggia in the front elevation, the hall is slightly extended at the rear, and opposite the main entrance is a door or window, which serves to frame the view of the landscape.

The temple front emphasizes the main entrance to the house and adds considerably to the status of the building. The use of a temple front in domestic architecture was intended to suggest the divine status of the landowner. Since the front side is more prominent than the rest of the house this was also the best place to put the family's coat of arms, which is usually carved in the centre of the temple front.

The steps leading up to the *piano nobile* lend distinction to the house. The introduction of the raised *piano nobile* makes contact with the garden subordinate to the view of the landscape from the loggia. According to Palladio the raised main floor has two advantages. Firstly it no longer requires any servants' quarters, which are now housed in the basement. Secondly, it is a more pleasant place to be because the floor is raised above the damp soil, it commands a better view of the farmlands, and can itself be seen to better advantage from the distance. The physical dominance of the villa achieved through its central position and the raised position of the main floor symbolizes total control of the landscape.

The original layout of the gardens is unknown. Old engravings suggest that the forecourt was an open space. The low flat ponds, which hardly rise above the grass, and the low walls around the courtyard suggest the same. An open forecourt ensures that the villa can be seen from afar and that it commands a view of the fields. The forecourt was a public space onto which the barns, the dwellings of the agricultural workers and the stables opened.

Villa Emo, Fanzolo

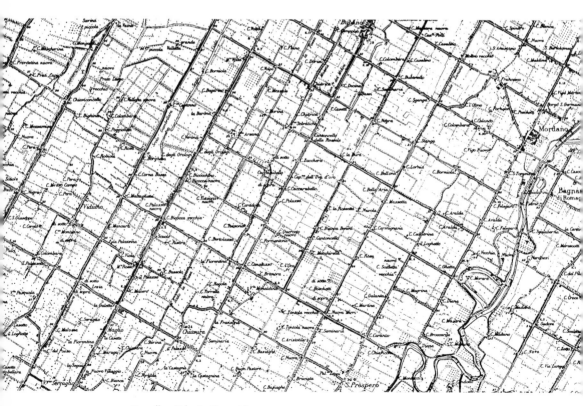

Po valley. Colonization grid

Villa Emo, Fanzolo. Aerial view

AGRICULTURE AND ARCADIA

The *raison d'être* of the Veneto villa was the reclamation of the countryside, in which the villa owner, in his role of divine padrone, occupied a central position. The villa was the centre from which the extensive farmlands were managed. The fields were mainly cultivated according to the so-called Roman *centuriatio* system, which still existed in a rudimentary form. This system consists of square plots some 625 square metres. The villa sites conform to the pattern of this system.

The way in which the relationship between landscape and villa was created should be considered against the background of ideas on landscape and nature at the time. In Palladio's villas there was no garden as was understood in the 14th and 15th-century Italian villa tradition. In so far as there was a garden it was a ceremonial introduction to the flight of steps leading to the *piano nobile*. The gardens in front of the house either decorated the courtyard or are a substitute for it, if the outbuildings were too small to constitute a courtyard by themselves. The flat, bare lawns or gravelled areas which fill these squares impede neither the view of the villa itself nor that of the farmlands from the villa. The kitchen gardens are situated on the edge and, as in Villa Barbaro, are camouflaged by tall hedges and rows of trees. The trees at the front have a representative function. The few elements used in this part of the garden – low walls, gates and trees – direct the view towards the horizon. Across the garden, house and landscape are linked to each other in an aesthetic rendering of the view. Vistas from the loggia and the hall are channelled along avenues towards the landscape. Landscape and villa are therefore joined together in a single architectural structure. The separate elements formalizing this arrangement are set up along the axes thus formed. To create the *integrazione scenica* various elements can be left out or added. According to Palladio the road is also an element of this *integrazione scenica*; it is an environment in itself, a little higher than the fields it crosses, shaded by trees and offering pleasant views.

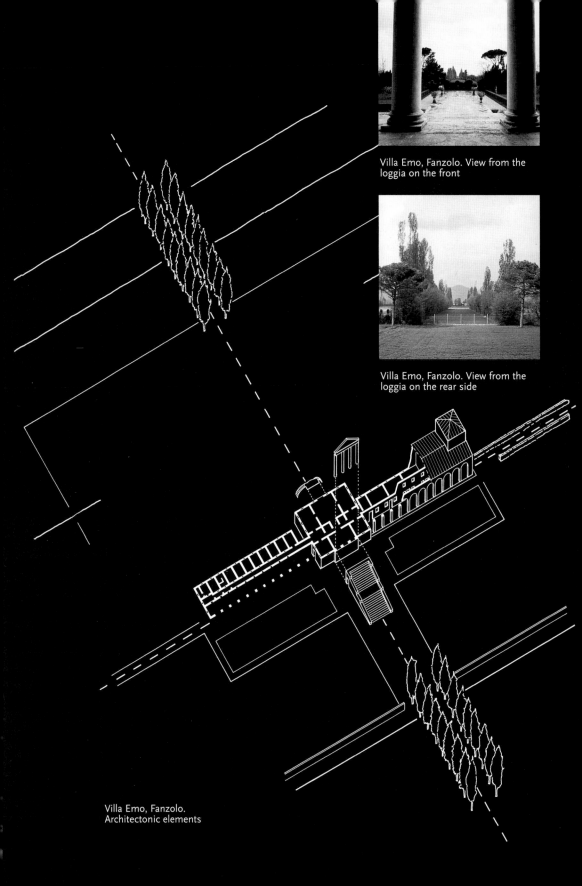

Villa Emo, Fanzolo. View from the
loggia on the front

Villa Emo, Fanzolo. View from the
loggia on the rear side

Villa Emo, Fanzolo.
Architectonic elements

The Arcadian idyll, the original motive behind villa life, was subordinate to the tough reality of the agricultural economy. Delight in nature within the enclosed domain of the villa was done away with. What had been lost on the outside could be regained in the interior. In the frescoes covering the walls of the reception rooms the ideal of rural life could be recreated and the landscape restored to its Arcadian significance. Arcadia, as the perfect illusion, was thus added to the villa.

THE EMPTY GARDEN

The main axis of Villa Emo follows the direction of the existing *centuriatio* division of the land. This direction was emphasized by projecting the axis in long tree-lined avenues at the front and rear of the main building, while anchoring the villa in the centre. From some distance away the position of the villa in the landscape is clearly marked. From closeby, however, the buildings are hidden behind high hedges and the entrance gate. From the front terrace the broad flight of steps leads to the *piano nobile*, and from the loggia there is a view, over the garden and its enclosure, of the landscape that from this position is ordered by the projection of the central axis. The steps to the loggia are considerably wider and less steep than those depicted in the *Quattro libri*. This gives the impression of a forecourt sloping right up to the loggia, reinforcing the central position of the building volume. The development of a transverse axis through the centre of the galleries was fairly exceptional given the general predisposition to mono-axiality. This axis passes through a side entrance of the garden and is terminated by a chapel on the opposite side of the road. The outbuildings also remain programmatically separate, and there is no direct entrance from the central *piano nobile*. The loggia is recessed into the main block and its side walls display murals. This re-emphasizes the concentration on the single direction of the main axis and, thus, on the negation of the side wings. It is only in the front elevation that the continuation of the gallery brings house and outbuildings into a unified whole.

The difference in the treatment of the front and the rear elevations is striking. As is the case at Villa Piovene at Lonedo, an absolute separation seems to be suggested between the symbolic significance of the front and the 'rustic' agrarian character of the rear of the buildings. The impression of dignity continues from the front of the house into its interior. This difference between the front and the rear of the villa is continued in the landscape setting. The kitchen gardens are to the rear, from where you look out along the axis imposed on the landscape, across a wide, open stretch of land between rows of trees that seem to merge imperceptibly into the agricultural fields. However, the rows of trees in front of the villa are planted much closer together to form an avenue. Within the rectangular parcel of land on which the villa complex stands, the empty garden creates a distance between its agricultural and ceremonial features.

The ideological agrarian programme, which postulated land reclamation in the Veneto, can be seen in what is probably its most complete form at Villa Emo. In his solution to this programme at Villa Emo, including the villa's setting in working farmlands, Palladio provides his most complete and advanced example of the agricultural villa. The tension between formal architectural vocabulary and references to traditional Veneto farm elements is here transformed into an almost nonchalant dialogue between the two. That these remain independent and identifiable within the total scheme does not only put matters into perspective but also even leaves room for the suspicion that the maestro might be making a somewhat ironic insinuation about the dignity of his client.

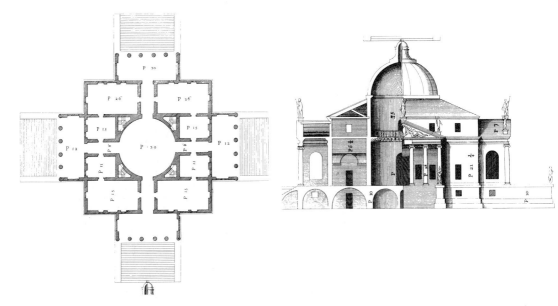

Villa Rotonda, Vicenza. Plan and front view. From Andrea Palladio, *Quattro libri*, 1570

Villa Rotonda

In 1566 the papal prelate Paolo Almerico returned to his native Veneto after having served under a number of successive popes in Rome. He asked Palladio to build him a summer residence on a hill about 500 metres south-east of Vicenza. In his *Quattro libri* Palladio wrote that 'The site is as pleasant and delightful as can be found, because it is upon a small hill, of very easy access, and is watered on one side by the Bacchiglione, a navigable river; and on the other it is accompanied with most pleasant risings, which look like a very great theatre, and are all cultivated, and abound with most excellent fruits, and most exquisite vines, some of which are limited, some more extended, and others that terminate with the horizon; there are loggias made in all four fronts; under the floor of which, and of the hall, are the rooms for the convenience and use of the family'.

In the *Quattro libri* the villa is included in the chapter on urban villas because it did not have an agricultural function and though not situated in the town itself was, nevertheless, in the immediate vicinity of one.

In 1569 the villa was ready for occupation. It was only completed, however, after Palladio's death by the architect Vincenzo Scamozzi who, among other things, replaced the semicircular dome in Palladio's conception with a less pronounced vault over the central hall. The design of the dome is supposed to be based on that of the Pantheon and was intended as a reference to the owner's status. The oculus on top was originally open (as in Scamozzi's Villa Pisari La Rocca at Lonigo): a water outlet in the floor of the hall leads to a well in the basement. The present main entrance and the buildings flanking both sides of the southern access avenue were also added by Scamozzi in about 1620. Of the artists who worked on the decorations, Palladio mentions only Lorenzo Vicentino, who was responsible for the statues on the pedestals of the loggias.

Villa Rotonda, Vicenza

THEATRE AND BELVEDERE

The situation of Villa Rotonda was described by Palladio as a large theatre which presented a changing but always beautiful spectacle on all sides. This would explain his decision to provide the villa, designed as a belvedere, with identical loggias on all four sides. In planning the interior of this four-sided symmetrical construction, a round central hall presents a logical solution. As corn lofts were unnecessary because the villa did not have any agricultural function, the hall was continued up to the roof, with a gallery over the *piano nobile*, and later, at the end of the 17th century, painted with illusionist architectural and sculptural elements to look like an open-air *tempietto*. The semicircular dome would have made the villa a salient feature in the landscape and fixed it in the centre of the panorama that unfolds on all four sides. It is therefore regrettable that Scamozzi did not have the courage and sensibility to construct the dome according to Palladio's design.

Due to its centralized symmetrical shape, descriptions of the villa usually suggest it is situated as an isolated object. The villa does indeed stand out in the landscape because of its location on a plateau and also because it is rotated 45 degrees to the north, independent of the local topography, so that all façades of the house receive sunshine each day. Closer examination, however, reveals that despite its apparent autonomy the villa has been placed in the landscape with the utmost care. When the complex is approached, the villa is gradually revealed. The entrance facing the northwest loggia is recessed into the hill. Looking back beyond the entrance from the loggia, a chapel can be seen on the axis on the opposite side of the road at the edge of the town. This axis, linking the house, the entrance and the chapel, formally establishes the estate's relationship with the town. A walk around the villa reveals how its setting in the landscape is handled differently on each side.

From the Strada della Riviera, below the north-east terrace, the villa is connected

Villa Rotonda, Vicenza.
The scenic stage management

Villa Rotonda, Vicenza. Views from the four loggias

to the buildings on the edge of town by the retaining wall of the terrace, although it juts out from the line of the other buildings. It is also linked to the road, and the river running parallel to it, by a grassy raised embankment at right angles to the terrace wall. This raised feature on the north-east side of the villa complements the recessed entrance and, on the edge of the terrace, makes the relationship between the developed land and the open landscape explicit.

Walking along the Strada della Riviera the landscape rolls on behind the villa, but at no single point does the picture lose touch with the wooded slopes of Monte Berico. Cut out of the woods is the *giardino segreto*, which can only be reached from the basement. It is only on the east side, where the loggia reveals the most unobstructed view of the landscape, that the villa separates itself from the edge of the wood and is elevated in its surroundings. This is, therefore, the only side on which the retaining wall along the edge of the plateau meets the lower part of the site directly, without modifications or additions.

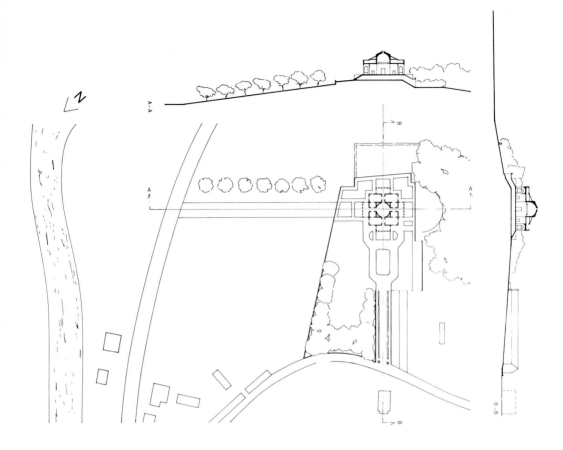

Villa Rotonda, Vicenza. The villa and the plateau

The state of the site around the villa is reflected in the shape of the terrace and the treatment of its edges. Because of the villa's asymmetric location on the terrace, the changing perspective effects and thereby the different and shifting positions of the background, are projected onto the terrace wall. The entire system of differentiating the landscape setting of the villa would, finally, have been anchored and unified by the semicircular dome, rising high above the house. This function can now only be observed in the repetition of the loggias on all four sides of the house.

The way in which the all-round symmetrical plan of the house is stage-managed in the landscape, by treating each of the four directions of the plateau differently, and its influence on the terrace walls, confirms the mastery of this last villa project by Palladio. The garden as an autonomous space between the villa and the landscape has disappeared from the *integrazione scenica*. Precisely because there was no agricultural programme the landscape could be integrated, without ideological prejudice, into the composition as an independent component. The natural plasticity of the landscape determines its interaction with the villa. Here, Palladio reached the limits of the possibilities of designing the landscape with an entirely controlled, formal architectural system. This could result in two possible developments. One was a further subordination of the landscape to a central perspective structure, as can be seen in French garden architecture, and the other – and this is anticipated in the setting of Villa Rotonda – is a severing of the cosmic unity between landscape and architecture, which was fundamental to Enlightenment thought, which concerned itself with the contrast between nature and culture.

The architecture of Palladio, especially in this project, stood between two worlds and was to prove of service to both of them. The final significance of Villa Rotonda in the architectural theory of the last three hundred years lies, then, in the fact that the credo of Western thinking about the contrast between ratio and *genius loci* was here made concrete in an architectural manifesto which was actually constructed and which still exists as an example of architectural achievement. This marks not only the point where ideologies diverged but also a fundamental contradiction in modern Western thought.

CHAPTER TWO

THE MAGICS OF
THE FORMAL

THE 17TH-CENTURY FRENCH RESIDENCE

Vaux-le-Vicomte, Melun

The idea of the ultimate landscape

THE ABSTRACT CONCEPT OF NATURE

During the 17th century, the scientific concept of nature and space was theoretically established. As well as art, scientific fields such as astronomy, geography, physics and mathematics began to unfold. The extent and complexity of knowledge became so great that all of science could no longer be represented in one person, the *uomo universale*. Voyages of discovery went beyond the horizon of the then known world to be drawn up later on maps. In abstract thought even mathematics began to overstep the boundaries of what was regarded as conceivable.

The pushing back of frontiers in science and travel rested on an expansion of political power. As Sun King, Louis XIV was the absolute embodiment of a Roman

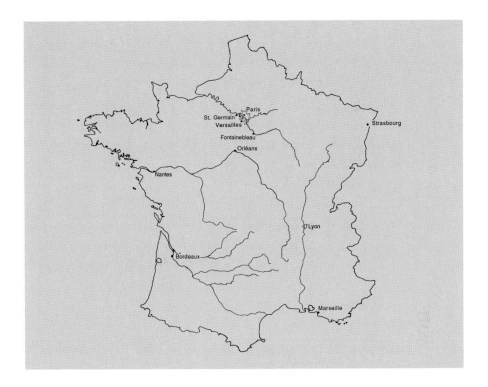

emperor. Paris was the new Rome, which in the second half of the 17th century acquired an imperial allure.

The development of the concept of nature and space in the first half of the 17th century is best illustrated by the theories of the French thinkers René Descartes (1596-1650) and Blaise Pascal (1623-62). Together they laid down the foundations for the work of Isaac Newton (1642-1727) in the second half of the 17th century. Descartes isolated the scientific concept of nature from its theological context. During the Renaissance the concept of a natural order was still closely tied to the concept of God. In his statement *Cogito, ergo sum* (I think therefore I am), Descartes postulated the primacy of human reason. For him, natural phenomena could still only be explained according to mathematics.

In his work *Discours de la méthode* (1637), Descartes presented analytical geometry and by so doing put the metric principles of Greek geometry (Euclides) into perspective. Algebraic notations were employed in order to study complicated mathematical theorems. The coordinate system made it not only possible to establish every position and configuration in space, but also the idea of a completely abstract, mathematical space, with an unlimited number of coordinates and dimensions. In theory, Descartes separated geometry from conceivable space. Together with Pierre de Fermat (1601-65), he also contributed greatly to the science of optics.

Blaise Pascal wrestled with the question of how far mathematics made it possible to fully comprehend nature. As opposed to the rational 'I think therefore I am', he put forward the philosophical 'La probabilité, est elle probable?' At the age of 31, Pascal did not see science as capable of explaining the first principle of nature. He tried to approach the boundaries which human reasoning set on the concept of nature: mathematics was for him a means with which to approach the inconceivable. In his thinking, infinity played an important role. He thought of the congruence of the

The transformation of a straightforward depiction of St John on Patmos into an anamorphosis on a wall. The distorted figure is stretched backwards. From Jean-François Niceron's *Thaumaturgus opticus*, 1646, tab. 33.

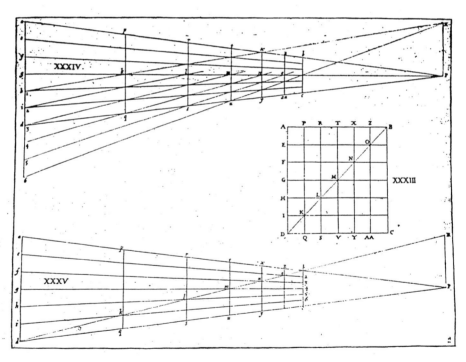

Jean-François Niceron. Mathematical construction for distorting a square, 1638. When looking at trapezium xxxv at height R above P, this appears like the original square xxxiii to rise from the surface of the paper.

mathematical arrangement of the microcosm and macrocosm in terms of mathematical forms. He wrote: 'Reality is an infinite sphere, whereby the centre is situated everywhere and the circumference nowhere. It is ultimately the largest tangible symbol of the almighty gods, that our imagination gets lost in this thought.' And he argued: 'Nature always recommences the same things, the years, the days, the hours; even spaces and numbers follow close on each other's heels. In this way a kind of infinity and eternity exists. Not that all this could be infinite and eternal, but these finite things multiply into the infinite. Thus it seems to me that only the number they multiply is infinite.'

Pascal also used mathematics in terms of existential questions. 'According to the calculus of probability you have to exert yourself to seek the truth, for if you die without venerating the True Principle, you are lost.' Along with Gérard Desargues (1591-1661), Pascal also developed the projective geometry concerned with conics. This was extremely important for the further theoretical development of perspective construction. For Pascal, beauty existed in 'a certain concordance between our nature and the matter that gives us enjoyment.' He went on to define this more precisely, not in terms of measurements or proportions, as Vitruvius did, but through symmetry. 'Symmetry has its basis in the fact that no other reasons exist to do it differently; one also sees this in a person's face. This is the reason why symmetry is only desired in the width and not in the height or depth.'

In the second half of the 17th century, Isaac Newton, supported by the work of Descartes, Pascal, Kepler and Galilei, developed a universal natural theory in his *Principia mathematica* (1687). He formulated not only the universal law of gravitation, but also developed (along with Pascal, Fermat and Leibniz [1646-1716] in particular) a differential and integral calculus. In theory these methods brought a mathematical control of the continuum within reach. Newton's contemporary, Leibniz, reduced counting to its most elementary form in the binary system. Newton, like Pascal, also sought to base his natural theory in theology.

THE MAGIC OF ANAMORPHOSIS

During the first half of the 17th century perspective construction was mathematically grounded. Well-known perspectivists, who contributed to its development, included Salomon de Caus and Père Niceron. The mathematical control of perspective made both a scientifically accurate perspective construction possible as well as its manipulation.

As the rules relating to scientific perspective were not only used to depict an actual space, but also as a means of arranging it, this can be termed perspective manipulation. A standard work in which this was theoretically discussed was

The construction of a perspective synthesis by Andrea Pozzo of actual space (auditorium) and illusionary space (stage) in a theatre, c. 1685

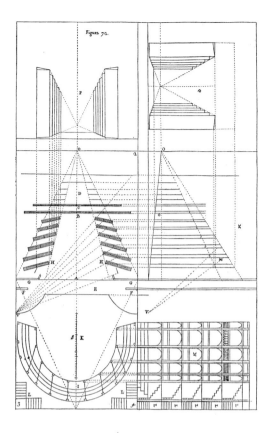

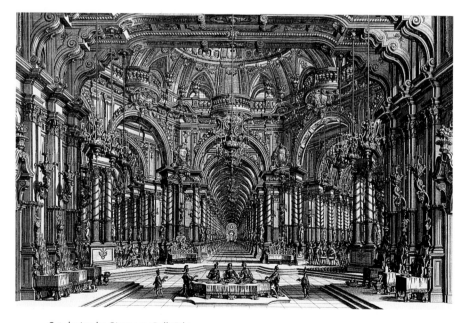

Set design by Giuseppe Galli Bibiena, 1740

Perspective curieuse ou magie des effets merveilleux (1638), by the French Franciscan Friar Minor, Jean-François Niceron (1613-46). Niceron knew all the treatises already published before his on perspective, from Alberti (1435) to Du Cerceau (1576), Vignola and Danti (1583), Sirigatti (1596) and Salomon de Caus (1612).

Niceron devoted the entire second book of his treatise to the study of geometric figures, which were so distorted that these only appeared to be properly proportioned when seen from the correct angle or viewpoint. When seen from other viewpoints they were indecipherable. To achieve this effect, Niceron inverted Alberti's straight forward perspective construction as it were. In Alberti's straightforward perspective construction a square grid lying horizontally on a vertical picture-plane is depicted as a trapezium, with the distance between the horizontal lines increasingly foreshortening the further back they lie.

Niceron, on the other hand, studied how an actual square grid could be distorted in order for it to appear as a regular square grid when seen in perspective. To do this, the actual grid was stretched backwards, thereby 'reversing' normal perspective construction. The foreshortening in the perspective picture plane was in fact compensated for by increasing the measurements of the actual plan the further back it went. In this way it appears as a regular square grid in the perspective picture plane. Niceron used the same diagonal construction which can also be used with normal perspective construction to determine the narrowing of distances between lines parallel to the picture plane. This diagonal is formed by the line through the viewing distance and the cluster of lines converging at the vanishing point. On the intersections parallel lines can be drawn.

Niceron's scheme was an extreme example of this same construction: the distance point lies close to the vanishing point. His scheme has to be 'read' from a point lying just above vanishing point. The stretched trapezium then appears in the perspective as a square (apparently tilted upwards). This is a so-called perspective anamorphosis whereby the picture plane, in which the figure appears correctly proportioned, is an imaginary one. Because of this, an anamorphosis can be constructed in any position or form of an actual surface. The depiction is separate from the underground, but this is not because the background recedes into the depth of the plane, as in normal perspective, but because in an anamorphosis the image, in fact, tilts forward from the surface.

TROMPE-L'ŒIL

French theoretical development on perspective manipulation occurred at a time when an experimental period of this was drawing to a close in Italy. After the 15th and 16th-century experimentations, *trompe-l'œil* was being perfected in 16th and 17th-century Italian painting, theatre design and architecture. In so-called *quadratura* (*trompe-l'œil*), 16th-century Italian painters employed perspective in order to escape architectural reality. By adjusting the vanishing point and the horizon to the position of the observer in actual space, the observer gained the impression that the painted space was an extension of existing reality. On the viewpoint, fixed by perspective construction, a continuum of real and illusionary spaces existed.

Quadratura Renaissance painters such as Melozzo da Forli and Andrea Mantegna tried to manipulate the actual distances to the ceiling or dome. The latter's spatial restrictions were kept at a greater optical distance by illusionary paintings of architecture and the use of light effects (*clair-obscure*). Domenico Ghirlandaio, Michelangelo and Peruzzi were among those who perfected illusionary architecture. Leonardo da Vinci, who meticulously examined the composition of flora, perfected the painting of open foliage. He painted interiors with powerful looking, towering

André Mollet. The ideal French garden, 1651

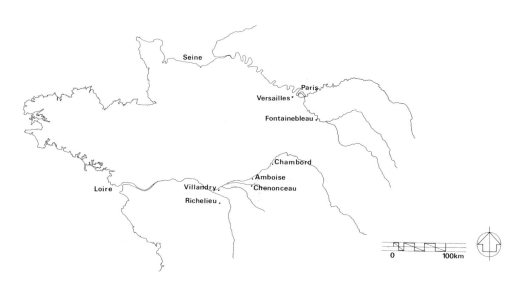

The Loire and the Seine were the most important locations for 16th and 17th-century châteaux around Paris.

tree trunks, their branches and shoots stretching across an entire ceiling that then resembled an open and transparent pergola.

During the 17th century, the Jesuit Andrea Pozzo (1642-1709) was so adept at perspective as *trompe-l'œil* that by painterly means he was able to transform any background into the desired effect. On the barrel vaulting spanning the nave of Sant' Ignazio in Rome, the walls of the church were continued as illusionary architecture 'as far as the heavens'. The painting on the vaulting was done by stretching a network of lines at the height of where it began and then, it being in a dark church, to illuminate this from the viewing point. The shadow from this indicated the precise distortion of the surfaces on the vaulting. Using this grid, the flat perspective drawing of the church walls on the vaulting could be executed. The chosen projection plane is therefore imaginary; it hovers, as it were, in the space under the vaulting. Pozzo's accelerated perspective appears to descend out of the vaulting.

Illusionary space was not only painted but also created using three-dimensional means. Experimentation of this kind was especially carried out in theatres. In 1583 Vignola (1507-73) maintained that the major problem in arranging a theatrical scene lay in establishing the correct perspective relationship between the three-dimensional stage props and the painted decors. The background should be constructed in such a way that it formed a perspective unity with the requisites on stage. As with *quadratura* painting, this construction had a fixed optimal viewpoint for observing this illusionist spatial continuity between three-dimensional reality and the painted picture plane. From all other points, the illusion varied from being less than perfect to completely distorted, thus, in fact, concealed. It is only from the so-called seat of the monarch, at the centre of the auditorium, that, from the standpoint of perspective construction, the representation on stage fully revealed its secrets.

Guido Ubaldus (1545-1607), Scipione Chiaramonti (1565-1652) and Giulio Troili (1613-85) also had the stage raised higher the further back it receded in order to manipulate the apparent depth of the stage and to improve the view. In the 17th century the background in the theatre was no longer just a painted surface. 'Vistas' were created in order to convey the illusion of infinite, continuous space. These were views framed by a series of architectonically constructed viewing 'windows'. The measurements and the placing of these 'windows' were perspectively manipulated and were in keeping with a painted panorama. An example of this are the five wooden streets executed in accelerated perspective and built by Scamozzi (1552-1616) as views to be placed behind the five portals of the three-dimensional decor in Palladio's Teatro Olympico in Vicenza (1580-84). In this way perspective trickery enabled city dwellers to bring their city into the theatre.

A further development in 17th-century theatre lay in abandoning three-dimensional props. This was made possible by the invention of the *coulisse* – a mobile screen or interchangeable wall. In this way decors acquired incredible mobility and versatility, which burgeoning opera at the time demanded. Giulio Troili used eight *coulisses* on stage, which he arranged one behind the other at increasingly smaller distances. This narrowing of distances in the regular indentations of the screens was done in keeping with the natural perspective of the space. The use of the coulisse made an unprecedented suggestion of spacial depth possible. The *non plus ultra* of such illusionist perspective in theatre sets was achieved in the work of Bibiena, an Italian family of set builders. Notwithstanding, the theatre remained dependent on painting for depicting spatial infinity. Accelerated perspective was ultimately directed by painterly means towards the vanishing point.

Geomorphology and châteaux
in the south-west area of Paris, c. 1650
The châteaux are still 'moderate' in size
and lie in a natural panorama.
  A. St Germain-en-Laye
  B. Versailles
  C. St Cloud
  D. Meudon
  E. Tuileries
  F. Luxembourg
  G. Sceaux

SAINT-GERMAIN-EN-LAYE

PORTRAIT DES CHASTEAVX ROYAVX DE SAINCT GERMAIN EN LAYE

Alexander Francini. The Italian layout
(since disappeared) of Château Neuf on
a slope of the Seine in St Germain-en-
Laye, 1614

In the mid-17th century two French treatises were published on garden art. *Le jardin de plaisir* (1651) was written by André Mollet. His father Claude Mollet was the head gardener of the French king and the *Théâtre des plans et jardinages* (published posthumously in 1652 and dedicated to Nicolas Fouquet) was attributed to him. André Mollet offered several interesting suggestions regarding the treatment of a view. He suggested placing a perspective painting at the end of an avenue to create the idea of a continuation of space. He also treated the avenue as if it were a vista enclosed by a set in a theatre.

In his work Salomon de Caus (1576-1626) dealt with the 'scénographie ou raccourcissement de la chose visible' and also discussed a perspective painting for an external wall. Seen through a frame, such a painting appeared to be the spatial continuation of the actual garden. The Jesuit Dubreuil, among others, wrote about two painted screens arranged in a garden as *coulisses* with, behind, a painted decor of a garden. To an observer standing at an allotted distance from them, the images on the screens merged into one uninterrupted spatial illusion.

Thus painting was employed in landscape architecture as an artificial device for creating spatial depth. In the first outline plans for the ideal garden, included in André Mollet's treatise and for which the Tuileries Gardens served as a model, the treatment of the view was taken a step further. The plans are bilaterally symmetric on each side of a main axis, which terminates in an exedra or echo – a primitive architectural device used to bring the perspective horizon forward (accelerated perspective) and to make the space appear deeper. (It is similar to the apsis and the dome in architecture.) The echo represents the natural panorama, in the same way the dome represents the cosmos. The axis with its bilateral symmetry, which meets this, is therefore the most important visual axis.

THE CHÂTEAUX ON THE LOIRE AND THE SEINE

During the second half of the 17th century huge changes took place concerning the number, size and design of country estates around Paris. In the period preceding the general pacification of the land and until the early 17th century, the French kings had sought sanctuary in their fortified châteaux. Many of these, such as Bury, Blois, Chambord and Chenonceaux were situated in the basin of the river Loire.

Fontainebleau, Chantilly, Anet, Dampierre and Verneuil lay in the basin of the Seine, some 50 kilometres from Paris. These châteaux also had strategically placed waterworks. From around the mid-16th century châteaux began to be built within the Paris area, such as Meudon, St Cloud, the Palais des Tuileries, St Germain-en-Laye and the Palais du Luxembourg. In these châteaux the country estate atmosphere was more important than their ability to defend. Although Charles VIII, on returning from his campaign in Italy, had already brought back Italian artists in 1495 who worked, among others, on Amboise and Blois, the Italian influence on country estates, especially in Paris, was still an important one. This was expressed in both the site and the construction. Here the Italian Medici family, connected to the French royal family by marriage, played a crucial role. Catherine de' Medici (1519-89) was the wife of Henry II, while Maria de' Medici (1573-1642) was married to Henry IV.

One of the first Paris châteaux was Meudon (begun 1520). It lay high on the southern valley wall of the Seine, overlooking the landscape and city of Paris. The Italian Primaticcio built a grotto (1552) on the mountainside next to the château. Catherine de' Medici sold a site, also on a steep southern slope along a bend in the Seine, to the Italian banker, Jerome de Gondi. He built a château (St Cloud) halfway up the slope from where there was a panoramic view of the Seine.

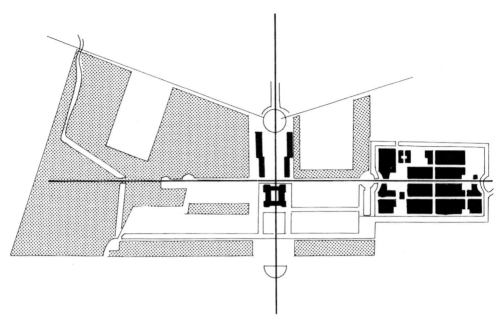

Richelieu, the ideal city as part of the residence

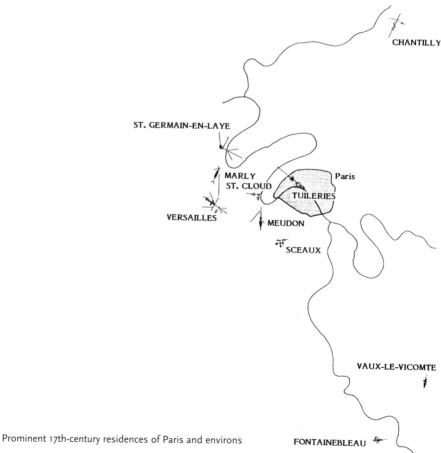

CHANTILLY

ST. GERMAIN-EN-LAYE

MARLY
ST. CLOUD
VERSAILLES
MEUDON
SCEAUX

Paris

TUILERIES

VAUX-LE-VICOMTE

Prominent 17th-century residences of Paris and environs

FONTAINEBLEAU

On the city boundary of Paris, Catherine de' Medici built the Palais des Tuileries (1562) with a geometric Renaissance garden. Bernard Palissy also constructed a grotto there, while between 1597 and 1605 the Italian, Alexander Francini, designed for Maria de' Medici a monumental flight of steps, grottoes and terraces on the banks of the Seine for château Neuf in St Germain-en-Laye. From the terraces there was a commanding view across the Seine valley. The design was like a monumental version of the slope-designs of Vignola for Horti Farnesiani (Rome) and Villa Lante (Bagnaia). With the series of nymphaeae placed one above the other in the principle axis, it is also similar to Villa d'Este in Tivoli. In 1615 Maria de' Medici had the Palais du Luxembourg built after the design of the Palazzo Pitti in Florence. The garden was laid out as far as possible in the manner of the Boboli gardens.

The development from the 16th-century French castle (Loire region) to the early 17th-century open château (Seine area) can, morphologically speaking, be summed up from four different aspects. These also illustrate the individual manner in which the French château opened towards the landscape. In the plan of the building the enclosing of the courtyard was broached on one side and the round towers were changed into rectangular pavilions. In the façade, the accent shifted from the corners (defence) to the centre (opening). The façade consisted of five parts: a central pavilion, flanked by other parts of the building and corner pavilions. In the plan for the grounds the narrow strategic entrance was changed into a drive leading onto a large entrance front. The many enclosed and separately sited parts (buildings, gardens, entrances) were geometrically arranged. As well as a defensive function, the water in the plan also took on an aesthetic importance (pools and canals). In the plan of the garden the neat symmetry changed into a simple bilateral symmetry.

RICHELIEU: THE IDEAL TOWN

In Touraine Cardinal Richelieu built a new town, Richelieu, begun in 1631 and based on the plans of Jacques Lemercier, part of which formed the garden and parklands around a château. The River Mable, which was made into a rectangular canal in the park and which bounds the town at right-angles, determined the layout of the plan in the topography. The town and the park layouts have their own measurement system, while the château, park, landscape and the town itself are linked by two axes which intersect each other at the château. The axis passing through the château connects the building, park and outside landscape. The other axis, passing through the town, remains within the boundary of the estate and connects the town with the spatial axis of the residency. The town plan has no independent spatial relationship with the landscape: this is brought about via the axis of the château. The axis passing through the city is a transverse axis in the park. The town is a part of the layout connected to the central part of the park and, like the garden plan, it is based on axiality and symmetry. For the first time, château, town and landscape are organized into one ideal plan at Richelieu.

THE ARTIFICIAL LANDSCAPE OF PARIS

Every early 17th-century château in and around Paris was 'homely' and on a local scale, just as in Italy. The geometric plan was of limited dimensions and served as foreground for the view. The traditional agrarian pattern of the landscape was barely affected by these incidental villa projects. Later in the 17th century, especially in the second half, radical changes took place under the reign of Louis XIV. The population of Paris doubled in size between 1590 and 1637 to more than 400,000 inhabitants. Wars and poor harvests created famines. Due to taxes and debts French peasants were forced to sell their land, while a lack of technical progress created structural failings in agricultural exploitation.

The regional network of landscape architecture in 17th-century Paris

The decline in agrarian activity resulted in rural communities losing their autonomy and in a decrease in the amount of land that was used for agricultural purposes. The traditional medieval agrarian structure had to make way for the free play of economic forces. Burghers, the aristocracy and financiers profited from the situation by acquiring as much ground as possible. For these new landowners, agrarian exploitation took second priority: there was no way rural life could be enjoyed by having views of ploughed fields and vineyards. The agrarian landscape was closed off from the field of view. The king, members of parliament, princes, magistrates and the urban aristocracy, by buying up concentrations of land lots, all sought to form as large estates as possible. By being in control of such vast tracts of land, they could also demonstrate their power. Land exploitation that went hand in hand with this was wholesale forestry development, which formed the backcloth to the country houses built during the second half of the 17th century. Paris in general was developed into a formal ideal city and became part of an artificial landscape.

THE CONCEPT OF FORMAL STAGE MANAGEMENT

The older châteaux, like the Italian Renaissance villas, possessed several striking features in the Seine landscape, even though the differences in height were smaller. Around the mid-17th century the city began to displace agricultural exploitation, and land around the Seine was reallocated and developed. New residencies were the bearers of a far-reaching process of reorganization.

Assisted by the science of mathematics, the depiction of nature and space within the artificial landscape of a residency took on an abstract and universal character. In the garden the depiction of nature, with its gradations of colour, texture and movement, was arranged like a linear classification system and linked to the Italian mythical and pictorial arsenal (grottoes and cascades) and to French elements, such as the canal. Knowledge of theoretical perspective enabled the use of perspective manipulation. Thus the link between image and reality became obscured. Anamorphosis was the most advanced device. Together with the discovery of the *coulisse*, the use of overlapping outlines and light/shade effects, this was an important means of bringing 'infinity' into the boundaries of the plan.

In the garden the picture plane (the terrace) and the line (the axis) are the most important devices of spatial organization. The spatial axis creates depth, clarity and order within the image. The city is part of the design. It is set against the garden like a mirror image, while the house, in between the two, both separates and connects with 'nature' and 'culture'. In the landscape outside the domain, the axes connect with avenues, which form direct links between the residences themselves. They also connect with the large-scale hunting forests on the level, elevated plateaus and with the city of Paris. In this way the entire region, although it cannot be seen in its entirety from any point, has been artificially made into one entity. The thinking observer must reconstruct this abstract skeleton, as if in an anatomical lesson, in order to have an idea of the actual form of the natural landscape. The whole construction can be seen as a synthesization of the natural landscape.

The geometric scheme consists of a hierarchical measurement system with the house as the centre. It links together the local scale and the scale of the private territory, the city and the region. The geometric grid is determined by a principle axis. The mirror symmetry of the axis is projected onto the natural form of the geomorphology (a valley). On the edges of the axial zone (both in the garden and the city) there is a conflict between the geometry of the plan and the natural form of the terrain. This has not been worked out as a series of local situational considerations (as for instance at Ville d'Este), but as camouflage for the irregular terrain.

The architectural landscape devices are, in principle, comparable to those used in the rational landscape design of the Italian villa. An important difference, however, is that they have been worked through as far as the boundaries of the rational allow, are presented at an abstract level and reinforce each other's effect. The themes of the landscape's architectonic treatment have been extended to the regional landscape and the city. The formally designed system incorporates and, simultaneously, constructs the entire space. Yet, despite its abstract and universal nature, the ambiguity of the formal design remains in the tension between natural geomorphology and artificial symmetry, between the real and the illusionary spatial image, between tangible material and abstraction.

Carlo Maratta. Portrait of
André le Nôtre, *c.* 1680

Vaux-le-Vicomte

During the second half of the 17th century Paris was a leading cultural and political centre. Around the city far-reaching changes were also being made to the landscape. A number of impressive residencies were built, and the most important landscape architect involved with these was André le Nôtre (1613-1700), the son of Pierre, the *Premier Jardinier des Tuileries*. He introduced his son to landscape art, who then proceeded to broaden his knowledge among the painters, architects and thinkers of the day.

This was also in keeping with the ideas of the age, such as those expressed by Jacques Boyceau, the *Intendant des Jardins du Roy*, who regarded a knowledge of architecture, drawing, painting and geometry as essential to a landscape architect's training. André le Nôtre became famous for the work he was commissioned to do for Nicolas Fouquet (1615-80), Louis XIV's appointed *Surintendant des Finances* in 1653. He had Vaux-le-Vicomte built (1656-61), the first of a series of large, new country houses outside Paris. Le Nôtre's design for Vaux-le-Vicomte fulfilled an important prototype. It complied with the new ideas of the age and gave French landscape art its own identity, the expression of which was in keeping with political aspirations. The most important historical details of the original plan are known. The present layout of Vaux-le-Vicomte is partly a restoration of this: the broad outlines of which remain unchanged.

MENUET-TRIO-MENUET: THE CEREMONIAL INAUGURATION

On 17 August 1661, King Louis XIV, accompanied by several noblewomen, travelled by coach from Fontainebleau to Vaux-le-Vicomte. Nicolas Fouquet, his young ambitious finance minister and enlightened patron of many artists, had invited over 6,000 guests to a glittering party to celebrate, along with the king, his new residence at Vaux. Around five years earlier, Fouquet had drawn together a highly-gifted trio:

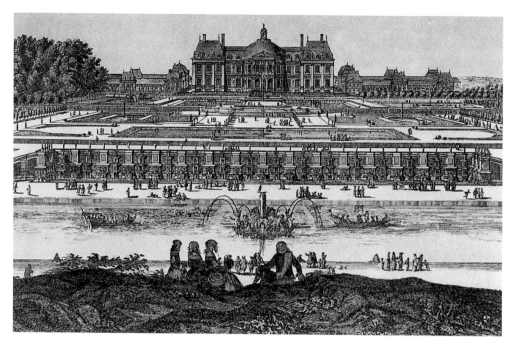

Israël Sylvestre. Vaux-le-Vicomte. The garden and château from the south

Vaux-le-Vicomte. The entrance, island with château and garden

architect Louis II Le Vau (1612-70), the landscape architect André le Nôtre and the painter and interior decorator Charles Lebrun (1619-90).

On a site covering several hundred hectares, containing a few settlements and Vaux village, the three artists were ordered to create a country house for the chief treasurer according to the prevailing ideas of the cultural and intellectual elite. A memorandum, written by Fouquet on 21 November 1660, indicates that a large number of workmen were involved in constructing the house and gardens. The settlements were shifted, hills excavated and rivers repositioned. In nearby Maincy, Fouquet had accommodation and a hospital built for his workers as well as large workshops and a carpet factory to execute Lebrun's colossal designs.

Despite his reckless behaviour, the quick-witted minister nevertheless took certain precautions when he heard that his enemy and arch rival, Jean Baptiste Colbert, also a minister of Louis XIV, had been in Vaux, secretly, to spy on the controversial work. 'Dispatch the bricklayers working on the canal for as long as is necessary, so that there are as few workers as possible to be seen.' Perhaps even in his rashness, Colbert's witty response, in his presence, to the king's complaint on visiting the Louvre that he had no money to finish the great building, was not lost on Fouquet. 'Sire, you need be finance minister for only a year to build to your heart's content.'

Fouquet received his royal guests with bold gallantry. The dazzlingly attired throng first went for a walk in the garden where they were entertained by the large waterworks. Jean de la Fontaine, one of Fouquet's most loyal friends, sang to them his *Songe de Vaux*:

> *Fontaines jaillissez*
> *Herbe tendre, croissez*
> *Le long de ces rivages*
> *Venez petits oiseaux*
> *Accorder vos ramages*
> *Au doux bruit de leurs eaux.*

Nymphs in gilded gondolas invited the guests to go boating, while hidden behind trees and thicket musicians enticed them into the labyrinth, grottoes, marble recesses and other hidden places. Then the guests visited the château where Lebrun's decor was admired. The already slightly 'touchy' king was apparently irritated by Fouquet's recurring heraldic inscription: *Quo non ascendam?* (To where can I not rise?). Wagging tongues also maintained that an allegorical painting, in which those who saw it thought they recognized the young queen, had also caused the king's displeasure. A written word of warning by Madame du Plessis-Bellièvre, one of the minister's spies, quickly stuffed into Fouquet's hand, was to no avail.

After the tour there was a lottery with expensive prizes for all those invited; jewels for the ladies and weapons for the gentlemen. Meanwhile the acclaimed gourmet chef, Vatel, had ordered the tables to be laid. The tableware, with more than 36 dozen solid gold plates, must have been an exquisite sight. Says Jean de la Fontaine, 'The delicacy and rarity of the dishes was great, but the witty gracefulness with which his lord the minister and his wife entertained their guests was even greater'. After supper the assembled guests made their way to the garden again. In the *Allée des Sapins* a theatre set had meanwhile been erected, designed by Lebrun together with 'magician' Torelli.

> *Deux enchanteurs pleins de savoir firent, tant par leur imposture,*
> *Qu'on crut qu'ils avaient le pouvoir de commander 'la nature'.*

Israël Sylvestre. Vaux-le-Vicomte. View of the flower parterre during construction

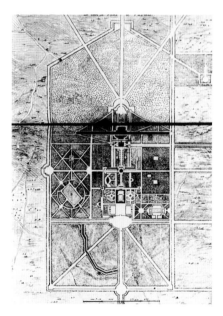

Israël Sylvestre. Engraving of the plan of Vaux-le-Vicomte, c. 1660

André le Nôtre. Plan of Vaux-le-Vicomte, c. 1656

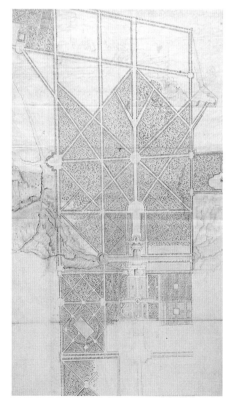

A large rock suddenly changed into a shell opening up, out of which stepped the nymph of the fountain who commanded the gods to descend from their marble pedestals and entertain the king. At this point fauna and bacchantes appeared from all manner of ornaments and statues and started to dance a ballet. The ballet was followed by a comedy *Les Fâcheaux* by Molière, especially written for the occasion. By the time it had finished it was dark and guests were making their way to go inside again, when suddenly a shower of fireworks illuminated the château yet again as a monumental stage decor.

The Sun King returned to Fontainebleau. Three weeks later, on 5 September 1661, Nicolas Fouquet was arrested in Nantes and imprisoned on the king's orders. Despite pressure from Colbert and the king also seeking revenge, Fouquet's trial, in which he was accused of embezzling state funds, lasted over three years and took what seemed a favourable turn for the accused. The judges sentenced the defendant to exile. The king, however, quashed this sentence and increased the severity of the punishment to lifelong imprisonment. All of Fouquet's possessions were confiscated and Colbert assumed control of his ministry.

On Colbert's advise, the king himself then set Vaux's three designers to work to create a new fitting residence for him at Versailles. Fouquet remained in prison until his death. Many maintained that he was a thief and had drained an already impoverished country and people of money and gold for his own reckless capers. Others, including many artists, remained loyal to him even in prison. The most loyal of all was Jean de la Fontaine, who for years in his poems pleaded in vain to the king for clemency.

Remplissez l'air de cris en vos grottes profondes
pleurez, nymphes de Vaux, faites croître vos ondes.

THE PRESENT LAYOUT

After Fouquet's arrest, the most beautiful furniture, carpets, paintings, sculptures and even trees were removed from Vaux and used to adorn the Louvre and Versailles. Twelve years later, in 1673, the estate was handed back to Madame Fouquet. When her eldest son died childless, in 1705, she sold the property to Field Marshall Villars. His son proved incapable of managing the estate; among others he had the water supply system in the garden dismantled in order to sell the lead. In 1764 the property was sold to the Duke of Choiseul-Praslin. His family owned the estate for six generations and, despite the motto of the National Convention to destroy all symbols of monarchy, the château remained undamaged during the Revolution.

After 1850 the gardens were neglected and in 1875 the estate was publicly sold. The new owner was a Paris industrialist, Alfred Sommier. Together with his son, he carried out numerous restoration projects. Around 1910, the restoration of the garden, based on the still existing broad layout and sketches, was virtually completed. The landscape architect Achille Duchène played a major role in the restoration. One of Alfred Sommier's great grandsons, Count Patrice de Vogüé, is the estate's current owner.

The present layout is broadly in keeping with the original plan. This is evident from André Le Nôtre's drawing and the engravings by Israël Sylvestre and Gabriël Pérelle (1665). A few details have changed: the *Grilles d'Eau* (*les Petites Cascades*) at the eastern termination of the transverse axis along *les Petits Canaux* have not been entirely restored, neither has the *goulette* (the cascading water chain of pools interconnected by small canals) along the principle axis at the *Parterre de Gazon* (the so-called *Alleé d'Eau*).

In Le Nôtre's drawing and Sylvestre's engravings, the dimensions of the pond

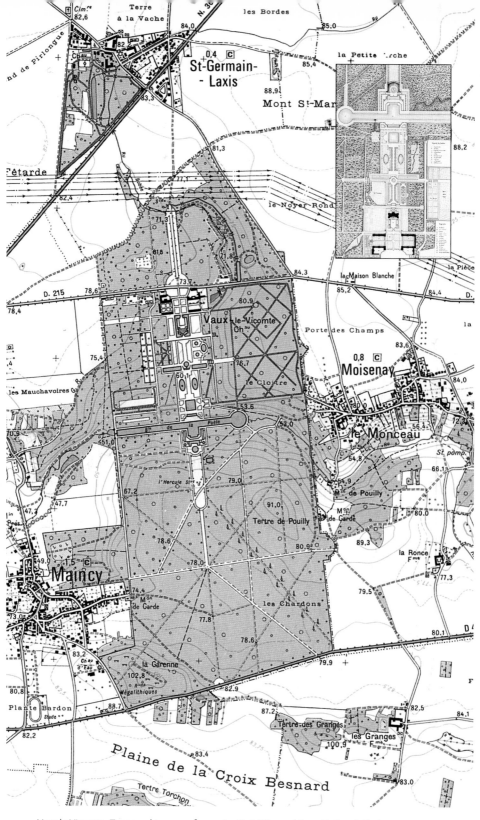

Vaux-le-Vicomte. Topographic map of 1977. Institut Géographique National, Paris
Insert: Plan of Vaux-le-Vicomte, 1887

in the *Parterre de la Couronne* seem larger than those of the ponds in the *Parterre de Gazon* (*Les Tritons*). However, in Sylvestre and Pérelle's perspective drawing this does not appear to be the case. For this reason it is difficult to give a definite judgement on the original proportions. Moreover, the two round ponds Sylvestre drew at the foot of the château, at the beginning of the *Parterre de Broderie*, are missing from the present layout. There are also no urns and pedestals in Sylvestre's engraving but herms, placed around the main round pond and against the forest wall, along the *Parterre de la Couronne* and the *Parterre de Diane*.

The origins of the present plantings is a separate issue altogether. In Israël Sylvestre's engravings, the rear of the garden, past the *Grand Canal*, was then still bounded by young, open forest. The edges of the forest, in the foremost part of the garden, were less uniform than they are now. The trees (elm, oak and chestnut) were not clipped, although they were underplanted with hornbeam. In its present state, the system of avenues in the forest is partly overgrown.

Pérelle and Sylvestre's engravings of the parterres also indicate that the internal configuration of the *Parterre de Broderie* (buxus with red chippings) was different. Moreover, the *platebandes* (edging borders) of this parterre were empty and did not include the present topiary forms. These were not in evidence along the other parterres either, although there was a row of tub plantings along the terrace at the foot of the château. The *Parterre de Diane* was not a lawn but was lavishly filled with flowers and the occasional pond. Going on the recommended varieties of plantings fashionable in garden art at the time, there must have been fragrant herbs like thyme, lavender, mint and marjoram as well as cut flowers such as carnations, violets, irises and lilies. Aside from the flower parterre, the rest of the garden plantings were extremely plain (grass, buxus, hornbeam and oak).

SITE

A modern topographical map shows an extensive forest complex to the north-east of the city of Melun. In a relatively open river valley landscape spreads a dense forest running north to south. Within this lies an elongated open space (the garden) and the house. On the edge of this solid forest are two villages, Moisenay le Monceau and Maincy, situated on the north and south slopes of a river valley running east to west. If we take the solid forest as being a 'wall' between the garden and landscape, then this can be seen as having an 'inside' (garden) and an 'outside' (landscape).

Most lines of the garden, including the principle axis and the other avenues, terminate in the forest wall, while, conversely, the patterns of agricultural landscape run into the outside wall as it were. The patterns of the layout and the landscape interact where a small river, the Anqueil, flows straight through both the forest and the garden, where a smaller tributary, the Bobée, penetrates the forest at the village of St Germain-Laxis to the north, and at the point where the principle axis to the north continues more or less to this same village.

The most important link with the outside world is the slightly curving route to Melun, which intersects the principle axis at *Avant Cour*. Between Maincy and Moisenay vestiges of the old footpaths also run through the forest. On the landscape side, the forest wall has hardly been styled as an 'outside wall'. Only occasionally can an exedra-like termination of an axis still be seen. As a result the outside forest wall no longer expresses the nature of the internal layout: the forest isolates the garden from the landscape. At the same time it acts as a 'buffer' in which practicalities like a vegetable garden and vineyard can be 'stored' out of the way.

There are certain differences between the existing situation and the plan engraved by Israël Sylvestre, a contemporary of Le Nôtre. The principle axis of Sylvestre's plan

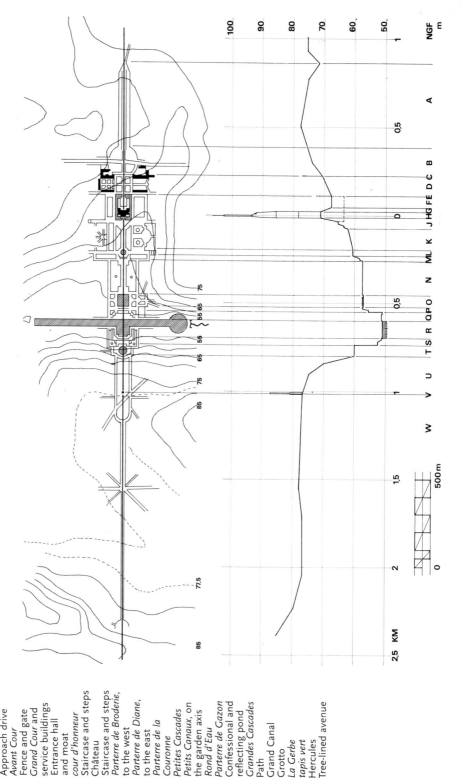

Vaux-le-Vicomte.
Plan and elevation of
the main axis
A. Approach drive
B. *Avant Cour*
C. Fence and gate
D. *Grand Cour* and
   service buildings
E. Entrance hall
   and moat
F. *cour d'honneur*
G. Staircase and steps
H. Château
I. Staircase and steps
K. *Parterre de Broderie*,
   to the west
   Parterre de Diane,
   to the east
   *Parterre de la
   Couronne*
L. *Petites Cascades*
M. *Petits Canaux*, on
   the garden axis
   Rond d'Eau
N. *Parterre de Gazon*
O. Confessional and
   reflecting pond
P. *Grandes Cascades*
Q. Path
R. Grand Canal
S. Grotto
T. *La Gerbe*
U. *tapis vert*
V. Hercules
W. Tree-lined avenue

Vaux-le-Vicomte.
Entrance to the garden
along the transverse axis
in front of the château.
The layout is flat across
the width of the main
axis; beyond this it
follows the site's natural
slope.

ran through the forest wall into the landscape, together with two diagonal side axes. The most important transverse axes continued west in the landscape. The pattern of the layout did not terminate in the wall but was continued in the landscape. The landscape side of the wall was bounded by a tree-lined promenade.

The pattern of the landscape (country roads and streams), especially in the extensive northern and southern parts, continued into the forest wall. The new scheme was laid over the landscape-pattern, as it were, whereby the old routes were retained in the forest. Only in the main part of the garden was the landscape as 'underlay' erased. When compared to the present form, Sylvestre's engraving clearly integrated the layout's patterns into the landscape, especially in the forest area.

Le Nôtre's is the most important drawing. In this plan the diagonal system of avenues was better designed than in Sylvestre's engraving. In the radial forest the old agrarian pattern of paths was erased. Outside the forest, the avenues were bounded by open fields. The system of avenues was the most important link between the actual garden and the landscape outside.

To sum up, the present plan comprises a garden which is isolated from the open landscape by a dense forest wall. Orthogonal, diagonal and peripheral avenues form the links between the garden, forest and landscape. The garden's symmetrical axis, piercing the landscape, is the most important internal element, while the Anqueil, piercing the garden, is the most important external one. Together they form a coordinated system that constitutes the framework of the layout. Despite the present spatial isolation of the actual garden, this anchors the complex in the landscape.

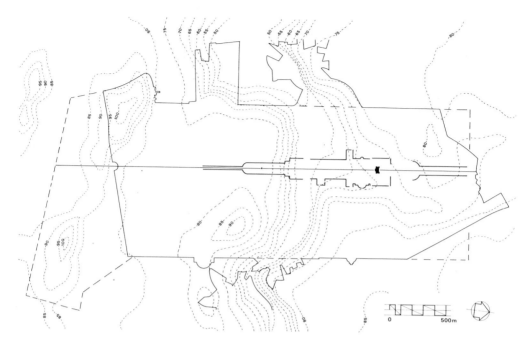

Vaux-le-Vicomte. The outlines of the estate and garden projected onto the contour lines

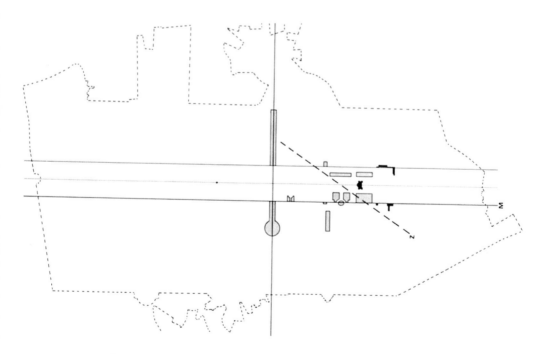

Vaux-le-Vicomte. The main axis, the diameter of the estate (M) and the natural axis of the side valley (Z). Together with the asymmetric elements along the garden perimeter, they create a balance between the natural shape of the terrain and the symmetry of the main axis.

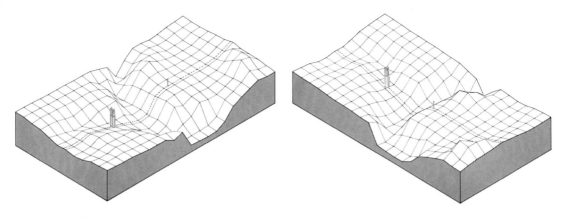

Vaux-le-Vicomte.
Geomorphology and main axis (the vertical measurements are 13 times exaggerated)

INTERACTION WITH THE GEOMORPHOLOGY

The garden at Vaux-le-Vicomte is a large independent space enclosed by forest. The effect of this seclusion is heightened even more by the local geomorphology. This comprises the Anqueil valley and a side valley (Bobée) flowing into this from the north at an oblique angle. Both river valleys are irregular, with a steep southern and an eastern valley wall, respectively. The axis of the layout lies at right angles to the direction of the main valley. The *Grand Canal* excavated along this forms a 'fold', as it were, in the plan, folding the principle axis into a northern and southern section of roughly equal length. The northern half lies in a side valley, the latter lying at a 20-degree angle from the principle axis.

The southern half lies on the elevated plateau. Moreover the principle axis does not converge with the north-south geometric middle of the forest section, but has been shifted in a westerly direction to the side valley. The garden's eastern boundary partly converges with the geometric middle of the forest section. Thus, the principle axis of the garden has been shifted as much as was necessary from the geometric centre of the forest section in order to project it in the heart of the side valley. Subsequently, the garden's width is determined by the natural width of the side valley. In this way the existing depression of the side valley can be optimally used for the technical and spatial organization of the axis. By carefully determining the position of the principle axis, excavation work is kept to a minimum. The slope of the valley basin makes it possible to make maximum use of the river water for the garden's waterworks.

The deviation of the side valley in relation to the principle axis has been visually corrected. The cross-section of the central axial zone has been erased. The *Parterre de Broderie* has been laid out in an artificial bedding with equally high banks on the sides, thereby camouflaging the terrain's natural transverse slope. The plan of the perimeter areas has been adapted to the natural valley form by varying the transverse measurements and creating differences in height of the off-centre parts of the garden. Thus the deviation of the side valley in relation to the principle axis can still be 'read' from the larger transverse dimensions of the north-east parterres (e.g. *Parterre de la Couronne*) and the south-west section of the small and large canals.

This complex interaction between the garden's axial symmetry, the geometric middle of the forest section and the natural course of the river valleys creates a visual balance between the plan's symmetry and the terrain's natural form. The strict geometric symmetry in the plan is restricted to the central area of axial symmetry, which has an autonomous significance, quite separate from the terrain's natural form.

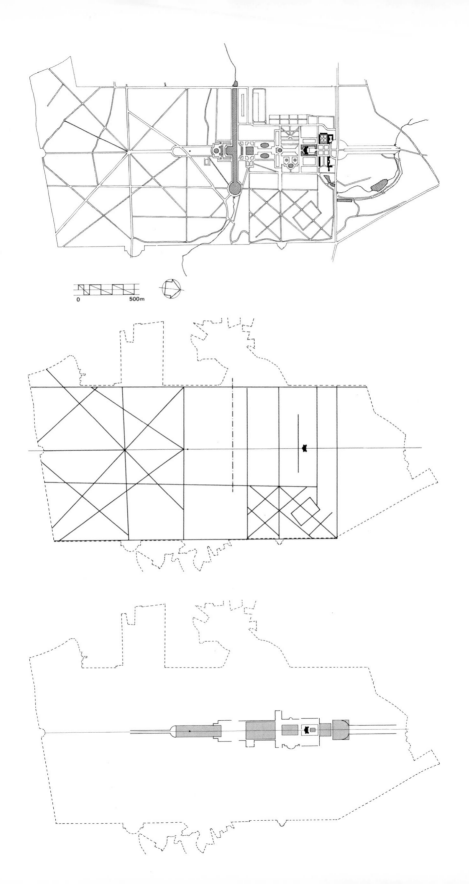

The château complex, garden and estate

0   500m

The orthogonal grid and the diagonal axes
of the estate

Vaux-le-Vicomte.
The sequence of planes (terraces) in the garden

In June 1987, under the author's direction, the axis of symmetry was measured, the measurements of which are significant for the geometric system and the spatial organization. The former is determined by the measurement systems of the building, garden and forest complex.

The island, with the château and *cour d'honneur* bordered by raised parterres, is surrounded by a moat and is the most important element on the principle axis. The château's north and south façades (70 metres wide) consist of protruding end pavilions, a recessed *arrièrecorps* and a main (protruding) *avantcorps*. However, the organization of depth and the proportions of the building parts are different in both façades. On the north front the end pavilions protrude more, the central one is smaller and the wall as a whole has a concave form. On the south side, the large domed central pavilion protrudes much more and gives the wall a convex form. This concave to convex distortion inclines the building in a south-ward direction along the principle axis. At a distance the regular indentations in the façades suggest a series of separate building parts, which in the layout, however, have apparently been combined.

The plan as a whole comprises a series of rectangles that overlap each other diagonally. The château's separate service buildings (*Les Communs*), situated to the north, are included in this scheme as the end pavilions, which have been shifted the furthest across the diagonals to the front. As a result the forefront has a total width of more than 250 metres. The overlapping of the building parts makes it difficult to estimate their true size. The building's actual depth (35 metres) is also manipulated visually by this. The scale of the château varies, as it were, according to the angle and distance from which it is seen.

The northern entrance drive terminates 350 metres before the château in a sequence of three consecutive open spaces: *Avant Cour*, *Grand Cour* and *cour d' honneur*. Their respective surface areas (2.4 hectares, 0.8 hectares and 0.2 hectares) rapidly decrease towards the château.

The most important part of the axial symmetry is between the château in the north and the statue of Hercules in the south (1,000 metres). In the width (100-150 metres) the mirror symmetry remains limited to the central zone. As with the north side of the château, the central area of the axis of symmetry is also constructed longitudinally from a series of three spaces on the south side: the terrace with the *Parterre de Broderie*, the terrace with the *Parterre de Gazon* and reflecting pond, and the *tapis vert* past the canal. The surface area of the second terrace is larger than that of the first (4.5 hectares and 1.5 hectares, respectively). The surface area of the *tapis vert* is no bigger than that of the second terrace, though the former is not level and lies exposed against the steep slope of the main valley, making it appear longer than it actually is.

The series of spaces on both the north and south sides overlap each other at the point where the château stands. In this way the château is gradually linked with both the scale of the front terrain as well as that of the garden.

The principle axis longitudinally (3,400 metres) comprises a sequence of three separate parts: the northern approach drive to the château (900 metres), the axial symmetry between the château and the statue of Hercules (1,000 metres) and the southern tree-lined avenue (1,500 metres), respectively. The entrance drive lies in the upper reaches of the side valley and is focused on the decor of the building, situated halfway into the valley. In the second section the visual play with water and terrain levels dominates the physical accessibility of the axis. Once more the background to this, the statue of Hercules, is the beginning of a following stage along the principle axis. It stands on the intersection of the axis with a transverse avenue and two diagonal ones. This *patte d'oie* is the beginning of an extensive radial forest and marks

163

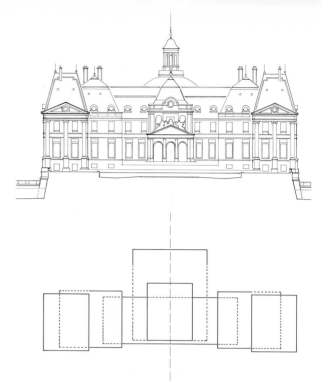

164

Vaux-le-Vicomte. Plan and
front view of the château.
Both are constructed from
overlapping rectangles.

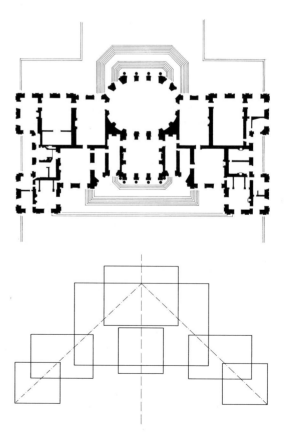

both the depth and width of the complex (1,350 metres).

The longitudinal measurements on the axis and the various distances between the transverse axes increase from the central section (the building) in a northerly and southerly direction. Together with the principle axis and the eastern tree-lined avenue running parallel to this, the transverse axes form an orthogonal grid of *carrés* with a module size varying from 4 hectares (in the central zone of the complex) to 40 hectares (in the forest). The increasing size of the *carrés* towards the periphery and the diagonal avenues are the links between the scale of the garden and that of the forest complex as a whole. This third level of scale, embracing the château and the garden, can be referred to as 'the estate', a rectangle covering a total surface area of 455 hectares.

To summarize, the geometric organization of the plan consists of an orthogonal grid. The axis is the central line in the geometry. The grid module is larger towards the edges of the plan. This expanding measurement system has basically three levels of scale: the house, the garden and the estate. Their measurement schemes also have an internal graded structure of proportions. By laying the measurement schemes over each other, a hierarchical system exists with a continuous series of jumps in scale between the interior and the landscape along the axis.

THE SCENOGRAPHY OF THE AXIS

The axis is not only the central line in the geometry but also in the spacial stage management. The wide drive to the château begins in the north on a slight ascent. At first only the tip of the château can be seen but after a few hundred metres the road descends almost imperceptibly, revealing the lower part of the château with its façade fitting precisely into the frame of trees. At the point where the drive joins *Avant Cour* the view takes in the entire château, including the service buildings (*Les Communs*), which function as projecting stage wings. Due to the sloping forecourt and the jumps in scale, which appear both in the width and depth measurements towards the château, the spatial depth of the terrain appears particularly impressive. It is, however, impossible to gauge the distance to the château.

Between *Avant Cour* and the following *Grand Cour* is a screen. In the central section of the picture plane this screen filters out elements of the background. The screen, on either side of a wrought iron entrance gate, consists of three parts which have a diminishing transparency. The first part comprises four pieces of wrought iron trellis between herms: imposing square columns, topped by sculptured heads of the Greek god Hermes. The middle part consists of a portal with an iron trellis in the opening. Finally, the screen on the side of the *Communs* is terminated by a wall divided into four sections.

At the point where the drive meets *Avant Cour* there are vistas through the open portals of the screen to the colonnades, which denote the side entrances to the garden beyond the *Communs*. From the centre of *Avant Cour*, where the east-west access road crosses the principle axis, the vistas through the portals are directed at the side entrances of the *Communs*. Thus the hierarchy of entrances and connections is precisely defined on *Avant Cour*. Closer to the entrance gate, the motifs of the railings are partly in keeping with those of the château's façade. Certain of the gate's carved lines correspond with those of the set of steps leading to the château, while the apex of the entrance gate blends visually with the lamp on the dome.

The *Grand Cour* is bounded on both sides by the end pavilions of the *Communs*, connected to each other by walls with the entrance in the middle. The elements and measurements of *Grand Cour* correspond both diagonally and longitudinally to each other; the two open portals in the screen, for instance, being a projection of the width of the château. Because of the static nature of this four-sided symmetry, *Grand Cour*

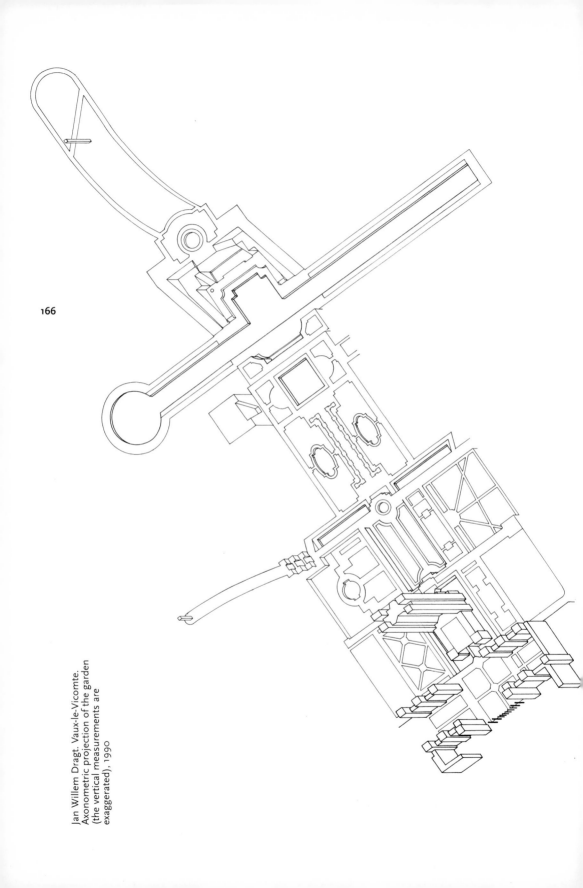

166

Jan Willem Dragt. Vaux-le-Vicomte.
Axonometric projection of the garden
(the vertical measurements are
exaggerated), 1990

Vaux-le-Vicomte.
Section of the
château along the
main axis

Vaux-le-Vicomte.
The visual link between
points G,F,E, the width of the
avenue, the screen and the
entrances to the château

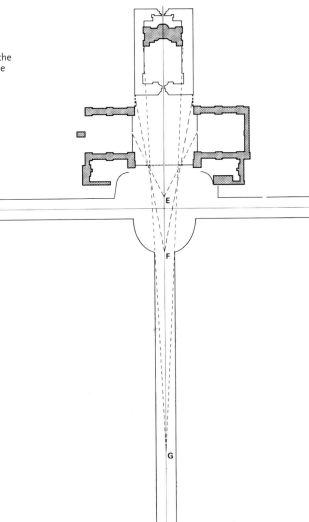

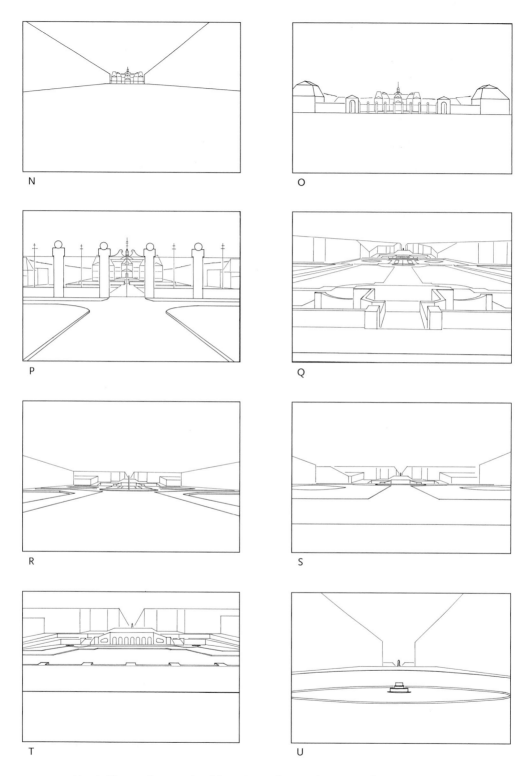

Vaux-le-Vicomte. Scenography of the main axis from north (N) to south (U)

Vaux-le-Vicomte. Hercules

forms a noteworthy 'pause' en route to the château. The visitor is still able to exit the theatre via two side arcades.

Notwithstanding, everything remains focused on the setting of the château. The *cour d'honneur*, surrounded by a moat, is approached via a second, smaller entrance gate. It is here that the gradual unveiling of the entire château ends. The indentations of the various elements of the façade, shoved one before the other like stage wings, and the tapering width of the stone flight of steps accentuate the entrance hall, which seems to have been pushed back into the heart of the building. The use of a large column order in the end pavilions as well as a smaller one in the entrance part heightens this effect. It also makes it more difficult to measure the proportions and relates the size of the forecourt to that of the interior.

Due to the *bel-étage* being raised above the souterrain the building appears to be in an elevated position. Four flights of steps interrupt the slope of the terrain and lead to the entrance hall. Three glass doors give access to a squarish entrance hall with two stairways tucked away behind side walls. The entrance hall terminates the axis and the series of forecourts on the north front of the château. From the hall, in a northerly direction, the entire front terrain can be seen.

Opposite the entrance are three pairs of large, closed doors. When these are opened the massive château is transformed into a sun-orientated, transparent construction. The building, which at first seems to terminate the axis, is in fact the beginning of a new series of spaces. This metamorphosis is spatially made possible in the interior by the low, square entrance hall adjoining the high oval *Grand Salon*. This is three floors high and is crowned by a dome. Lebrun made a design (never carried out) for the painting of this, in which the architecture of the *salon* is illusorily extended upwards to a painted round opening in the centre. This imaginary opening in the dome was projected onto the floor of the *Grand Salon* in the form of a marble com-

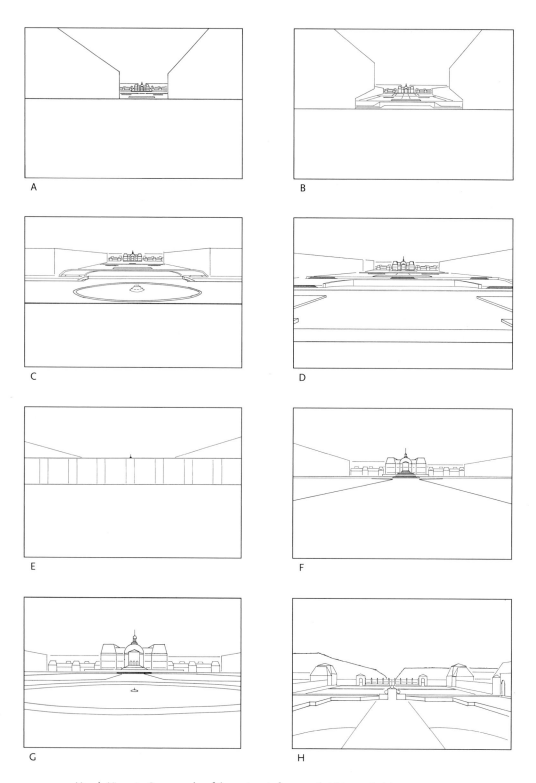

Vaux-le-Vicomte. Scenography of the main axis from south (A) to north (H)

Vaux-le-Vicomte.
Smooth transition in
the terrain, incorporat-
ing the flight of steps
next to the *Grandes
Cascades*

171

pass. This meeting of heaven and earth is the formal centre of the layout. From here, through the open garden doors, the spatial axis can be seen as far as the southern horizon. Moreover when the entrance hall doors are closed again, the southern spatial axis is projected onto the mirrors fitted into these doors on the side of the *Grand Salon*. In this flat depiction, the space is controlled in the same way as a perspective drawing. The measurements and proportions, however, remain puzzling. It is impossible to estimate the spatial depth of the design. When walking in the garden the integral image you had from the *Grand Salon* disintegrates into separate autonomous structures, both ambiguous as well as unexpected. The *Petit Canal*, for instance, beyond the *Parterre de Broderie* at the foot of the château, is only visible when you are on top of it, while the ponds (*Les Tritons*) situated further along in the *Parterre de Gazon*, which appear round from the château and seems to be the same size as the main *Rond d'Eau*, are oval and much bigger in reality. The site and dimensions of the square reflecting pond have been chosen so that it mirrors the entire château. The grotto, which seems to rest on the edge of the pond, is situated much further back. The deep set *Grand Canal*, despite its broad width on the axis, is only visible when you are suddenly standing in front of it. You immediately discover that the sound of falling water, heard in the garden, emanates from the cascades in the canal's north wall. The set of steps framing these *grandes cascades* have a consistent rise (height = 15 centimetres) and an increasing depth, from 35 centimetres to 54 centimetres, which gives them a concave form that seamlessly blends into the terrain. The *Grand Canal* appears as straight as an arrow until you walk around it and come across a large round pond at its far end, hidden behind the smallest possible mound. On the other side of the canal, the two lions, marking each side of the flight of steps along the grotto, appear the same size. In fact, the one is 32 centimetres higher than the other, which stands against the background of the grotto.

Vaux-le-Vicomte. Main vista of the garden

On the sloping *tapis vert* is a statue of Hercules which appears to be life-sized, though it is impossible to judge its real dimensions due to the lack of reference points. In fact, the middle section of the plan, with its walking route, is taken over by the *tapis vert*, which extends along the axis beyond the canal. Thus the human figures, which could act as a reference point for Hercules's true size, are kept hidden on the edge of the forest. From close up the statue, an allegory of Fouquet himself and his work, is immense. The Titan holds one hand behind his back, inviting the observer to look round to see if he is not hiding the three golden apples from the mythical garden of Hesperides. The statue also refers you to the cultural and perspective centre of the layout. It is only here, by synthesizing and summarizing the kaleidoscopic experiences, that the essence of the spatial organization can be understood.

THE INCORPORATION AND MANIPULATION OF THE HORIZON

It is evident from the foregoing descriptions that moving through the layout, for instance a walk with the owner of the estate as host, enables you to discover the secrets and particular elements of the garden. Yet the space, as with 17th-century theatre, was first completely controlled and understood from a static viewing point, where the kaleidoscopic experiences blend into one perfect optical illusion. This is the majestic viewpoint in front of the mirrors of the *Grand Salon*. There are three distinct aspects to the view that unfolds before you: spatial depth, visual control of this spatial depth and the illusion of perfect order. From this viewpoint, the space appears to take in the entire world.

On level terrain the horizon is determined by a (hypothetical) tangent from the eye to the curve of the earth's surface. Because of the spherical shape of the earth (R = 6,370 kilometres), the horizon will appear to be 4.5 kilometres away at an eye level of 1.8 metres. Atmospheric influences aside, as the eye level increases, so the horizon will lie further away (for instance, 16 kilometres at an eye level of 20 metres). Objects beyond the horizon are only perceived if they protrude above it (hill tops, ships' masts etc.). Theoretically, therefore, the visible spatial depth is determined by the height of the viewpoint and that of the observable objects beyond the horizon.

It follows from this that the concave or bowl-shaped surface area is the most suitable to 'compensate' for a restricted view, which is intrinsic to the spherical shape of the earth. This partly explains not only the geographical siting of many Italian Renaissance villas (above a valley with a panoramic view), but also the chosen geomorphologic site at Vaux. Here it is extremely difficult to guage the position of the perspective horizon in the rear terrain with the naked eye. Measuring with a levelling instrument, the intersection of the main axis with an imaginary horizontal surface at eye level, when seen from the *Grand Salon*, lies halfway the *tapis vert*, some 850 metres from the château. Thus, the horizon at Vaux lies within the boundaries of the plan. Beyond the horizon the *tapis vert* continues its ascent to natural infinity. On this line, between land and sky, the statue of Hercules finally determines the total spacial depth of the layout.

When measured, the actual spatial depth is roughly 1,000 metres, but objective, measured data does not decide subjective interpretation. The objective position of the perspective horizon and the garden's actual spatial depth are manipulated by the way the spatial axis has been architectonically organized.

The descent of the ground in front of the *Grand Canal* shifts the perspective horizon forwards (accelerated perspective) so that the space appears deeper. The reverse effect occurs by widening and extending the terraces (*Parterre de Broderie* and *Parterre de Gazon*). The perspective horizon is then shifted backwards and the space appears to have less depth. Behind the *Grand Canal*, the ascent of the ground, the

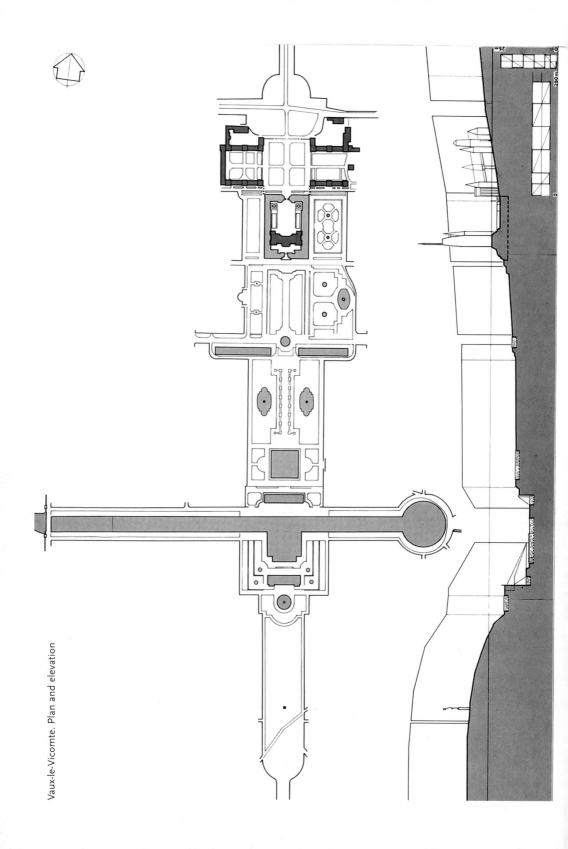

Vaux-le-Vicomte. Plan and elevation

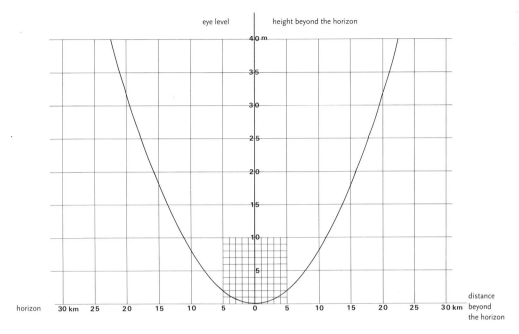

eye level | height beyond the horizon

40 m

35

30

25

20

15

10

5

horizon 30 km 25 20 15 10 5 0 5 10 15 20 25 30 km distance beyond the horizon

The link between eye level, the distance to the horizon and the observerable height beyond the horizon

Vaux-le-Vicomte. The shifting of the horizon due to the sloping surfaces

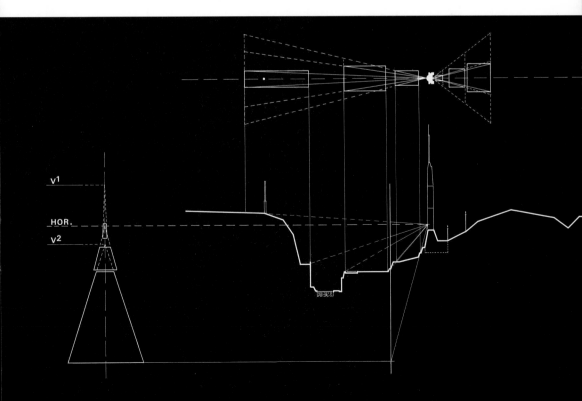

V¹

HOR.

V²

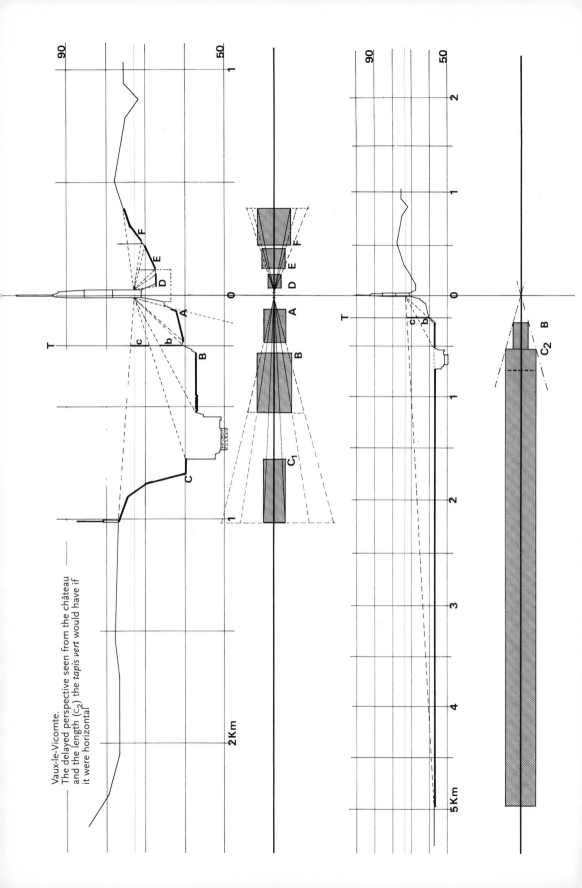

Vaux-le-Vicomte.
The delayed perspective seen from the château and the length (c_2) the *tapis vert* would have if it were horizontal

Vaux-le-Vicomte.
Charles Lebrun's design for a *trompe-l'œil* on the dome of the *Grand Salon*

enlargement of the features (grotto and Hercules) and the convergence of the forest walls cause the perspective horizon to shift backwards, so that the space again appears to be less deep. Where the layout narrows at the *tapis vert* the opposite effect is suggested again. The perspective horizon is shifted forwards and the space appears deeper than it actually is. Due to this perspective trickery the actual spatial depth of the axis cannot be determined. In this context, the 'infinity' of the natural panorama has been 'constructed' in the garden by architectonic means.

THE VISUAL CONTROL OF INFINITY

An increase in scale occurs within the *Parterre de Broderie* and *Parterre de Gazon* sequence. The final size of several parts of the plan increases the further away they are from the château so that perspective foreshortening is 'delayed'. The furthest surface on the axis is the *tapis vert*, which has roughly the same perspective depth as the terrace with the *Parterre de Gazon*. This effect is not created by increasing the scale of the *tapis vert* but by it tilting forwards.

Another increase in scale occurs at the front of the château in the series *cour d'honneur, Grand Cour, Avant Cour* and the approach drive. Such an increase enables extremely deep spaces still to be kept visually under control as the viewing distance increases. The landowner saw not only 'infinite' space but also kept it under control. In the château he found himself at the eyepiece of a telescope, as it were, which was made in the landscape and with which he could bring infinite space within the reach of his eye.

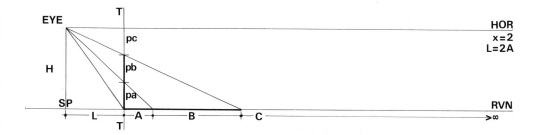

$X=L/A$

$$z_n=L\times z_n \ (x=L/A)$$
surface n

x =	z factor	1	2	3	4	5	6	7	8	9	10	etc.
	1	1,00	∞									
	2	0,50	1,50	∞								
x =	3	0,33	0,67	2,00	∞							
	4	0,25	0,42	0,83	2,50	∞						
x =	5	0,20	0,30	0,50	1,00	3,00	∞					
	6	0,17	0,23	0,35	0,93	1,17	3,50	∞				
	7	0,14	0,19	0,27	0,40	0,67	1,33	4,00	∞			
	8	0,13	0,16	0,21	0,30	0,45	0,75	1,50	4,50	∞		
	9	0,11	0,14	0,18	0,23	0,33	0,50	1,83	1,67	5,00	∞	
	10	0,10	0,12	0,15	0,20	0,26	0,37	0,55	0,92	1,83	5,50	∞
	etc.											

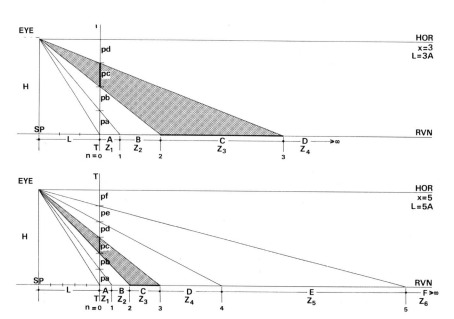

A series of increasingly longer surfaces, whereby with x (x=L/A= the total number of surfaces with the same perspective depth) the factor with which L has to be multiplied in order to obtain the length of the surface n (z_n), can be deduced.

A theoretical question that occurs here is, where the optical boundaries lie, if one wishes to eliminate perspective foreshortening. This can be dealt with by using a simple model. Imagine a viewpoint is chosen with an eye level of 1 m ($H = 1$) on a level terrain, at a distance of 2 m ($L = 2$) from surface A with a length of 1 m ($A = 1$). We thus see this surface on the perspective picture plane projected as pA. For pA read: $pA/A = H/(L+A)$, from which it follows that: $pA = 1/3$, which is $1/3$ of the picture-plane height because $H = 1$.

If we want to place a surface B behind A with the same perspective depth as A ($pA = pB$) then: $pA+pB/(A+B) = H/(L+A+B)$, from which it follows that B = 3 m, thus is three times as long as A. A third surface C would have to be endlessly long if its projection on the picture plane (pC) is to be as big as pA and pB. If we increase the viewing distance to A, the perspective depth of A (pA) becomes shorter. With $L = 2A$, three surfaces can theoretically be laid out, one behind the other, with the same perspective depth. If $L = 3A$, $pA = 1/4$, so that four surfaces with the same perspective depth can be laid out. This sequence can be represented as a formula: $x = L/A$, in which $L =$ the viewpoint distance and $A =$ the first, or reference, surface.

Value x, which indicates how many surfaces of equal perspective depth can actually be laid out consecutively behind each other (theoretically is that one more, $x+1$, if you include the surface to the horizon), is thus determined by the relationship, or scale, of the front terrain to the reference surface. This can be referred to as the 'axiom scale'. The shorter the reference surface becomes (and/or the longer the viewing distance), the more surfaces of equal perspective depth can be laid out in succession.

Instead of a foreshortened sequence, as with 'normal' perspective, now, with x as a given value, a series of increasingly long spaces can be determined in which the scale (z) is indicated between the viewpoint distance (L) and the length of the actual surface (z_n), so that $z = z_n/L$ and $z_n = L \times z$. When, for instance, $x = 2$, the series of increasingly long spaces is equal to (z): 0.5-1.5-∞ (infinity).

In all of this the absolute value of the height of viewpoint H does not matter. Value H does, in fact, determine the size of the perspective depth measurement (pA, pB etc.), but at the same time it also determines the effective picture-plane height. When H is increased, both increase correspondingly, so that the image as a whole is made bigger (and therefore clearer), but remains the same. This has the practical advantage that in the graphic construction needed for the perspective analysis of a profile, the vertical scale can be exaggerated with regard to the horizontal one.

The above was based on a simplified model. At Vaux-le-Vicomte there were complications because of the different heights of the terrain. Due to the château being built on a rise the view is more extensive. This effect is heightened by the upward slope of the rear terrain.

Nevertheless, at Vaux-le-Vicomte the series of lengthening spaces is in principle determined by the scale of the viewpoint distance and the reference surface. When we take the first terrace (*Parterre de Broderie*) as a reference surface, then $L/A < 1$, and a second surface with the same perspective depth is then impossible in the given linear profile of the garden. When the second terrace (*Parterre de Gazon* with reflecting pond) is taken as a reference surface, then $L/A > 1$, thus making the creation of a subsequent surface with the same perspective depth possible. If this were horizontal, the surface would have to be roughly 4,700 metres long, but as the *tapis vert* tilts forwards this could remain considerably shorter. Another surface lying behind the *tapis vert*, again of the same perspective depth, would only be possible if the rear terrain climbed a further 15 to 20 metres. This height is approached with the statue of Hercules. By 'eliminating' the perspective foreshortening and diminution, the spatial axis functions like a telescope. In this way the double illusion is created by depth projecting towards the observer.

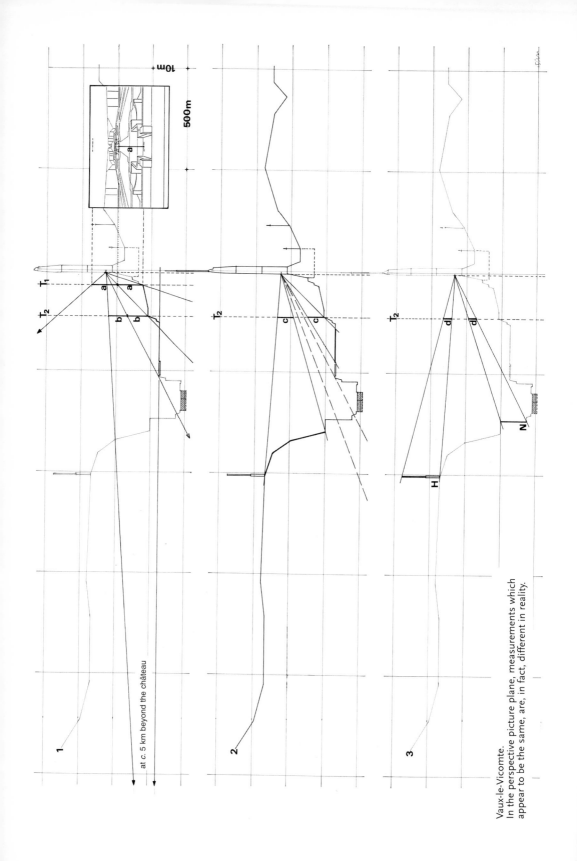

10m

500m

T₁
T₂

a a
b b

1

at c. 5 km beyond the château

T₂

c c

2

T₂

dl dl

N

H

3

Vaux-le-Vicomte.
In the perspective picture plane, measurements which
appear to be the same, are, in fact, different in reality.

As a result of the perspective foreshortening being made 'neutral' in the main measurements of the plan, visual control of the terrain could be maintained over a maximum distance. Also in the detailing, the mutual relationships of, for instance, the forms and dimensions of the ponds and parterres can be seen as 'correcting' the perspective distortion. For this reason the perspective correction, besides making huge distances controllable, has another effect. The more the perspective distortion is perfectly corrected by amendments in the actual plan, the surfaces and features will no longer be round or square and the same size in this plan, but in the perspective picture plane. This means that the order (and significance) of the layout is no longer in the geometric scheme of the actual plan but in the (imaginary) perspective depiction thereof.

The spatial axis is an anamorphosis constructed in the landscape, the hidden meaning of which can only be discovered from the viewpoint at the centre of the 'stage': i.e. in the flat perspective in the mirrors of the *Grand Salon*. There the illusion of perfect order reveals itself, while confirming the landowner's position as mediator of God's plan in human society.

A SYNTHETIC ARCADIA

Vaux-le-Vicomte is situated in an agricultural landscape. The forest is a means of separating the garden from this. Lying along the garden axis are first the *Parterre de Broderie*, then the *Parterre de Gazon* and the *tapis vert*. As in a classified system, these represent gradations of naturalness in the direction of the horizon within which the statues of Ceres, Flora and Pomona emphasize the cultivated aspect and those of Pan, Faunus and Bacchus the pleasurable one. The forest, as a form of uncontrolled growth, can be seen to represent unspoilt nature. This would seem to be the case from the statues of fauns positioned sporadically along the garden perimeter and the statue of Diana, goddess of the hunt, standing in the parterre of the same name. However, its clipped hornbeam perimeters reduce the forest to an architectonic garden wall. The way the forest interior has been laid out according to its various practical functions (kitchen garden and vineyard with a system of avenues) has restricted it too much for it to be seen as representing a natural landscape within the estate boundaries.

Water is another important element in exemplifying nature in the garden, and Vaux has four streams. The water flows (partly underground) from north to south (in the direction of the side valley where the garden is laid out), from the Bobée into the château moat and the terrace ponds, including the *Rond d'Eau*, *Les Tritons*, the former *Allée d'Eau*, and the *Arpent d'Eau* (reflecting pond) to the *Grandes Cascades* in the north wall of the *Grand Canal*. A second stream flowing east to west is formed by the *Grilles d'Eau* (*Petites Cascades*), the *Petits Canaux* and the *Rond d'Eau*. This is a higher, smaller and more northerly counterpart of the *Grand Canal*. In the *Grand Canal*, situated east-west, the natural flow of the Anqueil has been channelled and flows on the east side into a round basin. At the point where it intersects the garden axis, the *Grand Canal* has been widened into a large reflecting pond. On the west side, the water flows out of the canal via a dam. A fourth stream has been created along the steep southern slope of the garden, where it flows, via a pond and fountain (*La Gerbe*) into grottoes built into the southern canal wall. These consist of seven high niches next to each other, flanked by two triangular grottoes cut out from under the steps, in which lie the river gods Anqueil (east) and Tiber (west). The water from the grottoes is caught by a basin placed there for the purpose.

The waterworks mark convergences of the axial scheme and heighten the hori-

Vaux-le-Vicomte.
The sequence of parterres
(the *Broderie* and the *Gazon*)
and the widening of the axial
zone to the canal

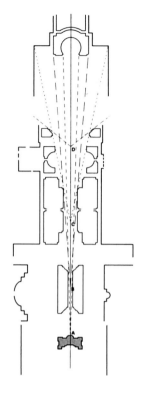

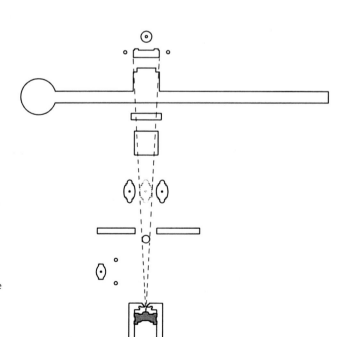

Vaux-le-Vicomte.
Changes in size and shape
of the water basins by
increasing the distance
from the château

Israël Sylvestre. Vaux-le-Vicomte. The *Petites Cascades* in the 17th century

zontal and vertical articulation of the garden. At the point where the three main streams converge, the grotto and the cascade have been placed symmetrically across from each other. Between lies reflecting water, an evocative and mythical symbol of a cyclic natural process. Architecturally, the grottoes and the cascade are treated in the same way as the walls of the *Grand Canal*. They enclose an elongated space, autonomous partly due to its deep situation. The reflecting pond in this space is not visible from the château, though this flaw is corrected by another reflecting pond lying further along the garden axis, which when seen from the château appears to be situated at the foot of the grottoes. Thus is the image of a synthetic Arcadia still made perfect.

THE ULTIMATE TRANSFORMATION

Vaux-le-Vicomte stands isolated from the surrounding landscape. The agrarian pattern has disintegrated due to the urban nature and the huge surface area of the estate. Its link to the outside world is formed by the axial cross of the main avenue and the transverse canal. The estate's landscape architecture comprises a visual, a geometric and a spatial system.

The visual representation of nature is achieved by specific combinations of plantings (*Parterre de Broderie, Parterre de Gazon, tapis vert* and forest) and water elements (streams, cascades, reflecting ponds and canals).

The plan consists of a geometrically 'expanding' measurement system which imposes order on the leaps in scale and hierarchically links the components of the house-garden-estate-landscape sequence. The plan is anchored in the site conditions by a balanced interaction between the symmetry of the layout, the natural geomorphology and the shape of the estate. The siting, length, width and organization of the principle axis and transverse canal are all determined by this.

The garden's spatial system is a perspective manipulation of the natural bowl

Vaux-le-Vicomte. The layout from the southern end of the spatial axis

shape of the terrain. The horizon lies within the boundaries of the plan. Despite the clear organization, the spatial depth cannot be gauged. As with an anamorphosis, elements of the plan have been distorted in order to create a perfect image from a given viewpoint. In this sense the plan and the image are not linked.

When compared to Villa Medici, Vaux-le-Vicomte has both similarities and differences. The former is situated high up (250 metres above the floor of the Arno valley) with an open view across a large valley (15 kilometres). At Vaux-le-Vicomte the valley is much smaller (1 kilometre) and the house is on a lower site (20 metres above the valley floor). Despite the enormous size of the plan (455 hectares, as compared with the 0.6 hectares of Villa Medici) a reduction of space and scale is created. Instead of it being integrated into the landscape (as Villa Medici is), Vaux-le-Vicomte is closed off from the surrounding agrarian context. Here, too, the visual system, which is still rudimentary at Villa Medici, has been treated as a universal (anatomical) depiction of nature. The grid plan has evolved into a hierarchical and symmetrical system. The horizon at Villa Medici lies far outside the boundaries of the plan while at Vaux-le-Vicomte it lies within these. Through perspective manipulation the spatial depth is both suggested as well as visually controlled. The visual order has shifted from the actual plan to an imaginary perspective picture plane.

At Vaux-le-Vicomte the same themes of architectural landscape have been employed as those found at Villa Medici, however, at Vaux they have been treated differently. The low, sloping site in the small valley recalls the setting of Villa Giulia. The play between symmetry and the site conditions is also an important theme at Villa d'Este. This is also the case at Palladio's Villa Rotonda, where the dome, as at Vaux, occupies the centre of the space. The incorporation and manipulation of the horizon is similar to Bramante's spatial arrangement at Cortile del Belvedere. The house-parterre-*bosco* sequence is to be seen in its simplest form in the Frascati villas. Palladio, for instance, also used the series entrance hall, forecourt and avenue running through the landscape at Villa Emo. The accentuation of the spatial axis is a central theme of the Boboli Gardens, while at Villa Gamberaia the principle axis is also broken up by a transverse axis. The terraces at Villa Medici were constructed on a landscape scale. The *trompe-l'œil* on the garden axis and the façades of the building was a means of putting monumentality into perspective at Villa Aldobrandini.

At Vaux-le-Vicomte all these special treatments have been united into one plan and further elaborated upon. In this sense it is an absolute transformation of the rational prototype. It is essential that within the unity of the formal prototype, tension is preserved between the site conditions and the geometric plan, between the pictorial representation of nature and its mythological interpretation and between actual and illusionary space. In the formal prototype the oneness of space is all-embracing (from the interior to the landscape) and entirely constructed, though this can no longer be the work of a single individual. Within the unity of the formal prototype, landscape architecture (in the person of Le Nôtre) has become an independent specialism.

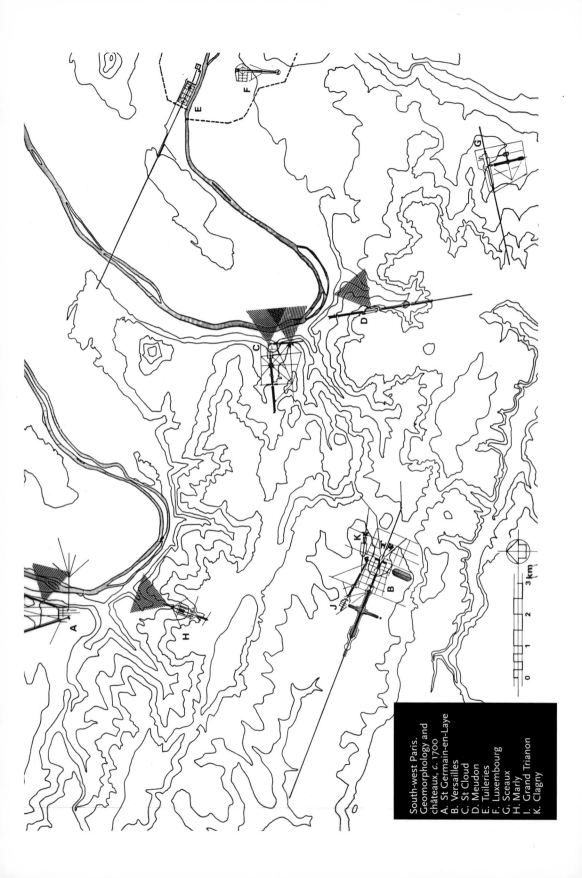

South-west Paris.
Geomorphology and
châteaux, c. 1700

A. St Germain-en-Laye
B. Versailles
C. St Cloud
D. Meudon
E. Tuileries
F. Luxembourg
G. Sceaux
H. Marly
I. Grand Trianon
K. Clagny

St Germain, St Cloud, Meudon, Sceaux, Marly, Trianon and Clagny

During the second half of the 17th century, Vaux-le-Vicomte was used as a model for reconstructing old properties and building new ones. Among those reconstructed in the area south-west of Paris were Versailles, St Cloud, St Germain-en-Laye, the Tuileries Gardens, Sceaux and Meudon. The new properties included Trianon (de Porcelaine), Clagny and Marly.

At St Cloud (1661) Le Nôtre designed a new axis for Philippe d'Orléans, the *Allée de la Balustrade*, located high above the Seine. At right angles to this, in a side valley of the Seine, he created a new spatial axis in which the upper reaches of the side valley, the château and the Paris panorama below were linked by one axial scheme.

In St Germain-en-Laye, Le Nôtre designed two new spatial axes for Louis XIV. The first (*c.* 1665) was orientated towards the north wing of Château Vieux and incorporated this irregular structure into a large-scale formal layout. The second, the *Grande Terrasse* (1669), was laid out 60 metres above the Seine. The plan consisted of a 2,400-metre-long (30-metre-wide) promenade. For Le Nôtre this entailed a careful hollowing-out of the elevation in order to transform the monotone image of the layout (grass and gravel) into something playfully illusionary. The axis was intended to connect Château Neuf at St Germain with the planned Château du Val. Seen longitudinally, the completed *Grande Terrasse* is suspended above the Seine valley like a gigantic balcony.

Even thrifty Colbert had his 16th-century château at Sceaux (1670) embellished. In a north-south direction, across from the château, the Avenue de l'Octogone was laid out. This ran through a valley and comprised the avenue, a long cascade, the *Bassin de l'Octogone* and a *tapis vert*. An axis of symmetry, which passed through the château, was extended in a westerly direction. Later, parallel to – and west of – the avenue the *Grand Canal* (begun 1690) was excavated.

At Meudon, Servien, the finance minister of Louis XIV, began with the building of a large terrace. This measured 253 by 136 metres and was situated on a ridge overlooking the Seine. From the terrace is a commanding view of the landscape and the city of Paris. This terrace, which partly formed the foundation for the château, was subsequently (1679) incorporated into a kilometre-long spatial axis. This ran from the Seine in the north, across the longitudinal axis of the terrace, straight through a side valley with a lake, to as far as the high southern horizon.

The Trianon de Porcelaine (1670) was an exotic pavilion amidst great floral splendour at the northern end of the *Grand Canal* at Versailles. At the southern termination of the canal was a menagerie. In 1687 the Trianon de Porcelaine was replaced by the Grand Trianon. The axis of the layout passes through the central open colonnade of this building and connects with the *Bassin du Dragon* in a south-easterly direction. This pond, together with the *Bassin de Neptune*, forms the termination of the most important transverse axis at Versailles.

Just to the north-east of Versailles, Louis XIV had the Clagny country house built for Madame de Montespan (begun 1674). To the south-west the château's axis, with its bilateral symmetry, passes through Lake Etang de Clagny and links the building to Versailles.

Marly (begun 1679), six kilometres north of Versailles, was an exclusive royal weekend retreat. The house was the final structure in one of the two symmetric rows of six guest pavilions built along an axis. The spatial axis, directed towards the Seine valley and St Germain, consisted of large terraces with promenades and water elements.

In summing up the 17th-century residences located south-west of Paris, it

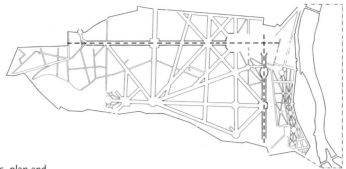

St Cloud, Paris.
System of avenues, plan and
elevation of the spatial axes

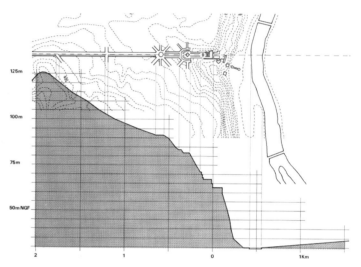

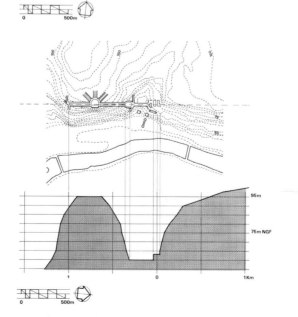

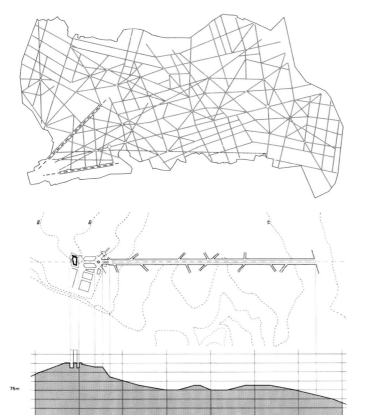

St Germain-en-Laye, Paris.
System of avenues, plan
and elevation of the spatial
axes

75 m

50 m NGF

0   1   2   3 Km

0   500 m

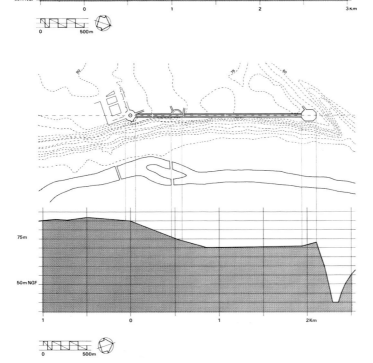

75 m

50 m NGF

1   0   1   2 Km

0   500 m

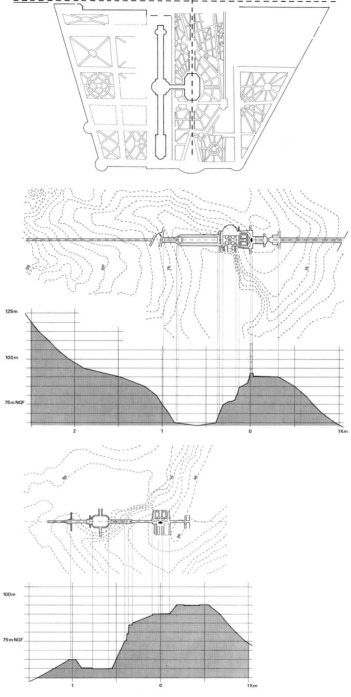

Sceaux, Paris.
System of avenues, plan and elevation of the spatial axes

appears they shared several features of landscape architecture with each other and also with Vaux-le-Vicomte. Their siting is linked to a natural bedding or basin, which in terms of scale (a few kilometres) is subordinate to a plain or large main valley (several kilometres). The irregularity of the natural site was disguised and brought into balance by artificial axial symmetry. The natural lie of the elevation was used to incorporate the horizon into the garden and to manipulate the spatial depth perspectively.

THE NETWORK OF AXES AND AVENUES IN THE PARIS AREA

On the *Carte des Chasses du Roi des Environs de Versailles* (1764-73) the effects of 17th-century encroachment on the area lying south-west of Paris is evident. The modest châteaux built in the beginning of the century were still sited on strategic spots, high above the banks of the Seine (St Germain, Meudon, St Cloud) and on dry tracts in the middle of marshland (Louvre, Versailles, Sceaux). In the second half of the century they were drastically enlarged and reorganized. Internally, this redesigning was dominated by the laying of spatial axes. The arrangement and measurements of these were dependent on the building and/or the condition of the terrain. The siting of the spatial axis corrected, as it were, the natural, sloping position of the upstream side valley in relation to the main valley. The spatial axis was positioned at right angles to the main valley. The importance of the geomorphology is also evident in the choice of location of new residences such as Marly, Trianon and Clagny. The visual effect of the hollow elevation of the spatial axis is similar to the already-mentioned theatre stage rising the further back it recedes. For using water in the formal plan, a longitudinal site in a valley was also of great importance.

As well as acting like a 'telescope' towards the landscape, the spatial axis, in the plans of some Paris residences, also acts as an 'onlooker' towards the city. At Versailles the landscape and the city face each other, like tableaux on opposite sides of a spatial axis. The axis of bilateral symmetry, with the château in its visual centre, has a vanishing point in the landscape and one in the city. At St Cloud and Meudon there is an indirect visual relationship to the city. The city appears, as a segment of the panorama, on the horizon of the spatial axis. At Versailles, the Tuileries and Luxembourg there is a direct link with the city. The spatial axis also continues into the city.

The spatial axes are extremely long, reaching as far as the horizon. Nevertheless, the spatial axis is also of limited scale, its length never exceeding a few kilometres. At the horizon it ceased to be a distinctive formal space and became an avenue: from a visual axis it became an axis of movement or a route. Together with the diagonal and transverse avenues, such an axis formed part of a network that connected the regional residences. The city too was linked in this way. When the city wall of Paris was demolished in 1670, the boulevard became a ring road that joined numerous star-shaped, radiating routes.

In this manner a formal link at a regional level was created in which two types of axiality played a role. The strategically placed spatial axes were the 'carriers' within the network. They were the 'telescopes', the visual axes in which the landscape was 'illuminated' in an abstract manner and on a large scale. Here, landscape and town were united into one spatial construction. Then there were the connections between the residences themselves and the city, the unfashioned spaces or avenues, the earlier-mentioned axes of movement. They formed a functional infrastructure for the entire district; they were the ceremonial routes taken by the royal court when travelling in coaches, hunting parties or parades.

Aqueducts and canals were also elements of the infrastructure. In order to feed

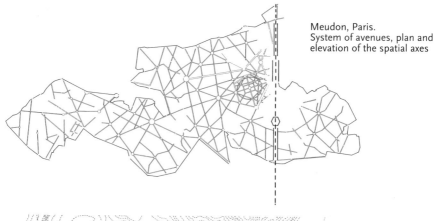

Meudon, Paris.
System of avenues, plan and
elevation of the spatial axes

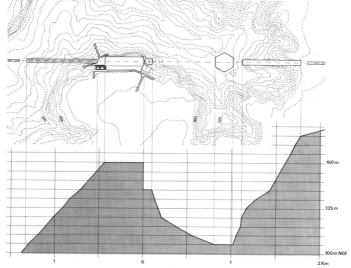

150 m

125 m

100 m NGF

1   0   1   2 Km

0   500m

Meudon, Paris. View to the north-east
from the terrace

Meudon, Paris. The formal spatial axis from the
terrace. In the present situation the valley is
overgrown. On the opposite side of the valley the
axis continues as the *tapis vert*.

Meudon in the 18th century, Paris. *Carte des Chasses du Roi*, 1764

Meudon as it is today, Paris. Institut Géographique National, Paris

Israël Sylvestre. Meudon, Paris. Main vista of the formal spatial axis from the terrace, *c.* 1690

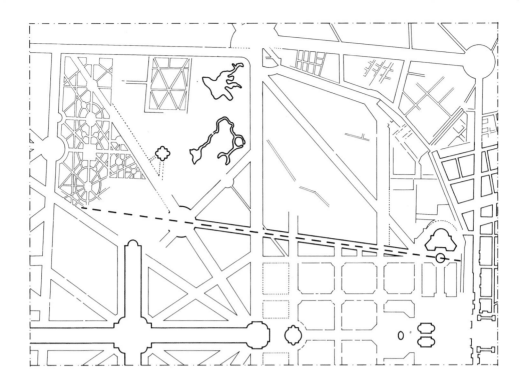

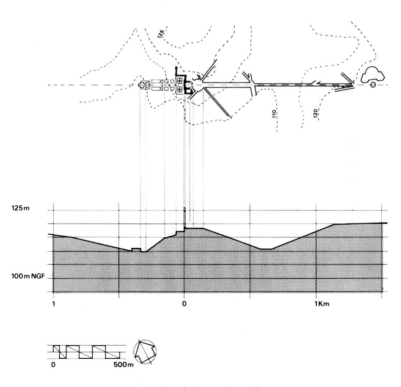

Grand Trianon, Versailles.
System of avenues, plan and elevation of the spatial axes

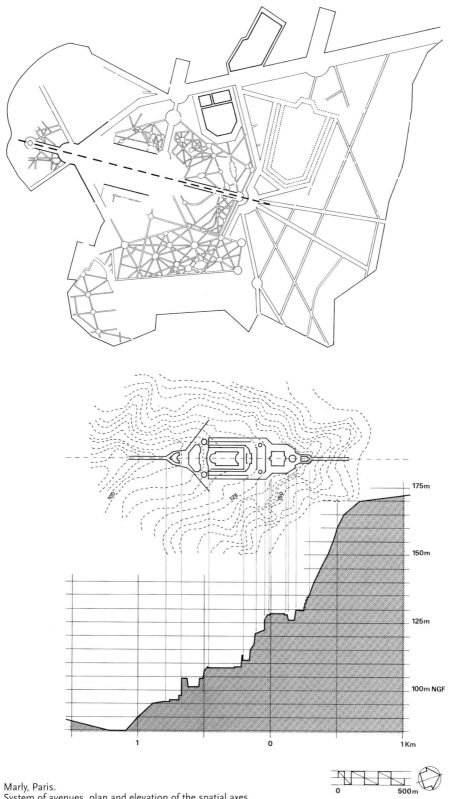

175m

150m

125m

100m NGF

1   0   1 Km

0   500m

Marly, Paris.
System of avenues, plan and elevation of the spatial axes

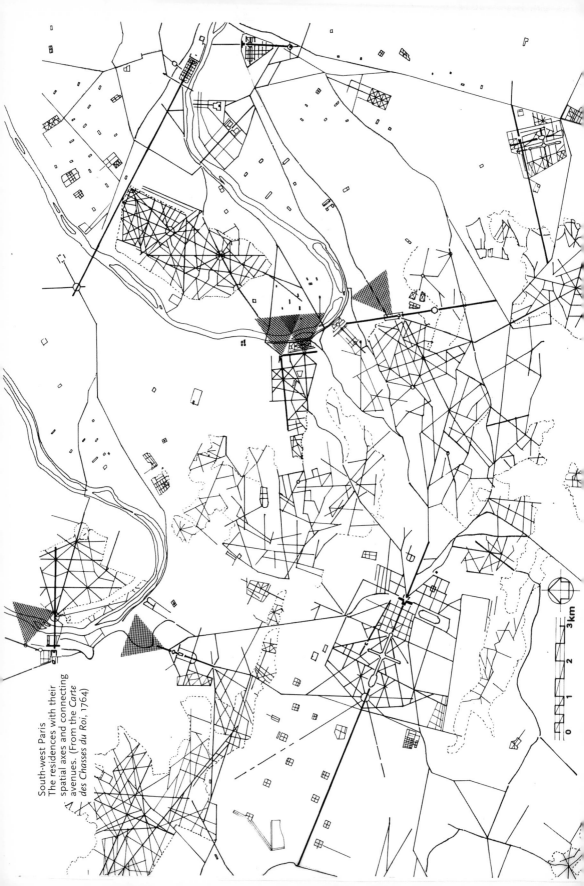

South-west Paris
The residences with their
spatial axes and connecting
avenues. (From the *Carte
des Chasses du Roi*, 1764)

0 1 2 3 km

Marly, Paris. The water pump in the Seine with St Germain-en-Laye in the background (engraving, c. 1681)

the numerous fountains at Versailles (approximately 1,400 in 1680), water was taken from the lakes of Trappes, St Quentin, Bois d'Arcy and Bois Robert, among others. Every water source was tapped and the entire area was dissected by a network of pipes and canals that carried the water to the royal reservoirs. When it became apparent that this would not produce enough water, the famous hydraulic works near Marly were built, where 14 wheels and 223 pumps transported 5,000 m^3 water daily out of the Seine. Then in 1684, Vauban, assisted by 22,000 soldiers, began building an enormous aqueduct to convey the water from the River Eure to Versailles.

Maintenon.
The aqueduct from River
Eure to Versailles

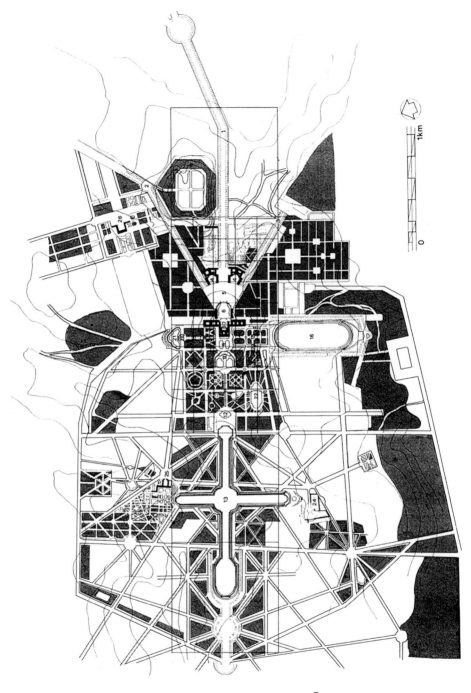

Versailles. A drawing of
the overall layout
1. Avenue de Paris
2. Avenue de St Cloud
3. Avenue de Sceaux
4. Grandes Écuries
5. Place d'Armes
6. Cour des Ministres
7. Cour Royale
8. Cour de Marbre
9. Parterre d'Eau
10. Bassin de Latone
11. Allée Royale
12. Bassin d'Appollon
13. Grand Canal
14. Parterre de Midi
15. Orangery
16. Lac des Suisses
17. Parterre du Nord
18. Bassin de la Pyramide
19. Allée des Marmousets
20. Bassin du Dragon
21. Bassin de Neptune
22. Bosquets
23. Les Cent-Marches
24. Grandes Écuries
25. Clagny
26. Clagny
27. Butte de Montbauron

Versailles

In 1630 Louis XIII had a hunting lodge built on a strategic spot in Versailles. It stood on the upper reaches of a large side valley of the Seine, where this valley splits into two and bears to the west towards an elongated marshy plateau high above the Seine. In 1661, after seeing Vaux-le-Vicomte, the king decided to extend and embellish the lodge. As the landscape architect responsible for the layout, Le Nôtre encountered forces in the geomorphology of the site that would defy even his talent for design. Unlike Vaux, the final spatial design was not created with one master stroke within the space of a few years, but was developed in a series of consecutive plans spread over a 25-year period. At the same time, the one plan repeatedly evoked something of the other. The unprecedented scale with which Le Nôtre lay open the landscape meant that, for the balance of the whole ensemble, it had to be continually enlarged by architects Louis le Vau and Jules Hardouin-Mansart, and vice versa. Moreover, Louis XIV saw so many of his own aspirations embodied in Le Nôtre's ideas and proposals, and he was on such intimate footing with him, that Colbert feared the king was hopelessly under the spell of the brilliant designer: 'Your majesty will surely understand that he is in the hands of two men [Le Nôtre and Le Vau], who drag your majesty from the one project into the other'. But Colbert preached to no avail. Under the Sun King's own personal supervision, and with the help of an army of labourers, the marshy, obscure site and the insignificant château were transformed into the *non plus ultra* of formal spatial art.

THE MAIN AXIS AND THE GRAND CANAL

When Le Nôtre began remodelling the Petit Parc, the original Renaissance garden (by Jacques Boyceau) surrounding the lodge, he retained its grid division. The forest quadrants were architectonically redesigned into *bosquets*. For the rest Le Nôtre devoted all his energy to liberating the main axis. At the same time Le Vau revised the front of the château entrance so that here, as at Vaux, a series of progressively smaller spaces served to form a ceremonial approach to the palace. The terrace to the rear was raised, the *jardin bas* dug out behind it, and both were linked by a horseshoe-shaped, semicircular set of steps (*Fer à Cheval*). The end of Petit Parc was still marked by a *patte d'oie*. In 1667 the descending *Allée Royale*, behind the *jardin bas*, was widened and made into a *tapis vert*. However, from the old house, situated more to the fore, the *jardin bas* and the *tapis vert* behind could not be seen due to the difference in height. The vista ran along the foreground, across the terrace and disappeared between the treetops of the *Allée Royale* into the indeterminate, marshy landscape.

At the foot of the sloping *Allée Royale*, before the extensive marshland, a crucial point had thus been reached in the layout. At Vaux a further extension of the main vista, at the end of the descending slope, was made possible by the sloping position of the surface behind behind the *Grand Canal*, whereby the perspective foreshortening was 'lifted'. At Versailles, beyond the end of *Allée Royale*, there was also a hill that restricted a glimpse of the valley, but Le Nôtre must have found this too trivial to allow it to form the termination of a vista. He proposed to the king that the hill be dug out, the valley drained and a large canal built along the length of the principle axis. Even for the king this was such a radical idea that he first consulted specialists at the Academy of Sciences, who judged the project favourably. After three years (1668-71) the canal was completed. Louis le Vau then adapted the old château to the scale of the new layout by building his 'envelope' around it (1671), with a large open balcony on the spot where the later Hall of Mirrors would be built. From this more elevated viewpoint, however, the canal was still too short in perspective terms. It was therefore

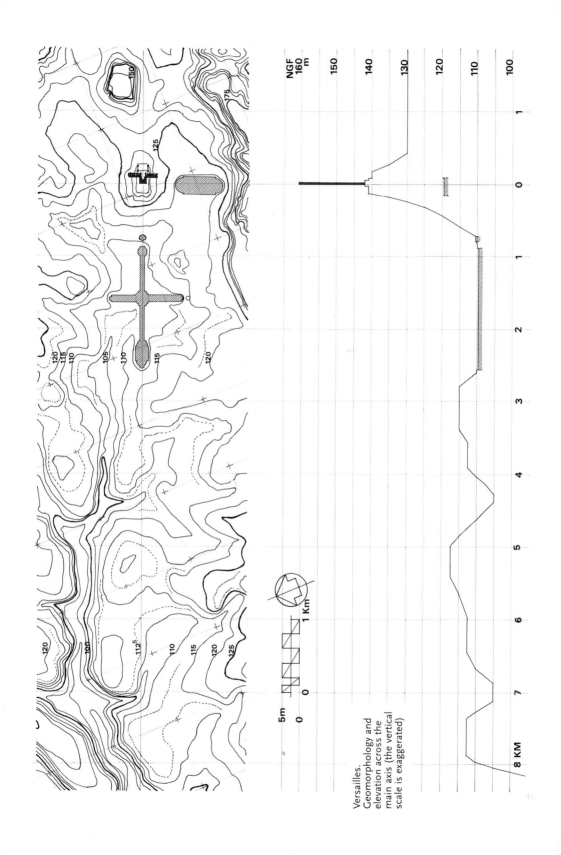

Versailles.
Geomorphology and
elevation across the
main axis (the vertical
scale is exaggerated)

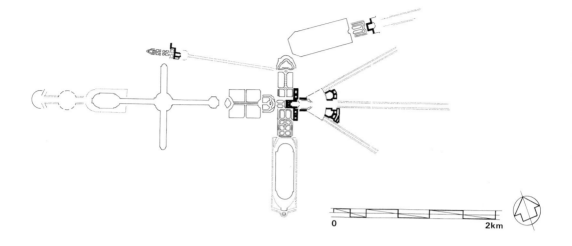

Versailles. The spatial axes of Versailles, the Grand Trianon and Clagny

Aueline. Versailles. The northern half of the transverse axis to the west of the château from the *Bassin du Dragon*

Versailles. The southern half of the transverse axis to the west of the château, with the *Parterre d'Orangerie* and the *Lac des Suisses*

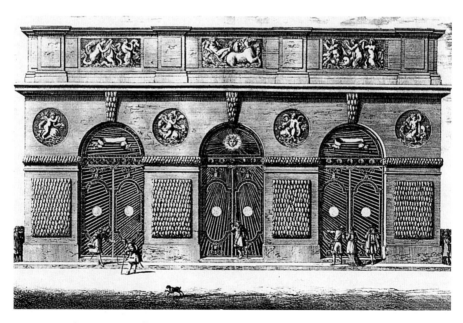

Pierre le Pautre. Versailles. Thetis's grotto, 1672

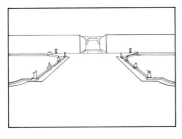

1. From the Hall of Mirrors

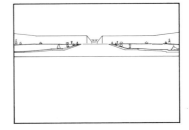

2. From the Grand Terrace

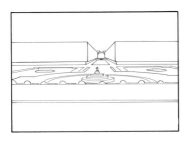

3. From the steps at *Jardin Bas*

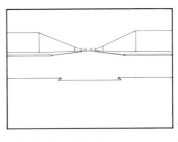

4. At the Grand Canal

Versailles. Main vistas across the principle axis in a westerly direction

made even larger (1671) and then spanned the total length of the natural plateau. In this way the exceptional length of the canal (1,500 metres) accommodated the perspective foreshortening as a result of the great distance between the château and the beginning of the canal (900 metres). The reflecting water ensured that it would remain visible as a luminous surface between the avenues of trees of the *Allée Royale*. In order to heighten this light effect, a semicircular mound, or *vertugadin,* was employed as a reflector behind the termination of the canal. The axis continued past this as an avenue, stretching kilometres further to the horizon. The total length of the axis on the west front of the building was eight kilometres.

Upon the execution of the various projects the most important elements of the main vista were completed. From the palace balcony the vista (perspective) now consisted of the following majestic sequence: the *Grande Terrasse* (white), *tapis vert* (green) and the reflecting *Grand Canal* (silver). These three consecutive elements were of increasing length (and breadth) so that they appeared to be proportionally well-balanced in the perspective picture plane. Also in the detailing, such as the increase in size of the three receding *bassins* in the *Grand Canal,* this postponing of the perspective was used. In this way an anamorphosis was created: a perspective with orderly proportions that, as it were, folds out forwards .

THE TRANSVERSE AXES

After 1678 Jules Hardouin-Mansart began adding the enormous north and south wings of the palace, the Hall of Mirrors and the new orangerie on the south edge of the *Grande Terrasse* with the large, well-known flight of steps (*Cent Marches*). At the same time the transverse axis, behind the château, was made in accordance with the scale of the new layout. On the southern termination of this axis Le Nôtre designed the *Lac des Suisses* on an area of marshland (1680-82). This formed a reflecting sur-

Versailles. The spatial axis from the *Bassin d'Apollon*

face, whose dimensions were in keeping with the perspective link with the parterre above the orangerie. On the north side, where Le Nôtre had linked the *Parterre du Nord*, the *Bassin de la Pyramide* and the *Bassin du Dragon* perspectively together, he designed the *Bassin du Dragon* as a final set piece. This brought the total width of the valley (two kilometres) visually under control in a transverse direction. This was also the case with the transverse arm (1.2 kilometres) of the *Grand Canal*, which links the *Ménagerie* (to the south) with the *Trianon de Porcelaine* in the north. Both axes assume the maximum length possible given their geomorphological situation and are not symmetrical in relation to the main axis. They are larger on the south side than on the north side, while the main axis of symmetry is asymmetrically positioned in the terrain of the valley.

A VISTA OF WATER, AIR AND LIGHT

Modifications to the water parterres on the *Grande Terrasse* (*Parterre d'Eau*), directly behind the château, where the transverse axis bisects the main axis, were finally completed. In 1684 the *Parterre d'Eau* from 1674 (with one main round *bassin* and four subsidiary triangular ones) was replaced by two large, rectangular water mirrors or *Miroirs d'Eau*, in which the perspective of the main axis was 'framed'. In an uninterrupted sequence of the Hall of Mirrors, the *Miroirs d'Eau*, the *tapis vert* and the *Grand Canal*, the main vista opens out as far as the horizon. The central axis and the two most important transverse axes 'overpower' the given geomorphological situation, as they occupy the entire length and width of the basin-shaped plateau. Due to the postponing of the perspective along the central axis, the terrain is brought under visual control by means of a maximum optical depth. The horizon lies within the constructed landscape and is brought towards the viewpoint of the observer as if seen through a telescope. Past the *clair-obscure* of the central axis the space dissolves into an atmospheric perspective. Beyond the reach of the eye from this viewpoint, the system of diagonal and transverse avenues links the château to the 1,500-hectare estate and surrounding area.

THE CITY AS A REFLECTING IMAGE

In 1671 Louis XIV decided to make Versailles the seat of the government. Much of the neighbouring land, including the old village of Versailles, had already been bought up by the Crown. Thus the reigning monarch gathered not only his court around him but also the entire machinery of government as well as civil servants. His residence became the capital of the country. Mansart was given the task of studying the architectonic and planning problems created by this transition. The terrain in front of the château, like that to the rear of it, was completely reorganized. In 1673, the agrarian pattern, the existing routes and the old village of Versailles (slightly to the south of the palace) were obliterated. Where possible the site was made level and the square in front of the château raised.

The main axis of the residence, which on the rear side varies in width from 50 metres at *Allée Royale* to 150 metres across the *Grand Canal*, was given a uniform width of 100 metres on the front side. It slopes downwards from the forecourt to the upper reaches of a side valley of the Seine. The main *chaussée* is 'on-going', local access is provided by the four *contre-allées* (parallel roads), screened from the main *allée* by rows of trees. About two kilometres from the château the axis bends to the north-east, following the course of the side valley and the road which descends to Paris from the plateau. There the line was absorbed by the regional system of avenues. Unlike the axis on the rear side which, by almost exceeding the boundaries of what is geomorphologically and optically possible, brings the landscape visually under con-

Versailles. Vistas across the main axis towards the château

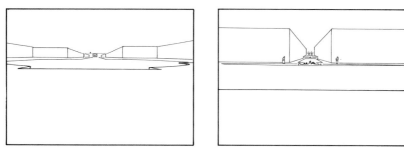

1. From the rear side of the *Grand Canal*

2. At the foot of the *Allée Royale*

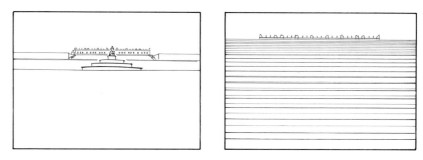

3. At the *jardin bas*

4. At the foot of the steps at *Parterre d'Eau*

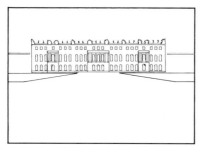

5. From *Parterre d'Eau*

Versailles. The *Grand Canal*, looking back from the termination of the main axis

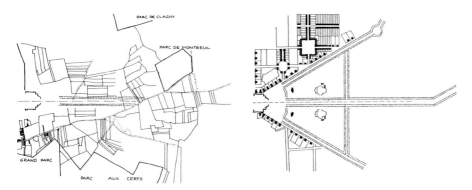

Jean Castex.The transformation of the landscape on the city side of the château, 1673

trol via perspective manipulation, the main axis on the front side, past the *Place d'Armes*, is not perspectively manipulated. In the plan of the new city this axis is determined by two parallel lines. Nevertheless, the geomorphology offers the possibility of a much greater, optically controllable vista on this axis, namely over the 'hollow' of the upper reaches of the side valley of the Seine. Not making use of this possibility could indicate that the main axis of the layout on the front side should be 'read' in the reverse direction: the direction towards the château. The length of the axis is then not so much determined by a maximization of the visually controllable vista from the château but, conversely, by the distance at which the château becomes 'readable'. It is largely an axis which enables the free flow of traffic and a route which leads to the château, upon which – due to a connection between the profile of the axis and the dimensions of the château – a gradual revealing of the floors and wings is stage-managed. Past the approach drive, on the squares in front of the palace (*Place d'Armes, Cour des Ministres, Cour Royale* and *Cour de Marbre*), the unveiling of this decor culminates in a hierarchical series of spaces. Due to the accelerated perspective, conveyed by this, the space appears to deepen and the relatively modest proportions of the old château are integrated into the scale of the new layout. It is the last act in the ceremonial route to the perspective centre of a world empire.

THE PATTE D'OIE AS URBAN PANORAMA

Diagonal axes are projected to the north and south of the main axis. Together they form a *patte d'oie* (three-pronged road), whereby the imaginary shared intersection lies in the *Cour de Marbre*. Seen from the château, the diagonals form a triangle. The top angle of this measures approximately 60 degrees: the lateral extent of human vision. In this way the width of the front terrain, which at the base of the triangle equals some 500 metres, can be absorbed at a glance. The angle, at which the diagonal axes diverge from the main axis, is partly determined by the geomorphology of the site. Butte Montbauron (on which large water reservoirs are situated), as a natural obstacle, determines the angle between the northern axis (Avenue de St Cloud) and the main one (Avenue de Paris). Fourteen hundred metres from the château, the Avenue de St Cloud (75 metres wide) curves to the north, climbing the slope of the side valley to St Cloud. The southern, shortest axis (Avenue de Sceaux; 70 metres wide), is symmetrical in relation to the northern diagonal and runs in the direction of Sceaux, terminating at Butte Gobert. Because of the wings built by Le Vau and Mansart along the *avant-cours,* the field of view from Cour de Marbre is restricted to the

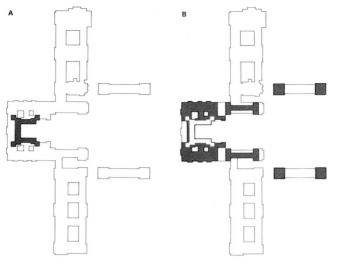

Versailles.
Extensions to the
original hunting
lodge of Louis XIII

A. 1624, Salomon de Brosse (?)   B. 1661-71, Louis le Vau

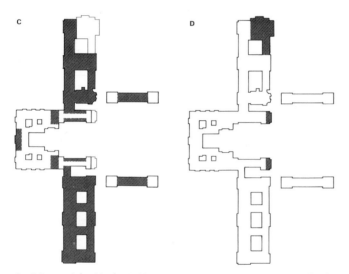

C. 1678-1710, Jules Hardouin-Mansart   D. c. 1756, Jacques-Ange Gabriël

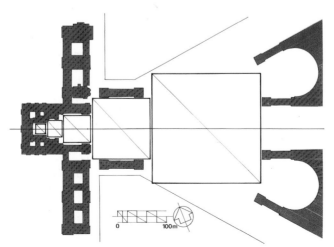

Versailles.
The hierarchical
sequence of spaces
on the city side
of the château

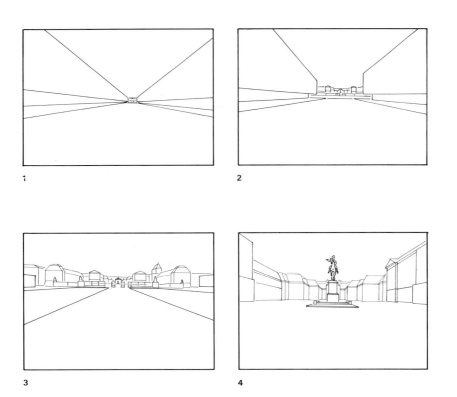

1

2

3

4

Versailles. Ceremonial entrance from the Avenue de Paris

main triangle. Further along the avenues are mansions for the nobility and important government officials, which, from the time the town layout was begun, were built according to strict regulations and models and disguised the still unordered landscape. In 1679, Mansart built the *Grandes Écuries* (royal stables) facing the château, in the angles of the three axes. These formed the final set piece in the view from the château. The area between the horizon and the *Grandes Écuries* has not been designed, neither in the axes which continue as roads, nor in the panorama which is visible as a stripe above the *Grandes Écuries*. The latter have been shifted in front of the horizon, as it were, completing the layout and forming its decor. The depth is emphasized by the slight angle in the arrangement of the two buildings and by the depth of the horeshoe-shaped squares behind. By placing the curved *Grandes Écuries* and the linear indented château opposite each other, the *patte d'oie* has taken on an urban form. The ceremonial entrance and the grand view are united in one complex.

After 1671, following the laying out of the *patte d'oie*, work began on extending the new city behind the façades of the mansions bordering the sides of the triangle. This was built in two parts and in two periods: the Quartier Nôtre Dame, to the north of the Avenue de St Cloud (begun 1671), and the Quartier Saint Louis, to the south of the Avenue de Sceaux (begun 1680). In Quartier Nôtre Dame the king leased building plots, tied to privileges and building regulations, to burghers and merchants. In the Quartier St Louis the king placed free building plots at the disposal of court personnel and servants who, after 1680, when the entire government moved to Versailles, came to live in the new city. Both quarters are situated next to the *patte d'oie*, behind the mansions, and outside of the monarch's field of view. The central triangle between the diagonal axes interrupted the continuity of the town plan. This was strengthened in that all the administrative services were concentrated in this main

Versailles.
Ceremonial entrance with jumps in scale
towards the *Cour de Marbre*

Versailles. The view is shielded in the width on the city side of the château.

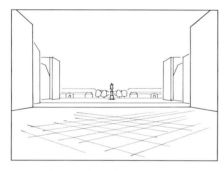

1. From the *Cour de Marbre*

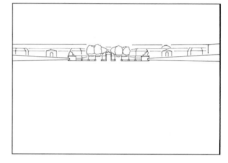

2. From the *Cour des Ministres*

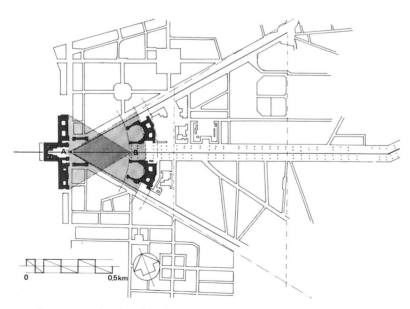

Versailles. Two visual angles of the château; A and B are 60 degrees

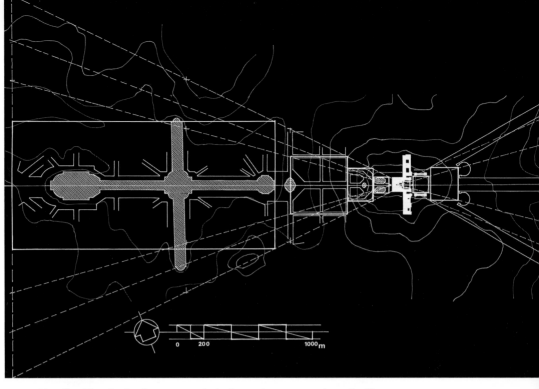

Versailles. The plan has been perspectively distorted to create a telescopic effect.

sector. Nevertheless, at the end of the 18th century, one still had to bypass the main triangle to get from one quarter to the other. The *patte d'oie* split the town plan into two parts. The central triangle was aligned with the château, while the palace, with its elongated wings, screened off the landscape behind. Only the monarch had an overview of the entire layout.

THE GRAND ENSEMBLE
From the foregoing it appears that the architectonic devices found at Vaux-le-Vicomte have also been employed at Versailles. Yet, one may also sense an evolution. At Versailles the spatial axis is more clearly articulated. As in a theatre, the foreground and background are seperated by *coulisses* (in the form of a forest). Internally, the forest coulisses form elaborately designed *bosquets*. At Vaux the most important viewpoint is in the *Grand Salon*, with its mirrors on the ground floor of the château. At Versailles this is the Hall of Mirrors on the first floor. At Vaux, due to the sloping position of the final surface of the hierarchical sequence, the main vista could be terminated by a relatively small longitudinal measurement. At Versailles, due to the level, horizontal rear terrain, an enormous extension, stretching as far as the extreme boundary of the plateau, was needed and reflecting water was used to bring this last segment of the main vista visually under control. Unlike at Vaux, it is not Hercules that terminates the vista and 'lifts' the horizon like a vertical giant. At Versailles the *Grand Canal* appears to stretch to the horizon and touch the sky. Depending on the position of the sun, it is still just visibly separated from the horizon by the amphitheatre-like slope (*vertugadin*), rising behind the end of the canal, and the continuation of the main axis as an avenue behind this. Here the geometric perspective dissolves into an atmospheric haze. At Versailles the spatial depth of the natural panorama is artificially represented. It is brought into the garden as an optical construction. Due to the

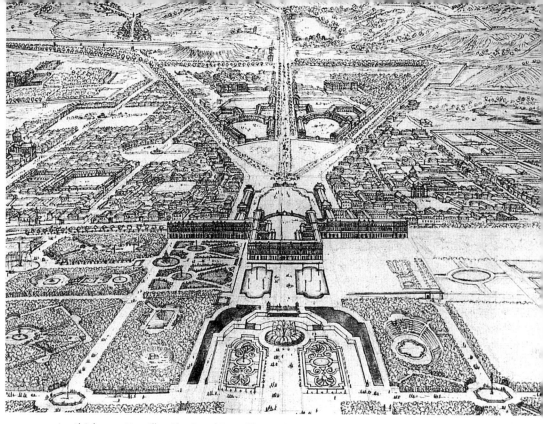

Israël Sylvestre. Versailles. The *Grand Ensemble,* 1687

Gabriël Pérelle. Versailles. The *Grand Ensemble,* 1690

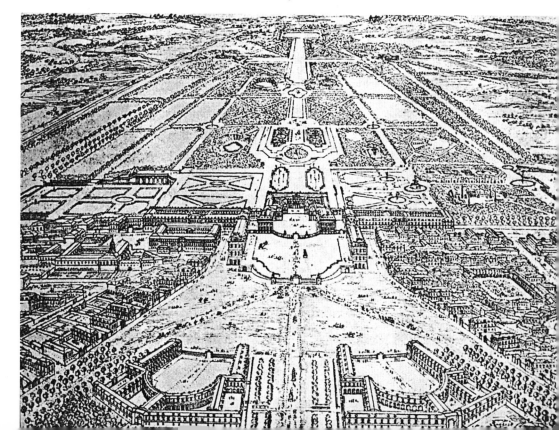

sheer magnitude of the final dimensions, the construction, unlike at Vaux, does not work in the opposite direction. Looking back from the termination of the central axis, the palace no longer plays a role in the view. Now the layout works as a telescope in reverse. Only at the *Bassin d'Apollon*, where the middle section, wings and floors of the building are visible, by traversing the axis, is the palace an interesting component.

The *Bassin d'Apollon* also plays a key role in the mythological interpretation of the main axis. This converges more obviously than at Vaux in the spatial sequence of the axis. Starting at the source where the water appears (a symbol of birth and earthly origin), via the fountains (representing effervescent life), the series leads to the water surface of the *Grand Canal* – a symbol of infinity. Originally the *Parterre d'Eau* represented an ancient cosmogony, or creation story, with the four elements, fire (Pluto), air (Boreas), earth (Saturn) and water (Neptune). Later, a more geographical allegory represented the French rivers. The Latona in the *bassin* of the *jardin bas*, which cannot be seen from the château, can be associated with the birth of Apollo. Via the sloping *Allée Royale* this image is linked to the *Bassin d'Apollon*, the sun god, placed at the centre of the field of view. Finally, the *Grand Canal* reflects cosmic space. In its entirety the east-west axis represents the path of the sun and is a symbol of the benevolent rule of the Sun King.

In its totality, the longitudinal axis at Versailles is roughly as wide, but three times longer (10 kilometres) than that at Vaux-le-Vicomte, while the estate as a whole is about twice as broad (3 kilometres) and the surface area of the entire plan is three times as large (1,500 hectares). Despite its greater size, the plan's unity, as at Vaux, is controlled by the gradually increasing scale and by the axes or avenues radiating out into the periphery of the estate. An important distinction, however, is that at Versailles the town has become a part of the spatial construction: the landscape and the town face each other on a reflecting axis. In principle, both have been designed using the same devices. The most important formal structure used in both the garden and the town layouts is the (measurement) grid, the axis and the symmetry. The result is that the landscape and the town layouts are united in one artificial Grand Ensemble.

A. From 52 BC (the Roman town)

D. 1400 (the remodelled Louvre inside the city walls)

B. 1180 (the medieval town)

E. 1560 (the Tuileries outside the city walls)

C. 1210 (the old Louvre as a fortress outside the city walls)

F. 1620 (the Tuileries inside the city walls; *Cours-la-Reine* outside)

G. 1700 axis by Le Nôtre, boulevard

The Louvre and the Tuileries in the Paris plan

The Tuileries Gardens

After indicating the four cardinal points, the priest, with his face turned south, proclaimed, 'This is the front and this is the back, this is left and this is right'. He then solemnly drew the *cardo* and the *decumanus* with his staff. It is quite likely that in 52 BC the town plan for Lutetia (Paris), like that of Florence, became part of the universal order in the same mystical way. Whatever the case may have been, the original plan of this Roman city documents two main roads: one extending in a north-south direction across the Seine at the Ile de la Cité and the other at right angles to this, running parallel to the river.

THE FORMAL ORIGINS OF THE PARIS URBAN LANDSCAPE

In 1180 Philippe Auguste began building a city wall which was fortified at its weakest points where it intersected with the Seine. One of these fortresses built outside the city was the old Louvre. When Charles V built a new wall at the end of the 14th century, the Louvre became part of the city and lost its strategic importance. After 1546, François I had a new castle built by Pierre Lescot on the square foundation of the old fortress, running parallel to the Seine. However, for Catherine de' Medici, queen of Henry II, it proved to be unsatisfactory. She deemed it to be too dark and confining as she desired to command magnificent views of the landscape. To this end, work started on a new country residence in 1563, 500 metres from the Louvre, outside the city wall, on the site of an old tile maker (*tuileries*). This was orthogonal to the next stretch of the Seine so that the gentle bend in the river was visible as a kink between the axes of symmetry of the Louvre and that of the new plan. Along the banks of the Seine, the Palais des Tuileries was linked to the Louvre by a covered gallery. At the same time a geometric garden was laid out at the new palace, parallel to the river and stretching as far as its next bend. In Philibert Delorme's design the garden was an irregular rectangle measuring 70 by 270 metres. It was an independent space, situated to the west of the palace, and enclosed on four sides by walls. The squares in the plan were filled with a colourful mix of Italian-inspired elements. Though the garden was autonomous in relation to the palace (like a medieval *hortus conclusus*), the geometric unity between the two can be seen in an engraving by Androuet du Cerceau of the original plan. Both the plan of the garden and the palace appear to have been organized on a grid.

As a result of the building of a new city wall (by Louis XIII in the early 17th century), the Tuileries also became enclosed within the city. It was now Maria de' Medici, widow of Henry IV, who was looking for a way of escaping the urban straitjacket. A solution was found by turning to the Italian example of the *cacine*, the Florentine promenade along the Arno. Outside the fortified wall, she had a similar tree-lined walk laid out along the Seine in 1616. This *Cours-la-Reine*, which quickly filled up with carriages, was laid out in a straight line along the next section of the river. The promenade lies as an autonomous, classical stoa in the riparian landscape.

The rectangular plan and measurement grid of the garden as well as the line of the promenade formalized the site of the Paris urban plan on the Seine.

A TELESCOPE TO THE OPEN LANDSCAPE OF THE SEINE

In 1664, architect Le Vau was commissioned to design new plans for the Louvre and to complete the Tuileries. At the time Le Nôtre was also brought in to lend spatial balance to the whole construction. As a basis for his new plan he used the measurement grid of the Renaissance garden. The surrounding walls were pulled down and a large terrace was laid out in front of the palace façade. The axis of symmetry, which

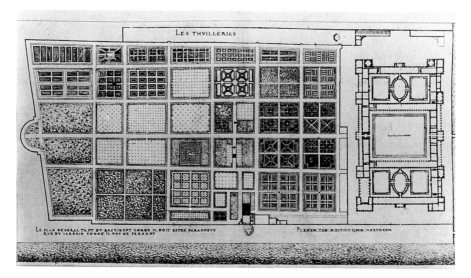

Androuet du Cerceau. The Renaissance plan of the Tuileries Gardens, 1578

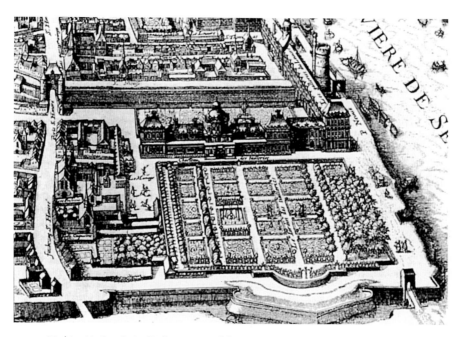

Mathieu Merian. Paris. Bird's eye view of the Renaissance garden, 1613

Israël Sylvestre. Paris. The *Cours-la-Reine* from the beginning of
the Champs-Élysées

in the Renaissance garden was still only a grid line, was transformed into a spatial
axis. Geometric differences in the original measurement grid, which created anoma-
lies in the bilateral symmetry, were 'corrected'. The site sloped towards the Seine and
both sides of the axis had different measurements. Le Nôtre made the plan appear
level and symmetrical by, among other means, laying out new raised side terraces
along the Seine. Lengthwise the plan was perspectively manipulated. One of the ways
this was accomplished was by increasing the size of the water *bassins* as they receded
so that the garden, as far as its boundaries, was brought visually under control when
viewed from the palace. Beyond the large open terrace, behind the palace, the old grid
was filled in with *bosquets* which bordered the new spatial axis as *coulisses*. Together
with the new, raised terraces along the sides of the garden, which visually opened up
the town and the river, these *bosquets* ensured that the whole plan was spatially focused
on one point. This was where the city wall was breached and the two side terraces terminated in a horseshoe-shaped form to frame a vista of the landscape across the city
moat.

In the Renaissance plan the axis of symmetry ended here in an echo (apsis),
which may be seen as a primitive form of 'accelerated' perspective. In the given situation more was not possible. In 1670, the city wall was pulled down so that the garden axis, past the garden boundary, could be extended. The spatial axis was continued
in the (levelled) landscape as a broad, ascending tree-lined *Grand Cours* (1667),
which, on the top of the Butte de Chaillot, three kilometres from the palace, dissolved
into an atmospheric vista. Due to the sheer size of the *Grand Cours* (over two kilometres) in relation to the foreground and its upward slope, the horizon, as a tangent
between heaven and earth, was brought into the Tuileries as if with a telescope.
Beyond the horizon the axis became part of the regional infrastructure of residences,
forming a direct link with St Germain-en-Laye.

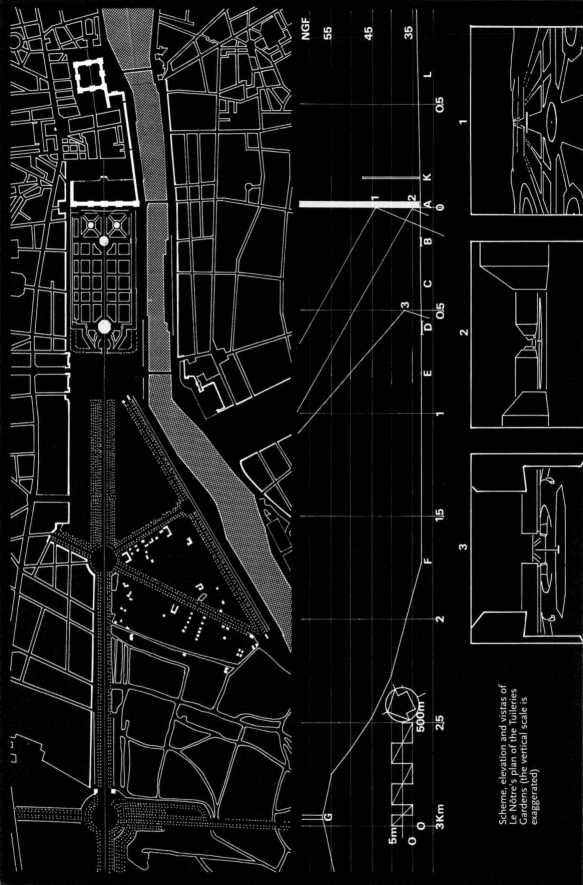

Scheme, elevation and vistas of
Le Nôtre's plan of the Tuileries
Gardens (the vertical scale is
exaggerated)

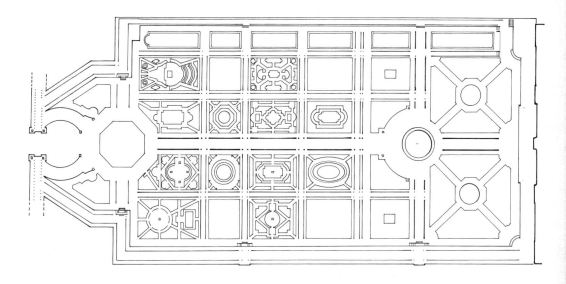

Paris. Scheme of Le Nôtre's plan for the Tuileries Gardens

Paris. An analysis of the measurements of the circles in Le Nôtre's plan for the Tuileries Gardens

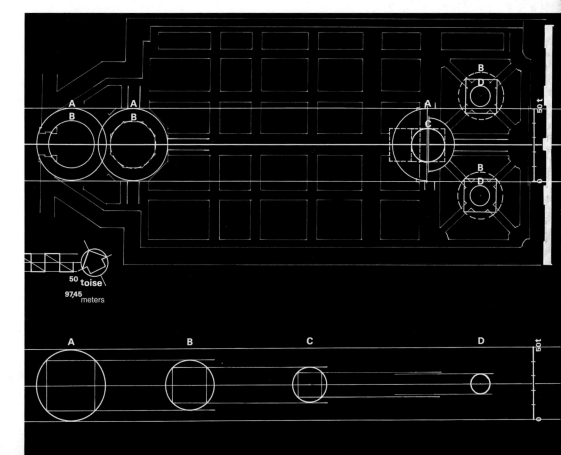

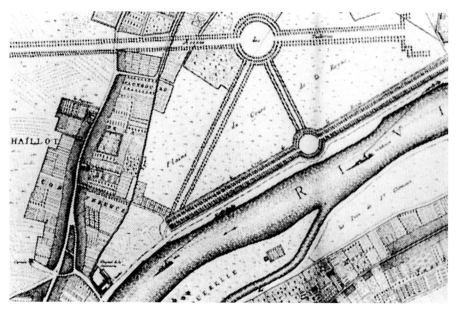

Jouvin de Rochefort. Paris. Le Nôtre's spatial axis continued as an avenue into the landscape beyond the city, 1675

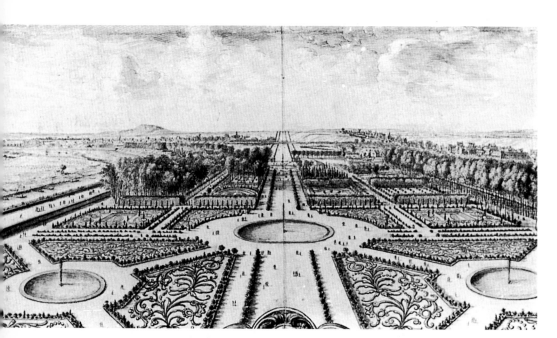

Israël Sylvestre. The Tuileries Gardens, Paris. View of the garden and the horizon from the palace, *c.* 1680

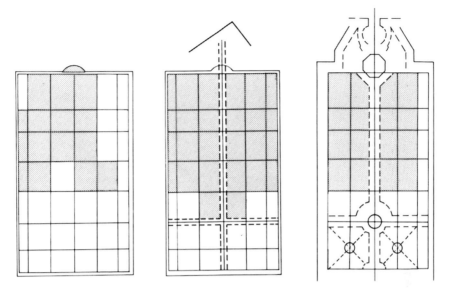

The Tuileries Gardens, Paris. The transformation of the Renaissance plan into Le Nôtre's formal plan

In order to better structure the terrain, it was planned to create a new northern diagonal axis which would be placed symmetrically to the *Cours-la-Reine* along the Seine. This would have created a *patte d'oie* at the point where the fortifications were breached. By placing the *Grand Cours* by two diverging avenues, the eastern city was, in principle, brought under visual control both in depth and width. The space was formalized as far as the eye could see.

THE PLACE DE LA CONCORDE AND THE OBSCURING OF THE VIEWPOINT

The new axis was aimed on the landscape. The urban plan developed in the same westerly direction as the spatial axis, that is, towards the landscape. As a result, the landscape design and the city did not face each other (as at Versailles) but overlapped and ran alongside each other. The spaces on the axis were transformed, one by one, into urban areas of the city, until the total length of the axis itself was incorporated into the urban morphology. This urbanization has evolved over a period of more than 300 years and the process of expansion still continues today.

During the construction of the Tuileries Gardens the urban fortifications along the western edge of the park lost their military significance (1670). A new role was found for its *tracé*: Louis XIV had 36-metre wide boulevards laid out, which as stately tree-lined promenades virtually formed a network of green throughout the entire city. Triumphal arches were erected at the junctions of these boulevards and the most important arteries. The latter were made arrow straight and, as radiating axes, linked the city with its environs creating a formal whole.

The *patte d'oie*, where the boulevard intersected the spatial axis, became a chaotic traffic junction. The idea behind designing the Place de la Concorde was to provide the junction with an architectonic accent and to control the flow of traffic. After several competitions the design for the square was executed by the architect Jacques-Ange Gabriël (1755-63). Along the square's short northern edge he composed a vista

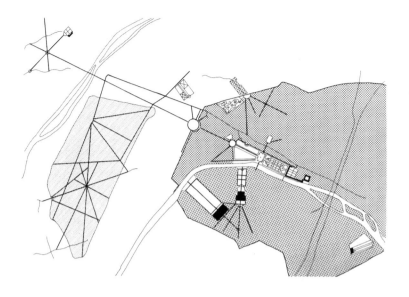

The Louvre and the Tuileries Gardens in the Paris plan,
1800 (axis across the Seine, Place de la Concorde, Rue
de Rivoli)

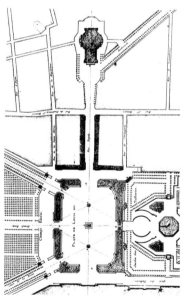

Paris. Jacques-Ange Gabriël's plan of
1755. Place de la Concorde

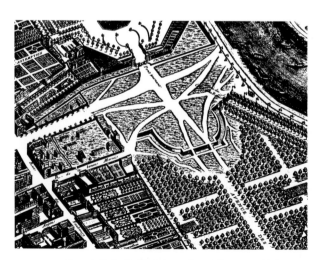

Turgot. Paris. Traffic intersection at the spot which
later became the Place de la Concorde, 1735

Paris. Place de la Concorde, 1843. Paris Bibliotheque National

through to the Madeleine Church which was 'framed' as a backdrop between two symmetrical palaces. The design of the Place de la Concorde was in fact restricted to this one architectonic 'screen'; on the south side it remained open towards the Seine and on the east and west sides there were no buildings. At the time, some Parisians, used to the façades of the old *Places Royales*, considered the new space too large and empty. Perhaps, though, leaving it open on three sides was a passive means of bringing the expanse of the landscape into the square. In Gabriël's design, however, there is a recognizable, active attempt to make the square into a spatial centre. The longitudinal axis of the square, with the vista to the Madeleine, was positioned orthogonally on Le Nôtre's spatial axis. The rectangular surface was framed and made autonomous by surrounding moats. The square's shape also cut through the triangular *patte d'oie*. By erecting a monument on the spatial axis at the point where it intersects with the axis leading to the Madeleine, Le Nôtre's vista to infinity was interrupted. The horizontal view was also impeded by monuments erected on the junctions of the Madeleine axis with the two diagonals of the *patte d'oie*. In fact, the most important viewpoints on the square have been taken up by monuments. As a result Le Nôtre's vista becomes fixed on the square. The statues 'elevated' the viewpoint to a monument, but the spatial effect of the *patte d'oie* was obscured.

THE ARC DE TRIOMPHE AND THE MATERIALIZATION OF THE VANISHING POINT

The *Grand Cours*, lined with elm trees, originally lay outside the city and ran across farmland and vegetable fields to the *rond-point* (a star-shaped intersection of avenues). Later the entire area along this, which was then known as Champs-Élysées, was planted with trees (from 1709 onwards). At the same time as the Place de la Concorde was laid out, the 150-metre axis through the Champs-Élysées was again planted with elm and lime trees (1758-67). The drier situated north side was especially used for ball games, parties and parades. In 1770, Jean Perronet, the director of the École des

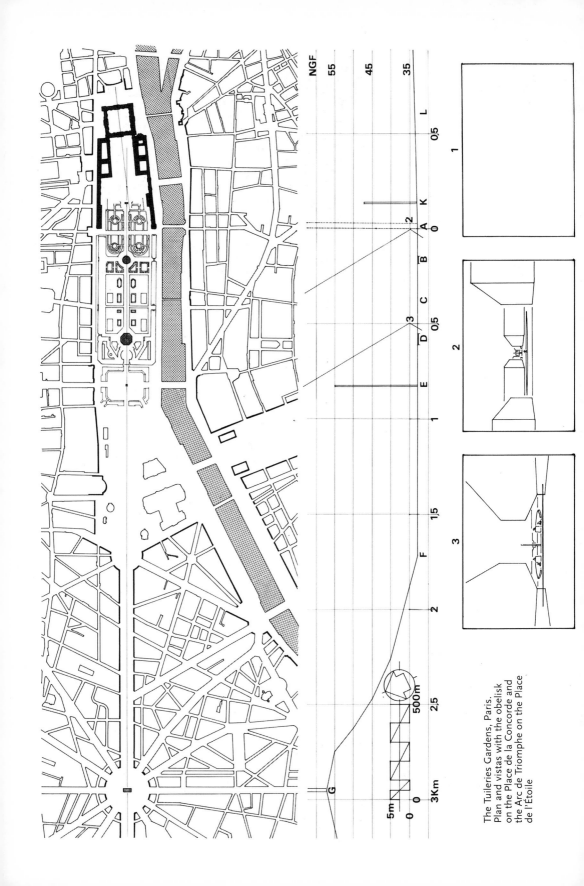

The Tuileries Gardens, Paris.
Plan and vistas with the obelisk
on the Place de la Concorde and
the Arc de Triomphe on the Place
de l'Étoile

Paris. Arc du Caroussel

Ponts-et-Chaussées, extended the axis, past the Butte de Chaillot, in a straight line to the Seine, where the Pont de Neuilly was built. In order to have a uniform slope along the entire route, the Butte de Chaillot was made five metres lower (1768-74). The octagonal square on this hill, dating from Louis XIV's time, was changed into a circular plan with five routes radiating from it (Place de l'Étoile).

During the 18th century numerous suggestions were put forward for erecting a monument on the Place de l'Étoile. After his return from Austerlitz, Napoleon finally decreed the erecting of two triumphal arches, one symbolizing peace, the other war (1806). Both had to be positioned on the axis of the Palais des Tuileries. On the landscape side of the palace the Arc de Triomphe, as a city gateway, was part of the toll boundary of 1784, while the Arc du Caroussel served as a gateway to the Tuileries on the east side. The size of the arches is in keeping with their distance from the palace. In the original layout this could be seen from the emperor's residence, the Palais des Tuileries.

The Arc du Caroussel was built in a relatively short period of time according to the plans of the architects Charles Percier and Pierre F.L. Fontaine (1808), but the Arc de Triomphe on the Place de l'Étoile took from 1806 to 1836 to build. Jean F.T. Chalgrin's design (1806-09) shows three interesting variations of the Arc du Caroussel. The latter was inspired by the classic Roman triumphal Arch of Constantine, which had three openings. The Paris monument is of modest size (height: 14.62 metres, breadth: 17.87 metres, depth: 6.54 metres), is richly detailed and displays a colonnade of pilasters resting on high socles. The Arc de Triomphe, on the other hand, consisted of only one arch (25 metres high), open on all four sides, and is a colossal, massive block measuring 50 metres high, 45 metres wide and 22 metres deep. The relief is sober and there is no colonnade of pilasters – as decreed by the court architect Fontaine, who maintained that 'a colonnade of pilasters is unnecessary for an arch

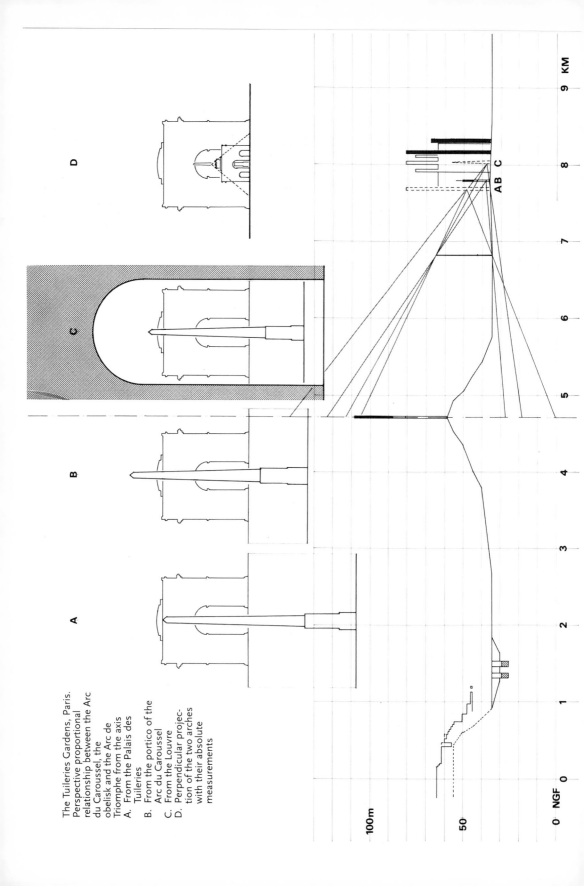

The Tuileries Gardens, Paris.
Perspective proportional
relationship between the Arc
du Caroussel, the
obelisk and the Arc de
Triomphe from the axis
A. From the Palais des
    Tuileries
B. From the portico of the
    Arc du Caroussel
C. From the Louvre
D. Perpendicular projec-
    tion of the two arches
    with their absolute
    measurements

D

C

B

A

9 KM

8

AB C

7

6

5

4

3

2

1

0

100m

50

0 NGF 0

Paris. The Champs-Élysées with the Arc de Triomphe defining the horizon, 19th century

Paris. Arc de Triomphe

which can be seen from far away and whose spatial beauty is formed by its mass and size'. Since a colonnade enables one to read the proportions more easily, the absence of one gives the structure a total lack of scale.

In its lack of scale, the arch resembles the huge statue of Hercules at Vaux-le-Vicomte. There, in the experimental garden of the formal design, this statue connects the natural horizon with the sky above. On the spatial axis of the Tuileries the *Grand Cours*, which leads up to the top of Butte de Chaillot, touches the natural horizon and, because of its length (two kilometres) and slope, brings the horizon forward. This optical effect was endangered however by the levelling off of the hill. Notwithstanding, the hill forms the parameters of the field of vision. There the main vista dissolves into the atmosphere. Positioning an object (in this case an arch) – even if it has no scale – on the natural horizon, is therefore, in fact, comparable to taking a step backwards. The arch delineates one point on the natural horizon. The shape of the arch prevents the sky and the earth from meeting. At the same time the opening in the arch suggests a horizontal continuation of the space in the depth, yet Perronet's extension of the axis remains invisible when standing before the arch. Thus, in this way, despite the arch's abstract design, the picture plane spatial infinity is reduced to a material representation.

THE CHAMPS-ÉLYSÉES AND THE DISMANTLING OF THE ARCADIAN IMAGE

Napoleon's Arc de Triomphe on the horizon of the Champs-Élysées also served as a gateway linking the old city with the new one. On the hills to the west, reaching as far as the Seine, a new imperial city was planned. Napoleon's downfall meant a set back in the realization of these plans. During the second empire (1852-70), Napoleon III, together with his prefect Georges-Eugène Haussmann, began a gigantic operation to modernize the city, which now had more than one million inhabitants. With his colleagues, Barillet Deschamps (surveyor) and Jean Alphand (engineer and landscape architect), Haussmann revamped the urban plan by creating traffic break-throughs, improving technical facilities for the network of streets, reorganizing public transport and systematically creating green spaces in the form of parks and squares throughout the city.

Up until then, traffic running from east to west followed the original higher route north of the Louvre and the Tuileries. To resolve traffic congestion in the heart of Paris, Napoleon III extended the new Rue de Rivoli, begun by Percier and Fontaine, along the north wing of the Louvre to the east and the Place de la Bastille,

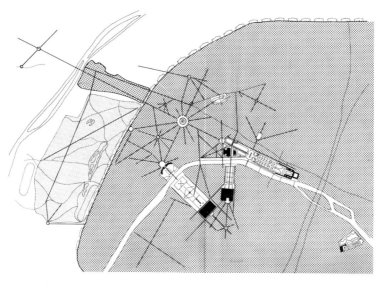

The Louvre and the Tuileries in the Paris plan, 1900 (Le Nôtre's spatial axis within the city)

Jean Alphand. Paris. Place de l'Étoile, 1867-73

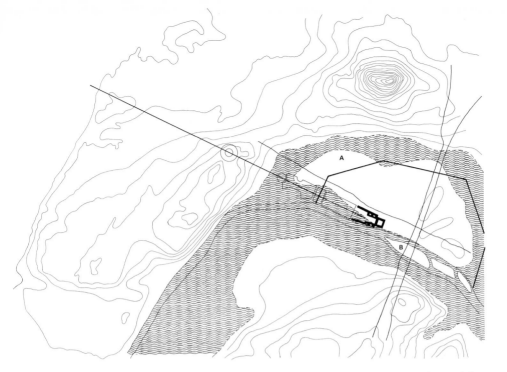

Paris. The projection of Le Nôtre's axis (and the boulevard) onto the geomorphology and the Seine's original course

Place de la Nation and Bois de Vincennes (1854-55). The part of the city between the Tuileries and the Louvre was demolished so that the northern wing connecting the two palaces could finally be built. When the Rue de Rivoli was completed the Tuileries Garden, which on the north side originally bordered the backs of buildings, was provided with new access to the city. The Champs-Élysées, which became the property of the city council in 1828, was provided with pavement and gaslights, and was the most popular promenade in Paris. Strollers, equestrians, carriages and ball games all contributed to the lively bustle. Cafés began to appear as did restaurants, winter gardens, circuses, puppet theatres and, finally, international exhibitions.

Further to the west, the Place de l'Étoile became the hub of a new district. Similar to the Place de la Concorde, the square is located at the intersection of Le Nôtre's spatial axis and a boulevard. The latter was laid out at the former toll border of 1784. With seven new avenues, which as a framework for a new city were extended as far as the Passy fields, the round square (diameter: 240 metres) was enlarged and transformed into a star with 12 'arms' (1857). The German architect Jakob Ignaz Hittorf built 12 buildings with uniform façades around the square, which are small when compared to the Arc de Triomphe. It was said that Haussmann planted three double rows of trees around the square in order to redress the scale. The large urban developments that went up along the new avenues coupled the Paris axis to the re-organized Bois de Boulogne (1852) and the Place du Trocadero (opposite the Champ-de-Mars) in the south, and to the villas around the new Parc Monceau (1860) in the north. This accompanied a drift of the aristocracy and the prosperous bourgeoisie to the western part of the city.

Haussmann's reorganization of the city resembled a later, urban version of the 17th-century rearranging of the crumbling medieval landscape around Paris. The *rond-point* of the 17th-century radial forest made it possible to range over hunting ter-

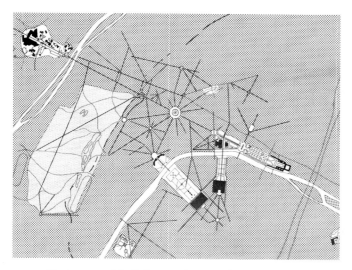

The Louvre and the Tuileries in the Paris plan, 1958 (La Défense within the city)

Paris. Plan and elevation of the axis from the Louvre to La Défense (the vertical scale is exaggerated)
A. La Grande Arche
B. La Défense
C. Pont de Neuilly
D. Pte. Maillot
E. Place de l'Étoile and the Arc de Triomphe
F. Rond-point
G. Place de la Concorde
H. The former Palais des Tuileries
I. Arc du Caroussel
J. Pyramide
K. Louvre

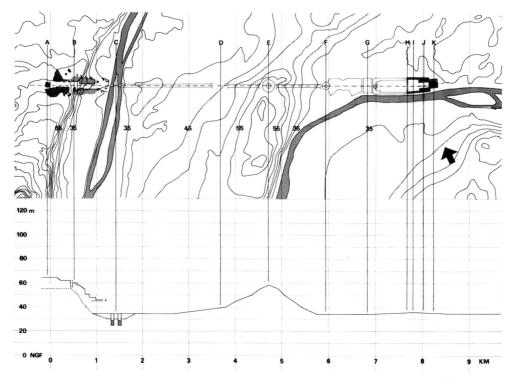

Paris. Vista through the Arc de Triomphe to La Défense

Paris. The axis from the Arc de Triomphe to La Défense

ritory and to survey every direction from strategic points. Haussmann's Place de l'Étoile is a *rond-point* in the city and plays a significant role in the infrastructure. Similar to the new avenues, over 30 metres wide with uniformly straight façades, it is primarily a space which allows for a more efficient flow of traffic. The Champs-Élysées, which joins the Place de l'Étoile, was no longer a *tapis vert* surrounded by trees in the open landscape. The traffic route was laid out on this axis so that it became a metropolitan traffic artery, which, hemmed in by uniform building façades, formed the backbone of an entire city sector. It became a 'parkway' which brought the landscape, in the form of the Bois de Boulogne, into the reach of Paris.

In the 19th century the entire 3,800-metre axis became part of the city. Even the natural horizon, which through optical manipulation had to be brought forward to remain visible in the old city, lay within the urban fabric at the time. At the same time the Arcadian sequence of pictures on the viewing axis was destroyed when the country, tree-lined avenue became a main traffic artery.

LA DÉFENSE AND THE LOSS OF BALANCE

Beyond the Arc de Triomphe, on the other side of the Butte de Chaillot, the axis continued in a straight line over the Pont de Neuilly to the Rond-point de la Défense, on the other bank of the Seine. Yet neither via the tree-lined avenue (after 1770), nor via the urbanized 19th-century avenue, did the view of this play a role in the picture plane, visible in the open portico of the Arc de Triomphe from the Louvre. The monumental arch with its colossal proportions stood lonely on the horizon for a century, framing nothing other than the sky.

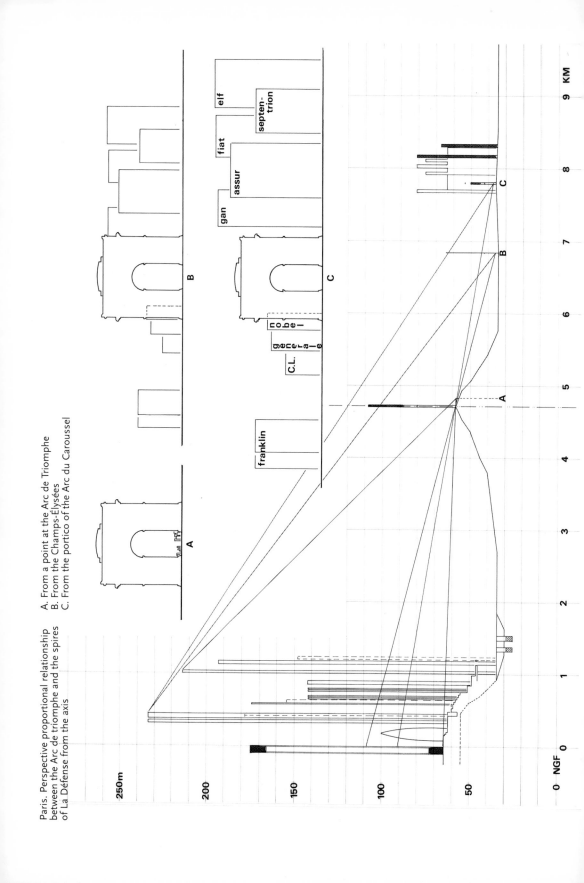

Paris. Perspective proportional relationship
between the Arc de triomphe and the spires
of La Défense from the axis

A. From a point at the Arc de Triomphe
B. From the Champs-Élysées
C. From the portico of the Arc du Caroussel

In 1931 the Départment of the Seine announced a competition for designing the axis from the Etoile to the Rond-point de la Défense. Proposals were submitted by Le Corbusier, among others, but the war interrupted further progress. In 1956 it was planned to extend the axis through the area of Nanterre, across the island Chatou in the Seine and through the area of Montesson to St Germain. This extension (still only on paper) more than doubled the length to a total of 17 kilometres. The EPAD, a public body set up in 1958, was to remodel the La Défense area and create a new business district. Again the targeted area centred on the intersection of the axis with a boulevard, this time Boulevard Périphérique. The old *rond-point* made way for a mega engineering construction with different levels for through traffic routes, local roads, underground parking and pedestrians. A platform, measuring 100 by 120 metres, which descends a level at a time, forms a link between the shops, restaurants and public services on ground floor of the tower blocks and the Seine.

La Défense is the antithesis of Le Nôtre's Tuileries where architecture, landscape and city formed a formal unity. At La Défense this formality is negated by the spatial diversity of the modern metropolis. On a clear day it can even be seen from the Louvre. Despite the distance seperating them (eight kilometres), the height of the towers (with a maximum height of 200 metres) makes them appear as though they are next to the Arc de Triomphe as the same size. Due to these blocks, the shifting of the urban skyline far beyond Le Nôtre's horizon can be seen in the old city. Against this background, the 'infinity' of the 17th century formal spatial axis degenerates into a paradox.

La Grande Arche and the step over the horizon

While the Arc de Triomphe no longer stood alone on the horizon, its portico was still 'empty'. The central area of La Défense was carefully left free of anything that would rise above the horizon and therefore be seen in the portico. In 1973, the architect Emile Aillaud launched an ambiguous project which, with its reflecting façade, terminated the axis, yet at the same time seemed to extend it. The architect Jeoh Ming Pei proposed two symmetric towers, linked by a parabola. But even in 1979 and 1980, when various architects were invited to make a new design for an object on the axis, one of the preconditions was that a structure should not exceed 35 metres so that from the Tuileries it would not be visible through the open portico. However, once it was realized that such a structure would be no match for the other towers, the height restriction was lifted. In an international competition (1982-83), it was in fact the emptiness, which up until then had been carefully protected like a historic monument, that was the design theme. An international communications centre (*c.* 45,000 square metres) and two new ministries (*c.* 75,000 square metres) were drawn up for the programme. It is interesting that the jury report on the 424 entries submitted, noted that the project had 'to break with the unitarian morphology of the towers'.

The Dane Johann Otto von Spreckelsen won first prize. His idea was to place a cube with an open front and rear as 'a new Arc de Triomphe' at the head of the axis. The plan's measurements (100 × 100 × 100 metres) and the angle of the cube in relation to the axis defer to the similar size and angle of the large Louvre square at the other end of the axis. The Grande Arche consists of large concrete 'bars'. Offices are housed in the two vertical walls, while the horizontal ones bear a covered square and roof gardens. The cube's walls are smoothly polished marble. The most important architectural aim of this project was to create an axial 'apex' at La Défense. The architect of the new arch spoke about 'a window onto the world', 'a meeting of peoples' and 'a view into the future'. Spreckelsen has been able to put these grandiloquent views into perspective. On top of his 'window onto the world' he has laid out a roof

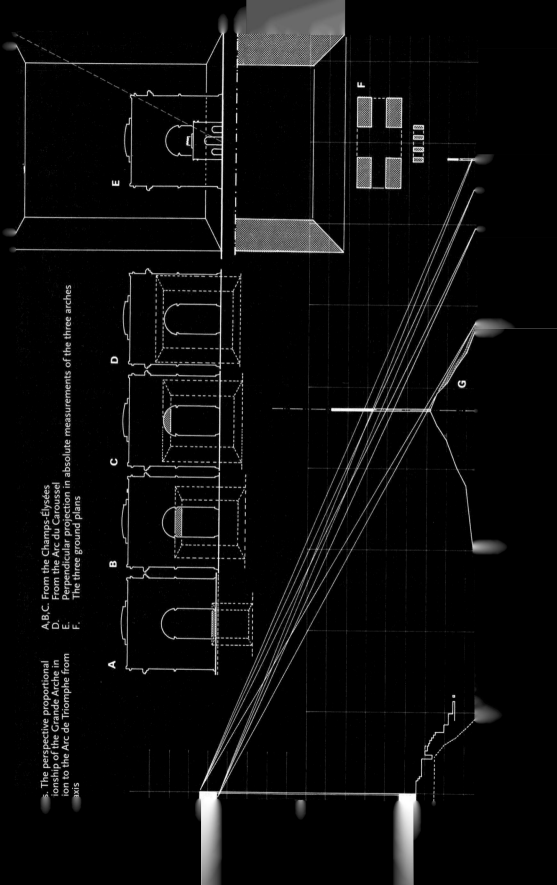

The perspective proportional
relationship of the Grande Arche in
relation to the Arc de Triomphe from
the axis

A,B,C. From the Champs-Élysées
D.   From the Arc du Caroussel
E.   Perpendicular projection in absolute measurements of the three arches
F.   The three ground plans

Paris. La Grande Arche

garden as a *fata morgana*, which is suspended between heaven and earth and, when viewed from the correct vantage point, is framed by the portico of the Arc de Triomphe.

Due to its height of 100 metres, the structure, across the Butte de Chaillot, can be seen through the portico of the Arc de Triomphe from the Tuileries Gardens. Traversing the Champs-Élysées, its upper part shifts like a horizontal stripe in the vista of the portico. The form of the new structure in the main vista (a horizontal line) is abstract and lacks even more scale than the Arc de Triomphe, which is why the depth of the spatial axis cannot be gauged. Nevertheless, Spreckelsen's arch shifts the visible termination of the main vista from the Butte de Chaillot to La Défense, which greatly alters the character of the foreground, middle ground and background of the spatial axis. The background is now formed by La Défense, while the Arc de Triomphe constitutes the middle ground like a *coulisse*. Le Nôtre's original plan has been entirely reduced to the foreground. The axis has been lenghtened from three to eight kilometres, though it is doubtful whether this is accompanied by an increase in perceived spatial depth. The space behind the Arc de Triomphe cannot be perceived and the urbanized background imposes itself like some grotesque backdrop. Here the natural horizon really has been exceeded. The spatial depth is no longer illusionary but real; the tension between appearance and reality has dissolved.

CHAPTER THREE

THE GEOMETRY
OF THE
PICTURESQUE

THE 18TH-CENTURY ENGLISH LANDSCAPE GARDEN

236

'Capability' Brown's landscape at Petworth, West Sussex

The landscape experiment of the Enlightenment

THE INDIVIDUALIZATION OF TIME AND SPACE

Reason, freedom and equality were the slogans of the Enlightenment, the 18th-century spiritual and political reform movement that had virtually all of Europe in its grip. Armed with reason, 18th-century citizens wished to liberate themselves from existing religious and political structures and from other inherited forms of authority. In practically every area new ideas and practical organizational forms arose. John Locke (1632-1704) laid the basis for research and empiricism in the sciences and for a separation of legislative and enforcement powers. The social reformer Anthony Ashley Cooper, 3rd Earl of Shaftesbury, emphasized personal integrity. Human nature was thought to be inherently good but could be corrupted by external conditions. Reason formed the new basis for ethics and aesthetics. David Hume (1711-76) advocated individual experience as a starting point for human knowledge and moral

insight, while Adam Smith (1723-90) called for a liberalization in economic activities and opposed governmental interference.

Parliamentary democracy reached an apex in early 18th-century England. With what would be a limited electorate by today's standards, parliament was representative for the then balance of power within society. A liberal vanguard came into being which propagated new ideas and put them into practice. After the victory of the Duke of Marlborough against Louis XIV's army at Blenheim on the Danube in 1704, England became the strongest military power in Europe. This led to expansionist foreign policy in which America and parts of Asia and Africa were colonized. James Cook circum-navigated the world's seas in the interests of England's expansion as a colonial power, discovering New Zealand, among other territories, and landed on Australia's New South Wales.

The age of Enlightenment inspired the development from formal to practical thinking. Scientifically based principles underlined the processes controlling nature and society. In 1687 Isaac Newton (1642-1727) wrote his *Philosophiae naturalis principia* in which he set down the laws of gravitation which were to be decisive in explaining the creation of the universe. Experimental breakthroughs produced empirical science. Joseph Priestly experimented with electricity and isolated oxygen from air; Henry Cavendish succeeded in separating water into oxygen and hydrogen. Many scientific discoveries found an almost instant application. England was the undisputed pioneer in the area of technological advances and was the first country to switch from manual to industrial mass production in the second half of the 18th century. Industrialization and the development of world trade made it the world's richest nation. In 1735 Carolus Linnaeus (1707-78) wrote his *Systema naturae* in which nature was classified according to a system for the first time. This was further expanded upon in 1753 in his *Species plantarum* which became the basis for modern botany. This knowledge

Balscott, Oxfordshire. Pattern of the landscape before enclosure (from T. Sharp, *English Panorama*)

Balscott, Oxfordshire. Pattern of the landscape after enclosure (from T. Sharp, *English Panorama*)

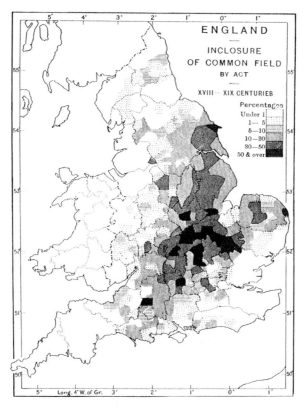

The extent of the parliamentary enclosures (from E.C.K. Gonner, *Common Land and Inclosure*, 1912)

was applied to agricultural techniques, horticulture and experimental farming methods.

Nature became the mirror image of the social order: the structure of the cosmos was represented politically by parliamentary democracy. Freedom and 'naturalness' were mutually corresponding counterparts. The striving within nature was the basis of economic rivalry. The landscape garden was, in a sense, the metaphorical model of this society: the free will of the Englishman was reflected in the winding stream and the growth of the tree.

Another aspect is that nature was bestowed with sentimentality, sensation and intuition. Nature was idealized as the source of goodness in humankind. Jean-Jacques Rousseau (1712-78), for instance, espoused a return to human 'nature' in which only the essential mattered. Marc-Antoine Laugier's architectural criticism presupposed an imaginary primitive architecture in which only the essential parts would exist.

During the Enlightenment an individual understanding of time emerged as well as an awareness of one's own destiny and one's own will. Classical space lost its import, the traditional view of spatial unity was abandoned while the experience of the individual was of paramount importance. What had previously been resolved in architecture according to traditional experience now became problematic. New theories arose on perception and the experiencing of space.

THE DYNAMICS OF THE GEORGIAN LANDSCAPE

Between 450 and 1066 the first Anglo-Saxons settled in England, establishing their own communal farmlands and social structure. This system reached the peak of its development in the 13th century and in some areas remained largely unchanged until the 18th century. Its archetypal form flourished in the Midlands, the hilly central part of England, where the open fields stretched to the horizon. Surrounded by commons and large grazed or untamed forests, they formed the backdrop of the first landscape gardens.

Between 1570 and 1770, after the difficult period of colonizing the natural landscape was over, England's countryside flourished. Agriculture thrived as never before: for two hundred years (seven generations) the country was prosperous enough to provide everyone with a decent living. During Elizabeth I's reign this had already resulted in a general economic revival and renewed building activity in villages and towns. It was only towards the end of the 17th century that the four most northern English counties experienced large-scale redevelopment, which was probably a continuation of the first Elizabethan wave that by now had reached the borders. Between 1660 and 1720 there was a second wave of redevelopment across the rest of England, especially in the Midlands, during which entire villages were sometimes rebuilt and many schools and poorhouses founded.

During the 18th century the commons were divided amongst the so-called yeomen (freeholders who cultivated their own land). Until around 1730 this was mainly done among themselves without government interference, but from 1750 onwards enclosure became regulated by law. Agreements between individual owners and the government were enshrined in either a private act of parliament or the parliamentary act and award. These parliamentary enclosures radically changed the face of the English landscape between 1750 and 1850, especially during George III's reign. One million hectares of land was affected and some 700,000 hectares of wasteland was reclaimed by a 'private act of parliament'. This methodical Georgian landscape was most noticeable in the Midlands, particularly in Northamptonshire.

Land appropriation was carried out on the basis of a map, an enclosure plan and a road plan by a committee especially set up for the purpose. Heathland in

An 18th-century turnpike road at Hampstead

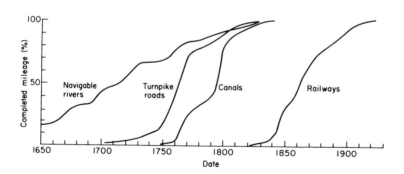

The development of transport means (graphics from Eric Pawson, *Transport and Economy*, 1977)

Norfolk, for instance, was converted to an arable area for rye, barley and wheat. Heavy clay areas, better suited as pasture, were for the most part planted with grass. Where possible the committee made rectangular, preferably square, enclosures. The optimum size for more efficient rotation grazing lay between two and four hectares. The carrying out of land enclosure was efficient even by contemporary standards and resulted in an extraordinary increase in production.

This process of rationalization completely transformed the old landscape pattern with its small fields, twisting cart tracks, headlands and footpaths into a modern chessboard of small enclosures and a network of new by-roads running as straight as an arrow in all directions and from village to village. Land was chiefly enclosed by planting with quickset (whitethorn or hawthorn). On the more elevated stoney plateaus, such as in Derbyshire, the land was enclosed using piled-up natural stones unearthed during the cultivation of the wasteland. Trees were sporadically planted, chiefly ash but also elm and oak. During land appropriation, the enclosures of one owner were clustered together as much as possible, which necessitated the building of new farms outside the villages. As a result of this process, some 3,000 villages changed their appearance beyond recognition. Because of the myriad plantings the Georgian landscape became more visually dense than its previous traditional open fields. The medieval main roads (fosse ways) had hedges where they were previously exposed to the open landscape.

After 1700 transport developed at a rapid pace. From 1720 onwards many new roads were laid out. Thomas Telford worked on the planning and construction of hard roads, while John McAdam improved the foundations and surface using freestone gravel. The hard surface elicited improvements to the carriage, which now carried mail and passengers considerably faster and more comfortably. New turnpikes also linked the urban centres with coastal harbours. Everywhere in Britain turnpike trusts appeared, responsible for road maintenance and collecting toll fees, as well as setting out signposts and milestones for travellers. Development of turnpikes reached its peak around 1750 and by about 1770 the network of roads was more or less complete.

Canals were more suitable than roads for transporting industrial raw materials like coal and iron ore. Josiah Wedgwood financed the laying of canals for transporting his fragile china and pottery. The foremost pioneer of the canal waterways in England was the 3rd Earl of Bridgewater who, together with his engineers, John Gilbert and James Brindley, designed a canal from his coal mines in Worsley to his factories in Manchester and Liverpool. The network of canals was so dense that every city of any importance used them as a cheap means of transportation. To lay the canals in hilly regions, tunnels had to be dug, dykes constructed and aqueducts built. This brought with it a new technique of constructing bridges and other engineering feats. The first cast iron bridge was built across the Severn in Coalbrookdale, Telford, between 1777 and 1781.

The greatest outcome of the transport revolution was the railway. Robert Trevithic built the first steam train in 1809 and in 1813 William Hedley introduced his 'Puffing Billy', a steam train for transporting miners in Wylam, Northumberland. George Stephenson opened the first railway line, from Stockton to Darlington, in 1825. From then on development went unexpectedly fast. In 1843 the railway network covered just over 3,000 kilometres; hardly 30 years later more than 22,000 kilometres of track had been laid and passenger transport had increased fourteenfold.

Industry in Britain dates from the early 18th century, aside from mining and the systematic extraction of minerals, like iron ore, which had taken place since the Romans. The first real factory was John and Thomas Lombe's silk mill built in Derby

The Duke of Bridgewater at the Barton aqueduct

between 1718 and 1722. Lombe's five-storey mill was driven by hydropower and employed 300 workers. In the 1760s industrialization really took off. Darby's iron foundry was set up in Coalbrookdale in Shropshire on a tributary of the Severn. In 1765 Matthew Boulton opened his large Soho factory just outside Birmingham and, together with James Watt, began manufacturing steam engines in 1774. Josiah Wedgwood established his Etruria pottery factory at Burslem in Staffordshire, while Richard Arkwright set up his second mill in Cromford along the River Derwent in 1771. These four manufacturers accelerated industrialization and began to shape the modern industrial landscape.

Initial industrialization had a revolutionary impact on the 18th-century agricultural landscape. The new industries driven by hydropower established themselves not in existing villages but along the upper reaches of streams and rivers in the open, natural landscape. The size of the factories was unprecedented and as work was done in shifts the noise went on day and night. At night they were brightly illuminated, the whole provided a festive-looking spectacle. The new industrial barons originally built large country houses overlooking their splendid factories. In no time at all, workers' houses began to be built around the new factories, cottages at first but later terraces. A forest of large bottle-shaped kilns appeared in the Potteries, the region in

Staffordshire in which the china and earthenware industries were then concentrated.

Grime and overcrowding came with the steam age towards the end of the 18th century as a result of the burning of fossil fuels and the emergence of the chemical industry. The iron industry, which flourished wherever there was coal and iron ore side by side, created huge slag heaps in the Midlands, Yorkshire, Lancashire and South Wales. In Ravenshead at St Helens, Lancashire, the British Plate Glass Manufactory was set up in 1773 and more glass factories followed. In 1780 a large copper smelting works was built near Pary's Mountain on Anglesey. The water became polluted, the atmosphere toxic and the trees perished. In Lancashire, the Potteries, Yorkshire, South Wales and the Black Country of the Midlands, the 19th-century industrial landscape, 'the landscape of Hell', as Hoskins called it, cast its advancing shadow.

THE MODERNIZATION OF COUNTRY LIFE

At the end of the 10th century the nobility began to exercise more control over hunting wild game, which they wished to preserve for themselves. After 1066 the Normandy kings incorporated agricultural land into their hunting forests so that settlements were destroyed and the inhabitants driven away. They introduced legislation which curbed the use of the forest and which made hunting a royal privilege. In this way the Royal Forests were created, sometimes partly surrounded by a fence or by a wall and a moat. They were recorded and administered as royal possessions in the so-called Domesday Book of 1086. The New Forest, drawn together by William the Conqueror, is one of the best know examples, though there were even much larger forests. This system of Royal Forests extended across a large part of England. In the 13th century there was an immense belt of forest, stretching from Windsor on the Thames, across Berkshire and Hampshire, to the south coast. The Royal Forests reached their maximum size under Henry II: one third of the entire nation. The nobility were also allowed to lay out their own hunting preserve, or were given one by the king as a reward for their services.

Often these hunting parks were the beginning of the 18th-century landscape gardens. Knowsley, now the largest park in the north of England, was created in 1292 when Sir Robert Latham received a 'wood which is called a park' from the king. By wild animals grazing on it, Knowsley developed into a forest with open areas of grassland, though this was by no means a park landscape as we now know it: park originally meant no more than an enclosed area or warren.

The top of British society in the Middle Ages comprised some 50 families who ran the country, held political sway and exercised military power. These great lords founded many new estates after the Middle Ages. At the heart of this domestic colonization, which came in successive waves, lay political and economic motives. Under the political strategist Henry VIII, the monasteries, with their already well-organized and administered estates, were being dissolved. In their place the king favoured the landowners, who functioned as satellites of the court. In the second place, the economic success of agriculture was a strong driving force in stimulating the acquisition of more land. Between 1570 and 1640, particularly under Elizabeth I and following the acquisition of foreign colonies, new country houses sprang up all over England (apart from the northern counties).

In the 17th century the country house became an objective of the gentry, that class of untitled moneyed people comprising landowners, merchants, doctors, lawyers and the like. As noble titles could be bought – the proceeds financing the royal household – the number markedly increased. Palaces were built to rival those of the king, or in order to receive him, and a new class of country nobility came into being.

During the first half of the 18th century many new stately homes were built as

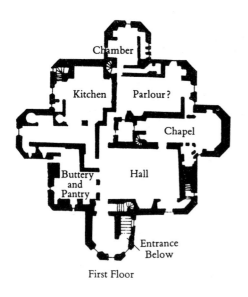

Chamber

Kitchen   Parlour?

Chapel

Buttery
and   Hall
Pantry

Entrance
Below

First Floor

a Northumberland. Warkworth Castle, 1474

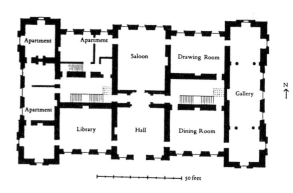

Apartment   Apartment

Saloon   Drawing Room

Gallery

Apartment

Library   Hall   Dining Room

50 feet

N

c Worcestershire. Hagley Hall, 1753

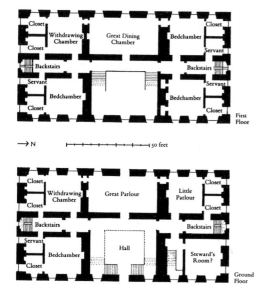

Closet   Closet
Withdrawing   Great Dining   Bedchamber
Chamber   Chamber
Closet   Servant

Backstairs   Backstairs
Servant   Servant
Bedchamber   Bedchamber
Closet   Closet
                                        First
                                        Floor

→ N   50 feet

Closet   Closet
Withdrawing   Great Parlour   Little
Chamber   Parlour
Closet   Closet

Backstairs   Backstairs
Servant
               Hall   Steward's
Bedchamber   Room?
Closet
                                        Ground
                                        Floor

b Berkshire. Coleshill House, 1650

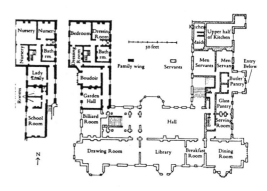

Nursery Nursery   Bedroom Dressing   Kitchen Upper half
                              Room   of Kitchen
Nursery   Bath   Dressing   Bath   50 feet   Maids
               rm.   Room   rm.
                                            Family wing   Servants   Men   Men   Entry
Rooms   Lady   Boudoir   Servants Servant Below
           Emily
                              Garden   Butler
           School   Hall   Pantry
           Room   Billiard Room   Glass
                    Room   Pantry
                                              Hall   Serving
N   Room
↑   Drawing Room   Library   Breakfast   Dining
                                      Room   Room

d Nottinghamshire. Thoresby Hall, 1864

The development of the ground plan of the country house (from Mark Girouard, *Life in the English Country House*, 1978) an expression of the new political élan of the aristocracy. The development of the landscape garden now marked an urban colonization of the countryside. The Palladian stately home was, in a sense, a copy of an urban dwelling printed in the still sleeping agricultural landscape. Between 1720 and 1724 this *villeggiatura* resulted in an explosive increase in the number of estates. Moreover there was a clear emancipatory trend which made owning land a status symbol for the urban commercial classes. With a healthy financial economy and flourishing trade, money was available that had to be sensibly and safely invested: estates were seen as the answer.

The years after 1760 were peak ones for the laying out of parks on a large scale. Trade and industry, however, shifted the main sources of prosperity to the city, thereby undermining the economic reason behind the country estate's very existence. Thus few new estates were founded after 1770.

The ideology of 18th-century colonization was aimed at improving the estate's economic structure. The new lords of the manor were good stewards of their estates. Initially they were especially interested in plantations rather than agriculture. Between 1710 and 1720 the ornamental farm was popular, even if it was chiefly due to aesthetic motives. Riskins and Castle Howard had modern, scientifically established kitchen gardens. Stephen Switzer's extensive rural gardening and Lord Bathurst's forest gardening in Cirencester were forestry experiments, inspired by tradition and status but also by the expectation that wood in times of uncertainty would yield a profit. However, forests have seldom produced a good return on investment, one of the reasons being the import of cheap wood from the Baltic States.

In the second half of the 18th century the landowners felt that agricultural modernization could strengthen the economic basis of their estates. Originally the appropriating of the common lands and the cultivation of the wasteland mainly led to more tenant farmers and an increase in revenues for the landowners. From around 1770 onwards the latter set up experimental farms on their estates in which new drainage techniques, improvements to fertilization methods and crop rotation were tried out. This resulted not only in more tenant farmers but in an increase in productivity and higher rents. In this way the landscape garden was an important factor in the changing technological conditions of the countryside. Thomas Coke, or Coke of Holkham, later Earl of Leicester, turned a bleak expanse of grassy heathland into fertile farming land by ploughing up the underlying calcareous loam and spreading it over the sandy top soil. He helped his new tenant farmers do the same thing in exchange for a higher rent, so that in 15 years' time he had quadrupled the return on his estate. Jethro Tull created a revolution with his sowing drill, while Robert Bakewell discovered new ways of breeding and laid the basis for a new irrigation technique. The second Lord Townshend, nicknamed 'Turnip Townshend' because he encouraged the growing of turnips, designed a crop rotation system, which ensured that no field would be left lying fallow: he grew wheat in the first year, turnips or beet in the second, barley or oats in the third and peas, beans or clover in the fourth year. Improvements almost doubled the income of the landowners, which contributed greatly to the popularity of the 18th-century estate.

The medieval residences of the nobility were power houses, their authority based on military strength, administrative control and command over a territory. The house afforded a shelter for the landowner's entire household, including his staff. A feature of the house was the Hall in which communal meals were taken and disputes settled (for this reason the houses were often known as 'Halls'). The late 18th-century country house, however, was distinguished by its 'green baize door', a padded door separating the servant's wing from the landowner's private quarters. Changes like this reflect a social and cultural evolution in country living that had been taking place.

The breaking down of the rigid, social hierarchy of the household affected the design of the 18th-century country house. Coleshill House in Berkshire, designed around 1650 by Roger Pratt, was a milestone in this evolution. Pratt's discovery was to place the parlour on the ground floor and the great chamber on the first floor, in the centre of the house, as a space across two floors and to incorporate the main staircase into this. Though this made the entrance more impressive, the Hall of the barons was thereby lost. Instead the great chamber on the first floor was used for communal meals.

The formal assemblies for concerts, conversation or other happenings gradually made way for more informal forms of social contact, such as house parties and circulating around the various quarters of the house. This also had an effect on the design of the landscape garden: the circuit walk was the direct counterpart to circulating around the house. There was a walking circuit in the Pleasure Grounds and a longer circuit through the park, intended for equestrians and carriages.

More rooms were increasingly used for special purposes, such as the morning room, the billiard room and the smoking room. Around 1770 the main spaces of the house were in direct relation to the garden in the form of rooms on the ground floor and balconies. The *piano nobile*, still on the first floor of the classical house, was now on the ground floor, while the servants' quarters also dropped down one floor to the basement. The houses sometimes sank literally into the ground; a dry moat around the house was necessary to enable light to enter the souterrain. This thwarted the country nobleman's contact with the garden and was later solved by allocating a wing of the house for the servants, thus creating an asymmetric arrangement of the layout. The garden came into the house in the form of potted plants and vases of flowers or even took up an entire room in the form of a conservatory.

Thomas Hill's *The Gardener's Labyrinth* from 1577 depicted the garden from the Tudor Age as a walled parterre. In the 17th century the treatises on gardening were practical, aimed at facilitating country living. They brought the influence of the waterworks from the Italian gardens, the larger scale of the French ones and the parterre arrangement and embellishment of Dutch garden design, though generally retaining indigenous elements such as mazes and mounts. In *The English Husbandman* from 1613, Gervase Markham recommended decorating the parterre with various motifs which played an important role in English garden design and which were used until Kent introduced a 'modern taste'. In 1664 John Evelyn, in his *Sylva, A Discourse of Forest Trees*, advised landowners to decorate their estates with 'trees of venerable shade and profitable timber'. From 1700 onwards this led to the import of various tree species such as Mediterranean oaks, pines from Corsica, Georgia and New England as well as spruce from Scandinavia and North America. New horticulturists specialized in cultivating, among others, lime, maple, walnut, horse chestnut, laurel, mulberry, cedar of Lebanon and cyprus.

In the 18th century the treatises entirely changed character. Due to colonization, design theory was aimed at economic development and a new, representative design for country estates. Echoing the views of Joseph Addison and Shaftesbury, Timothy Nourse in his *Campania foelix* of 1700 recommended siting a country house in an open landscape. A happy life in the country was only possible in a rural setting. Wherever possible, fencing had to be abandoned in favour of an unrestricted view of the surrounding landscape and to make it appear as if it were all a part of the garden. In this sense Stephen Switzer's *The Nobleman, Gentleman and Gardener's Recreation*, published in 1715, was a breakthrough. In his *Ichnographia rustica* of 1718, in which

Switzer pragmatically elaborates on the economic bases of the estate, his design studies have a more natural style.

Over the next decades landscape architecture evolved from being paradigmatic to experimental. The application of classical rules made way for design experiments, which extended not only into the garden but also into the landscape. Conventional garden theory could not entirely keep up with these experiments. The poet William Shenstone did not call his 1764 writings on the treatment of the landscape garden *Some Unconnected Thoughts on Gardening* for nothing. In 1765 Thomas Whately wrote his *Observations on Modern Gardening*, while Horace Walpole published his *Essays on Modern Gardening* in 1785 in which the treatise was changed into a 'critique of landscape architecture'. At the end of the 18th century, the main concern was with the aesthetic principles of landscape architecture. A battle raged around the 'picturesque', which was somewhat at odds with the demands of reality. Richard Payne Knight published *An Analytical Enquiry into the Principles of Taste* in 1794; in that same year Uvedale Price wrote his *Essays on the Picturesque*. In 1803 Humphry Repton replied with his essay *Observations on the Theory and Practice of Landscape Gardening* in which the balance between the picturesque and common sense was restored.

In the beginning of the 19th century garden art became a science. John Claudius Loudon, for instance, wrote his *Encyclopaedia of Gardening* in 1822. There were magazines such as Loudon's *The Gardener's Magazine* in which gardening was popularized. Interest shifted from the laying out of country estates to the Victorian suburbs. In 1836 Loudon wrote *The Suburban Gardener and Villa Companion*. From 1831 onwards Joseph Paxton drew attention to design in the public domain in industrial towns, such as the park and subscription gardens in his magazine *Horticultural Register*. The landscape garden was already no longer an important assignment.

THE PICTURESQUE TRADITION

Palladianism, as an expression of a more liberal society in Britain and the emergence of the Whigs, was an unprecedented force. It became influential at court and showed all the signs of a takeover. The first onslaught came in 1718-19 when Colin Campbell, shortly before Lord Burlington's second trip to Italy in 1718, filched the job of chairman of the Board of Works from Christopher Wren, thus passing over Vanbrugh. The second came when Burlington returned from abroad with William Kent on his side. These new politics went hand in hand with an impressive publishing agenda.

In the first part of the 18th century a number of influential publications appeared in support of the new artistic movement. In 1715 the Venetian Giacomo Leoni, who was living in England, published the first part of his study on Palladio. In the same year Colin Campbell published *Vitruvius britannicus*, or *The British Architect*, dedicated to George I, which was a manifesto of the new movement as well as a direct attack on Baroque art, which during the 17th century had served the absolutism of state and church throughout Europe. The poet Alexander Pope and the painter Jonathan Richardson the Elder wrote similar manifestoes related to literature and art.

Part III of Campbell's *Vitruvius britannicus* from 1725 was devoted to the country house, which meanwhile had become immensely popular. Palladianism was now the architectonic form with which the oligarchy of Whigs identified and the book proudly presented the houses built in this style. In fact, the first steps in the Palladian development of the 18th-century country house were taken by Campbell himself with the prototype Wanstead mansion in Essex (1714-15, demolished in 1822), in which, according to John Summerson, the house was conceived for the first time as a palatial unity. Houghton Hall later followed for Robert Walpole, Britain's prime minister (1720), and Holkham Hall (also in Norfolk) for the Earl of Leicester based on a design

Roger Pratt. Coleshill House, 1649-62 (demolished)

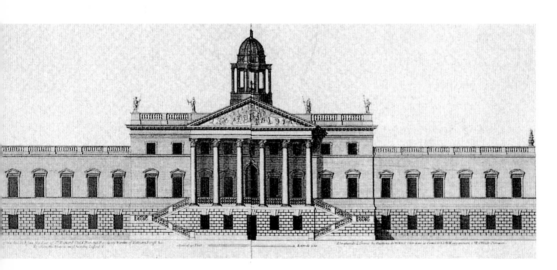

Colin Campbell. Wanstead House, 1714-15 (demolished 1822)

by William Kent (1734). With Mereworth, a derivative version of the Villa Rotonda at Vicenza, Campbell achieved a new effect in landscape architecture by placing the villa on the garden's main axis. The standard type of the Georgian villa was resolved in Campbell's third design for Stourhead House (1721-25). In 1746 the development was completed.

The natural landscape design was the obvious stylistic counterpart of Classicism, as is apparent, among other books, in Robert Castell's *The Villas of the Ancients Illustrated*, published in 1728. The Palladian country house found its answer in Kent's experimental classical landscapes, which were rooted in the differentiated visualization of the pictorial tradition. This ideal harks back to picturesque conventions that had already been developed in set designs and murals since Roman antiquity. Two main themes were always in the foreground: the theatre and human response to nature. The theatre dealt with the close relationship between observer and stage management. A second theme touched upon the tension between the paradisiacal ideal of absolute harmony with nature, the unfettered pastoral happiness, on the one hand, and a disturbed relationship on the other, in which the chaos in nature is seen as a threat.

Eighteenth-century landscape compositions are usually associated with the paintings of Claude le Lorrain and Nicolas Poussin (1594-1665), especially those after 1624, as well as with those of Salvator Rosa (1615-73) and Gaspard Dughet (1615-75; sometimes known as Gaspard Poussin), in which the Roman landscapes were idealized in the garden's iconic references. Having found their way to the landscape garden, these references were linked with the visual characteristics of the English agricultural landscape, with the expanse of the open fields, the spatial effect of the rolling hills, the winding paths, the northern light and the atmospheric perspective. The latter was once described by Sigfried Giedion, after having seen *Simplon Pass*, a painting by Joseph M.W. Turner from around 1840, as 'a humid atmosphere which dematerializes the landscape and dissolves it into infinity'.

Theatre, which is inextricably linked with the picturesque tradition, played an influential role in painting, architecture and landscape architecture – the spatial evolution of which made a link between these arts possible. The three genres of Greek theatre in the 5th century BC were tragedy, satire and comedy. Satire, which takes its name from the chorus comprising satyrs (half man, half beast), was performed in a landscape setting. In 1545 Sebastiano Serlio designed a simple theatre space, based on Baldassare Peruzzi's perspective designs, in which the stage and the backdrop were linked with the auditorium by a real perspective. He, like Vitruvius, distinguished three types of stage space: the *scena tragica* for tragedy, the *scena comica* for comedy and the *scena satirica* for satire, represented as a garden with rustic objects such as grottoes, rockeries and trees. Kent virtually copied the *scena satirica* in his landscape gardens, for instance in Venus's Vale at Rousham.

In a metaphorical sense this landscape theatre was intended to allow the observer to 'participate' in the performance. During the 17th and 18th centuries garden design, painting and theatre design were fused together in the concept of the *theatrum mundi* in which the world – in its wondrous as well as ordinary aspects – was graphically represented. The theatre and the garden were interchangeable in the sense that both were a 'collection' or compendium (the garden as a collection of curiosities) as well as a stage. Urban life was also a stage: William Hogarth depicted the city as a continuous theatrical performance. In the landscape garden, Hogarth's 'stage of life' was placed on a cultural level.

250

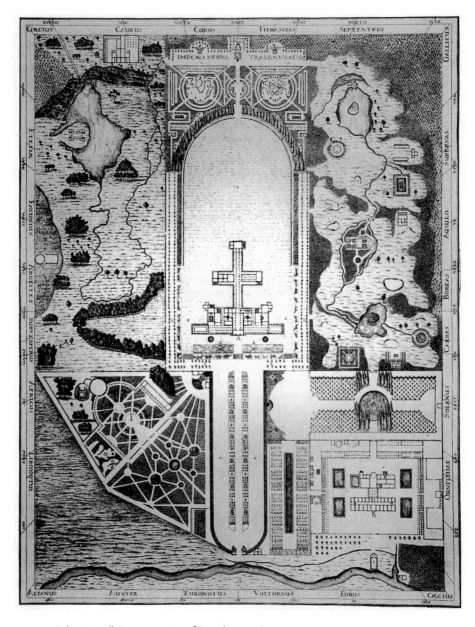

Robert Castell. Reconstruction of Tusculum, 1728

For those living in the 18th century, the English landscape had mythical origins. There were the incomprehensible symbols of the Stone and Bronze ages, such as Stonehenge and the White Horses on the chalk slopes of Salisbury Plain. There were also the remains of the Celtic landscape from the Iron Age, such as the fields and forests which according to tradition were inhabited by Druids, the tumuli, the hill fortresses and *oppidia*, such as Danebury in the chalk hills of Hampshire. Then there were the sacred open spots of the early medieval landscape where the great kings gave counsel or did battle. Together they formed the *topoi* in a mythical landscape that had no geometric elements and which was labyrinthic, infinite and without scale.

The Celts played an important role in 18th-century thinking on design. Their language, social structure and customs were maintained in England after the collapse of the Roman empire. After the 11th century their culture was continually threatened but held out in England's remoter parts. Celtic art, steeped in complexity and intricacy, derived inspiration from the spiral form and incorporated this into complicated fabrics with imaginative, spiritual motifs. The 18th-century Gothic style was linked to this culture.

The *locus* was visible in the road structure, the towns and the rationality of the Georgian landscape and anchored in Roman cultivation. It was a rational concept of place, which was geometrically determined by the place in the design matrix – in the man-made spatial and architectonic system.

In the 18th-century landscape garden the *topos*, the sacred spots in the mythical landscape, clashed with the *locus*, the rational basis of cultivation and garden design. The mythical landscape mingled with the rational. The *genius loci* was a hybrid concept in the landscape garden that encompassed both the *topos* and the *locus*.

The work of Lancelot 'Capability' Brown (1716-83) lent a stylized form and content to the landscape garden between 1750 and 1780. Brown came from an entirely different background than William Kent, who embodied the pictorial tradition and the rhetorical style of the early 18th century. Brown was a gardener but he was more a pragmatist than a theorist. The basis of Brown's design lay in, what were for the time, generally accessible notions of beauty, movement and 'representative' natural forms. Christopher Hussey points out that Brown's early career coincides with publications by Hogarth and Burke formulating these aesthetics. Brown began as an independent landscape architect in 1751; William Hogarth published *The Analysis of Beauty* in 1753 and Edmund Burke his *Philosophical Inquiry into the Origins of our Ideas of the Sublime and the Beautiful* in 1756. According to Hussey, Brown's understanding of landscape was so similar to Burke's explanation of beauty and Hogarth's 'serpentine line of beauty' that they represented three complementary expressions of the spirit of the age.

Burke propounded that every emotional experience has a physical basis and he distinguished between two essentially different sensations: the Sublime (challenge, danger, wariness or fear), which was the driving force of the picturesque movement, and the Beautiful (comfort or satisfaction). Smallness, smoothness, gradual variation and delicacy of form were attributes of beauty. His description of beauty strongly resembled the sensation of speed and movement. It is strikingly similar to a landscape by Brown, whose style directly evoked the senses, the visual experience of movement and serenity. Brown focused on the physical and visual features of the natural landscape and gave it an abstract architectonic form. His park landscapes were 'picture planes' upon which the beauty of the natural landscape, stripped of distracting non-essentials, was displayed.

In the 17th century England's natural landscape was, generally speaking, still not an object of artistic or aesthetic appreciation. The rationalization of the agricul-

Scena Satirica. From Sebastiano Serlio, *Libri d'Architettura*, 1545

tural landscape, however, evoked counterforces in which nature was identified with human destiny and became glorified as well as romanticized. There was renewed appreciation for the rugged and untamed hilly landscape, previously considered 'wasteland'. This was accompanied by a new kind of tourism in England, an extension of the tradition of visiting stately estates, that had already existed since the 17th century, and pioneered, among others, by Celia Fiennes, Daniël Defoe, Richard Pococke and Arthur Young. Around 1770, the travel lust among the English to visit wild natural landscape markedly increased. Their travel objectives were the Alps and the Pyrenees as well as England's Lake District. According to Gilpin the wild landscape of the Lake District lent itself to a painting and was 'picturesque', in contrast to Brown's 'groomed' landscape. Using a spherical mirror, the so-called Claude glass, an attractive landscape could be cut out and its reflection painted.

Richard Payne Knight and Uvedale Price, both country squires, developed a theory on the picturesque. Alongside Burke's 'Sublime and Beautiful' the picturesque was considered somewhat contrived as an independent, aesthetic category. One important difference was that while Burke described perception, Price referred to a landscape's visual characteristics. Knight later distanced himself from the latter view, maintaining that it was untenable to regard 'picturesque' as a quality of a landscape.

From around 1770 the picturesque began to be part of landscape design and a new wild garden came into fashion with fallen trees and hollows overgrown with ferns, set in a natural landscape with spectacular geological features like steep ledges and ravines. Humphry Repton, after much deliberation, came to realize that the relationship between landscape design and painting was not so close as the theorists of the picturesque made it appear. He believed it had its practical basis, after all, in gardening. Nonetheless, after 1800 it was the accepted view, to which Repton also subscribed, that a house should be bounded by a beautiful garden backing onto a more or less natural, picturesque park from where the agricultural landscape had disappeared.

The picturesque marked the end of the classical landscape ideal of the Enlightenment. The march of industrialization in the mid-18th century began to obscure the Arcadian dream. The landscape garden can be placed between the Arcadian ideal of country life and the emerging industrial metropolis. The form developed on the knife edge of the picturesque tradition and the landscape architectonic experimentation of the Enlightenment, in which a more abstract and more dynamic spatial technique evolved. In a wider context the landscape garden paved the way for the 19th-century urban revolution. The picturesque landscape theatre profoundly determined the appearance of 19th and 20th-century cities. Its devices appear essentially modern; the decline of rural life and the arrival of the industrial society marked the beginning of an 'urban' landscape architecture, which even in our own age has not fully explored its great gamut of possibilities.

Henderskelfe *c.* 1694

Castle Howard

I believe here will be (beyond all contest) the Top Seat and Garden of England.
Vanbrugh in a letter to Lord Carlisle, 1721

The landscape of Castle Howard still makes an overwhelming impression, after almost 300 years, to those approaching it for the first time. Contemporaries also regarded it as extraordinary and remarkable, while for us the spaciousness of the Carlisle landscape still has a special significance. Christopher Hussey regarded Castle Howard as a 'masterpiece of the Heroic Age of English landscape architecture', a direct architectonic evocation of the Elysium of Greek mythology. Castle Howard surpasses the categories of 'garden' or even 'landscape'. Visitors to the estate are confronted by a battle of building styles derived from Classical Greece, Palladianism and the colourful history of England. The buildings and statues in the landscape were the prerequisites for a perfectly stage-managed theatre. The English critic Horace Walpole echoed philosopher Edmund Burke's sentiments in referring to the staged infinity of Castle Howard as 'sublime'. Wherein lies the secret of the Carlisle landscape? How was this great scenic creation achieved?

HISTORY
The Carlisle landscape is the result of a creative collaboration spanning over 25 years between the owner of the estate, Charles Lord Carlisle, and his architects, John Vanbrugh and Nicholas Hawksmoor. Carlisle was the initiator with a sixth sense for landscape, while Vanbrugh's conceptual genius created exuberant and powerful theatrical compositions. Hawksmoor, a skilful architect, was able to translate Vanbrugh's dramatic ideas into pure architectonic creations which have a remarkable allure.

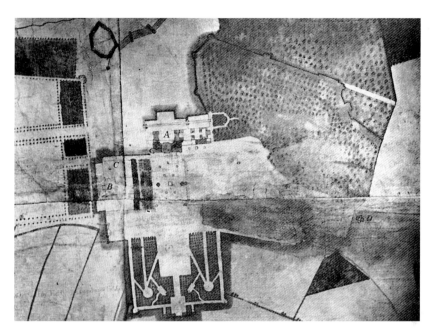

Map of the estate *c.* 1727

Charles Howard, 3rd Earl of Carlisle, was born in 1669 in Naworth, a small castle on the border of England and Scotland. Carlisle rapidly carved out a career for himself at court and held various key positions. In 1702 he withdrew from public life and devoted his energies to Castle Howard until his death in 1738. Castle Howard was intended as a visual affirmation of the position and history of the Howard lineage and its tradition of executing great works. Naworth Castle was considered unsuitable for this and Carlisle's eye fell on Henderskelfe Castle near York, an ancient property of the Dacres, which the Howards had owned since the reign of Queen Elizabeth I through the marriage of his ancestor Lord William Howard to Elizabeth Dacre. Moreover, the fertile land and valuable woods of Henderskelfe Castle seemed a profitable investment for the future. Building was also made necessary by a fire that gutted the castle in 1693, leaving it unsuitable as a permanent abode.

John Vanbrugh of Vanbrook (1647-1726) was the son of a prosperous and cultured merchant in Chester, and grandson of Van Brugg, a Protestant immigrant from Ghent. In 1683 Vanbrugh joined the infantry under Lord Huntingdon, where he rose to the rank of captain and by all accounts led a roguish existence. In 1689 he was imprisoned by the French for three years in the Bastille as he was suspected of spying. After his release and discharge from the army, Vanbrugh became a quite successful dramatist and as such took an active role in the artistic world of London.

Vanbrugh was a man of the world: convivial, warmhearted and about the same age as Carlisle. As a member of the patriotic Kit-Cat Club, an exclusive dining club for Whigs, he was on a friendly footing with the most influential political and cultural personalities of his day, such as the poet Joseph Addison and the dramatist William Congreve as well as Carlisle. The Club embraced the Glorious Revolution of 1688 and with that its constitutional principles. Vanbrugh's talent as a playwright made him

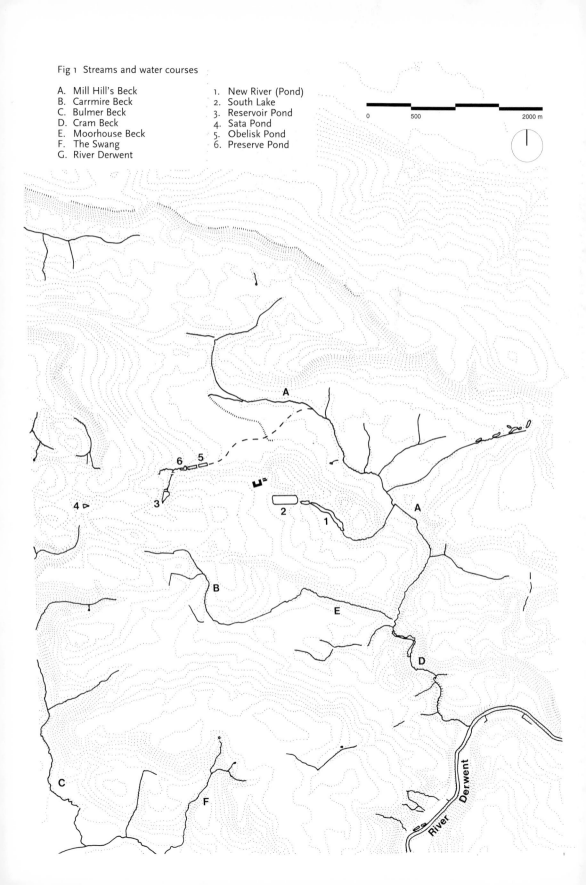

Fig 1 Streams and water courses

A. Mill Hill's Beck
B. Carrmire Beck
C. Bulmer Beck
D. Cram Beck
E. Moorhouse Beck
F. The Swang
G. River Derwent

1. New River (Pond)
2. South Lake
3. Reservoir Pond
4. Sata Pond
5. Obelisk Pond
6. Preserve Pond

0   500   2000 m

valuable to the Whigs, who were out to acquire, as well as demonstrate, new political and cultural status. He was totally inexperienced as an architect when Carlisle commissioned him to build a new house in 1698 and Castle Howard was his first architectural creation.

Nicholas Hawksmoor (1661-1736) was a more 'simple' personality and was far less acquainted with his clientele than Vanbrugh. He was by no means a subordinate or an assistant: in technical terms he was Vanbrugh's superior. Hawksmoor began collaborating with Vanbrugh around 1700, becoming his partner and later his friend. After Vanbrugh's death in 1726 he became Carlisle's chief architect. The original division of roles was consistently maintained for the outside world: Hawksmoor was there to underpin Vanbrugh's ideas, no matter how gradually they began to coincide with his own.

GEOMORPHOLOGY AND TOPOGRAPHY

Castle Howard lies 24 kilometres north-east of York in the Howardian Hills, between the vales of Pickering and York. North of the hills lies the Jurassic Plateau of the Yorkshire Moors and on the south front the chalk plateau of the Yorkshire Wolds. The rolling Howardian Hills are formed of soft slate and sand with narrow seams of grit and limestone, varying in height between 150 and 350 metres. To the north the hills are bounded by the steeper-sided Slingsby and Coneysthorpe banks, which on the north-west side become the higher plateau of the Yorkshire Moors. The River Derwent flows past the south-east foot of the Howardian Hills at Malton.

The central part of the Howardian Hills is saucer-shaped and slopes eastward. In the middle of this the house lies on a saddle-shaped tract of land that ends on the east side in a round hill (Wray Wood). This was the site of old Henderskelfe Castle and the hamlet of Henderskelfe.

The name Henderskelfe, literally meaning 'one-hundred springs', refers to the water-retaining strata; the becks around Castle Howard reflect the abundant presence of water. The South Lake and the New River are fed by springs; the Great Lake, north of the house, was created by damming a beck on the north-east side of the valley. This is fed by the Cascade Ponds via the Obelisk Ponds and the higher situated fish ponds at The Dairies, which together form a visual unity with the lake; it is also probably fed by running underground water on its north-west side. The water is carried away in a south-east direction via Cram Beck, which discharges into the River Derwent (fig. 1).

The shape of the earlier Henderskelfe village is documented in a drawing from around 1694. The new house was built on the east side next to Henderskelfe Castle. The old village street was transformed into The Broad Walk, while the eastern part became the Grass Walk. The road from York to Henderskelfe, that went through an area known as The Commons, was abandoned and the earlier country road to Slingsby, which ran across a watershed at Henderskelfe through a small dip of Slingsby Bank, was transformed into the Great Avenue. In this way the topography of Henderskelfe has been preserved in the formal layout of the garden (figs 2 and 3).

THE HOUSE

In 1698 Carlisle asked the architect William Talman (1650-1720) for advice regarding the building of a new house. Together with the garden architect George London (d. 1714), Talman drew up a plan. Carlisle was not impressed by the design and, wanting something different, he then decided to enlist the help of Vanbrugh, who designed an entirely different house and changed its aspect.

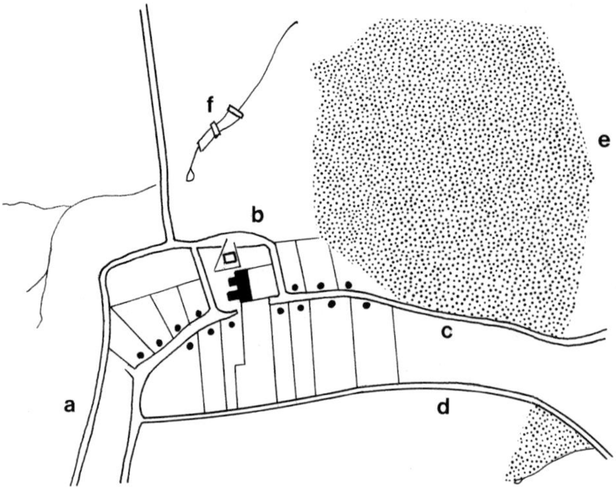

Fig 2 Henderskelfe

a. Country road to York
b. Village street
c. Village street
d. Back street
e. Wray Wood
f. Fish ponds

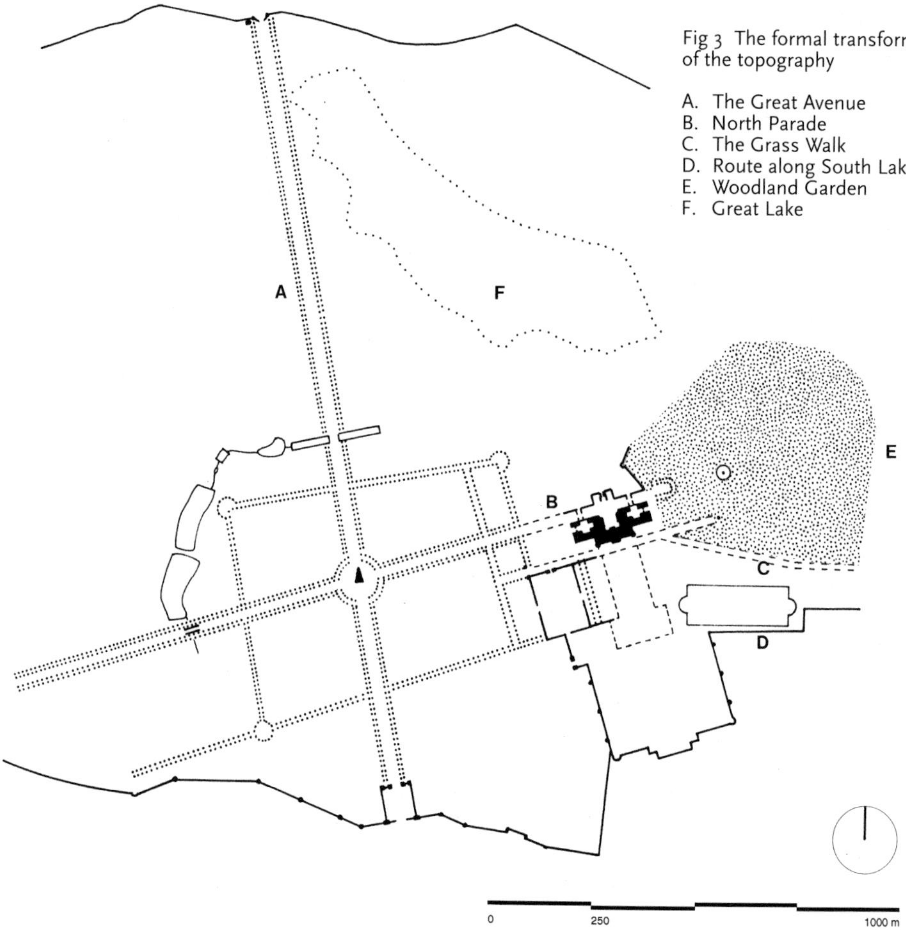

Fig 3 The formal transformation of the topography

A. The Great Avenue
B. North Parade
C. The Grass Walk
D. Route along South Lake
E. Woodland Garden
F. Great Lake

0   250   1000 m

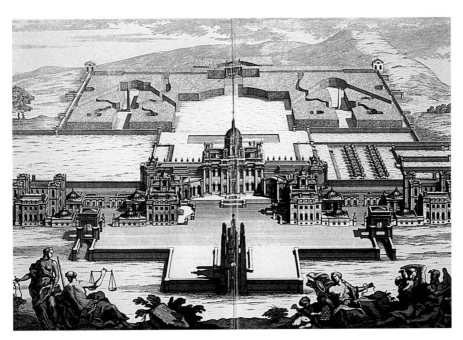

The Grand Design. From Colin Campbell, *Vitruvius brittanicus*, Vol III, 1725

In Talman and London's proposal the house directly faced an approach running from east to west, in the same direction as the old Henderskelfe Castle. Wray Wood lay at the rear of the house so that the courtyard was protected from the northeast wind. The garden was a formal one with *rond-points* and diagonal avenues that intersected each other in the courtyard, which was the visual pivot of the design. The formal ponds and canals of the parterre on the north front were aligned with the courtyard, which was so that from the house the waterworks could always be seen from an angle. A kitchen garden and a lawn was designed for the south front of the house while a radial design was planned for Wray Wood. On the south-west front of the house a circular model village had been designed, which according to Hussey was the first English prototype for a landscape garden. However, this was never built (fig. 4).

In Vanbrugh's proposal the house was turned by a quarter so that the front façade faced open space. This change of aspect is perhaps Vanbrugh's most important contribution to the development of the landscape garden. This ostensibly small modification actually implied a radical break with the formal tradition in that it assumed that the starting point for the stage management was not a formal scheme but the view, and, in a more profound sense, the morphology of the Howardian Hills. Thus the given irregularity of the site, which was later always being elaborated upon, became part of the layout in a single stroke (fig. 5).

One advantage of the design was that the garden side and the parterre were exposed to the sun. Vanbrugh drew attention to this by using a different colonnade for the garden façade and treating it in a more flamboyant manner than the front one, which gave rise to caustic comments from the neoclassicists. Vanbrugh laconically defended himself by remarking that nobody could ever take in the two façades in one glance anyway. One practical objection to the design was that the house and the fore-

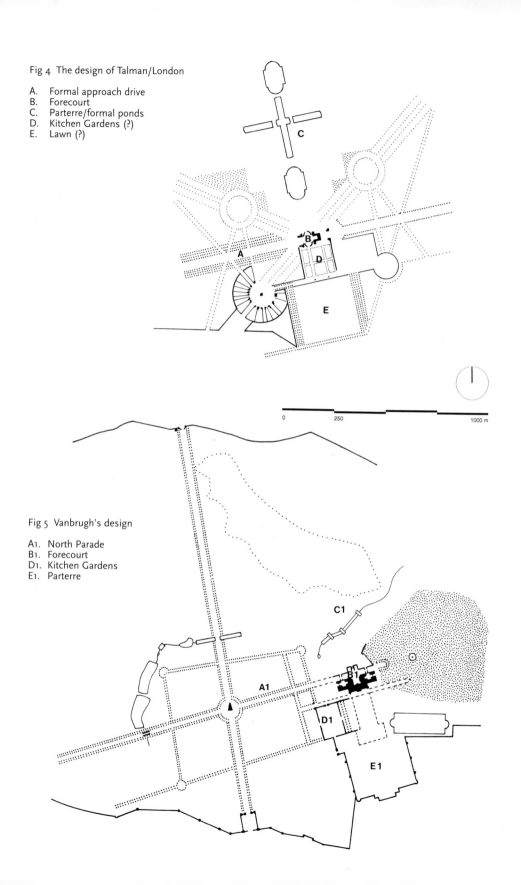

Fig 4 The design of Talman/London

A. Formal approach drive
B. Forecourt
C. Parterre/formal ponds
D. Kitchen Gardens (?)
E. Lawn (?)

Fig 5 Vanbrugh's design

A1. North Parade
B1. Forecourt
D1. Kitchen Gardens
E1. Parterre

0   250   1000 m

View from the Temple of the Four Winds (photograph by J.K.M. Te Boekhorst)

court, contrary to the conventions of the country house, were exposed to England's dreaded north-east wind. As Laurence Whistler once wrote: 'In England, views are windy. The tender glories of English distance have to be paid for in warm clothing'. Carlisle accepted this objection as inevitable. Notwithstanding, Vanbrugh, for his part, went to a great deal of trouble to make a comfortable and energy-conserving house.

The house was modelled after Palladio's Villa Trissino in Meledo (never completed), with a central block and protruding side wings which enclose the forecourt. The building mass is extremely articulated and lively-looking with a crescendo in the slim dome of the central block. Originally the forecourt was walled and had fortified entrance gates, but this idea was dropped during the building phase. On further consideration Vanbrugh decided against an ascending head-on approach to the house. In his mind the view to the north front had already been transformed into an impressive panorama with the Great Lake. However, it was to be a further 70 years before this vision became a reality: the lake was only laid out between 1795 and 1799.

THE FORMAL LAYOUT

The layout for Castle Howard consisted of a grouping of three different elements: a cross of avenues, a formal arrangement of the house with the parterre and a kitchen garden. These elements were held together by a square space with lawns on a level part of the Henderskelfe Hills (the Commons), enclosed on three sides by a sequence of woods. This space was divided in four by the approach drive (later the Great Avenue) and the North Parade, which intersected each other in the middle. The Pyramid Gate from 1719 was built on the edge of the level area, while in 1714 an obelisk was erected on the crossroads in memory of the 1st Duke of Marlborough, the victor of Blenheim (fig. 6).

Fig 6 The formal layout

1. North Parade
2. Entrance Gates
3. Broad Walk
4. Parterre
5. Wilderness (woods within the walls)
6. Kitchen Garden
7. Castellated wall

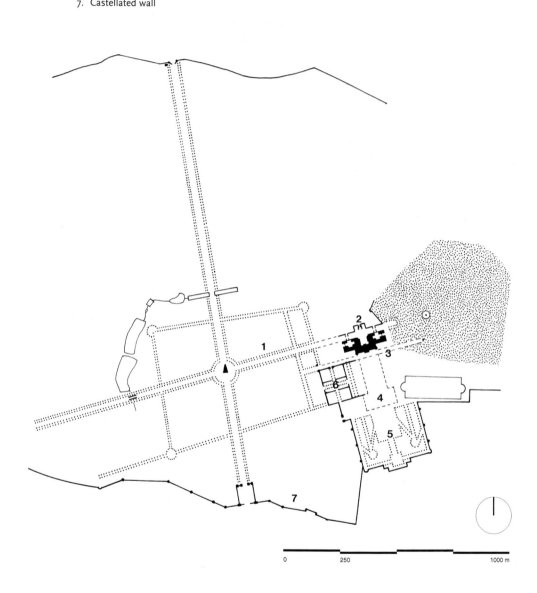

0   250   1000 m

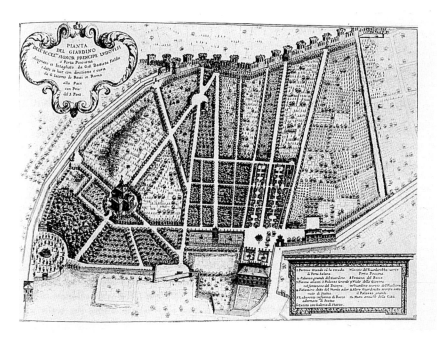

Villa Ludovisi in Rome. From Giovanni Battista Falda, *Li Giardini di Roma*, 1683

The Great Avenue and the North Parade along with the principle axis of the house and parterre form the lines of an imaginary grid that reflects the natural landscape of the Howardian Hills. Around the principle axis this grid merges with the design matrix of the house.

The parterre, under which most of Henderskelfe lies buried, forms the second element of the layout. Its division is a transformation of the model of the walled Venetian garden, which was worked out in a tripartite zoning system. At Castle Howard this manifested itself in the form of steps, a formal pattern of diagonal, tapering obelisks and a Wilderness or 'Woods within the wall', with a stylized maze after the French model. The original parterre covered a total of 30 hectares – which is twice as large as the present one – and was almost certain to have been laid out as shown in part III of Colin Campbell's *Vitruvius brittanicus* from 1725. The dismantling of the parterre in 1760 was in keeping with the evolution of the Carlisle landscape: the wilderness serving as an *amora bosco* in the layout was made redundant when this function was taken over by Wray Wood. The present parterre, which was laid out in 1890, is a simplified version of a more detailed design with a fountain (new Pleasure Grounds) by William Nesfield (1793-1881) in 1850.

Around 1705 the kitchen garden, the third element of the formal layout, was fitted between the axial intersection of the lawns and the formal parterre. Much attention was given to the architectonic detailing. The contrast between this element and the open character of the rest of the landscape garden is striking. The kitchen garden was an 18th-century revival of the *giardino segreto* of the Renaissance villa.

THE WOODLAND GARDEN

Wray Wood, with 66 hectares of oak and beech trees, dominated the entire site from the beginning of the project. Around 1700 it consisted of enormous trees over a cen-

Fig 7 Woodland gardens

A. Wray Wood
1. Temple of Venus
2. Temple of the Four Winds
3. Fountain

B. Pretty Wood
1. Four Faces
2. Pyramid

C. Mount Sion Wood
D. Lowdy Hill Wood
E. Ready Wood
F. East Moor Banks

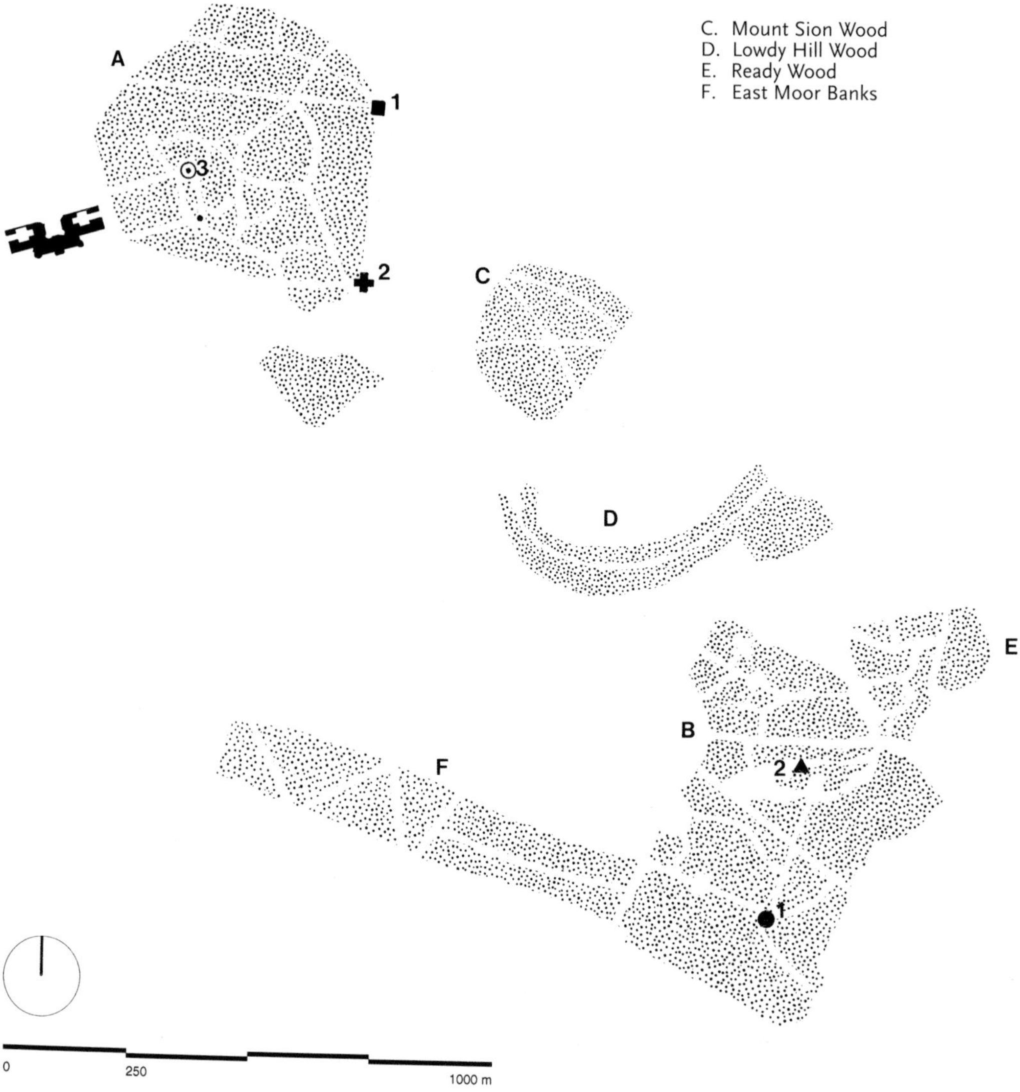

A

○3

■1

✚2

C

D

E

B

2▲

●1

F

0   250   1000 m

tury old and between 25 and 30 metres high, planted during the Elizabethan Age. The original idea of having the Broad Walk continue into Wray Wood was quickly abandoned. In 1706 work began on a woodland garden made according to a 'labyrinthian diverting model'. This experiment was generally regarded as a turning point in the development of the English landscape garden, some 15 years before Kent created something similar in the Elysian Fields at Stowe. At the peak of its development between 1718 and 1732, Wray Wood comprised a series of spaces linked by meandering paths, which according to John Dixon Hunt was designed after the model of the *amora bosco* at Villa Lante and Villa Pratolino owned by Francesco I de' Medici. The pictorial elements were inspired by Ovid's *Metamorphoses* and the fountains and basins by Stephen Switzer were particularly striking.

Even though it was the first and most important one, Wray Wood was not the only woodland at Castle Howard. Traces of a similar arrangement can also be found in Pretty Wood, Lowdy Hill Wood, Ready Wood, East Moor Banks and even Mount Sion Wood. The woodland gardens were already lost at the end of the 18th and early 19th century. During the latter century replanting was carried out in Wray Wood but the garden was never restored to its former glory (fig. 7).

THE SCENOGRAPHY OF THE GREAT AVENUE

The Great Avenue, stretching for more than six kilometres, is one of the most stunning designs in the Carlisle landscape. Developed in phases to become an autonomous creation, it derives its scenic architectonic significance largely from the way it reveals the morphology of the natural landscape. The avenue bisects and reveals the geological structure, which would have remained hidden in an east-west setting. Its length makes it possible to visually gauge the scale of the Howardian Hills between the vales of York and Pickering.

The Great Avenue was designed with the visitors arriving from York in mind, which explains why the screens were arranged from south to north. Carrmire Gate spans the avenue in a hollow and then the avenue climbs to the Pyramid Gate on the edge of the plateau of Henderskelfe, with a castellated wall on both sides. From Carrmire Gate the Marlborough Obelisk at the junction of the Great Avenue and North Parade can be seen through the opening of the Pyramid Gate. From the obelisk the terrain descends again and, past the Obelisk Ponds, the avenue runs along the lake shore until reaching the north entrance of the estate. It then ascends Slingsby Bank and, without any landmarks, becomes part of the local road network.

The pictorial scenography of the Great Avenue can be understood as a 'decomposition' of the formal model of axial symmetry. While at Vaux-le-Vicomte the principle axis complies entirely with the optical laws of a central perspective, so that each visual step on the axis was designed using a three-dimensional decor of surfaces and fixtures to frame a vista, the scenography of the Great Avenue is largely determined by the stimulating 'conflict' between the avenue and the dramatic geology of the Howardian Hills (fig. 8).

The architectonic set pieces on the axis form a series of compositions that correspond with the prominent points in the natural morphology of the landscape. The choice of a rustic gate as a motif in the valley of Carmire Beck instead of a bridge, like at the Obelisk Ponds or at the Oxford Bridge and Waters at Stowe, can be explained as a wish to announce the Pyramid Gate (the former entrance of the estate), thereby visualizing the extensiveness and status of the estate.

The first building phase of the Great Avenue covered the tract of land stretching from the north entrance to the Pyramid Gate. In the second phase the Great Avenue was extended. This segment was called the South Avenue, which stretched as

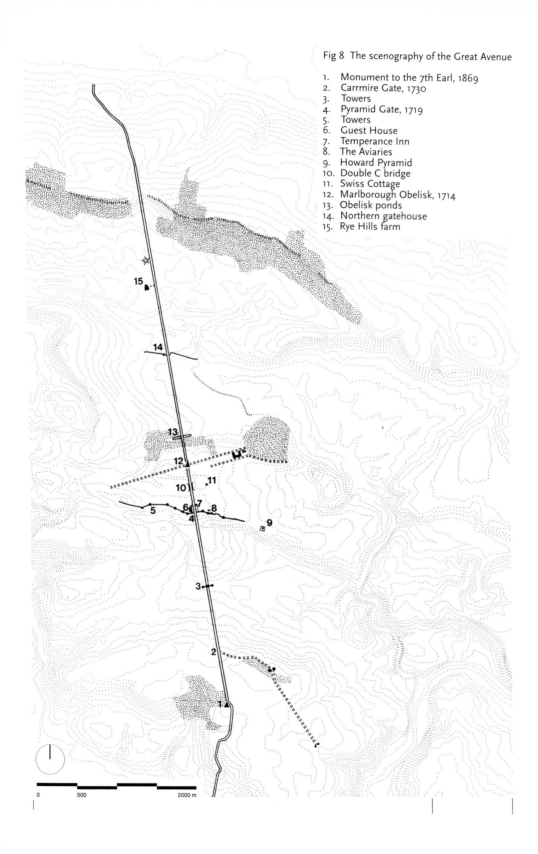

Fig 8 The scenography of the Great Avenue

1. Monument to the 7th Earl, 1869
2. Carrmire Gate, 1730
3. Towers
4. Pyramid Gate, 1719
5. Towers
6. Guest House
7. Temperance Inn
8. The Aviaries
9. Howard Pyramid
10. Double C bridge
11. Swiss Cottage
12. Marlborough Obelisk, 1714
13. Obelisk ponds
14. Northern gatehouse
15. Rye Hills farm

0   500   2000 m

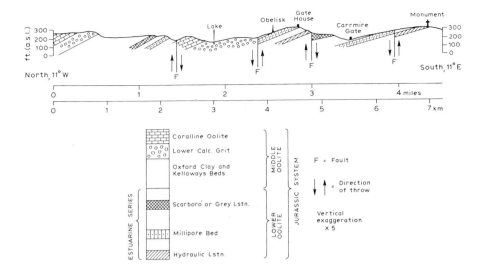

ft.(a.s.l.)

North, 11° W

South, 11° E

| 0 | 1 | 2 | 3 | 4 miles |

| 0 | 1 | 2 | 3 | 4 | 5 | 6 | 7 km |

Coralline Oolite

Lower Calc. Grit

Oxford Clay and
Kellaways Beds

Scarboro' or Grey Lstn.

Millipore Bed

Hydraulic Lstn.

ESTUARINE SERIES

MIDDLE OOLITE

LOWER OOLITE

JURASSIC SYSTEM

F = Fault

= Direction of throw

Vertical exaggeration × 5

267

The geology of the Great Avenue
(from J. Appleton, 'Some Thoughts on the Geology of the Picturesque', 1986)

The Great Avenue with Carrmire Gate and Pyramid Gate

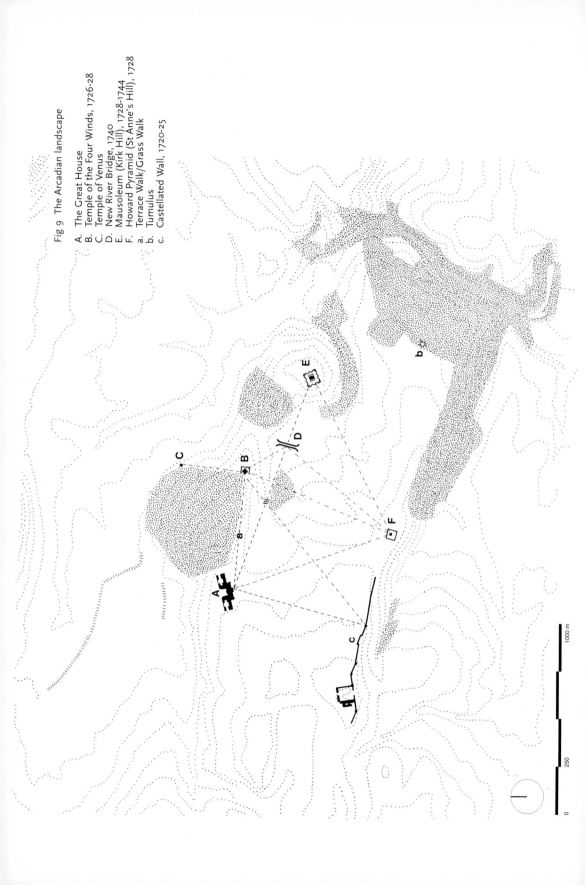

Fig 9 The Arcadian landscape

A. The Great House
B. Temple of the Four Winds, 1726-28
C. Temple of Venus
D. New River Bridge, 1740
E. Mausoleum (Kirk Hill), 1728-1744
F. Howard Pyramid (St Anne's Hill), 1728
a. Terrace Walk/Grass Walk
b. Tumulus
c. Castellated Wall, 1720-25

0   250   1000 m

far as Carrmire Gate, and possibly included the area between the north entrance and Slingsby Bank. Earlier the route from York ran along the Derwent, via a formal avenue, to the top of a ridge south of Welburn, where the visitor, emerging from the woods onto the hill at Exclamation Gate (built by Sir William Chambers in 1770), suddenly had a view of the grand design, with the south front bathed in sunlight which appeared to set the panorama alight. In the Victorian Age the Great Avenue was extended further south to join the local road network. This point was marked in 1869 by a memorial to the 7th Earl. However, Exclamation Gate fell into disuse and this sublime element of the scenography of the Great Avenue was lost forever.

The plantings of the Great Avenue reflect the three phases of its development. From the Pyramid Gate to Slingsby Bank the avenue is planted with double serried rows of lime, a scheme which was probably already employed in the first design and at the North Parade. Between the turning to Welburn and the Pyramid Gate, the avenue is planted with formal clumps of beech (recent replantings). This part of the avenue leads to a rustic corridor of hardwoods as far as the memorial to the 7th Earl. At strategic points along the avenue deliberate gaps in the plantings reveal the view in a transverse direction. The plantings terminate at the top of Slingsby Bank where a commanding view of the agricultural landscape of the Pickering Vale unfolds.

THE ARCADIAN LANDSCAPE

Carlisle and his architects had been preoccupied with Wray Wood, the parterre and the South Lake for almost 20 years. Around 1723 it was felt that these more or less independently developed designs should be placed more in context with each other. The key to this lay in a fortification located on the somewhat protruding south-east corner of Wray Wood, where a commanding view of the surrounding countryside could be taken in. Vanbrugh recognized the important significance of the spot and persistently urged the building of a classical temple in the manner of the Villa Rotonda, while Carlisle had only a rustic, crudely built belvedere in mind.

The Temple of the Four Winds, the Mausoleum and the Howard Pyramid on East Moor Bank have been strategically placed in each other's line of vision and form a visually coherent landscape or natural amphitheatre. The size of the monuments is in keeping with the natural morphology. All three works are symmetrical and are intended to be viewed from different angles. The Temple of the Four Winds is a slim building which, when seen from the Grass Walk and the Temple of Venus, is translucently thrown into relief against the sky. In contrast, the Mausoleum, which can be seen against the backdrop of Slingsby Bank from a great distance, is a quite massive structure, designed to suit the shape and scale of Kirk Hill. The Howard Pyramid appears as a beacon on the long horizontal ridge of St Anne's Hill. While the Temple of the Four Winds is aligned with the south front of the house, the other works in the Arcadian landscape escaped the formal controls of the layout and correspond directly to the morphology of the natural landscape.

The old village road of Henderskelfe was transformed into an informal architectonic route, the Terrace Walk or Grass Walk, which runs from the house to the Temple of the Four Winds and is then absorbed by the Arcadian landscape. From the temple the other monumental buildings can be seen from various angles. Hawksmoor's Mausoleum on Kirk Hill forms the visual climax and because of its scale is in direct conflict with the house. When the New River landscape was designed, a Roman bridge, built around 1740 by Daniel Garret, was placed between the two as a *coulisse* (fig. 9).

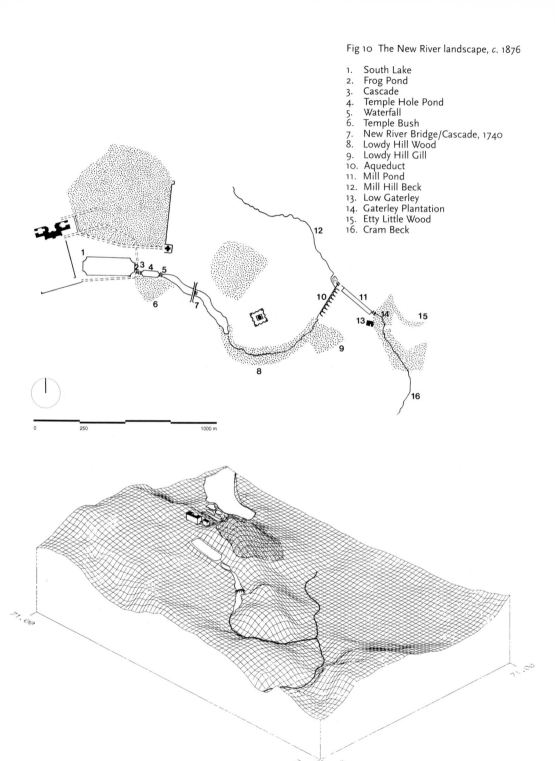

Fig 10 The New River landscape, c. 1876

1. South Lake
2. Frog Pond
3. Cascade
4. Temple Hole Pond
5. Waterfall
6. Temple Bush
7. New River Bridge/Cascade, 1740
8. Lowdy Hill Wood
9. Lowdy Hill Gill
10. Aqueduct
11. Mill Pond
12. Mill Hill Beck
13. Low Gaterley
14. Gaterley Plantation
15. Etty Little Wood
16. Cram Beck

0   250   1000 m

Fig 11 Digital model of the New River landscape

The Temple of the Four Winds

THE NEW RIVER LANDSCAPE

The New River landscape was completed in two phases. From preserved invoices of the time, it appears that work started in 1732 on the excavation of a 'serpentine river that will lose itself in a wood', as John Tracy Atkyns in his book *Iter boreale* (1732) described it. This river was not yet linked with South Lake.

In *c.* 1876 William Nesfield was commissioned to create a new, unified river landscape. He overcame the discrepancies in height between the South Lake and the serpentine river by building a series of ponds and cascades. The original spring in the Temple Hole Bush was hidden and probably used to feed the Temple Hole Pond. The New River landscape deviated from the classic spring/cascade/reflecting pool design, which until then had also been used at Castle Howard, in that the water elements were spread across the layout (fig. 10).

The Arcadian landscape and the New River landscape complement each other and, because of the morphology of the landscape and the Roman bridge, visually merge into a whole. The difference in the three-dimensional effect lies mainly in the vantage point from where the landscape is observed. In the Arcadian landscape one stands on the hilltops and takes in a commanding view of the countryside, while in the New River landscape one finds oneself in the enclosed space of the valley (fig. 11).

THE GREAT SCENIC CREATION

After 1725 Castle Howard became an open design, a landscape garden without visual boundaries, directly linked to the natural landscape by means of a panoramic design comprised of water areas, groups of plantings, villages and agricultural land. The final element was the Great Lake, covering 50 hectares, between the house and the village of Coneysthorpe, and laid out between 1795 and 1799. The serpentine lake creates a formal link between the house and the village: the latter was partly demolished and

The Great Lake with Slingsby Bank in the background

rebuilt for the purpose. Though the fish ponds at The Dairies lie higher up and are separated from the lake by a jetty, they have been visually incorporated into the whole. The lake finally achieves the panoramic unity which in 1724, and perhaps even in 1699, Vanbrugh and Carlisle envisioned, and which consolidates the rational and formal architectonic fragments of the layout within the physical, geographical parameters of the natural landscape.

When the various historic phases of Castle Howard could simultaneously be projected onto each other and placed in the morphology of the landscape, the complex visual unity of this landscape garden would become more apparent. The rational matrix of the Italian villa and the theatrical perspective design of the French garden were both surpassed in this great scenic creation to which Christopher Hussey referred (fig. 12).

Castle Howard's impact on the development of the 18th-century landscape garden was less evident than that of Stowe's. Castle Howard never served as a direct example, although looked at from today it was a key work in landscape architecture of the Enlightenment, in the same way Faust was of the theatre or Don Giovanni of the music world at that time. While in the Italian Renaissance villa and the formal 17th-century landscape – even at Stowe – the garden and the agricultural landscape were two separate worlds, at Castle Howard they were fused together to form a new synthesis. The facets of the architectonic landscape and the commonplace agricultural landscape seamlessly overlapped each other. It was as if the visual and spatial essence of the agricultural landscape had been laid out and reassembled again as a work of art. The various fragments of the Carlisle landscape formed a dialectical coherent arrangement. For these reasons the scenic creation of Castle Howard could be termed the first *montage* in the history of landscape architecture.

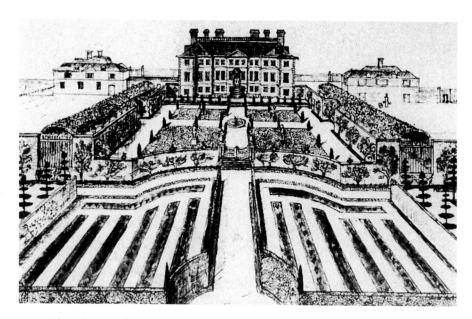

The 17th-century house with the garden at the south side, *c.* 1690

Stowe

Eighteenth-century Stowe is full of surprises. But nothing, in the end, is more astonishing about that extraordinary place than the continuity of change.
George Clarke, *The Moving Temples of Stowe,* 1992

At Stowe in Buckinghamshire the conceptual development of the landscape garden has been established in various parts of the garden. The garden itself, roughly 160 hectares, covers only a small part of the estate, which at one time comprised some 20,000 hectares.

Stowe's influence on landscape gardening was enormous. In the same way that Versailles epitomized French formal landscaping, Stowe was the showpiece of English landscape art. The garden has been frequently copied, from Russia – Tsarskoe Selo owned by Catherine the Great – to America – Washington's Capitol, for instance. Leading 18th-century English artists worked on the garden as well as famous foreign architects later on. Yet at the same time Stowe represents the 'dilettantism' of the Georgian era. The garden is an iconographic tenet, containing references to both painting and literature as well as to political and moral statements. In this sense Stowe is a reflection of 18th-century English culture, a living document of its social, political and aesthetic history.

Even today Stowe provides material for art historical and architectonic research, through which fresh facts come to light and new insights, including those on landscape architecture, are gained. To what extent, for instance, were rational and formal design schemes used when developing a layout? How many new compositional schemes can be distinguished?

HISTORY

The estate came into the possession of the Temple family in the 16th century. During the 17th century several family members distinguished themselves in the army and in affairs of the state. The 3rd Baronet, Sir Richard Temple, increased the family fortune, while his son, later to become Viscount Cobham, rose to lieutenant general in the 1st Duke of Marlborough's army and became a leading statesman. Cobham moved in the liberal circles of the Whigs and made his family one of the most influential in England. He was the founder of the 'dynasty and palace of Stowe'.

In 1713 the Tories came to power and Cobham, together with the Duke of Marlborough, was dismissed. At George I's coronation in 1714 Cobham once again found favour at court. In 1733, however, he was dismissed again and bitterly withdrew himself from public life, devoting his attention to embellishing his country estate. Behind the scenes he continued to be involved in politics, constantly commenting on affairs of the day from his garden. Like Carlisle, Vanbrugh and Kent, Cobham was a member of the Kit-Cat Club. Vanbrugh was architect to both gentlemen and was thus most likely to have been the central player in the exchange of ideas that took place during the experimental phase of both landscape gardens.

Cobham died childless in 1749 and bequeathed the estate to his younger sister, who was married to Richard Grenville of Wotton Underwood. Their son and heir, the extremely ambitious Richard Grenville Temple, later to become Earl Temple, increased the family property and worked on the landscape garden until his death in 1779. He also died childless and passed on the estate to his nephew, George Nugent-Temple-Grenville, later the Marquess of Buckingham, who supplied the finishing touches. Aside from a few details, Stowe appeared then as it does today.

After 1813 the estate detoriated rapidly: in 1848 the family became bankrupt. All possessions were auctioned except for the house and garden. In 1921 even these were finally sold off as one lot.

Brave attempts were made to keep the estate intact, among others by the architect Clough William Ellis, who purchased the Grand Avenue and brought it under the administration of a foundation. In 1923, Stowe was converted into a school, as this was the only means of rescuing it from total oblivion. In 1967 the National Trust became responsible for part of the gardens. In 1984 it acquired Oxford Avenue and in 1989 most of the estate, apart from the house and school buildings. Since then large-scale restoration has been carried out, one of the most spectacular ever undertaken in landscape gardening.

MORPHOLOGY AND TOPOGRAPHY

Stowe lies on the upper reaches of the River Alder in the undulating, clay farmland that descends around 155 metres in elevation to the Great Ouse at some 90 metres above sea level. To the north of Stowe is the medieval Whittlewood Forest, situated at the watershed between the Ouse and Tove river systems, which flow together in an easterly direction. Two side valleys of the Alder, on both sides of the principal axis of the house, have invited a broadly symmetrical design of the layout and have determined the garden's southern boundary.

The Hey Wey (Highway) ran through Stowe village on the Alder, linking Buckingham to a Roman road that joined Akeman Street at Bicester. The old Manor House was probably situated on Slant Road, a cart track linking Lamport to the Roman road, via the Hey Wey. This triangle was to play an important role in the subsequent development of the garden. This was walled and possibly had an orchard. Sir Richard, 1st Baronet, probably had the Manor House demolished between 1675 and 1680 and a new country house built which lay higher up the hill to allow for a view.

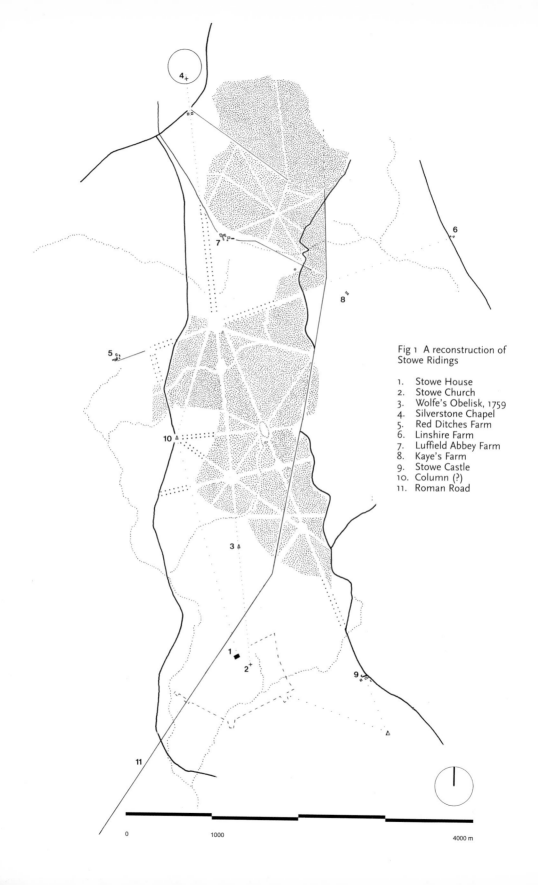

Fig 1 A reconstruction of
Stowe Ridings

1. Stowe House
2. Stowe Church
3. Wolfe's Obelisk, 1759
4. Silverstone Chapel
5. Red Ditches Farm
6. Linshire Farm
7. Luffield Abbey Farm
8. Kaye's Farm
9. Stowe Castle
10. Column (?)
11. Roman Road

0   1000   4000 m

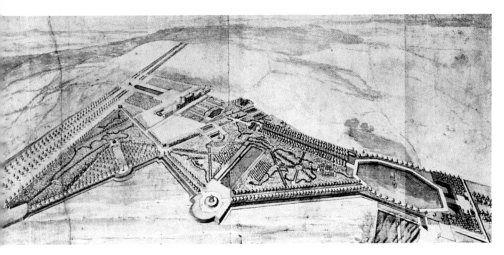

Charles Bridgeman. Perspective drawing, *c.* 1723

It was aligned with the steeple of Buckingham's medieval church. On the south side a parterre was laid out with terraces and a central footpath (Main Walk) leading to Slant Road. This was the garden which the later Viscount Cobham inherited in 1697, and which was the starting point for developing the landscape garden.

STOWE RIDINGS

The garden on the south side was initially of only secondary importance. Much more relevant was Stowe Ridings, an extensive plantation on the north side. Of this, roughly 50 hectares still remain; the northern part is now incorporated into Silverstone race track. A reconstruction gives an idea of the original size and design (fig. 1).

The layout was determined by a southern foothill of Whittlewood Forest. The wooded plantation was intersected by avenues used for tree felling, horse riding and hunting. The longest avenue stretched between the two church steeples of Stowe and Silverstone, while a secondary avenue pointed towards Stowe Castle. The avenues generally followed the morphology, intersected by the lines of vision. The avenue structure was also supplemented with various offshoots and refinements, though it is no longer possible to check the extent of these precisely. One intriguing detail is that, in a drawing by Sarah Bridgeman, the avenue leading to Stowe Castle was lengthened on the south side and joined an avenue at a now unmarked point, which started at the south-western bastion on the ha-ha (hidden sunken fence) designed by Charles Bridgeman. Was it originally intended to extend the structure to the south side and thus set the garden in a large configuration of avenues?

THE FORMAL SYSTEM

The development of the landscape garden began with the arrival of Charles Bridgeman in 1713. He designed the layout of the garden together with Vanbrugh, who had quite drastically remodelled the house in 1719. Vanbrugh's influence on the layout of the garden is recognizable in the extension of the principal axis, which was to be realized much later, and in the indirect approach taken. After his death in 1726, his role was taken over by James Gibbs (1682-1754), who designed most of Stowe's buildings.

The garden was extended along the principal axis. On the north side an elongated pond was laid out between two formal clumps of trees framing the vista. With

Fig 2 The formal system, *c.* 1719

1. Wings and side pavilions
2. Terrace Garden
3. Kitchen Gardens
4. Nelson's Seat
5. Nelson's Walk
6. Temple of Bacchus/Brick Temple
7. Garden of Bacchus
8. Lime Walk
9. Abele Walk
10. Canal
11. Mount
12. The Park

a. Roman road
b. Stowe Church
c. Slant Road
d. Hey Wey
e. Hog Pond

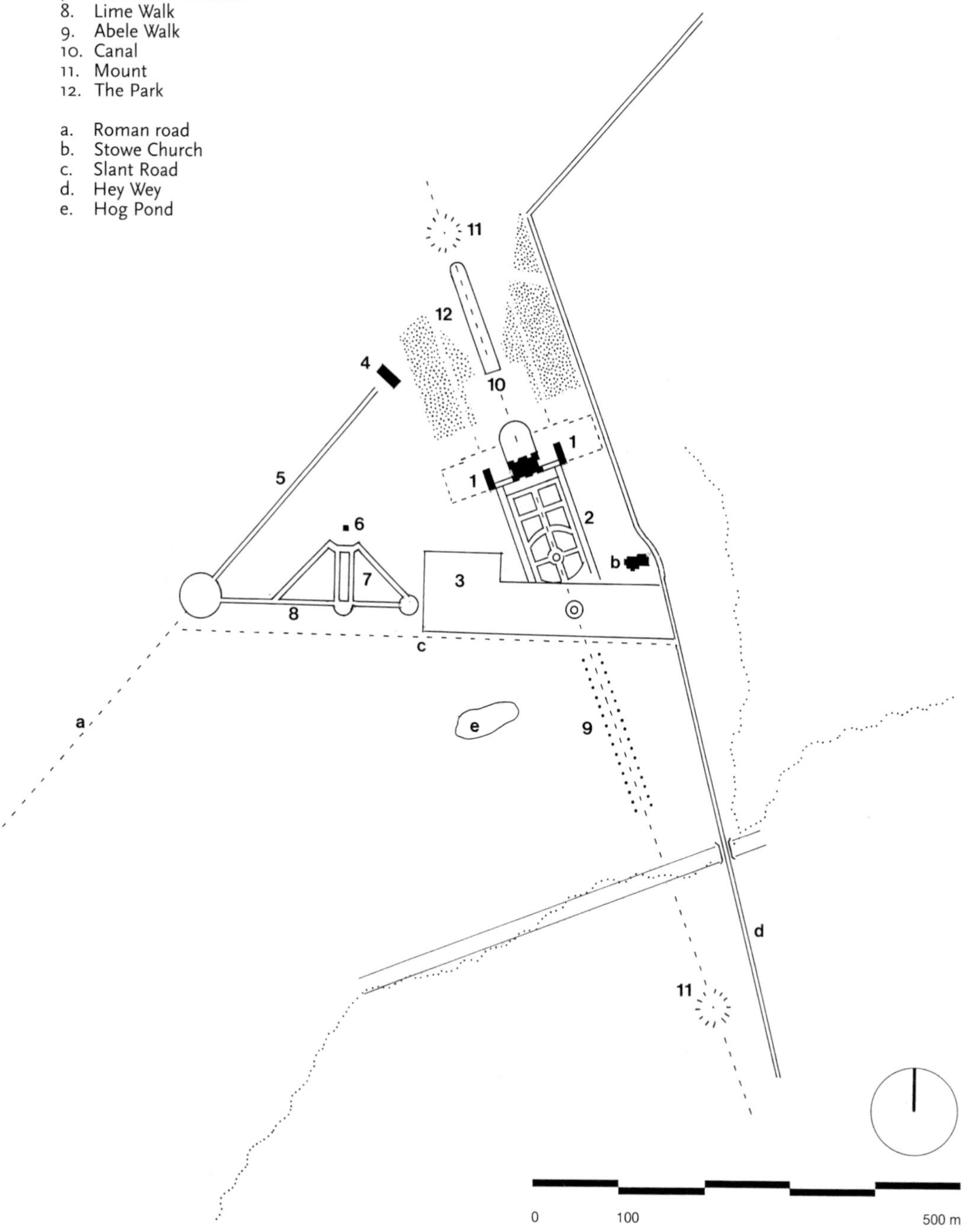

0   100   500 m

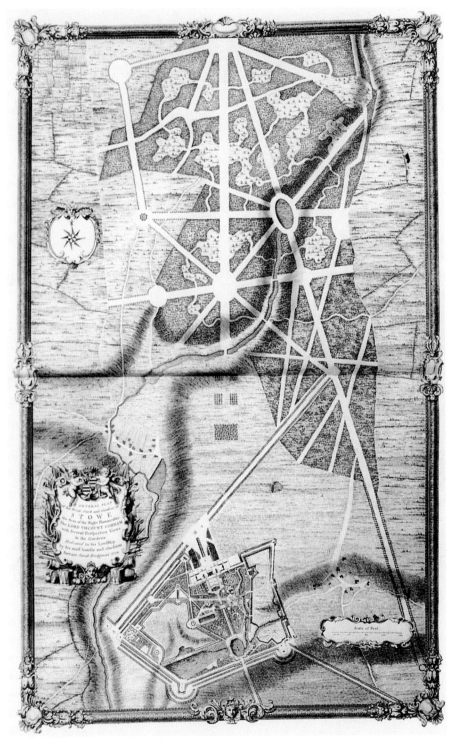

Ground plan. Engraving by Sarah Bridgeman, 1739

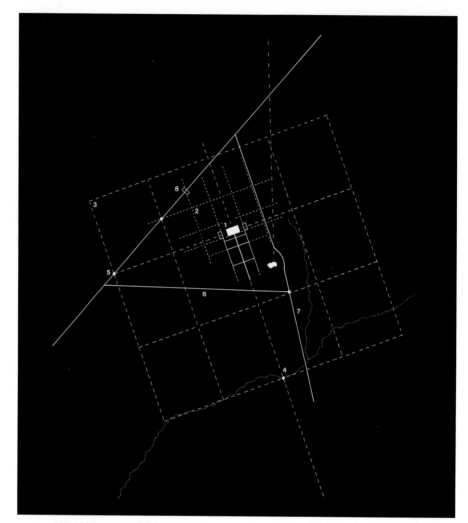

Fig 3 The topographic design matrix

1. The house
2. The architectonic design matrix
3. The topographic design matrix
4. Intersection of the main axis with the Alder
5. Intersection of the transverse axis with the Roman road
6. Slant Road
7. Hey Wey
8. Nelson's Seat

material from the pond, a lookout mount was built as a termination of the vista. On the south side the principal axis was extended beyond the kitchen gardens to the Alder, which was transformed into a formal canal. Using this ground, a second mount was built on the opposite bank of the river – the visual result being that the horizon was formally represented in the garden. The laying out of the pond broke up the Roman road and its south-west section was transformed into Nelson's Walk. It is probable that the surrounding area was levelled and bounded by a construction known as a stockade ditch. Slant Road to the south of the 'ould' garden remained (fig. 2).

THE TOPOGRAPHIC DESIGN MATRIX

The design problem confronting Bridgeman in developing the garden was how to create a link between the formal system of the principal axis and the more or less separately developed section of the garden in the western point of the original triangle. In a flash of inspiration, Bridgeman discovered the hidden order of the future land-scape garden, a topographic design matrix which merged the incongruous elements of the design problem. This drew together the formal system of the principal axis, the design matrix of the house, the topography of the estate boundaries and the morpho-logy of the Alder landscape. This grid enabled every line of force of the morphology and topography to be included in the matrix, while the area to the east of the garden also came into play. As a result Bridgeman created a geometric synthesis which Henry Wise had failed to achieve at Blenheim (fig. 3).

The measurement system for the house was made subordinate to the lines of force of the landscape. This preserved a certain autonomy in the vicinity of the house but joined it with the topographic design matrix. Nelson's Seat was built on the inter-section of the Roman road with a line of the architectonic matrix on the east side. The Bacchus Temple, however, was placed exactly on an intersection of lines of the topo-graphic design matrix. Bridgeman's design matrix 'mediated' between the house and the topography, making a merging of both measurement systems possible.

Bridgeman's transformation of Stowe can be seen as follows. The Bacchus Temple was turned until its axis was at right angles to Lime Cross Walk. A second treatment involved the use of several grid diagonals. The layout line between Bacchus Temple and Giulio determined the outer boundary of the Bacchus garden and organ-ized Sleeping Wood. With the intersection of this construction line and Lime Cross Walk, Bridgeman then drew a line (Roger's Walk) from Nelson's Seat, which inter-sects the grid diagonal between Giulio and Gurnet's Walk at a grid point, which became the site of the Rotunda. This transformed the estate's topography into an 'architec-tonic' triangle and integrated it into the formal organization of the garden (fig. 4).

THE LANDSCAPE THEATRE

Around 1720 Lord Cobham began a wholesale refashioning of this formal garden. The unwalled garden with terraces was replaced by a spacious parterre and a pond. The scenography of the principal axis was adapted accordingly; the intersection with Lime Cross Walk was incorporated into this. The octagonal lake was laid out in the River Alder with a somewhat elongated shape which the reflecting pond proportion-ally corrected when seen from the portico and parterre. The vista, framed by Vanbrugh's two pavilions, then continued as an avenue, thus making the Alder val-ley the middle section of the composition. The west side of the garden bordered the natural landscape in the form of the Embankment Terrace, a further development of the stockade ditch, which also provided an unrestricted view.

Lime Cross Walk was extended and became Great Lime Cross Walk, while two ponds accented the symmetry further along the principal axis. There was as yet no

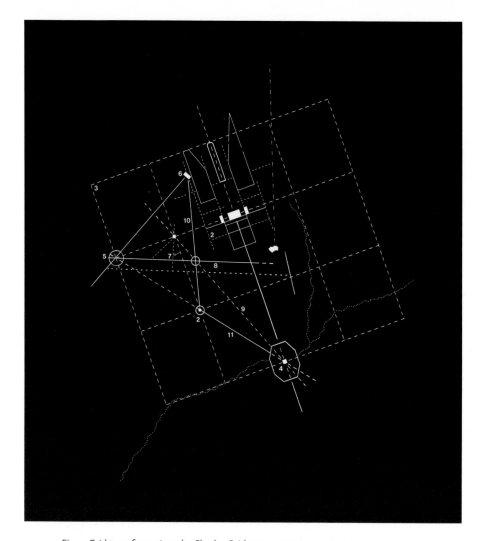

Fig 4 Grid transformations by Charles Bridgeman, 1720

1. The house
2. The architectonic design matrix
3. The topographic design matrix
4. Giulio/Octagon Lake
5. Rondel
6. Nelson's Seat
7. Rotation of Bacchus Garden
8. Great Lime Cross Walk
9. Construction line Bacchus Temple-Giulio
10. Roger's Walk
11. Gurnett's Walk
12. Rotunda

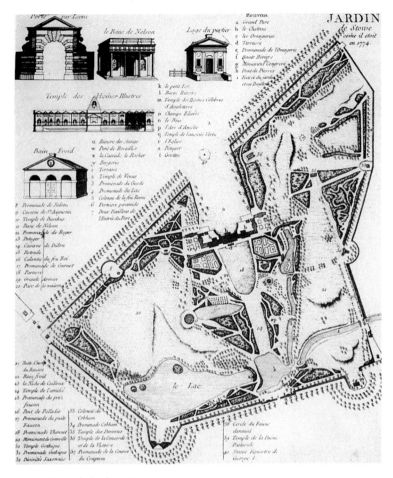

Ground plan by Le Rouge, 1774

formal termination: the avenue probably came out unmarked at Hey Wey, then still the access road from Buckingham. Vanbrugh designed the Brick Temple, facing the undulating landscape south of the garden. The widened garden section, halfway along the principal axis, was divided by the Garden of Venus, which had a reflecting pond and an earthen amphitheatre, one of Bridgeman's favourite garden features. At the far end of the pond, at its most protruding point, Vanbrugh positioned the Rotunda. This created a second landscape theatre, directed at the agricultural landscape to the west of the garden (fig. 5).

HOME PARK

The heavy clay soil in the west part of the garden was difficult to cultivate. It was thus decided to lay a new ha-ha (a hidden sunken fence) with an esplanade around it. This also enclosed the farmland with grazing cattle, and so the Home Park came into being. At the same time Eleven Acre Lake was made by damming the Alder. This created a new composition with an open middle area, the counterpart of Sleeping Wood. New structures on the west perimeter were visible from the Rotunda and vice versa. The first of these, a high pyramid, was Vanbrugh's last contribution to Stowe. He died in 1726 (fig. 6).

Fig 5 The landscape theatre, *c.* 1723

1. Side courtyards and steps
2. House Terrace
3. Orangery Walk
4. Equestrian Statue (George I)
5. The Great Lime Cross Walk
6. Roger's Walk
7. Gurnett's Walk
8. Rotunda
9. Garden of Venus
10. Theatre and Queen Caroline's Monument
11. Pond
12. Turf Terrace
13. Octagon Lake
14. Guglio Fountain
15. Lake pavilions
16. King George's Column
17. Temple of Sleep

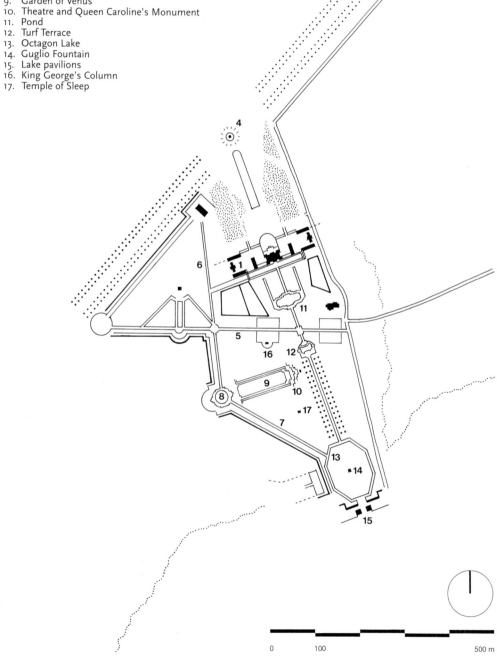

0   100   500 m

Fig 6 The Home Park, *c.* 1734

1. Rotunda
2. Bacchus Temple
3. Coucher's Obelisk
4. Pyramid
5. Gibbs' Building
6. Venus Temple
7. Hermitage
8. Embankment Terrace/Inner ha-ha
9. The Home Park
10. Eleven Acre Lake
11. Lake Walk
12. Artificial Ruins
13. Great ha-ha
14. Warden Hill Walk
15. Cascade
16. Pegg's Terrace
17. Boycott Pavilions, 1728
18. Oxford Avenue
19. Grand Avenue
20. Indirect Approach
21. Abele Walk

a. Roman Road
b. Lamport Road/Slant Road
c. New Inn Farm

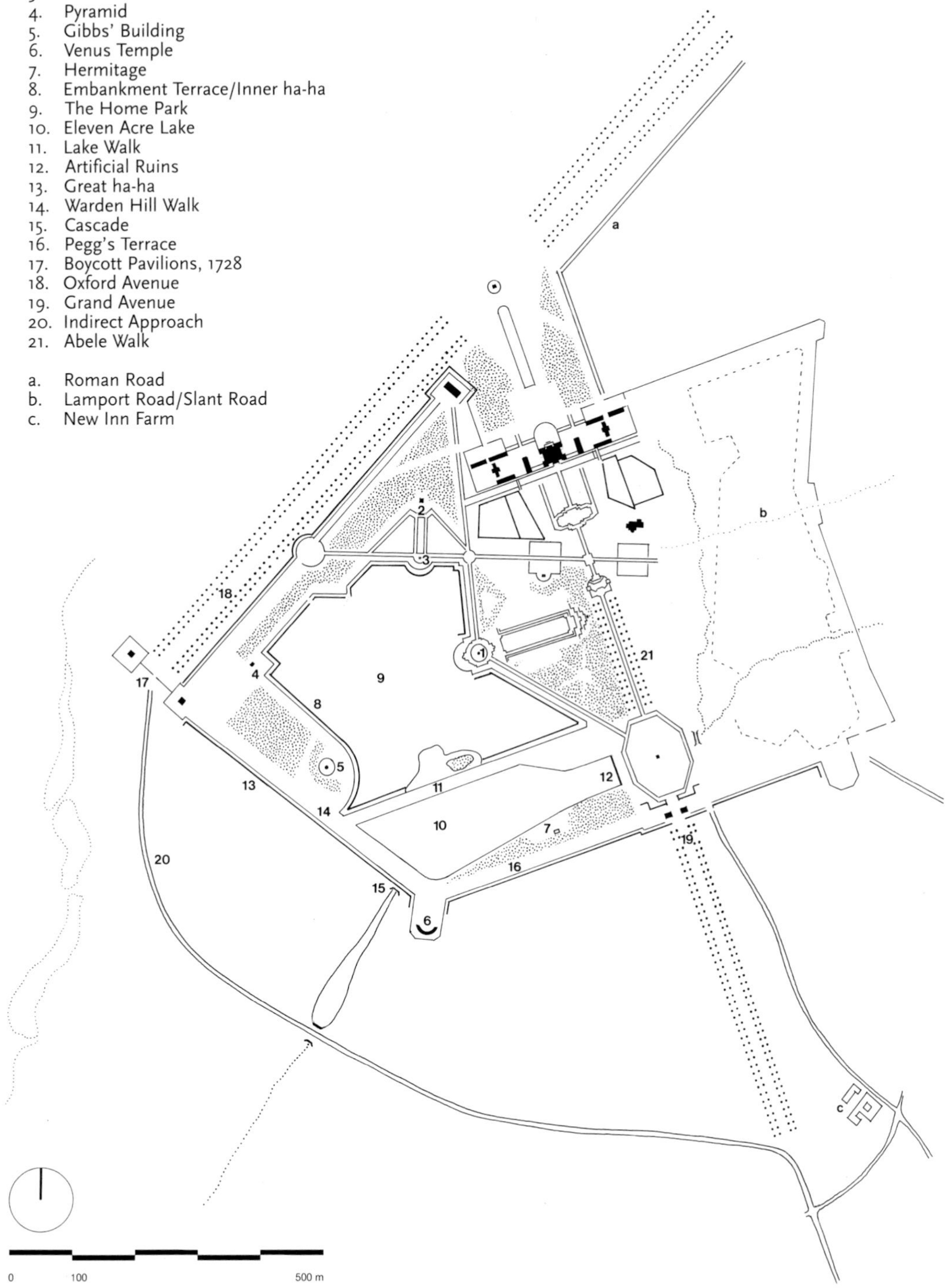

0   100   500 m

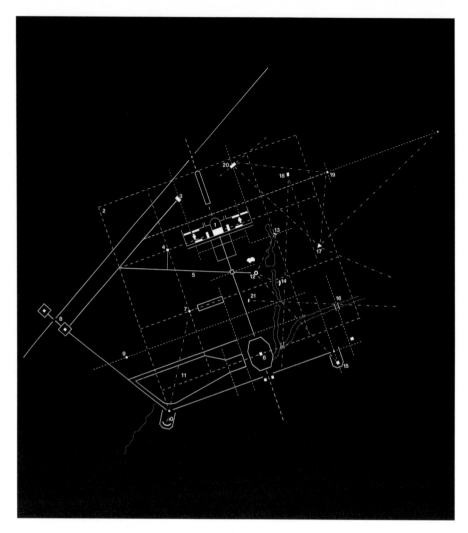

Fig 7 The escape from the design matrix

1. The House
2. The topographic design matrix
3. Nelson's Seat
4. Temple of Bacchus
5. Great Lime Cross walk
6. Giulio
7. Rotunda
8. Boycott Pavilion
9. Gibb's Building
10. Temple of Venus
11. Eleven Acre Lake
12. Temple of Ancient Virtue
13. Cold Bath
14. Temple of British Worthies
15. Temple of Friendship
16. Palladian Bridge
17. Gothic Temple
18. Ladies' Temple
19. Cobham's Column
20. Grecian Temple
21. Amelian Temple

Fig 8 Great Lime Cross Walk

1. Nelson's Walk
2. Brick Temple
3. Coucher's Obelisk
4. Embankment Terrace/Gurnett's Walk
5. King George's Column
6. Terrace Walk
7. Temple of Ancient Virtue
8. Temple of Vanity/Modern Virtue
9. Temple of British Worthies
10. Stowe Church
11. Stowe House

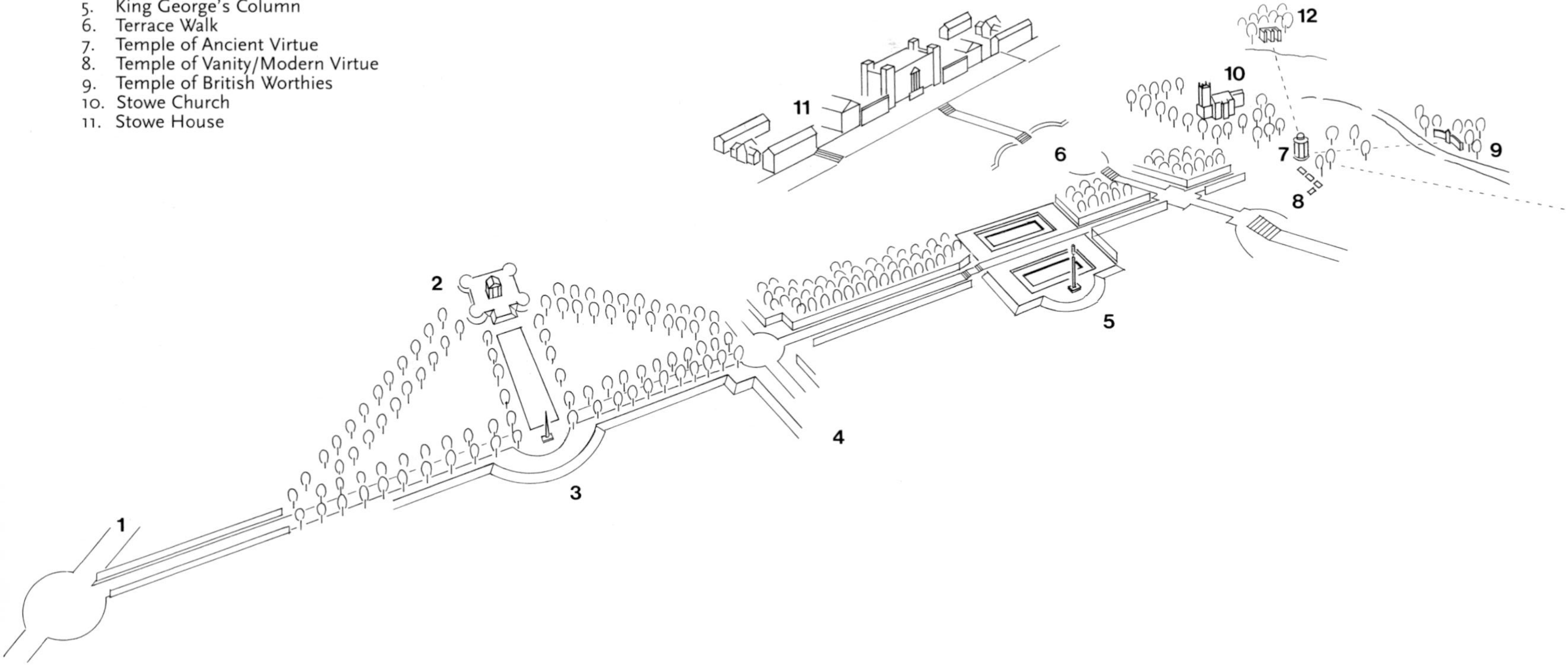

Fig 9 The Elysian Fields, *c.* 1739

1. River Alder/River Styx
2. Worthies River
3. Lower River
4. Upper River
5. Egerian Grotto and Shell Temple(s)
6. Temple of (Ancient) Virtue, 1736
7. Temple of British Worthies/Honour, 1735
8. Temple of Vanity/Modern Virtue
9. Shell Bridge
10. Chinese House/Temple, 1737-1750
11. Congreve Monument, 1736
12. Stone Bridge
13. Witch Wood
14. Witch House
15. Great Cross Walk
16. Stowe House
17. Stowe Church
18. Kitchen Gardens
19. Grenville Column/Monument
20. Cascade/Cook Monument (?)
21. Guglio
22. Pebble Alcove
23. Ha-ha
24. Pavilions
25. Octagon Lake
26. Season's Fountain
27. Cold Bath/Temple of Contemplation

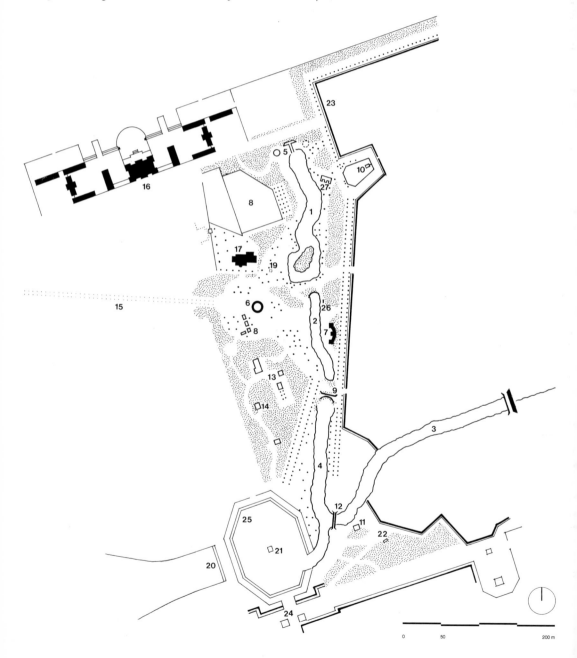

Georges Bickham. The Grotto with the Shell Temples, 1750

THE DEVELOPMENT OF THE LAYOUT

By extending the layout to the east, the symmetry was embodied in a rough pentagon shape with bastions. Elysian Fields formed the counterpart to Sleeping Wood with the Garden of Venus, while Hawkwell Fields (Hawkwell Meadow) was intended as a counterpart to Home Park. The boundary between both was planned to be used as a Walk, similar to Gurnett's Walk on the west side. The topographic matrix gradually lost its importance in favour of picturesque compositional schemes. The Temple of Ancient Virtue and the Temple of British Worthies 'escaped' the matrix and were the initial impetus for a picturesque organization of the garden spaces, in which architectonic elements were directly placed in the landscape's morphology (fig. 7).

Great Lime Cross Walk was used to link the new part of the garden with the rest. The diagonal put the symmetry of the principal axis into perspective and contrasted sharply with the naturalism of Elysian Fields. The dynamics of Great Lime Cross Walk was absorbed by the round form of the Temple of Ancient Virtue and disseminated in various directions. The temple dominated Elysian Fields and formed the counterpart to the Rotunda in Home Park. This composition had the special appeal of a hybrid: it was orderly and fanciful, harmonious and asymmetric, all at the same time (fig. 8).

ELYSIAN FIELDS

Elysian Fields was a clear example of an emblematic garden. The group of buildings is a comment on the political circumstances of the age; the message being visually conveyed to observers by holding up a classical landscape before them as a mirror. Kent's revolutionary concept was to create a garden as a series of three-dimensional paintings by using foliage, architecture, earth and water. His scenes offered an idealized and 'civilized' view of nature, which was youthful and transparent, with architecture and foliage in equal proportions (fig. 9).

Fig 10 Hawkwell Field, c. 1745

1. Temple of Friendship, 1739
2. Ladies'/Queen's Temple, 1744-48
3. Gothic Temple/Temple of Liberty, 1744-48
4. Palladian bridge
5. Lawn
6. Imperial Closet
7. Congreve Monument
8. Hawkwell Mead Walk
9. Hawkwell Hill Walk
10. Gothic Walk
11. Thanet Walk
12. Cobham's Column, 1747
13. Orangeries
14. Carriage Road
15. Hawkwell Meadow

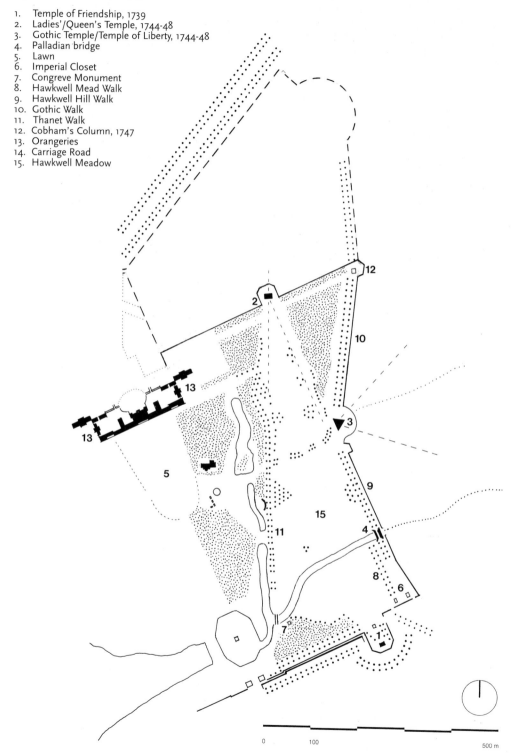

0   100   500 m

The Elysian Fields with the Temple of British Worthies

Similar to Chiswick and Rousham, Kent used a river as a motif but now on a sloping terrain. He solved this problem by designing three ponds linked together by cascades. The water composition followed the classical scheme: spring/cascade/ reflecting pond. The upper section, the Styx, was excavated so that space was created at its tip for a grotto, at one time flanked by two shell temples, while the pool was widened on the lower side and served as a reflecting surface for the Temple of Ancient Virtue. The middle section, the River Worthies, acted as a reflecting pond for the horizontal British Worthies monument when seen from the Temple of Ancient Virtue. The third section of the Alder, the Upper River, converged with the stream from Lamport and, on an unmarked bend, flowed into Lake Octagon.

HAWKWELL FIELD

Around 1740 a roughly oblong-shaped triangle, with a hypotenuse some 250 metres long, was cut out of Hawkwell Field. From the portico of the Ladies' Temple, which marked the top of the triangle, one had a vista across the eastern part of the garden and the undulating landscape to the south. On the lower side, the Temple of Friendship, built on a roundel of the southern ha-ha, completed the decor. When this layout is compared to the previous one, the Ladies' Temple appears to lie outside the then garden boundary, possibly on a bastion.

Hawkwell Hill was marked by the Gothic Temple (originally called Temple of Liberty) by James Gibbs, built between 1744 and 1748, and the ideological pinnacle of the eastern emblematic garden, a 'trumpet-call of Liberty, Enlightenment and the Constitution'. From its tower there was a commanding view of the surrounding landscape. On the eastern horizon two eye-catchers were built: Stowe Castle, a farmhouse in disguise, and the Bourbon Tower, a gamekeeper's cottage built to resemble a medieval tower.

Fig 11 The panoramic composition, 1750-1830

1.   The House
2.   Stowe Church
3.   The Lake
4.   Lake Pavilions
5.   Temple of Friendship
6.   Temple of Venus
7.   Cascade and Lake
8.   Boycott Pavilions
9.   Bourbon Tower
10. Wolfe's Obelisk
11. Doric/Amelian Arch
12. Corinthian Arch
13. New Inn Farm
14. Lamport
15. Akeley Farm
16. Stowe Castle
17. Chackmore
18. Home Farm
19. Dadford
20. Oxford Bridge and
     Water, 1761
21. Stowe Ridings

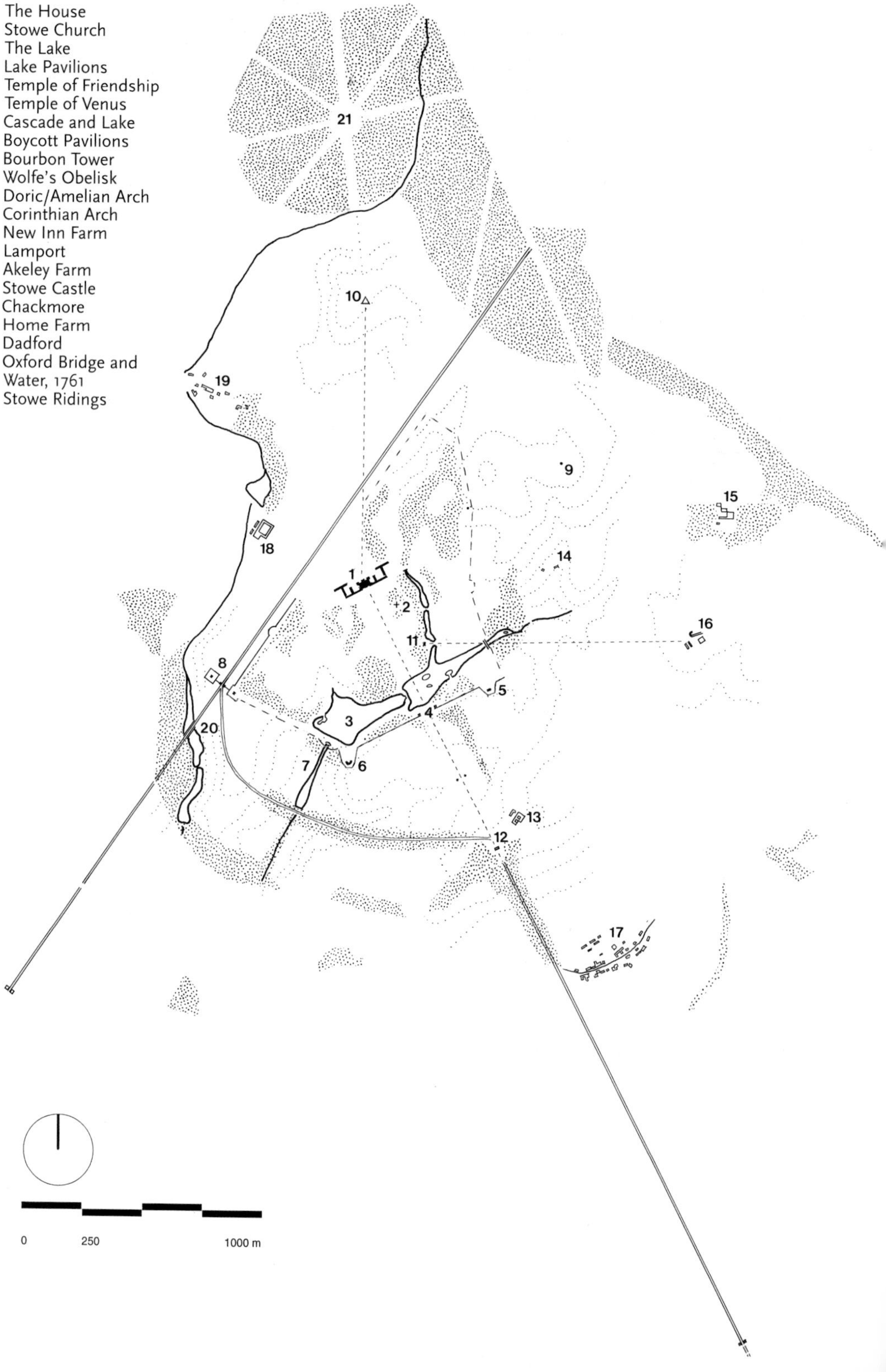

The Palladian bridge

Hawkwell Field was another example of a *ferme ornée* based on the Home Park model. The central area consisted of pasture and hayfields, the largest garden space up until then. The triangular space was bounded by avenues, their severe appearance being softened – albeit still formally – by means of *coulisses* (fig. 10).

GRECIAN VALLEY

What Cobham had in mind for the Grecian Valley went further than the pastoral idyll of the *ferme ornée* of Hawkwell Field. His intention was to design the perfect Arcadian landscape as depicted in one of Claude Le Lorrain's paintings. A Greek Temple, the largest and most exquisite ever built, was to be erected at the entrance to the valley. Death, however, came more quickly: Kent died in 1748, Cobham in 1749. After that, work came to a standstill until the moment when Grenville made the Grecian Valley a turning point in the development of Stowe gardens.

Grecian Valley was an elongated, partly artificial, excavated valley, roughly 180 metres long and between 20 and 30 metres wide. The Grecian Temple was placed slightly at a slant so that it was always obliquely visible. Around the valley was a meandering path that wove in and out of woods and clumps of trees: a scheme that can be interpreted as the prototype for Brown's belt. Statues were placed along the paths to reflect the theme of the Arcadian landscape. The plantings were more varied than Bridgeman's or Kent's and included cedar, larch and Scots fir.

According to an earlier proposal (by Kent or Brown), a lake was to be created in the valley and a triumphal arch facing the Grecian Temple erected on a roundel at the other end of it. Grenville rejected the idea for a lake, probably out of necessity, as there was insufficient water on this site. He had in mind a prominent place, however, for the triumphal arch.

Fig 12 The scenography of the Oxford Avenue

1. Stowe House
2. Equestrian Statue
3. Boycott Pavilions
4. Oxford/Ladymead Bridge and Water, 1761
5. Oxford Lodges, 1765
6. Entrance drive

a. Great Ouse River
b. Water Stratford
c. Brackeley Road
d. Welsh Lane
e. Boycott Manor Farm
f. Home Farm
g. Stowe Ridings

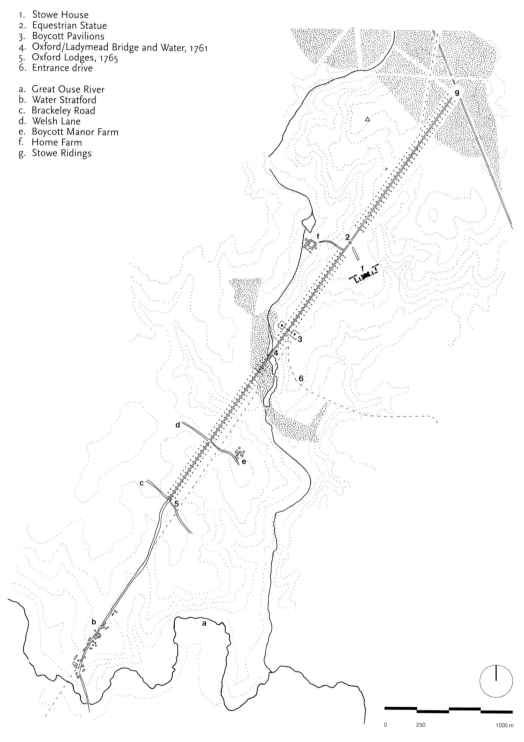

Oxford Bridge and Water

PANORAMIC COMPOSITION

Grenville's era, spanning 30 years between 1747 and his death in 1779, resulted in a rigorous expansion of the garden. Meanwhile an evolution in thinking about the garden had taken place, already evident from the Elysian Fields, Hawkwell Field and the Grecian Valley. Cobham had put the spacial boundaries of garden architecture to the test, while Grenville switched to the panoramic scale of landscape architecture and attempted to integrate the garden visually into the natural landscape.

The broadening and extending of the garden began by thinning out Bridgeman's plantings. More far-reaching, however, was the widening of the vista along the principal axis and the breaking up of the configuration of avenues in favour of criss-crossing vistas. The parterre was swept away and replaced by a lawn covering the entire width of the façade, while Vanbrugh's pavilions were set further apart from each other. The garden façade of the house had to be modified: to redress the proportions the existing portico was made bigger. The Embankment Terrace along Home Park was broken up and Lake Octagon and Eleven Acre Lake were 'naturalized'. The landscape theatres lost their importance: the pond in the Garden of Venus was drained and the theatre-hill smoothed. Out of consideration for proportion, the dome of the Rotunda was lowered and the columns shortened, while the vertical accents of the former 'architectural' garden were adjusted to the overwhelming horizontality of the panoramic landscape.

In 1765 a triumphal arch was erected on the hill at New Inn Farm, thereby extending the principal axis as far as the horizon. The Lake Pavilions and the Corinthian Arch now formed a triangle from the lowest point of Eleven Acre Lake to the highest point of the facing ridge. The plantings reflected this composition, when seen from the portico, in the form of *coulisses*, which underpinned the perspective effect of the architectonic composition.

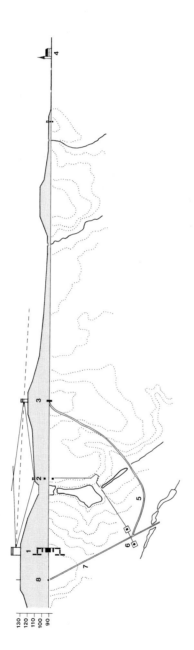

Fig 13 Compositional scheme: indirect approach

1. Stowe House
2. Lake Pavilions
3. Corinthian Arch
4. Buckingham Church
5. Entrance Road
6. Boycott Pavilions
7. Oxford Avenue
8. Equestrian Statue

North front of Stowe House. Engraving by J.C. Buckler, 1815

A new approach drive was scenically staged using single trees and clumps as well as a water garden. Oxford Bridge and Water were laid out by extending Oxford Avenue. Wolfe's Obelisk on the north side of the house divided the open space between the house and Stowe Ridings. The earlier architectonic garden, with its highly defined boundaries, was transformed into a panoramic composition in which the foreground, the middle section and the backdrop were drawn together in a new dynamic balance with each other (fig. 11).

THE SCENOGRAPHY OF GRAND AVENUE AND OXFORD AVENUE
At the foot of Boycott Hill, the Oxford Lodges, designed by Valdrè, were built. A stream was dammed and widened as far as Oxford Water, while Oxford Bridge was built in 1761. From Water Stratford on the Ouse, the road from Oxford now followed the line of the Roman road on a curve, via the junction with Brackley Road at Oxford Lodges, came onto the entrance drive. This descended through the woods until Oxford Water and the bridge. Boycott Pavilions marked the edge of the plateau on which the garden was situated. The avenue continued at a 30-degree angle past the house as far as Stowe Ridings (fig. 12).

Grenville also realized an idea which had probably already been in Vanbrugh's mind. As a continuation of the principal axis towards Buckingham, he laid out a grand entrance drive, over two kilometres long, and planted with rows of lime trees. Arriving from Buckingham, the visitor was confronted at the end of the drive with a view of the raised façade of the house, through the Corinthian Arch, as a *coup de théâtre*. The drive then turned off and the house disappeared behind clumps of trees, to reappear after the visitor had passed Boycott Pavilions and, via Oxford Avenue, arrived at its forefront. In this stage management the indirect approach of both Vanbrugh and Cobham is expressed (fig. 13).

Fig 14 Development scheme of the garden

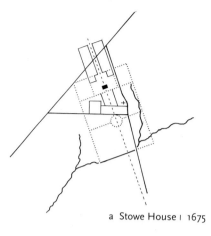

a Stowe House I 1675

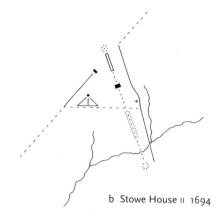

b Stowe House II 1694

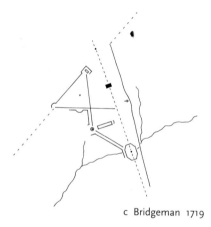

c Bridgeman 1719

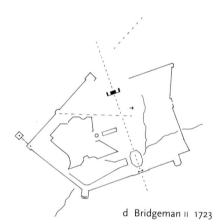

d Bridgeman II 1723

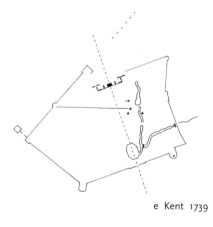

e Kent 1739

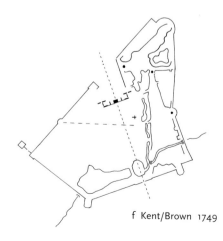

f Kent/Brown 1749

OVERVIEW

If the various historical phases of Stowe were summarized and projected into one plan, one could conceive of the scale and scope of its architectonic landscape, which in certain aspects was greater than that at Versailles. This conjures up an image of Stowe that was never a reality: it existed – and exists – only in the mind. The Grand Avenue and Oxford Avenue link the garden with Buckingham and the Ouse valley, while the central axis of the Ridings links the garden with the watershed between the Ouse and the Tove. Together they represent the morphology of the hilly landscape.

Stowe comprises five important phases in the conceptual development of the 18th-century landscape garden. The first was the plantation of Stowe Ridings with its formally ordered avenues. The second was the 'theatrical' phase of the western part of the garden by Bridgeman, which Christopher Hussey termed the most creative phase and which includes the Bacchus and Venus gardens, Great Lime Cross Walk, the ha-ha with its fortifications as well as Home Park. Then the formal features of the layout were developed, such as the symmetry of the western and eastern parts of the garden. After that came the third, naturalistic phase of Elysian Fields, the emblematic garden with its idealized nature and Hawkwell Field, the first conscious attempt to stage-manage the natural landscape as a *ferme ornée* within the garden boundaries. The fourth, Arcadian phase, with its natural decor of the Grecian Valley, resulted in sweeping changes to the architectonic garden. In the fifth, panoramic phase the garden was visually integrated into the natural landscape (fig. 14).

THE PICTURESQUE MOMENT

In terms of landscape architecture, Stowe is England's most complex landscape garden and is probably the best example of the 18th-century experimental tradition. It represents a new form of landscape architecture in both a conceptual and a technical sense. Between 1713 and 1780 three successive generations of owners, together with their architects and artists, created a picturesque landscape which had an almost inconceivable construction. Stowe, to use Christopher Hussey's words, is the *locus classicus* of picturesque landscape architecture.

The development of Stowe can be traced back to an initial topographic design matrix, which reconciled the geometry of the architectonic matrix with the *genius loci* and the irregularity of the site. Later on, the architectonic elements in the Elysian Fields, Hawkwell Field and the Grecian Valley 'escaped' the design matrix and were directly positioned in the morphology of the terrain. Between these elements was a network of visual relationships that also gradually extended beyond the boundaries of the garden itself.

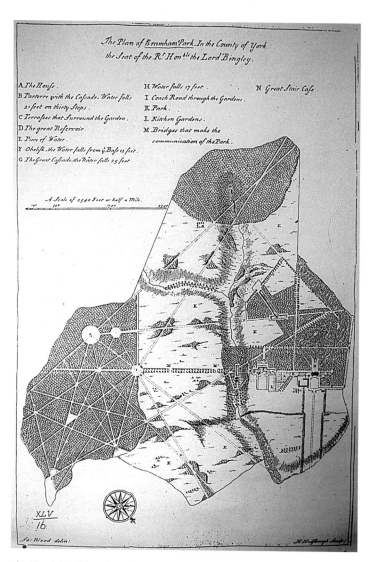

John Wood the Elder. Plan of Bramham Park, 1723-1725, seat of Lord Bingley in the County of York

Bramham

The acceptance of irregularities of site as a controlling factor in the design instead of symmetry for its own sake, [...] foreshadowed strikingly the dawning consciousness of landscape.
Christopher Hussey, *English Gardens and Landscapes, 1700-1750*, 1967

The landscape garden at Bramham House, designed by Robert Benson, with the help of his gardener Robert Fleming and the architect John Wood the Elder (1704-54), is regarded as one of the best surviving French style formal gardens in England. Bramham, however, is more a 'decomposition' of the formal garden. Notwithstanding the formal aspects of Bramham, Hussey saw it foreshadowing English landscape art. How did such a rational layout respond to the morphology of the natural landscape?

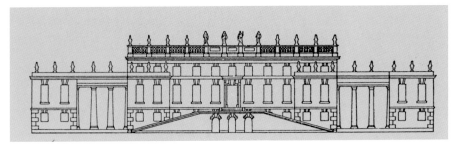

The forefront of the House

HISTORY

After a 'Grand Tour' through Europe, notably in Italy, Robert Benson (1675-1730) became a successful politician as Lord Mayor and Member of Parliament for York. In 1713 he was elevated to the peerage and became 1st Lord Bingley. In 1699 he acquired 611 hectares of Bramham Moor, east of Bramham Village, and probably began building the house in 1700.

His son-in-law, George Fox, became 2nd Lord Bingley. His son Robert died childless and the Bingley peerage ceased to exist for the second time. In 1792 his nephew George rescued the estate by going to live there. After his death in 1821, matters deteriorated again. In 1828 fire practically destroyed the house and there was no money to restore it. It was only in 1906 that a start was made to repair the house under George, 3rd Lord Bingley.

Since 1828 the garden had been entirely neglected. In February 1962 practically all the existing beech trees, mainly dating from the second half of the 19th century, were blown down. A start was made on restoring the garden and buildings, including the Great Cascade along the Broad Walk. The newly planted trees are now 30 years old and give a good impression of the garden at the time of 1st Lord Bingley.

TOPOGRAPHY AND SOIL COMPOSITION

Bramham House lies 15 kilometres north-west of Leeds, on the rather flat, eastern edge of the Pennines, some 65 metres above sea level. Bramham Beck drains into the Wharfe, a tributary of the Ouse. The soil composition is extremely varied, from boulder clay to sand, on a base of calcareous magnesian limestone in the northern part and lime deficient millstone grit, from an earlier geological period, in the southern part of the Black Fen.

The landscape garden is laid out around three branches of the upper course of Bramham Beck. The Terrace Garden was probably natural landscape. The Black Fen, as the name suggests, was a peat bog on the loamy plateau on the other side of Bramham Beck. Terry Lug, the home farm, responsible for the estate's agriculture, is on the north side of Bramham Beck and is relatively well drained (fig. 1).

THE HOUSE

Robert Benson probably designed the plan for the house and garden himself with the help of Thomas Archer, though John Summerson names Giacomo Leoni as architect. The house, completed in 1710, is symmetrical, with two colonnades on each side. The whole has been adapted to the east-west slope of the terrain. The siting of the house does raise questions. The principal axis points towards the view in a westerly direction, perhaps towards the old Bramham House in the village, although this is now blocked from view. Access is via the local road system and, aside from the entrance

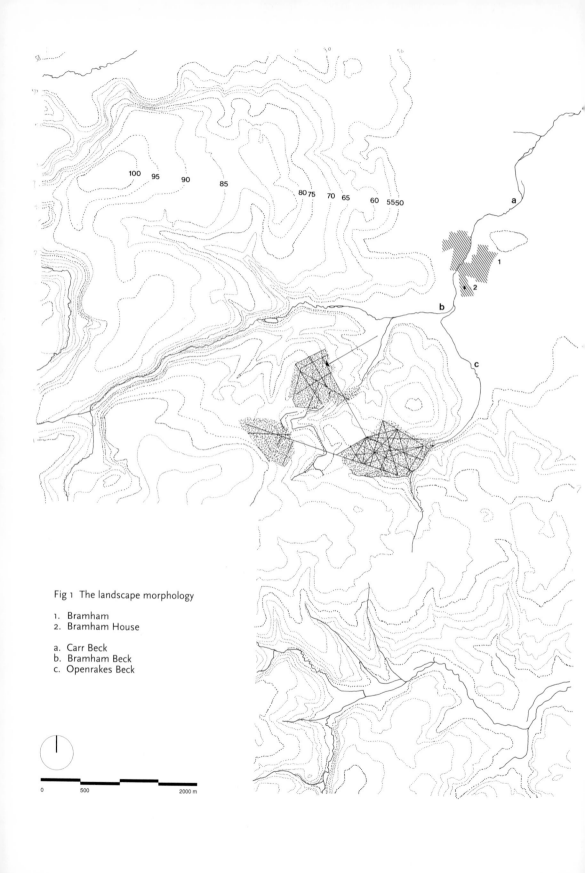

100 95 90 85   80 75 70 65 60 5550

a

1
2

b

c

Fig 1 The landscape morphology

1. Bramham
2. Bramham House

a. Carr Beck
b. Bramham Beck
c. Openrakes Beck

0   500   2000 m

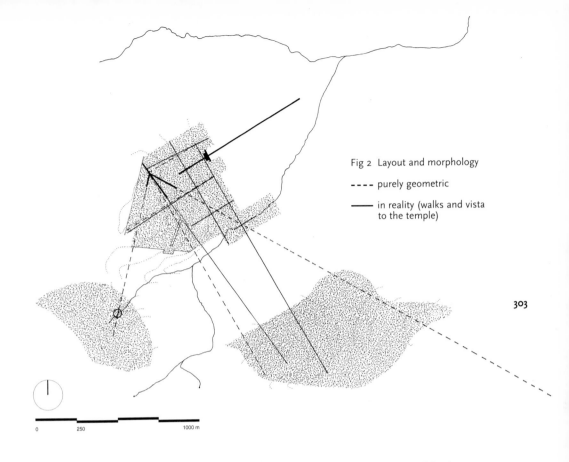

Fig 2 Layout and morphology

- - - - purely geometric

——— in reality (walks and vista to the temple)

0   250   1000 m

drive, has not been formalized. The drive is flanked by lime trees, planted both as single trees and in clumps. In a drawing by John Wood the Elder, a single row of trees on either side of the axis can be seen. The cascade on the principal axis of the house no longer exists, probably as a result of it drying up.

THE WOODLAND GARDENS

The earliest known drawing of the landscape garden was dated by Christopher Hussey between 1710 and 1713. It shows the same division as a drawing by John Wood the Elder, dated 1724-25, but without the Great Reservoir and the diagonal vista from the house.

The woodland gardens nestle amid areas of natural wooded parkland of roughly the same scale, giving the impression of a continuous, unified whole. The woodland garden around the house is known as the Terrace Garden, while that on the Black Fen was known in Benson's time as 'Boscobello', clearly an Italian inspired reference. As well as a parterre, the Terrace Garden consisted of a cascade and meandering paths leading through an artificial wilderness in young woodland, while the whole was surrounded by a ha-ha. The woodland garden on the Black Fen is star-shaped and is planted with diverse species of tree such as cedar, sweet chestnut, red beech, lime and Weymouth. The third woodland garden, on a hill containing the source of one of the tributaries of Bramham Beck, is probably what is left of the original wood. It has become overgrown, marked only by the architectonic treatment of a spring.

The three woodland gardens are connected by a system of vistas and avenues, walks and rides which also crisscross the natural landscape between the woodland gardens, which is planted with clumps of trees. In the Broad Walk, where this

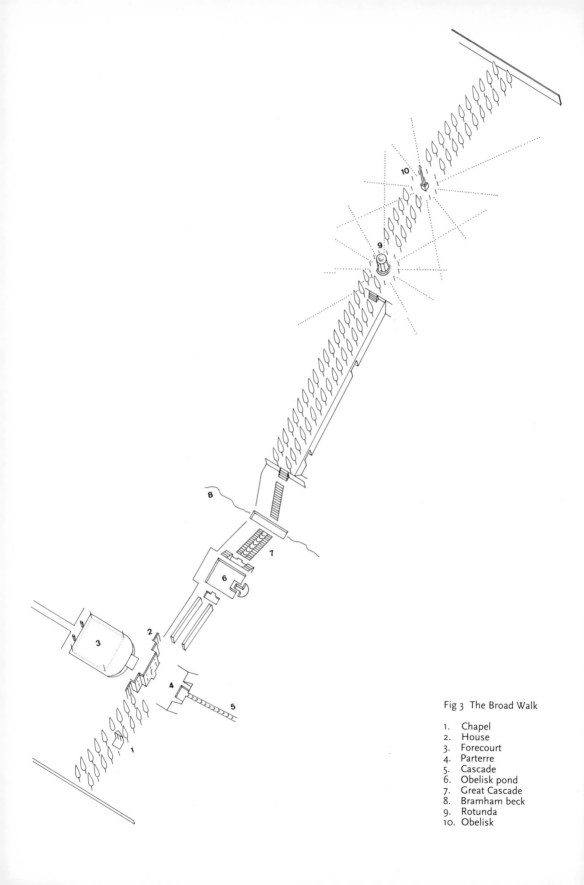

Fig 3 The Broad Walk

1. Chapel
2. House
3. Forecourt
4. Parterre
5. Cascade
6. Obelisk pond
7. Great Cascade
8. Bramham beck
9. Rotunda
10. Obelisk

The Broad Walk

crossing has been architecturally treated, two bridges have been included, which according to John Wood the Elder 'make the communication of the park'.

PLAN AND LANDSCAPE MORPHOLOGY

What at first appears to be a disorderly system of avenues and vistas in the layout can be understood as a 'transformation' of a rudimentary orthogonal grid, located on the principal axis of the house. Due to accommodating the terrain's natural conditions, the grid is distorted. The most important lines of this design matrix are the Broad Walk, orthogonal to the main axis, the Quarter Mile Walk, running visually along the house, parallel to the main axis (now blocked by the stables) and the axis of the Bowling Green, which crosses the Broad Walk at the Obelisk Ponds and Cascades (fig. 2).

In the grid several vistas have been aligned, such as the principal axis of the house and the *patte d'oie* from the Four Faces, that thus became a visual focus of the Terrace Garden. Due to having to accommodate the site's morphology, the angles between the points of the *patte d'oie* are not purely geometric and are unequal in length. The longest point pointed towards Bramham Cross, along the Great North Road, originally a Roman road, the central one towards the Temple of Lead Lud at the highest point of the Black Fen, while the third probably went to the spring in the third woodland garden. Thus a triangle was created between the Four Faces, the spring and the Temple of Lead Lud in which the morphology of the natural landscape was formally represented. The avenues of Black Fen point towards the three focal points of the system: the Rotunda, the Obelisk and the Temple of Lead Lud. Lord Bingley's Walk is the exception: it is possible that this avenue was part of a circuit that linked the various parts of the landscape garden with each other.

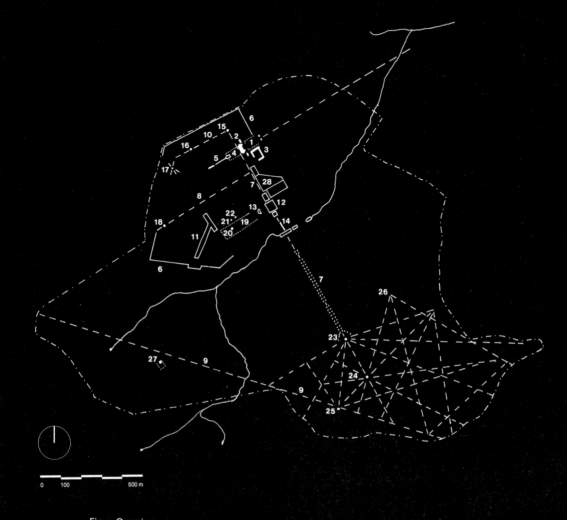

Fig 4 Overview

The landscape theatre of the Obelisk ponds

The Broad Walk was conceived as an architectonic route similar to Great Lime Cross Walk at Stowe. The cascade flowed into a formal basin at the foot of the valley, while on the south side there was a flight of steps. Due to increasing cultivation and water extraction for the Great Reservoir, the basin has now dried up at the point where the Broad Walk and the diagonal vista from the Four Faces to Bramham Cross intersect each other. The Bowling Green was treated as a landscape theatre, similar to the Bacchus and Venus gardens at Stowe (fig. 3).

The architectural elements of the landscape were partly built after Benson's death. When the 2nd Lord Bingley, George Fox Lane, occupied the house various temples, urns and columns were added to the garden. The obelisk at the end of the Broad Walk was erected in memory of his son, Robert. The Rotunda's design was probably based on Kent's Temple of Ancient Virtue at Stowe. The Temple of Lead Lud takes its name from the lead copies of antique statues on the temple's roof (fig. 4).

THE EMERGENCE OF THE LANDSCAPE GARDEN
Bramham illustrates *par excellence* the theory that English landscape design has its origins in the grid plan. The early and fragile beginning of what Christopher Hussey called the 'dawning consciousness of landscape' has been preserved in this garden through sheer coincidence. The main features of the plan were determined by a direct confrontation between the design matrix and the landscape morphology. The circuit walk was an important factor from the very beginning. The estate's most important avenues formed a triangle which were probably built to connect the three woodland gardens.

Anonymous. The ruin of Woodstock Manor, 1714

308

Blenheim

You have your end Madam, for I will never trouble you more.
John Vanbrugh in his resignation letter to Sarah, Duchess of Marborough, 1716

We have nothing equal to this.
George III in a letter to the Archbishop of Canterbury after visiting Blenheim in 1786

Blenheim Park is situated at Woodstock, about 12 kilometres north of Oxford. The park comprises some 1,100 hectares with a circumference of over 19 kilometres. Blenheim lies along the River Glyme, while not too far away is Rousham on the Cherwell. Both rivers converge at Oxford.

Blenheim, which owes its existence to a war, also represents a battle of ideas. The garden is interesting in that it represents the conflicting theories of Vanbrugh, Wise and Brown. How could a cohesive design emerge from such a confrontation?

HISTORY

Before the year 1000, Woodstock Park was enclosed and separated from Wychwood Forest, supposedly by King Alfred, as a hunting reservation for the Anglo-Saxon kings. The park was a favourite resting place of Henry I, who also enclosed it by means of a wall. Henry II had Woodstock Palace built with a retreat and a walled garden and lakes at Everswell (now Rosamund's Well). Henry III, Edward III and Henry VII all rebuilt and embellished Woodstock Palace. There then followed a period in which various English princes were born. Most of Woodstock Palace was probably demolished in 1617. During the Civil War, in 1646, the rest of Woodstock Manor, as it was then called, became a ruin.

Queen Anne presented Woodstock to the Duke of Marlborough (1650-1722) in 1705 in honour of his victory against the army of Louis XIV at Blenheim (SW Germany) on the Danube on 13 August 1704. Marlborough also received a sum of money, sufficient enough to have a new house built, which was intended to serve as a national monument. It was designed by John Vanbrugh, together with Nicholas Hawksmoor, and after Castle Howard it was their second most important commission. The foundation stone was laid in 1705.

In 1710 the Tories came to power. Marlborough was accused of embezzlement and discharged of his duties. In 1712 Queen Anne ordered the building of the house to cease. After the coronation of George I in 1714, Marlborough was rehabilitated but was not allowed to exercise political power anymore. He decided to complete the house and, as a token of Vanbrugh's loyalty, he procured a knighthood for him.

In 1716 the Duchess of Marlborough took matters into her own hands and dismissed all the workmen. She quarrelled over every detail with Vanbrugh, who finally threw in the towel in an emotional but brilliantly written resignation letter. Twelve years after the first stone had been laid, the dream house was still not habitable. In 1722, after a six year absence, the duchess summoned Hawksmoor to complete Blenheim. The duke died that same year and, because the chapel at Blenheim was not yet ready, was temporarily laid to rest in Westminster Abbey.

The 4th Duke commissioned Lancelot 'Capability' Brown (1716-83) to create a landscape garden in 1763. He began the work in 1764 and it took 10 years to complete. The Duke commissioned Sir William Chambers (1723-96) as architect, who added various embellishments. The 9th Duke inherited the estate in 1892 during the *belle époque*. Between 1892 and 1935 he carried out much replanting and started restoring Brown's landscape, as well as elements from before Brown's time.

MORPHOLOGY AND TOPOGRAPHY

The hilly landscape of Blenheim Park varies in height between 115 metres at High Park and 80 metres around Bladon. The Great Park is situated at a height of roughly 100 metres and the lake at 70 metres. The medieval landscape comprised pastoral oak woods, with single trees that were saved for their fruits. The name Furze Platt, along Akeman Street in the north-east of the Great Park, refers to an open, grassy overgrowth, probably an extensive meadowland. There are also various remains from Celtic, Roman and medieval defences. Grim's Ditch in the northern part of the Great Park was a Celtic fortification during the Ice Age, while Akeman Street was a vital Roman road. South of Bladon is a ruin of a former medieval castle (fig. 1).

THE LANDSCAPE OF VANBRUGH

The monumental landscape Vanbrugh envisaged for Blenheim comprised a formal approach drive, a Roman bridge and a parterre, all enhanced by the picturesque ruin of Woodstock Manor.

Vanbrugh already had a design in mind before he even set foot on the estate: similarities between the layouts for Blenheim and Castle Howard are striking. The whole complex was designed to create an impression. The main building is recessed and has four high corner turrets, the reason the house was originally given the name Blenheim Castle. The duchess thought the house was impractical and uncomfortable, because, among other reasons, of the great distance between the kitchen quarters and the dining room. Yet it also had several extremely practical devices, including one of England's first water towers. A machine, hidden under the Roman bridge, pumped water up via a wooden reservoir into a lead-lined basin above the entrance gate. By the stables there was another reservoir used for the west side of the house.

Fig 1 Morphology and topography

1. Oxford
2. Old Woodstock
3. Woodstock
4. Blenheim Palace
5. Rousham Palace

A. River Glyme
B. River Evenlode
C. River Cherwell
D. River Dom
E. River Ray
F. River Thames or Isis
G. River Windrush

a. Grim's Ditch
b. Aves Ditch
c. Hoar Stone
d. Tumuli
e. Round Hill
f. Motte & Bailey
g. Akeman Street/Roman Road
h. Site of Roman Villa
i. Round Castle (ruin)
j. Sturdy's Castle
k. Godstow Castle

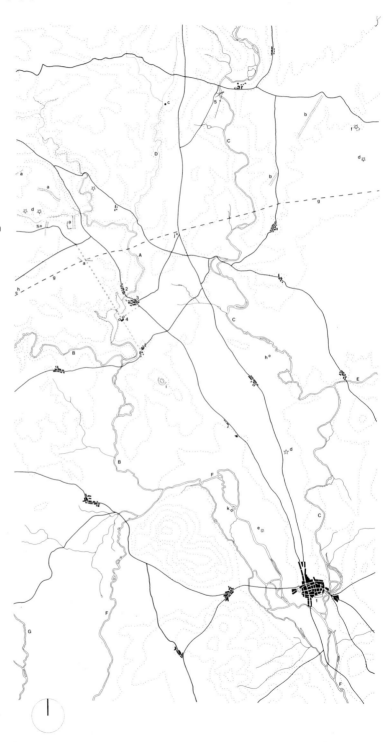

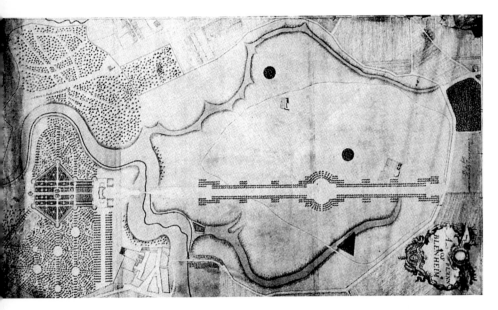

Charles Bridgeman's layout, 1709

In choosing a site Vanbrugh showed exceptional insight into the *genius loci* of the estate. The main entrance had to face north so that a garden could be laid out facing south. Only in this way could use be made of the steep Glyme valley on the north side. The stream itself was no more than a metre wide but had formed a broad valley with banks between 20 and 25 metres high. The principal axis of the house stretched between Ditchley Gate, on the northern boundary of the estate, and the village church at Bladon, on the south, with Bladon Heath Hill in the background. The principal axis divided the site into four unequal parts.

Sir Christopher Wren (1632-1723) advised building a bridge roughly four metres above the water level of the Glyme, with two semicircular offshoots of the approach drive bridging the remaining difference in height of 20 or so metres. Vanbrugh felt the resulting approach from below would not be distinguished enough and in 1708 designed a Roman-inspired bridge – a reference to the Roman forces who had once marched along Akeman Street – at virtually the same height as the forecourt so that the portico remained in view. The bridge comprised four pavilions and the arch measured roughly 13 metres in width, based on the width of the Glyme valley. The water was to flow under the bridge in the form of three formal canals. An 11-metre high arcade, intended to crown the bridge, was never built. A model of Bernini's river gods' fountain in Rome was to occupy a grotto under the bridge.

Vanbrugh envisaged a formal scenography for the three-kilometre long Grand Avenue in which there were four important visual moments or viewpoints. Approaching from Ditchley Gate, only the middle section of the house was to be seen, framed by trees and without the side wings. From the slopes of the side valley of the Glyme, both the building and its side wings could be seen in its entirety. At the point where

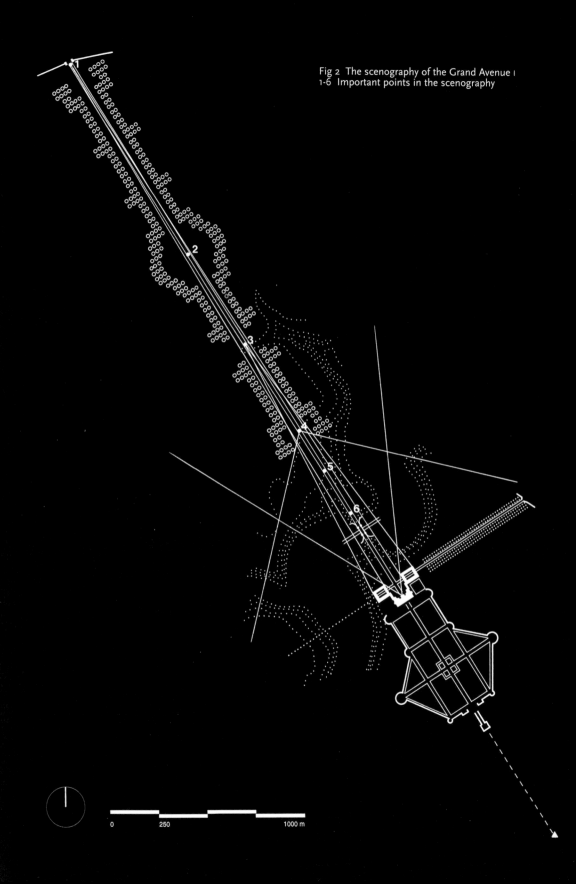

Fig 2 The scenography of the Grand Avenue I
1-6 Important points in the scenography

0   250   1000 m

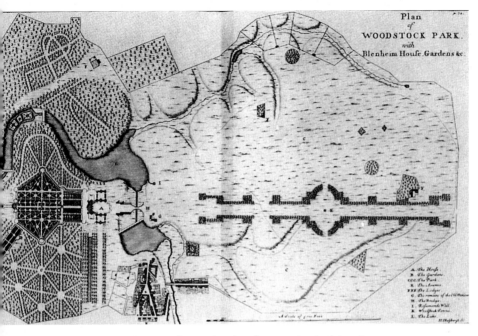

Colin Campbell. Plan for Woodstock Park. From *Vitruvius britannicus* part III, 1725

the plantings terminated, the visitor had a view of the bridge and the house couched in a sweeping panorama. The morphology played an important role here. The circle, which lies on a grid point of Henry Wise's design matrix, denotes the point at which the plateau of the Great Park begins to slope. From here the visitor had an overview of the vertical structure of the house. Attention was drawn to the side valley of the Glyme by means of an opening in the plantings (figs 2 and 3).

In the first phase the garden on the south side consisted of three different areas: the kitchen garden, the flower garden and the Great Parterre, with paths, ponds and fountains and planted with evergreens. On the south side the parterre gave way to a six-sided wilderness (The Woodwork), which can be seen as a formalization of the bend in the River Glyme. The whole was bounded by a curtain wall with bastions in the corners.

Due to the peculiarities of the topography, the approach to the house from Oxford posed a problem. From which point could the visitor best have a preview of the house? Vanbrugh's proposal to lead visitors, via the Mall, through the courtyard of the kitchen block instead of along the front of the house transformed the restrictions of the site into an advantage. Vanbrugh probably intended to mark the beginning of the Mall at Oxford Road with a triumphal arch, but things worked out differently. The Triumphal Arch, designed by Hawksmoor in 1722, was finally placed at the end of the village street of Woodstock, not as an extension of this but at an angle, with a link to the Mall, whereby the visitor is 'channelled' as it were to the park entrance via a *cul-de-sac*.

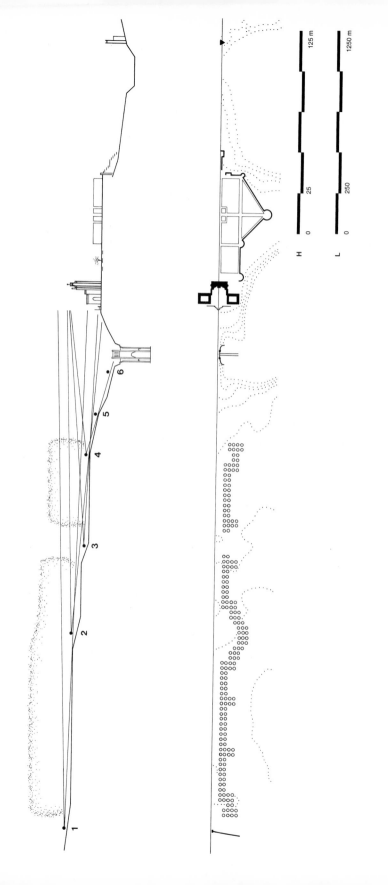

Fig 3 The scenography of the Grand Avenue II
1-6 Important points in the scenography

125 m

25

0

H

1250 m

250

0

L

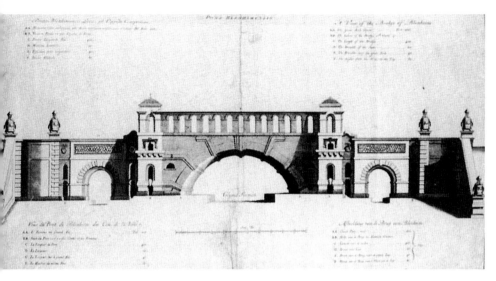

John Vanbrugh's Roman bridge. Engraving by Terasson, 1739

Vanbrugh urged that Woodstock Manor be preserved and later he wanted to erect a historic column on its site to commemorate the victory of the Duke of Marlborough. In 1731, however, the Column of Victory was placed at the beginning of Grand Avenue, after the Duchess had earlier considered positioning it at the junction of the Mall and the formal avenue leading from the Triumphal Arch.

THE LANDSCAPE OF WISE

Henry Wise (1653-1738) designed the plan for the landscape garden. Charles Bridgeman, who was just starting his career, assisted him, while Stephen Switzer helped him lay the waterworks. Wise hardly had time to make a coherent design for, due to the age of the Duke, the garden had to be planted within a year. Wise laid out the parterre with clipped trees in tubs. Within 18 months following the foundation stone, Grand Avenue and the Mall were planted, most likely with limes. To the south of the Mall, Wise designed a formal canal.

A sketch by Wise from 1705/06 has been preserved in which he attempts to find a solution for the Glyme in the form of a sequence of formal canals and basins on the north and south side of the house, linked to each other by a more or less natural reservoir in the low, meandering part on the west side. A sketch in *Vitruvius brittanicus*, part III, from 1725, shows the further development of this idea, with two reservoirs connected to each other by a formal canal. The design was never realized in this form, however.

Wise attempted to integrate the different parts of the garden by means of a design matrix which would incorporate Vanbrugh's formal system and the architectonic matrix of the house. He was only partly successful due to the extreme irregularity of the site. The matrix, however, did influence the scenography of the Grand Avenue and the wood in Lower Park (fig. 4).

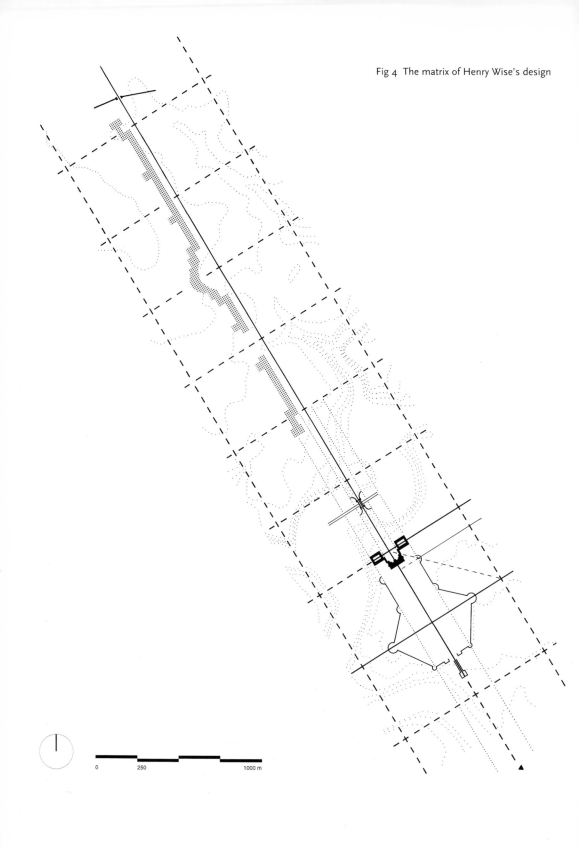

Fig 4 The matrix of Henry Wise's design

0   250   1000 m

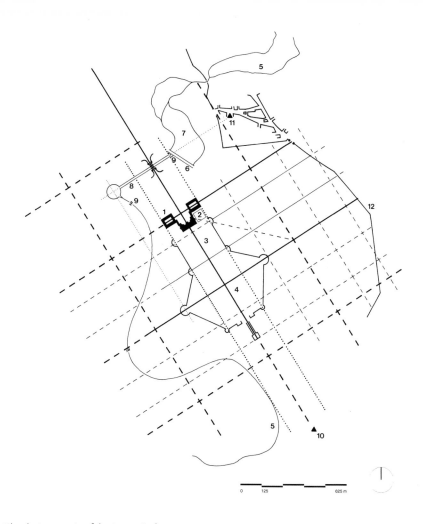

Fig 5 The design matrix of the Lower Park

1. Blenheim Castle
2. Flower garden
3. Great Parterre
4. The Wilderness/Woodwork
5. Glyme
6. Dam
7. Lake
8. Formal canal
9. Cascade
10. Bladon church tower
11. Woodstock church tower
12. Estate wall

——— Actual topographic matrix

– – – – Imaginery topographic matrix

········ Design matrix of the house

——— Actual design matrix of radial woods

– – – – – Imaginery design matrix of radial woods

········ Canal axes

On the east side of the parterre Wise was successful in achieving continuity on the basis of a grid that divided the site into four parts. The module was determined by the Mall on the north side, the principal axis and the axis of Woodwork. From the Bower Room an imaginary diagonal could be drawn across the flower garden and the first bulwark of the parterre. This resulted in intersection A, the fixed point in the plantation. A grid with a smaller module size formed the basis for dividing the site between the parterre and the east wall. The avenues of the plantation originate from grid transformations (fig. 5).

Fig 6 The landscape of 'Capability' Brown

The Great Park

1. Blenheim Castle
2. The Mall
3. Woodstock
4. Bladon church tower
5. Glyme
6. Evenlode
7. Queen's Pool
8. The Lake
9. Roman bridge

10. Ditchley Lodge
11. Roman way/Akeman Street
12. Furze Platt
13. Park Farm/Menagerie
14. The Paddocks
15. Fourteen Acre Clump
16. Big Clump
17. Icehouse Clump
18. Wall
19. Belt

20. Mapleton Pond
21. Ha-ha
22. Great Avenue
23. Column of Victory
24. Queen's Lodge
25. Triumphal Arch by Hawksmoor, 1722
26. Rosamund's Well

0   250   1250 m

THE LANDSCAPE OF **B**ROWN

Lancelot 'Capability' Brown (1716-83) put the final touches to the landscape garden. His parkland was suitable for farming, while the woods he planted were an investment for the future. For plantings he used elm, oak, beech, ash and lime, supplemented with a mix of Scots fir and larch with cedar to give a special accent. Brown radically reorganized the Blenheim landscape. The Great Park was bounded by a belt along the borders of the estate with openings at certain points which provided vistas across the park, or framed a visually important element. The ha-ha (hidden sunken fence) on the inside was concealed by clumps of ornamental trees and single ones. The belt walk was a further enhancement of Bridgeman's circuit walk, a route which offered both a view of the house and the surrounding natural landscape. Brown made a curve in the Grand Avenue, about two thirds of the way from Ditchley Gate, and continued it in a great bend along the lake before returning it to the principal axis at the bridge. The parterre on the south side of the house was dismantled and laid with grass, from which Brown made an open, sloping lawn surrounded by the Pleasure Grounds with clumps of trees and bounded by a ha-ha. The dismantling of the parterre did not do anything for the spatial cohesion of Lower Park, though from a panoramic viewpoint it convincingly anchored the massive house in the landscape garden (fig. 6).

The essence of Brown's contribution to Blenheim, which instantly became well-known, was the lakeside landscape of the Glyme valley. In his *Plan for the Intended Alterations*, probably dating from 1763, Brown proposed damming the river at Bladon in order to create a smoothly connecting reservoir, which was also considerably larger than before. It was the largest lake Brown ever designed and a worthy counterpart of Vanbrugh's palace and the great Roman bridge. The monumentality of Vanbrugh's landscape was suddenly put into perspective by the diagonal landscape of the lake, which brought the scale of the architectonic landscape visually in keeping with the geomorphology.

The level of the lake had to be raised to three metres in order to function as a reflecting surface for the panoramic composition. As a result the bridge was submerged deeper into the water so that its rooms on the underside were flooded. Armstrong's cascade near the dam at Woodstock Manor also disappeared under water. It is telling of Brown's precision that the water level came precisely to the beginning of the arch, which just about provides a balanced image and leaves the bridge visually intact. At the far end of the reservoir, Brown designed a cascade. Around the lake he made a panoramic composition; the view from the Triumphal Arch was stage-managed as a *coup de théâtre*. From the Queen's Lodge there was a view of the house across the length of Queen's Pool, while from the Temple of Diana,

319

Pleasure Garden

27. Flower Garden
28. Temple of Diana/New Temple Chambers
29. Temple of Health Yenn
30. Fountain
31. Grand Cascade
32. Boathouse
33. Middle Lodge

Lower Park

34. Kitchen Garden
35. Conservatory
36. The Groves
37. Lower cascade
38. New Bladon bridge
39. Long Acre bridge
40. Comborough Bridge
41. Bladon Lodge
42. Combe Lodge
43. High Lodge

Fig 7 The lakeside landscape

1. Blenheim Palace
2. Temple
3. Grand Cascade
4. High Park
5. Rosamund's Well
6. Queen's Lodge
7. Triumphal Arch
8. Woodstock
9. High Lodge

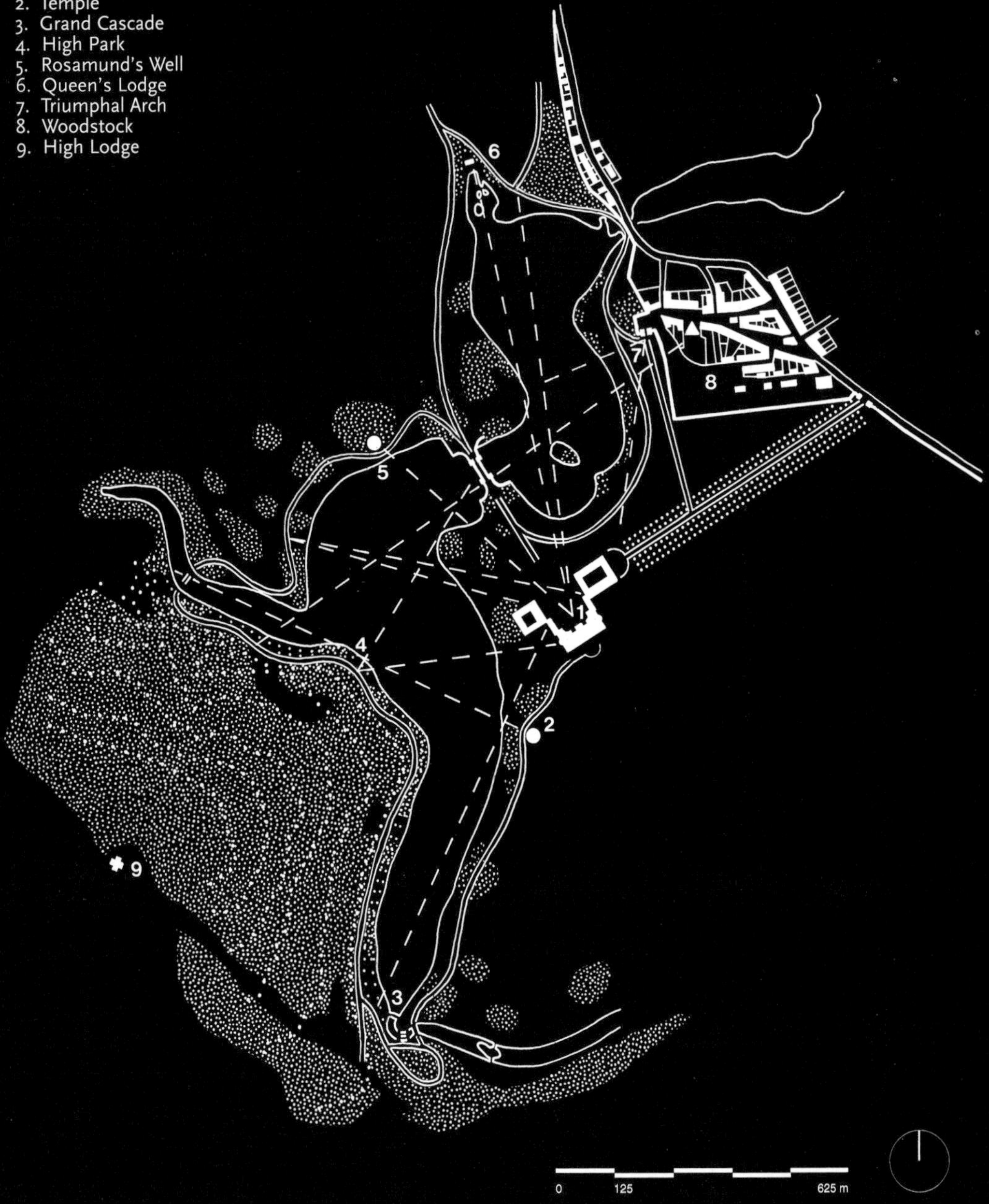

0   125   625 m

View from the Triumphal Arch

by Sir William Chambers, one could look across the west part of the lake. Above the cascade a viewing point was made from where, across the stretch of lake, the house could be seen (fig. 7).

THE DIALECTICS AND VISUAL SYNTHESIS OF THE ARCHITECTONIC LANDSCAPE

At Blenheim the main developmental phases of picturesque landscape architecture are directly evident. While Stowe derives its strength from the topographic design matrix and Castle Howard gleans its from the landscape theatre, Blenheim was exceptional for its formal dialectics. Its landscape seems to have been forged with a sledge-hammer; it is a visual *tour de force*, unique in the history of 18th-century landscape architecture.

Only traces of Wise's rational design matrix remain; the formal scenography of the Grand Avenue has been lost. As a result the confrontation between Vanbrugh's landscape and Brown's lakeside landscape fails to convey the boldness which lies hidden in the plan. Brown's damming of the Glyme combined the design dialectics of the architectural landscape to create a visual synthesis. His lake composition has something miraculous about it, or as Sir Sacheverell Sitwell, friend and advisor of the 9th Duke, put it: 'There is nothing finer in Europe; in its way this is one of the wonders of the 18th century'.

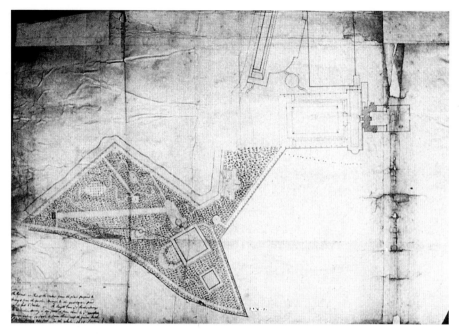

The New Garden by Charles Bridgeman, c. 1725

Rousham

The garden is Daphne in little; the sweetest little groves, streams, glades, porticoes, cascades and river imaginable; all the scenes are perfectly classic.
Horace Walpole (1717-97), *Correspondence* vol. X

The garden at Rousham is regarded as the best surviving design of William Kent (1685-1748) and is an important document for studying his work. Kent's plan was based on an earlier design by Charles Bridgeman (c. 1680-1738), executed around 1720. While Bridgeman and Kent were contemporaries, they represent different generations from the viewpoint of landscape architecture. Bridgeman's style was shaped by the formal idiom of Wise, while Kent's compositional technique was more picturesque than architectural, aimed more at corresponding tableaux and visually coordinating spaces than the tectonics of the plan. What were their contributions to the landscape garden at Rousham and what was their style of working?

HISTORY

Rousham House was built around 1635 by the grandfather of Colonel Robert Dormer, who settled there after a series of campaigns under the Duke of Marlborough. He commissioned Bridgeman to design a new garden, which was possibly laid out between 1715 and 1726. His brother, General James Dormer, also a Blenheim veteran, inherited Rousham after his death in 1737, and in that same year commissioned Kent to modify Bridgeman's garden. This was designed and executed between 1737 and 1738. The general died in 1741 or 1742 and his nephew Sir Clement Cottrell, the Master of Ceremonies of George II, inherited the estate but was hardly ever there. Around 1860, William St Aubyn enlarged the house, whereby many of the details of

Kent's design, such as the mullioned windows, probably disappeared. In 1982 a restoration plan was drawn up by the then Historic Buildings and Monuments Commission to restore Kent's landscape.

MORPHOLOGY AND TOPOGRAPHY

Rousham House is situated in a wooded landscape, close to the villages of Steeple Aston and Lower Heyford, halfway between Oxford and Banbury in Oxfordshire. The hamlet of Rousham probably dates from about 1200. The house lies on a level area of a plateau, facing south, while the garden lies on the north and west banks of the River Cherwell. The part that Kent developed covered some six hectares. The Cherwell flows from north to south, bounded by a steep bank of oolitic limestone, 15 metres in height, situated in a bend of the river, from which several springs originate (fig. 1).

BRIDGEMAN'S DESIGN

Before Bridgeman's arrival, the Tudor house was situated in the centre of the village, flanked on the east side by a walled vegetable garden. On the west side was the Warren, an enclosed wild park and probably the remains of a more extensive wood. To the rear was a walled garden with a parterre and terraces that descended to the river. In the bend of the river was a series of fish ponds (fig. 2).

An undated drawing by Bridgeman depicts the most important elements of his design. The parterre was replaced by a gravel walk and a slightly sunken Bowling Green. The five terraces were replaced by a grassy slope. The main division in Bridgeman's design of the walled woodland garden was based on two intersecting axes, suggested by the sharp angles of the boundaries. The garden contained a series of formal elements linked together by serpentine paths. The house and the new woodland garden were linked by one path along a retaining wall in the slope. Halfway, at a bend, Bridgeman designed a bastion as a 'rise' in the axis of the straightened river. He also designed two amphitheatres on each side of the parterre from where one could have a view across the valley. These landscape theatres established the most important characteristic of the later landscape garden.

KENT'S DESIGN

Kent remodelled the Tudor house in the Gothic style, adding wings to each side of the house. He designed several garden spaces which opened onto the meadows of the Cherwell, with roughly the same symmetrical structure and with a concave slope. The visual reach of the relatively small garden was enlarged by including the hills, on the other side of the valley, in the plan (fig. 3).

From an iconographic viewpoint Rousham, like Stowe, was an emblematic or 'learned' garden, each space having been given the significance of a classical scene. Along the edge of the plateau urns and stone sculptures were used, often to horizontal effect. Lead statues were placed in the niches of the house and lower down in the garden. The structures were also combined with a lookout point. Kent placed a statue by Scheemakers at the end of the Bowling Green as a visually important link: from the house it denoted the edge of the terrace and in conjunction with the Gothic Mill and the Triumphal Arch (an eye-catcher) gave depth to the valley.

In order to enlarge the north part of the garden, the road to Steeple Aston was shifted with the result that Heyford Bridge, dating from 1255, became part of the garden. Kent replaced Bridgeman's serpentine system of paths with a simpler structure and reduced the number of garden spaces. As an important new element he designed the Grass Walk, which made it possible to walk along the wall from the Paddock, via the Oval Pond, to the lower part of the garden. This now comprised three sections.

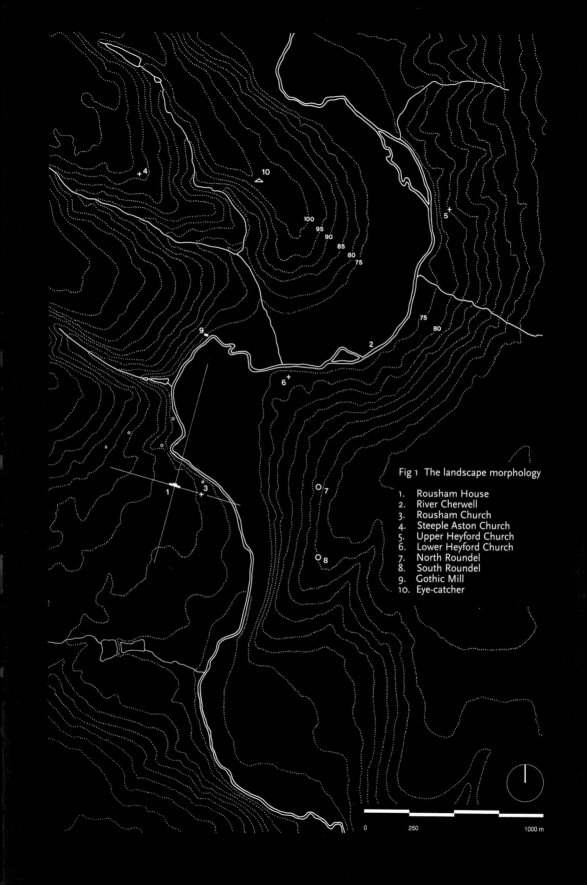

Fig 1 The landscape morphology

1. Rousham House
2. River Cherwell
3. Rousham Church
4. Steeple Aston Church
5. Upper Heyford Church
6. Lower Heyford Church
7. North Roundel
8. South Roundel
9. Gothic Mill
10. Eye-catcher

100
95
90
85
80
75

75
80

0   250   1000 m

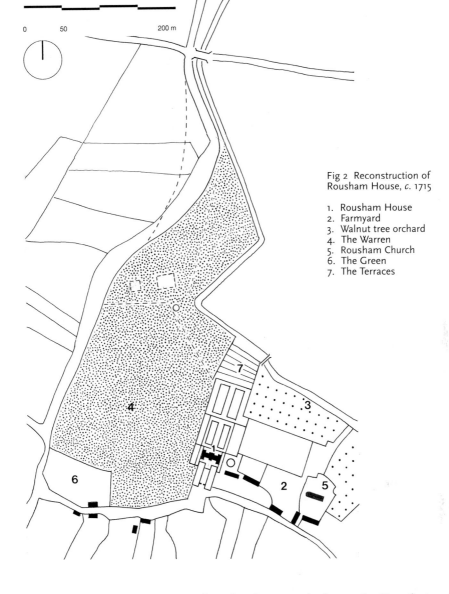

Fig 2 Reconstruction of
Rousham House, c. 1715

1. Rousham House
2. Farmyard
3. Walnut tree orchard
4. The Warren
5. Rousham Church
6. The Green
7. The Terraces

Along the river an open grove was planted and as a new lookout point Kent designed Townsend's Temple, named after the mason-architect, William Townsend of Oxford. At the end of the shortened Elm Walk, a statue of Apollo was placed with its back to the Walk. This was apparently intended to lure one into the Praeneste. Mavis Batey points out that virtually all of the statues at Rousham face outwards instead of inwards, as was then the custom, undoubtedly with the idea of enticing the visitor to do the same (fig. 4).

The key to improving the relationship between the Bowling Green, the Paddock and the woodland garden lay in a narrow part of the garden at Bridgeman's bastion. This was refashioned into a terrace with balustrade, the spatial pivot of the landscape garden with a view from each of its sides. On the terrace the visitor is unaware that the balustrade lies directly above Praeneste. From Elm Walk, the longitudinal axis of the lower-situated woodland garden, the arcade is visible from a diagonal area. Thus

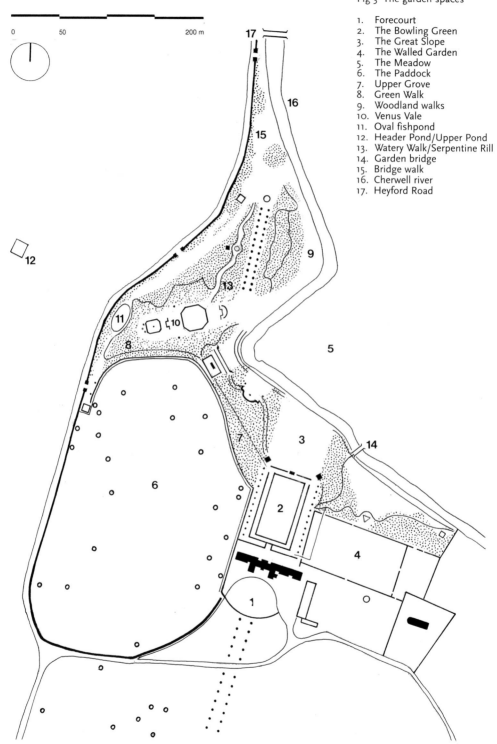

Fig 3 The garden spaces

1. Forecourt
2. The Bowling Green
3. The Great Slope
4. The Walled Garden
5. The Meadow
6. The Paddock
7. Upper Grove
8. Green Walk
9. Woodland walks
10. Venus Vale
11. Oval fishpond
12. Header Pond/Upper Pond
13. Watery Walk/Serpentine Rill
14. Garden bridge
15. Bridge walk
16. Cherwell river
17. Heyford Road

0   50   200 m

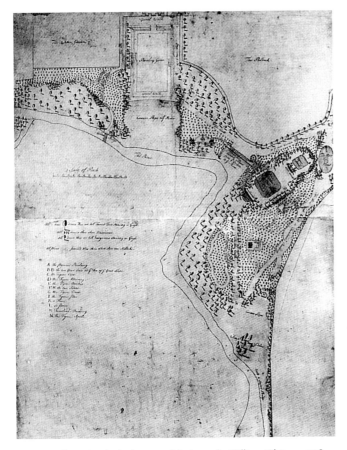

William Kent's design, possibly drawn by William White, *c.* 1738

there is an arrangement on two levels, the one linked to the other by the pivotal position of the terrace and arcade.

The waterworks at Rousham were fed by a number of springs high in the hills, where the water was collected in two header ponds and an oval fishpond just inside the garden wall. In this way modest, natural water pressure could be built up. The Octagon Pond was also fed by a water course along the slope, which later became the serpentine rill. From the two basins that lay one above the other, and which appear in Bridgeman's design, Kent designed a cascade according to the classical pattern of the Italian Renaissance villa. The Lower Cascade and Pool and the Upper Cascade had fountains some nine and six metres in height, respectively. The theatre to the east of Praeneste also has a 7.5-metre high fountain with shell-shaped basins. The Cherwell served as a reflecting pool.

Fig 4 The perimeter walk with views

1. Gothic seat
2. Townsend's Building
3. Viewing seat
4. Praeneste
5. Classic seat
6. Green seat
7. Gravel Walk
8. Rousham Church
9. Rousham House
10. Heyford bridge

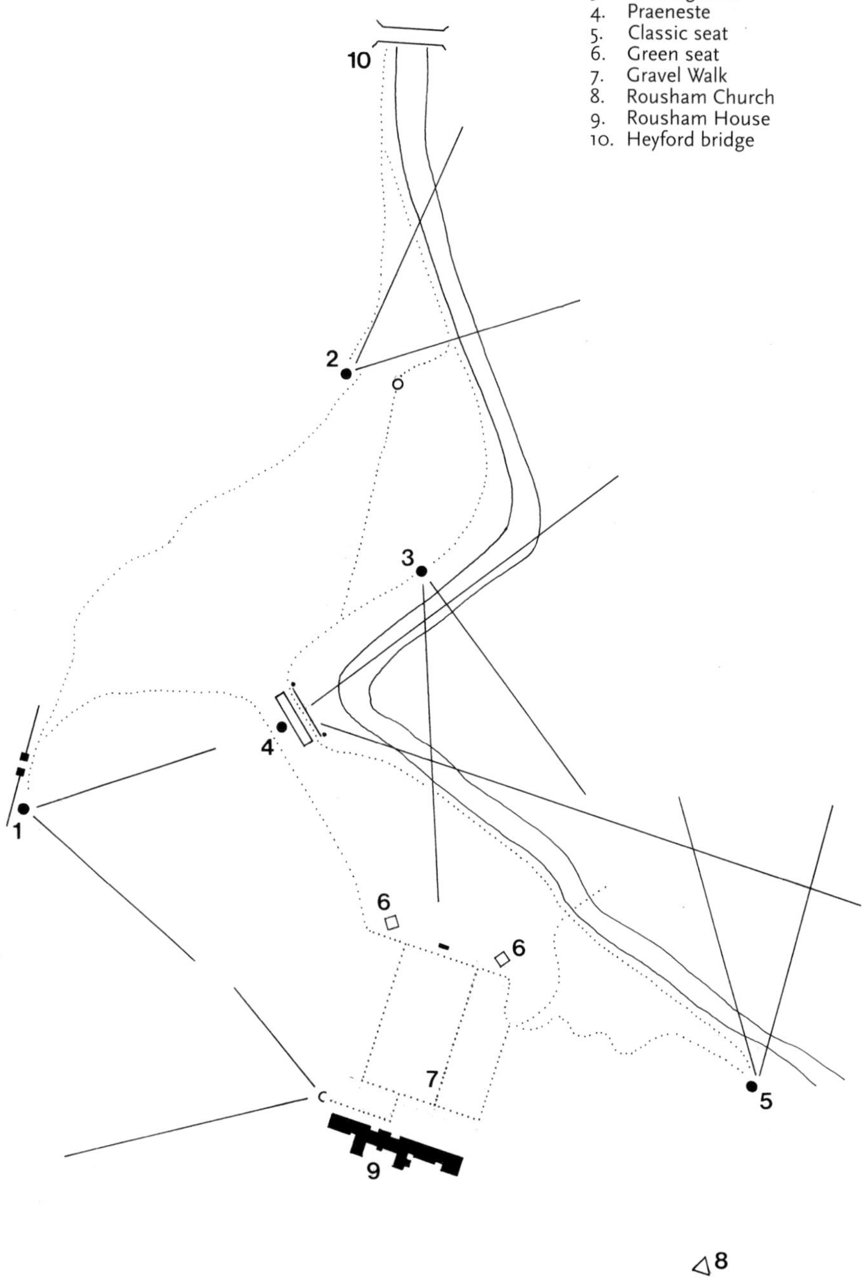

10

2

3

4

1

6

6

7

c

5

9

◁8

William Kent's design for Venus's Vale, *c.* 1738

The iconography of Venus's Vale embraces symbols of sensuality and fertility (the counterparts to the dying gladiator on the terrace above the Praeneste) as well as contains references to Spencer's *The Faerie Queen*. This fairytale theatre is dominated by Venus, flanked by swans and observed from the surrounding woods by Pan and a satyr. The drawing of Venus's Vale by Kent shows he intended an airy composition, with open views along the statue of Venus. Kent planted the sides with clumps of trees, pruned to allow light to enter this limited space in which one looks towards the hill and, in the afternoons, towards the sun.

The Warren on the west front of the house was transformed into the Paddock, an open meadow with clumps of trees surrounded by a ha-ha and Pleasure Grounds, with views on all sides. On the west side Kent designed the Palladian Gate, flanked by two urns and also the Cow Tower, a gatehouse which was used on the other side as a cow shed. Inside the tower a space had been cut out for a Gothic seat, from where the visitor had a favourable view of the remodelled house, embellished with Gothic ornamentation, and Rousham Church, with the North and South Roundel, on the eastern horizon, in the background.

In Bridgeman's design the parts of the garden on both sides of the parterre were not directly linked to each other. The path to the bastion was the only access to the woodland garden, which had to be taken in both directions. Kent designed a circular walk with many alternatives in which he made optimum use of the garden's perimeter. In this walk along the boundary of the garden, Rousham was presented as a *ferme ornée*, with the house, church and walled vegetable garden serving as a backdrop.

The walk was mainly along grass and ran, via the Oval Pond or New Pond, across the serpentine Grass Walk on the higher ground along the wall, and came out in the lower-situated part of the garden, dominated by Townsend's Temple. Via Elm

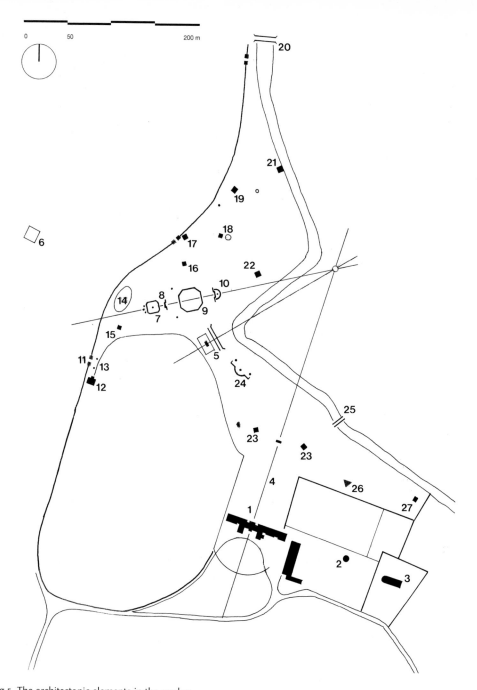

Fig 5 The architectonic elements in the garden

1. Rousham House	10. Lower cascade	19. Townsend's Building by Kent
2. Pigeon House	11. Palladian gate	20. Heyford Bridge
3. Rousham Church	12. Cow tower/Gothic seat	21. Boathouse
4. Parterre	13. Urns	22. Viewing seat
5. Terrace/Arcade	14. Road well/oval fish pond	23. Green seat
6. Header pond	15. High seat	24. Theatre
7. Upper pond	16. Garden privy	25. Garden bridge and cascade
8. Upper cascade	17. Forest chair	26. Pyramid House
9. Octagon pond	18. Cold bath	27. Classic seat

View from the parterre

Walk the walk continued through the new garden to the lower side of Venus's Vale, which had been designed from this viewing point. The turning point of the route was Praeneste, from where there was a view across the valley to Lower Heyford. The walk continued along the river to the eastern part of the garden with the Pyramid Building and the Classic Seat, from where there was a longitudinal vista of the Cherwell. The house could finally be reached again via the unwalled vegetable garden (fig. 4).

Kent retained the greater part of Bridgeman's design for the garden but enhanced the visual cohesion between the main spaces by coordinating the most important vistas. He had the axes intersecting at an unmarked point located outside the actual garden. By means of this imaginary intersection, the hidden link between the valley wall and the various garden spaces became visible so that the Cherwell valley and the surrounding hills were transformed into a large amphitheatre (fig. 5).

Kent created a theatrical landscape by 'retouching' the existing natural one. He made practical use of existing picturesque features such as the house, Rousham Church, Heyford Bridge and the church towers of Steeple Aston and Lower Heyford. He transformed a cottage in the middle section by using a Gothic gable for the Gothic Mill. On the barren hills to the eastern horizon he planted two clumps of trees, the North and the South Roundel. Refinement was achieved in the form of an eye-catcher in Aston Field, built against the northern valley wall. This was a folly intended, as its name implies, to 'animate' the horizon.

THE HIDDEN GEOMETRY OF THE PANORAMA

Kent's completion of Bridgeman's composition was a masterpiece. He opened up the garden and systematically directed the focus outwards. By using clever routing and by animating the horizon, Kent created the illusion of a boundless park landscape within this small garden. The arrangement of the garden spaces and vistas around an imaginary centre was unique and herein lies the secret of Kent's visual synthesis. He discovered the hidden geometric relationship between the various parts of the landscape garden and in so doing made the house, the various garden spaces and the surrounding hills part of a panoramic landscape theatre which also included the observer.

Claude Lorrain. Landscape with Aeneas at Delos

Stourhead

Apollo grant us a home of our own. We are weary. Give us a walled city which shall endure and a lineage of our blood.
Prayer of Aeneas at Delos

Around 1740 Woburn Farm, The Leasowes, Painshill and Stourhead were created, which were to be influential in the development of the landscape garden during the second half of the 18th century. It is significant that these gardens were designed by the owners and garden enthusiasts themselves, unassisted by landscape architects. They are all based on the concept of the circular walk: the path and immediate surroundings was the actual garden, while the rest was agricultural landscape or woods. The most famous and best preserved example of these is Stourhead, where an Arcadian landscape was created in the manner of paintings by Claude Lorrain and Salvator Rosa. Here the circular walk is staged as a sequence of vignettes, with the lake as the reflecting pool mirroring the scenes. The park also has an exceptional geology. How exactly has the Stourhead landscape been created?

View from the terrace of the Fir Walk to the Temple of Apollo

HISTORY

Historically speaking, the area around Stourhead is holy ground. According to tradition it is the spot where King Alfred, the founder of the English nation and leader of the Anglo-Saxons, defeated the Danes at the Battle of Edington in 878. Stourhead Park, covering some 2,100 hectares, was originally a much larger estate belonging to the Stourtons, already a powerful family during the Anglo-Saxon period. Robert Stourton was granted permission to build Stourton House around 1350. In 1448, Sir John Stourton, Henry VI's treasurer, was allowed to enclose 400 hectares of meadows, grazing land and woods around the source of the River Stour as a hunting park. After that the fortunes of the Stourtons steadily went downhill. In the 17th century they suffered for their catholic and royalist beliefs and, during the Civil War of 1642-46, their estate was ransacked by government troops and they incurred heavy debts. In 1717, the estate was sold to Sir Thomas Meres, who resold it that same year at a profit to the bank of Sir Richard Hoare. In 1720 it came into the possession of his son, Henry Hoare (1677-1725). 'Good Henry' was the second generation of a burgeoning financial elite. The buying of land was one of the few ways of investing financial profit, as well as being a prerequisite of power.

Fig 1 The geomorphology of Stourhead Park

1. House
2. Six Wells Bottom
3. St Peter's Pump
4. Diana's Basin
5. Lily Pond
6. Fish ponds
7. Garden Lake
8. Paradise Well
9. Paddock Lake
10. New Lake/Gasper Lake

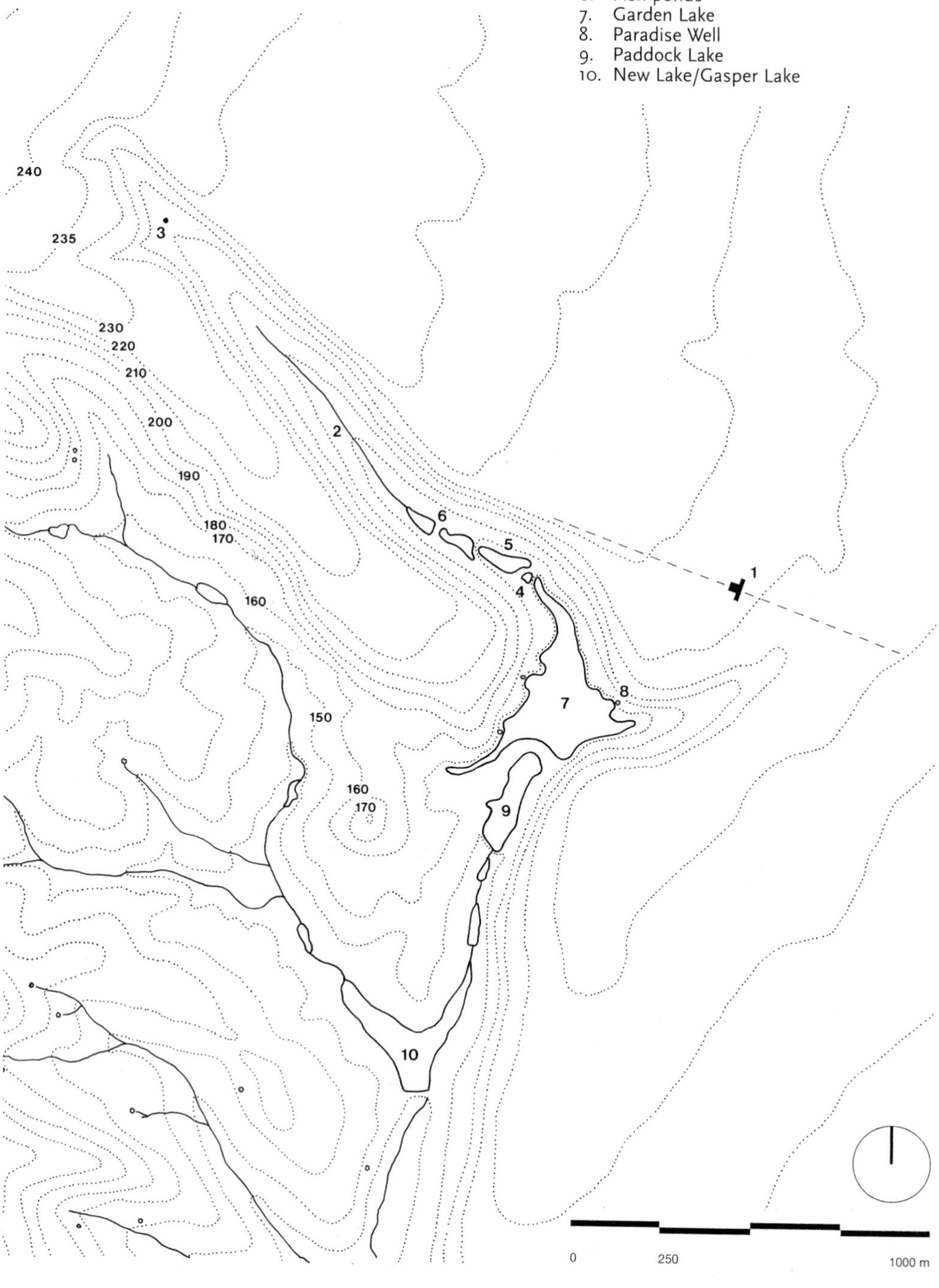

0   250   1000 m

His son, Henry Hoare II, 'The Magnificent' (1705-85), 1st Baronet and founder of Stourhead Park, was not only a sporting type but a man of taste, with an interest in painting and literature. As a banker, he was at the hub of the new court society under George I, who established the political power of the Whigs. Powerful gentlemen such as Carlisle and Burlington borrowed money from Hoare to build their country seats, as did Vanbrugh and Kent. In 1741 he moved to Stourhead and after the death of his wife in 1743 he set about designing the landscape garden, assisted by Henry Flitcroft, an established architect of the time.

In 1783 the grandchild of Henry Hoare II, Richard Colt Hoare (1758-1838), 2nd Baronet, inherited the estate. Under his guidance, the family came to own land, including Stourhead, which encompassed an impressive 4,500 hectares and the landscape garden was considerably enlarged. Stourhead changed very little during the Victorian Age and in 1946 all but 890 hectares of the estate was bequeathed to the National Trust.

GEOLOGY AND TOPOGRAPHY

Stourhead lies on the western edge of the Wessex chalk downs known as Salisbury Plain and borders the three counties of Wiltshire, Somerset and Dorset. These downs, created by folds of sedimentary Jurassic rock, form the scarplands of south-west England and they vary in height between 400 and 600 metres above sea level. They become increasingly higher to the west and are bounded by a steep ledge lying 900 metres above sea level before descending abruptly to 300 metres above sea level. The relatively soft rock is dissected by deep valleys or combes, their steep ledges are the source of several artesian springs that feed the surrounding rivers. The area around Stourhead is the watershed of the Brue, Wylye and Frome rivers, the latter meets the River Avon at Bath. The Dorset Stour flows through Dorset. Salisbury Plain is England's oldest inhabited landscape and there are many pre-historic and Roman remains of settlements and fortresses, including the famous Stonehenge, from the Bronze Age, some 30 kilometres away.

The Stourhead landscape therefore consists of two extremely different areas: the chalky, rolling, arable land of Salisbury Plain with its sparse vegetation, east of the house, and the scarplands intersected by the River Stour, with a steep bank hugging the Glastonbury Plain, to the west. The Stour was probably already dammed around 1700. In Six Wells Bottom and the junction with the side valley of Stourton Village there were originally a chain of ponds. In the valley there were supposedly a windmill and a few farmhouses. The rectangular pond at Paradise Well, where Flitcroft later built the Temple of Flora, was a drinking water reservoir for Stourton Village. By building a dam across the south west corner of the valley the fish ponds were flooded to create a lake (fig. 1).

STOURHEAD PARK AROUND 1722

In 1718 Stourton House was pulled down and in 1720 building started on a new house in the Palladian style, designed by Colin Campbell (1676-1729). It was called Stourhead House, a name that suggests the damming of the Stour was intended from the very beginning, and was a cube-shaped block similar to the central part of Villa Emo in Italy, also a Palladian building. The house existed for some 60 years in this simple form, until in 1792 two side wings, a Library and a Picture Gallery were added. In 1838 a portico with a flight of steps was added, built according to Campbell's original design.

The new house lay some 200 metres west of former Stourton House, with the entrance on the east front. It was reached from the south front, probably via the exist-

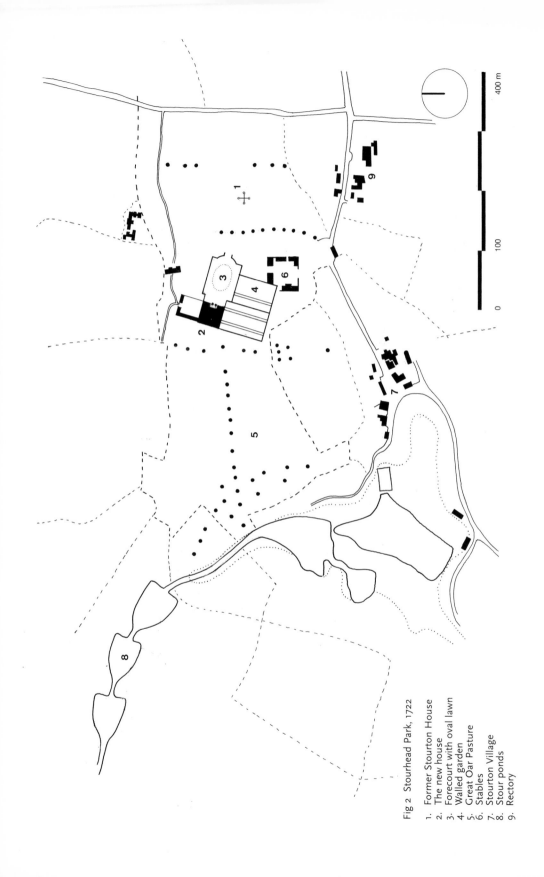

Fig 2 Stourhead Park, 1722

1. Former Stourton House
2. The new house
3. Forecourt with oval lawn
4. Walled garden
5. Great Oar Pasture
6. Stables
7. Stourton Village
8. Stour ponds
9. Rectory

Temple of Flora with cascade and spring. Engraving by C.W. Bampfylde, *c.* 1753

ing approach to Stourton House that branched off from the village road to Stourton. On the north front was a walled courtyard that was probably dismantled or moved elsewhere at a later stage. When the site is seen in the morphology of the landscape, the view of the forefront across the farmland, in keeping with the neo-Palladian nature of the agricultural villa, appears to have been the deciding factor in positioning the house (fig. 2).

THE GREAT OAR PASTURE

The first garden to the west of the house was a *ferme ornée* after the model of Home Park at Stowe. The Pleasure Garden comprised a walk around the Great Oar Pasture, its form directly derived from the natural morphology and surrounded by a ha-ha. Around 1746, along the edge of Six Wells Bottom, Fir Walk was laid out, a terrace covering the entire length of the valley wall. In 1746 an obelisk was built at its northern end. On the south side lay a terrace that probably had a commanding view of the eastern side valley and Stourton village.

In 1724 Stour valley appeared as it did at the time of Stourton House. The walled vegetable garden to the south of the house was dismantled and replaced by a lawn with beech trees. At the southern tip of this, Apollo's Belvedere was built. In the present situation, the Great Oar Pasture forms a whole with the parkland around the house, though the visual relationship with the valley garden has been lost through the growth of the plantings on the hill (fig. 3).

THE VALLEY GARDEN

The development of the valley garden began in 1744 with the building of the Temple of Flora and a grotto on the edge of the drinking water *bassin* at Paradise Well. The building of the dam in 1754 flooded the tableau at the Temple of Flora and the role of

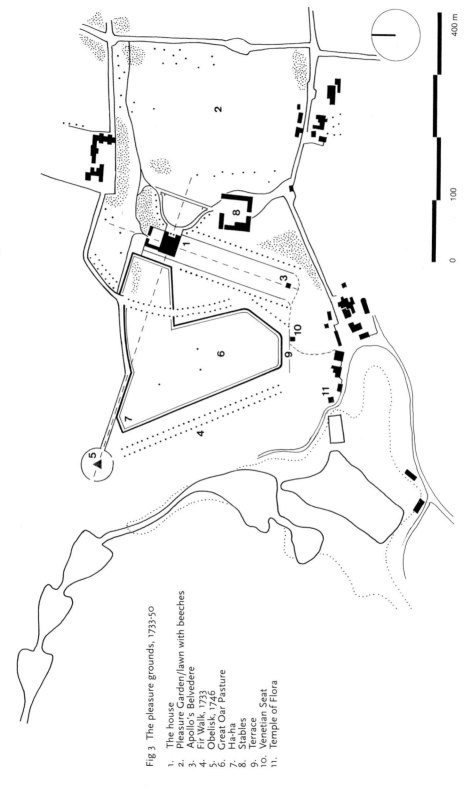

338

Fig 3 The pleasure grounds, 1733-50

1. The house
2. Pleasure Garden/lawn with beeches
3. Apollo's Belvedere
4. Fir Walk, 1733
5. Obelisk, 1746
6. Great Oar Pasture
7. Ha-ha
8. Stables
9. Terrace
10. Venetian Seat
11. Temple of Flora

0   100   400 m

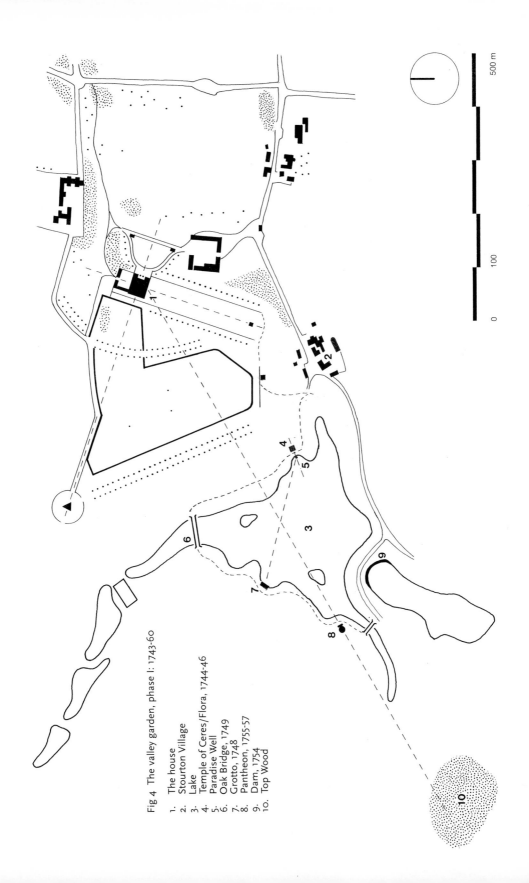

Fig 4 The valley garden, phase I: 1743-60

1. The house
2. Stourton Village
3. Lake
4. Temple of Ceres/Flora, 1744-46
5. Paradise Well
6. Oak Bridge, 1749
7. Grotto, 1748
8. Pantheon, 1755-57
9. Dam, 1754
10. Top Wood

500 m

100

0

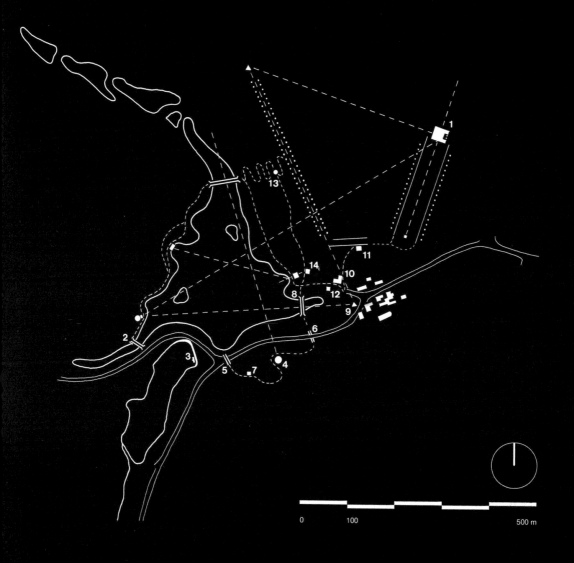

Fig 5 The valley garden, phase II: 1760-83

1. The house
2. Iron Bridge
3. Cascade, 1765
4. Temple of Apollo, 1765
5. Rock Bridge, 1760-65
6. Rock Underpass
7. Hermitage
8. Stone Bridge
9. Bristol Cross, 1765
10. Greenhouse (Gothic?)
11. Venetian Seat?
12. Chinese Umbrella
13. Turkish Tent
14. Orangerie

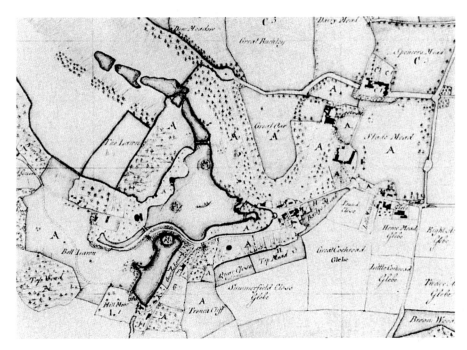

Layout of the estate, c. 1785

Paradise Well was partly taken over by the Grotto on the other side. The site of the Grotto, as with the Temple of Flora, was selected due to its proximity to a spring of the Stour. The water source was venerated like the Spring of Clitumnus by Pliny the Younger. The public road between Stourton and Blackslough ran across the dam on the edge of the plateau. Later the outermost circuit of the park along Alfred's Tower and the Covent was linked up with this (fig. 4).

The *Aeneid*, an epic poem by Virgil on the founding of Rome, played an important role in the initial phase of the garden. On the Temple of Flora, an inscription tells of Aeneas's initiation into the future of Rome. The Grotto, covered in tuff stone, is also dedicated to Aeneas. According to Kenneth Woodbridge, the painting *Aeneas at Delos*, by Claude Lorrain, is a key to the grotto's design.

After 1751, work came to a standstill until, in 1755, Hoare resumed again with the building of the Pantheon, originally called the Temple of Hercules. It became the chief element of the design and was placed at an angle across from the house, on one of the longitudinal axes of the lake, so that it could be seen from the Fir Walk and terrace. This Roman Temple consolidates the universal, classicist nature of the design and puts the Aeneid theme in a broader context.

In 1757, the Pantheon was completed and the lake given its present outline. A rock bridge was built across Zeals Road, the path of which went from the dam up the hill towards the more elevated Temple of Apollo, built in 1765. From here, as the apotheosis of the circular walk, there was a view across the entire lake. The path continued along the other side, going down and passing through a grotto *under* Zeals Road, until it emerged at the eastern arm of the lake. The difference in height between the grotto and the Temple of Apollo indicate the extent, as it were, from the reflecting surface of the lake (fig. 5).

Meanwhile at the foot of the Temple of Apollo a new tableau was created, the

View from the Pantheon in the direction of the Palladian bridge

concluding element of the design of the valley garden. From the Pantheon the visitor could look back towards the buildings of the village and St Peter's church which were somewhat at odds with the classical structures around the lake. What to do with the village? At Castle Howard the village of Henderskelfe disappeared under the parterre, while at Stowe only the church remained. Henry Hoare II, however, left Stourton Village as it was. A rustic, five-arched brick bridge, inspired by Palladio's bridge in Vicenza, was placed as a *coulisse* in front of it, thereby creating the impression of a river flowing through the village.

In 1765 Bristol Cross was added to this scene, a medieval cross that Henry Hoare acquired in 1764 and had re-erected in Stourton Village at the garden entrance, on the axis of Fir Walk, as a counterpart to the obelisk on the plateau and the Pantheon on the other side of the lake. Thus at the same time a geometric synthesis was created in this tableau between the various garden spaces and a merging together of the three pictorial genres: the Classical (in the form of the temples), the Rustic (the village) and the Gothic (elements from British history).

This was the landscape garden that Richard Colt Hoare inherited in 1783. The valley garden was largely completed and it was only necessary for him to add or modify a few of the details. Henry Hoare's building programme was revamped to obtain a stylistically pure effect, similar to that of an Italian villa. The Turkish Tent, another artifact, had already disappeared in 1792 and the Venetian Seat, the Chinese Alcove and the orangery were pulled down. In 1798 the wooden bridge spanning the northern arm of the lake was replaced by a ferry. In Stourton the cottages that spoiled the view of St Peter's church and the garden were torn down, while the remaining ones plus the church were given Gothic-style parapets. The inn was supplied with the family coat of arms, while a Tudor inspired lodge was built at the beginning of the driveway to the house.

The valley garden's system of paths was radically changed. Gravel paths were laid out along the shore of the lake and a path running along its northern arm incorporated this part of the design into the garden. Zeals Road was enclosed and an internal link created by making a path from the village across the Palladian bridge to the dam. The valley garden entrance was moved to the village so that the 'prescribed' route of the walk was interrupted. The descent from the house and the steep climb to the Temple of Apollo were skirted, while the effect of Henry Hoare II's scenography was lost.

Colt Hoare drastically altered the plantings around the lake by planting exotic trees and shrubs. The hill south of the lake was planted with laurel trees so that the Temple of Apollo stood out in a sea of green. The wood was also underplanted with laurel, which became so rampant it quickly had to be kept under control. Thus the transparent 18th-century plantings turned into an impenetrable thickset mass.

THE STOURHEAD LANDSCAPE

In a letter to his daughter Susanna in 1762, Henry Hoare II wrote of a plan that would crown all the other foregoing work. This was to be a tower dedicated to King Alfred on Kingsettle Hill, a few kilometres north-west of the house on the edge of Salisbury Plain. Alfred's Tower is at the end of a formal drive at the highest point along the western steep ledge, close to the former battlefield and on the borders of the counties of Somerset, Wiltshire and Dorset. This visually strategic position offers commanding views across the Somerset Plain and the Glastonbury Moors, against the backdrop of the Bristol Channel. The triangular tower, directed towards each of the three counties, was designed by Flitcroft and completed after his death in 1772. It is 53 metres high so that it can be seen from various points in the valley and from the house.

The carriage route marked the introduction of the horsedrawn carriage into the life of the country estate and the landscape garden of the second half of the 18th century. The development of the various circular walks and carriage routes reflect the increase in scale of the Stourhead landscape. A new drive was laid out from the north. The Tower Drive ran across the scarp along Six Wells Bottom to Alfred's Tower and, via the Hermitage (Convent), returned in a circular route to the dam and Stourton Village. The avenues in the panoramic landscape of the plateau form a counterpoint to the prescribed walk in the enclosed valley garden.

In 1820 Lake Gasper (now New Lake) was made, roughly 5.5 hectares in length and sited south of Turner's Lake Paddock at the village of Gasper. Its shape somewhat resembles Lake Stourhead but it has not been architectonically developed. By creating the carriage routes along the edge of the plateau, the panoramic congruity of the park-

Fig 6 The Stourhead landscape

1. Stourhead House
2. Stour
3. Stourhead Lake
4. Paddock Lake
5. New Lake/Gasper Lake
6. Six Wells Bottom
7. Tower Road
8. New Road
9. The Drove
10. Long Lane
11. Stourton Village
12. Stables
13. Rectory
14. Stourton Farm
15. Top Lane Farm/Home Farm
16. Beech Clump
17. Quarry
18. Neolithic fields
19. Fortress from the Iron Age
20. Round earthern rampart
21. Roman Camp
22. Beech Cottage
23. St Peter's Pump
24. Rustic Convent
25. Alfred's Tower

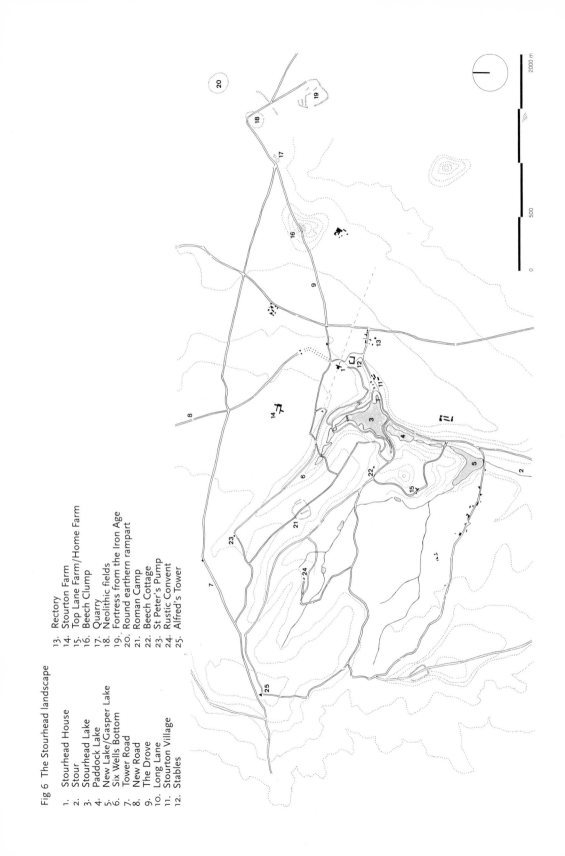

Alfred's Tower on the edge of Salisbury Plain

land became a new topic for consideration. Lake Paddock, Lake Gasper, Park Hill and Top Wood are all evidence that Colt Hoare was preoccupied by this (fig. 6).

THE ARCADIAN INITIATION

The plan of Stourhead Park consists of three different, yet interconnected, circuits. The circuit walk around the Great Oar Pasture distinctly recalls the pastoral compositional scheme of the Home Park at Stowe. The pictorial composition around the lake is the most detailed part of the plan, a further development of Kent's classical landscape, the first experiments of which were given form in the Elysian Fields at Stowe. The lake is the reflecting surface for the various staged scenes, divided up by screens of islands planted with clumps of trees and surrounded by the Arcadian decor of the lush, forested hills. The scenic drive to Alfred's Tower on Kingsettle Hill on the edge of Salisbury Plain integrates the spectacular geology of Stourhead Park into the composition. In this sense it is a forerunner of the late 18th-century landscape gardens, like Hawkstone, which were also sited in similar settings.

Harewood House seen from across the lake

Harewood

One of the most delectable of landscapes.
    Dorothy Stroud, *'Capability' Brown*, 1975

Harewood House is situated on the eastern flank of the Pennines, 12 kilometres to the north of Leeds. The landscape garden comprises some 600 hectares, while the estate now covers 2,830 hectares, bounded on the north side by the wide valley of the River Wharfe.

HISTORY

A border castle at Harewood was built on the edge of a plateau, just to the south of a ford in the River Wharfe, by Robert de Lisle in the early 12th century in order to keep invaders from the north at bay. In 1116 the Normandy nobleman William de Curcy erected the All Saints Church a short distance from the castle. In the mid-17th century the castle was abandoned and became a ruin. During the 16th century the estate was inherited by the Gascoigne family and combined with nearby Gawthorpe Hall. In 1580 it came into the possession of the Wentworths (Earls of Strafford). In 1738 it came into the hands of Henry Lascelles from Northallerton, a descendant of a noble family who had come over to England with William the Conqueror, and had lived, among others, at Henderskelfe Castle in Yorkshire. Lascelles had amassed a fortune from the proceeds of sugar plantations in Barbados.

Henry Lascelles son, Edwin (1712-95), was the originator of the estate's landscape garden. His nephew, Edward, inherited the estate and became the 1st Earl of Harewood in 1812. The house, including the extensive art collection, is still owned by the Lascelles family and is now occupied by the 7th Earl and his wife.

MORPHOLOGY AND TOPOGRAPHY

Harewood House lies in a landscape of fairly even, sandy hills running from east to west, between 200 and 500 metres above sea level, on a loamy undersoil intersected by marshy, badly drained river valleys. The Stank Beck runs through Harewood's park landscape from south to north and flows into the Wharfe. On the north side of the Wharfe is Alms Cliff, a 650-metre steep incline. Harewood village, a flourishing market town in 1209 with its own charter, was an important staging post for coaches in the 18th century. In 1753 the bridge spanning the Wharfe on the turnpike to Harrogate was replaced. Edwin Lascelles had the village, designed by John Carr of York, rebuilt as a model village and attempted to set up a ribbon factory but this was to founder. Around 1800 Lascelles had virtually the entire population of the village in his service. Halfway to the house is All Saints Church, remodelled in 1760 by Edwin Lascelles, which remained in use until around 1970 (fig. 1).

The 17th-century Gawthorpe Hall was situated on the Stank Beck, surrounded by meadowlands and the remains of a wood, and was linked by a road with All Saints Church as well as possibly with the ford in the River Wharfe. Most of the land was already enclosed, although around All Saints there were still common fields. The plateau south-east of the village was moorland. In 1771 Gawthorpe Hall was demolished to make way for a new house higher on the hill.

Immediately after his father's death, Edwin began building a new house, designed by John Carr (1723-1807). The site was probably decided partly on the advice of 'Capability' Brown. In 1759 the foundation stone was laid and by 1771 the house was habitable. Robert Adams contributed greatly to its interior, while Thomas Chippendale supplied the furniture. The house had a classic façade, with a portico and symmetric wings with side pavilions. The layout was asymmetrical, a so-called double circuit house, with public rooms on the right side and private quarters, with a different layout, on the left. Around 1850 Sir Charles Barry (1795-1860) built an additional third floor and replaced the portico on the south side with an enormous terrace and parterre. In so doing, the house changed from an 18th-century country manor into a 19th-century Italian *palazzo*.

THE LANDSCAPE OF BROWN, 1772-81

Harewood Park is one of 'Capability' Brown's late compositions. After his first visit to Gawthorpe Hall in 1757, Brown made a general plan for a new house and garden, although no sketches from his hand still remain. As a member of the House of Lords, Lascelles lived part of the year in London so that his steward Samuel Popplewell oversaw the building and the laying out of the garden. The garden was worked on without consulting Brown: much of the practical designing was left to a Mr Woods, the surveyor, to Thomas White, a pupil of Brown, and to a Mr Hutton, the estate gardener. The work focused initially on the Pleasure Grounds, to the west of the new house, where a mount and a ha-ha were laid out. A few years before Brown appeared for the second time on the scene, Lascelles had the Stank Beck dammed on the north-west side, thus creating an irregularly shaped lake which was to be the starting point of Brown's composition.

In 1772 Brown was consulted for the second time and designed *A Plan for the Intended Water and the Grounds*. He completed his work in 1781, two years before his

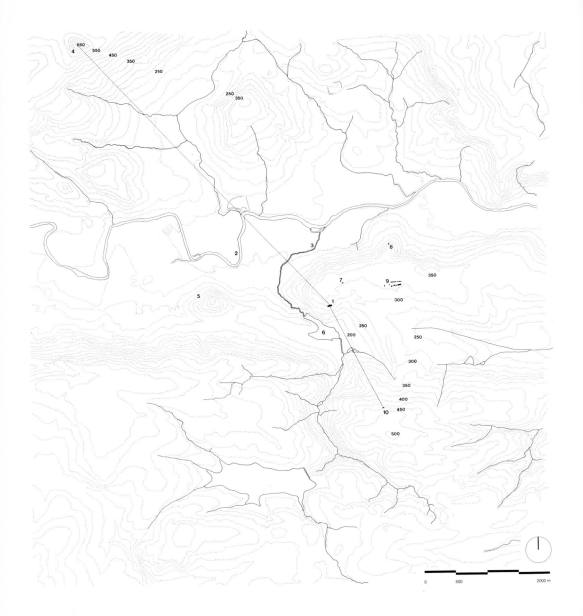

Fig 1 Landscape morphology

1. Harewood House
2. River Wharfe
3. Eccup Beck/Stank Beck
4. Almscliff Crag
5. Rawden Hill
6. Harewood Lake/Fish Pond
7. All Saints Church
8. Harewood Castle
9. Harewood Village
10. Sugar Hill (Temple)

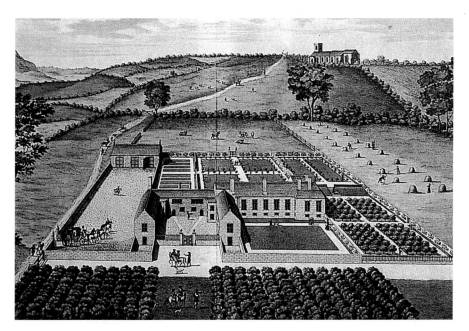

Gawthorpe Hall, *c.* 1720

death. This time he hired a foreman who paid the workmen, while Lascelles provided the tools, horses and materials. The meadowland and the fields on the south front of the house were refashioned into a park landscape with single and clumps of trees. The fences were removed and agricultural improvements such as levelling the terrain, building a drainage system and sowing better varieties of grass were carried out, as well as stocking the lake with fish. The aesthetic ideal also went hand in hand with improving cattle stock, producing wood and managing the estate's wildlife. The park was surrounded by a ha-ha, of which only sections now remain (fig. 2).

The hill to the north of the new house was excavated so that the house was sited on a ridge. In the belt of North Park a diagonal vista of Alms Cliff was cut out on the other side of the Wharfe. The Stank Beck in Piper Wood was transformed into several trout ponds, while the lake was formed by digging out a milldam upstream. Dickenson's Pond and Long Ing Pond, with a water level 10 metres higher than the lake, were dug out as a visual continuation of the lake as far as the principal axis of the house and Sun Sides, the lawn to the south. On the poorly drained gley soil of the river valleys, oak and elm were planted, on the sandy hills, birch, while holly oak, laurel and hawthorn formed the undergrowth.

A belt walk with seating, statues and follies was less suitable for Harewood due to the imposing asymmetry of the site to the south. Instead, Brown concentrated on designing the approaches to the estate as scenic drives. On the north side Harewood Drive joined the network of village roads and continued through a gatehouse in a forecourt, a landscape antechamber with All Saints Church as a landmark. Only after cutting into the belt could the house be seen from a favourable angle.

The scheme for the southern drive suggests a 17th-century 'Mannerist' route. The Lofthouse Drive branched off from the Leeds to Harrogate turnpike at a point which provided a grand vista of the house and the lake against the hazy background

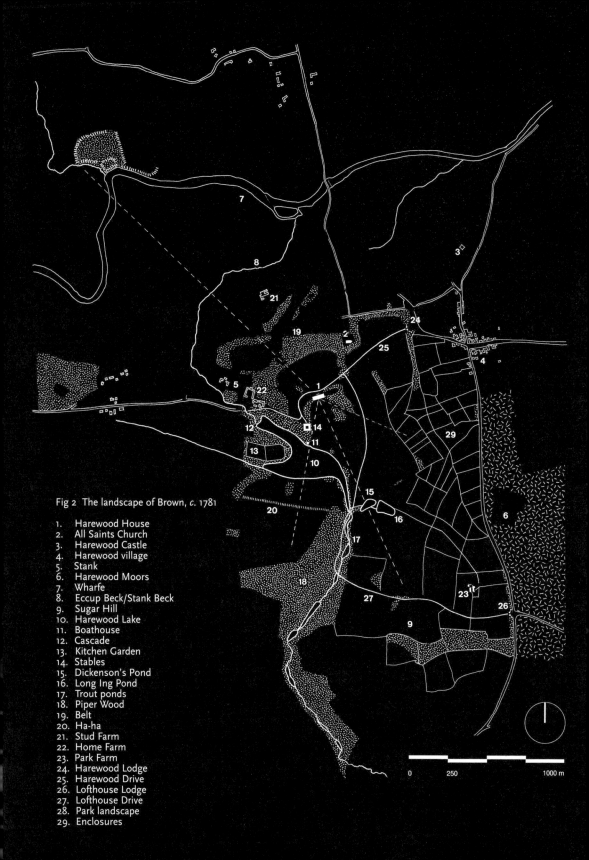

Fig 2 The landscape of Brown, c. 1781

1. Harewood House
2. All Saints Church
3. Harewood Castle
4. Harewood village
5. Stank
6. Harewood Moors
7. Wharfe
8. Eccup Beck/Stank Beck
9. Sugar Hill
10. Harewood Lake
11. Boathouse
12. Cascade
13. Kitchen Garden
14. Stables
15. Dickenson's Pond
16. Long Ing Pond
17. Trout ponds
18. Piper Wood
19. Belt
20. Ha-ha
21. Stud Farm
22. Home Farm
23. Park Farm
24. Harewood Lodge
25. Harewood Drive
26. Lofthouse Lodge
27. Lofthouse Drive
28. Park landscape
29. Enclosures

0   250   1000 m

The South Park from the terrace (photograph by J.K.M. te Boekhorst)

of the broad Wharfe valley. The drive followed the lie of the land along the edge of Sugar Hill, disappeared into Piper Wood and continued along the trout ponds in the valley of Stank Beck, intersecting, after Dickenson's Pond, the vista from the house to Sugar Hill for a second time in the opposite direction. After a broad sweep of the house, All Saints Church appeared and the house disappeared from view. In the belt the drive joined the northern one at right angles.

Brown's design did not aspire to architectonic order but made use of the morphology of the natural landscape. The asymmetry of the site was accentuated even more, rather than compensated for or disguised. Perspective was provided in the predominantly horizontal composition by the main band of trees of Piper Wood, which came down to the lake. Brown used the lake's irregular water as a reference surface on which the wavy lines of the composition could be visually traced. The eye is continually drawn to the distance on the left-hand side of the picture plane, but can only settle when it returns to the water surface in the pith of the composition on the extreme right-hand side.

THE ADDITIONS BY REPTON, 1800

Edward, 1st Earl, asked Humphry Repton (1752-1818) to make certain modifications. Repton proposed a new gatehouse and drive for the north side which joined the turnpike from Wetherby. The garden was made considerably bigger, from the east side to the Leeds to Harrogate turnpike, where a belt was laid out on the north side with North Park. This changed the visual reach of the park; attention shifted from Brown's classical landscape on the south side to the view over the Wharfe valley on the north side. The South Park was cleared for agricultural use so that many single trees were dug up and wire fences appeared. The lake's shoreline became undefined, caused by silt and flooding, while Dickenson's Pond and Long Ing Pond became overgrown. The spacial impression is less distinct than it was, but nevertheless Brown's landscape has essentially been preserved (fig. 3).

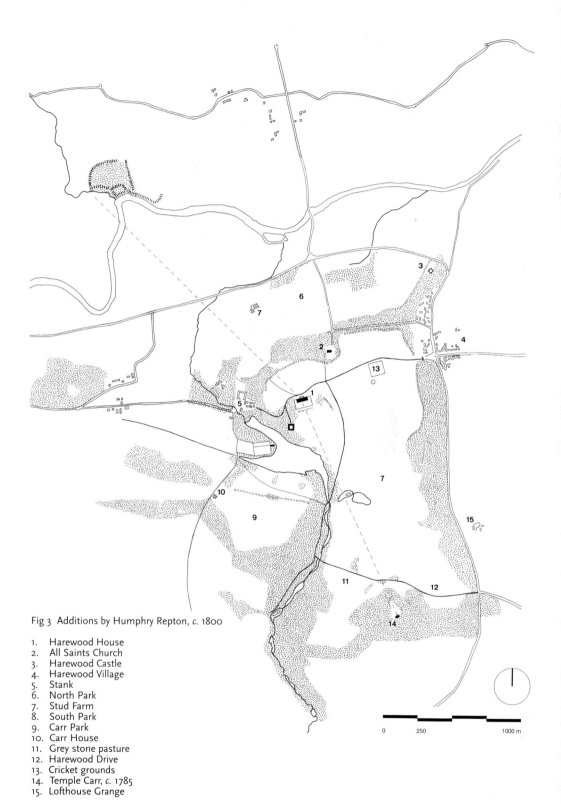

Fig 3 Additions by Humphry Repton, *c.* 1800

1. Harewood House
2. All Saints Church
3. Harewood Castle
4. Harewood Village
5. Stank
6. North Park
7. Stud Farm
8. South Park
9. Carr Park
10. Carr House
11. Grey stone pasture
12. Harewood Drive
13. Cricket grounds
14. Temple Carr, *c.* 1785
15. Lofthouse Grange

0   250   1000 m

J.M.W. Turner. Harewood seen from the south east at Lofthouse Gate

THE NATURAL PICTURE PLANE

The spatial effect of Brown's composition for Harewood eludes the geometric principles of a layout. Brown designed Harewood as a four-dimensional painting, a play of moving outlines that change with every season and every year, but always come to rest in the reflecting waters of the lake, the pivot of the entire composition. By a process of eliminating and amending, he designed a scene in which nature's abstract beauty can flourish.

In Brown's park drives the scenes are connected to each other in the form of a Manneristic arabesque which, in itself, anticipates movement. Thus Harewood takes on the form of a 'cinematographic' composition, pointing the way to the urban circulation pattern.

View from the belvedere northwards over the Shropshire plain (photograph by B. Kwast)

Hawkstone

A kind of turbulent pleasure between fright and admiration.
Dr Samuel Johnson, after visiting Hawkstone in July 1774

Hawkstone lies between Shrewsbury and Whitchurch, on the A49 to Liverpool and Manchester, in rough sandstone hills with steep slopes and deep ravines that jut out above the Shropshire Plain. Along with Hackfall and Piercefield in Gloucester, Hawkstone is one of the few landscape gardens that can rightly be termed 'picturesque' and was one of the most visited gardens in England at the end of the 18th century.

HISTORY

Hawkstone lies on the Welsh borders, since time immemorial the disputed boundary area between the English Midlands and the highlands of Wales: traces of fortifications from the Bronze and Iron Ages can still be found. William the Conqueror dispensed land to powerful barons who built fortresses, often founding settlements or boroughs at the same time. Hawkstone Hall was first mentioned in the preserved Pipe Roll of 1185 – an ancient annual record kept by the British Treasury – as a stronghold of Roger de Hauckestan (fig. 1).

In 1227, at the time of Henry III, Henry de Audley acquired the Manor of Weston and the right to build a castle. Red Castle, belonging to the Manor, was built on a solitary steep-sided cliff that was only accessible from the south side and already had military importance during the Iron Age. The Audley line died out and by the end of the 16th century the castle was a ruin. In 1556 part of the estate came into the possession of Rowland Hill via Thomas Lodge of London. Three generations of the Hill

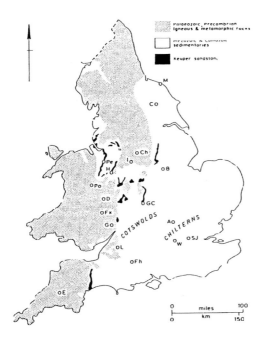

The geology of Picturesque England (H = Hawkstone)
(from J. Appleton, 'Some Thoughts on the Geology of the Picturesque', 1986)

family had led a quiet existence until through the efforts of Richard Hill (1655-1727), or 'The Great Hill' as he was known, they rose through the ranks of the aristocracy.

Rowland Hill (1705-83), 1st Baronet, inherited the estate in 1727 and together with his son Richard created the landscape garden. In 1756 Red Castle was added to the land at Hawkstone. Richard Hill (1732-1809), 2nd Baronet, inherited the estate in 1783 and immediately set about extending the landscape garden with great gusto. On his death in 1809 Hawkstone was one of the sights of England, visited by droves of people who often stayed for a few days.

Rowland Hill (1800-75), 4th Baronet and 2nd Viscount, had the house remodelled and extended the parkland. His extravagant lifestyle led to the estate's demise. In 1895 the effects of the Hall were auctioned and the house lay empty until 1906 when it was sold together with the park. In 1926 the Hall and Hawkstone Park Hotel were sold to the congregation of the Redemptorist Fathers, who built a church on the south side of the house in 1932. Land near the hotel is now a golf course. In 1990 the owner of Hawkstone Park Hotel began restoring the most important buildings on the hills of the park. In 1993 the park reopened again.

HAWKSTONE HALL, 1724-83

Hawkstone Hall, built of brick around 1700 in a depression in the slope at the foot of Terrace Hill, lies on the borders of the badly drained Shropshire Plain. No use was made of the hill to direct the view northwards towards the plain. Instead the house, built in different phases, lies at the foot and looks out along the hill. In 1721 two fore-

Fig 1 Geography

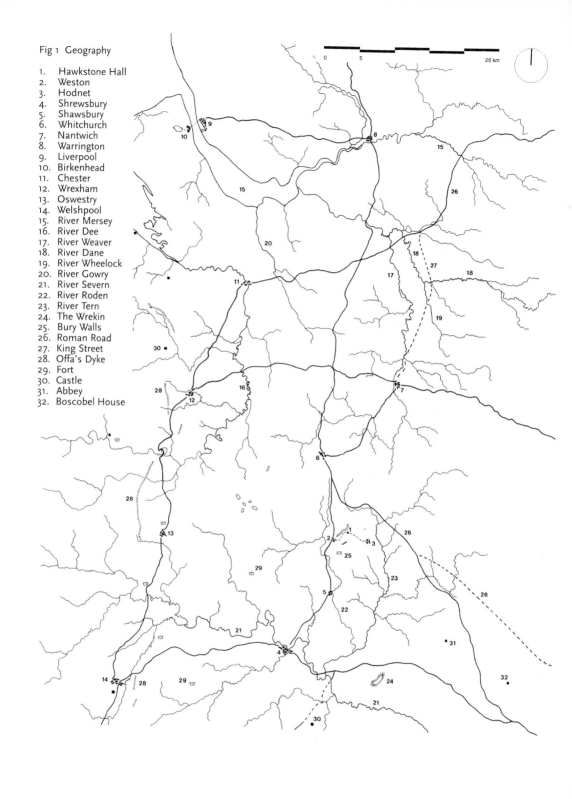

courts were built, which disappeared again during the next building phase, and a parterre laid out at the rear. In 1723 a new farmhouse was built north-east of the house and a formal approach with elm plantings. Along Terrace Hill paths were laid out, while on the slope of the path to Grotto Hill a Summerhouse and a Cold Bath were built.

From the house the spectacular steep ledges of the four hills cannot be seen; the horizon is formed by a wooded ridge. Hawkstone Hall was reached from the east via Hodnet and Marchamley, while north of Grotto Hill it was linked to Weston (fig. 2).

THE LANDSCAPE GARDEN, 1783-1809

The core of the landscape garden was formed by four sandstone hills, 220 metres high, that dramatically rise above the seemingly endless Shropshire Plain, some 80 metres above sea level. Hawk Lake or Hawk River, which has a serpentine form, was made between 1784 and 1787 by William Emes, a follower of Brown. The lake has an unusual shape, about two kilometres long and roughly 40 metres wide, and does not function as a reflecting pool – its surface can hardly be seen from the house – but was intended for boating. As part of the composition, the lake's shape is extremely effective. It lies like an eyebrow around one end of the garden, linking the house with Red Castle Hill and thus visually integrating the contrast between the horizontality of the Shropshire plain and the steep ledges of the hills into the garden.

There was a boat to ferry guests from the Inn around the lake so that they could admire the spectacular rock formations. It was also equipped with a canon to enable the sound to be heard reverberating against the rocks. Between Grotto Hill and Red Castle Hill there was originally a side lake that was separated from the lake by a dam and over which the road from Weston went. This part has disappeared possibly because it did not hold water very well (fig. 3).

THE SCENIC WALK

Sir Richard extended the circular walk and landscape garden as well as embellished it with several themes. Originally the design was similar to that at Stourhead. The walk began at Hawkstone Hall from where the unsuspected visitor, arriving via Hodnet and Marchamley, could not entirely see the steep ledges, which only came into view when standing on the edge. In 1790, at the west entrance of the garden, Hawkstone Inn was built (now Hawkstone Park Hotel) to accommodate the ever-growing stream of visitors. This inn, with a commanding view of the steep ledges, marked the starting point of the route through the park, so that the original effect of the surprise was lost. Visitors could take the circular walk via Grotto Hill, Fairy Glen and Terrace Hill, where the Hermitage was located, to the Menagerie and back. Various other day trips could be made, including one to Bury Walls. Many points of interest along the way were directly linked to the natural landscape, such as a vista, a rare planting or an unusual type of rock (fig. 4).

The Grotto, high in the hill, was dug out by Sir Rowland, possibly on the basis of an existing one and was opened in 1783. The hill was climbed originally from its west side, along the Temple of Patience, at the foot, which became commonly known as Gingerbread Hall. Later an entrance at Terrace Hill was made. Sir Richard had The Cleft, a narrow cave on the north-east side of the hill, made deeper and a tunnel dug out to the grotto, the inside of which was lined with cinders from the new Darby's iron foundry in Coalbrookdale. After an adventurous exploration of the grotto, the visitor emerged onto a 'balcony' and was suddenly confronted with the Awful Precipice, a ravine on the edge of the plain. Grotto Hill was crowned by a ruined Gothic arch as an eye-catcher, through which the visitor had a view of the fortress to the south.

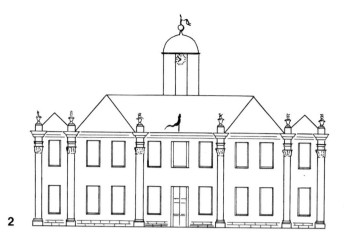

2

Fig 2 Hawkstone Hall, 1727

1. Hawkstone Hall
2. West front, 1720
3. Forecourt with lions
4. Hawkstone Park Farm
5. Kitchen Garden
6. Parterre
7. Ranger's Lodge
8. Hawkstone Farm
9. Marchamley
10. Elm Avenue
11. Hawk River/Lake

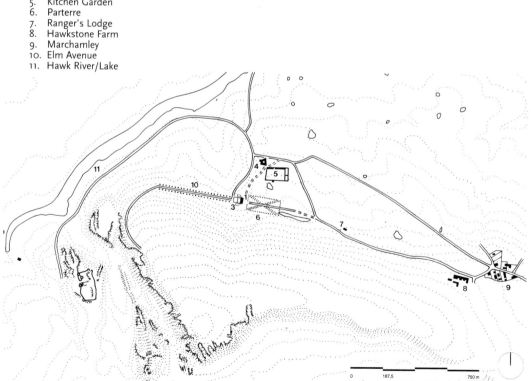

Fig 3 Hawkstone Park, 1783-1809

1. Hawkstone Hall
2. Obelisk, 1795
3. White Tower, 1784
4. Foxes Knob
5. The Grotto, 1765
6. Eye-catcher/Gothic Arch
7. Awful Precipice
8. The Red Castle
9. Neptune's Whim, 1787-1790
10. Windmill
11. Hawk Lake
12. Boathouse
13. Menagerie Pool
14. Citadel
15. Bury Walls
16. Hawkstone Abbey Farm
17. Abbey Cottages
18. North Lodge
19. Hawkstone Park Farm
20. Kitchen Garden
21. Ranger's Lodge
22. Hawkstone Farm
23. Marchamley
24. The Vineyard, 1784
25. Rake Park Lodge
26. Bury Farm
27. Weston
28. Rake Park
29. Belt

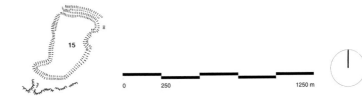

0   250   1250 m

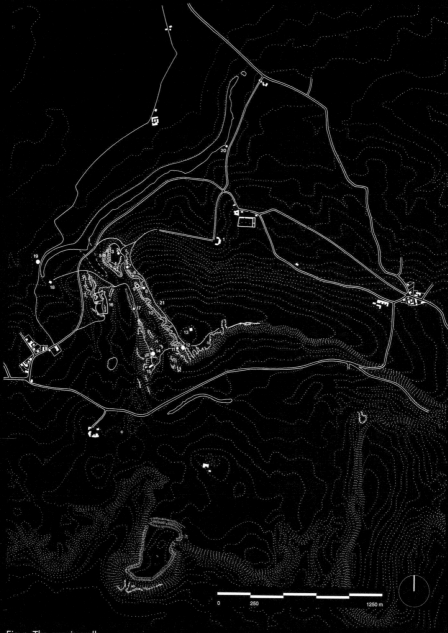

Fig 4 The scenic walk

1. Hawkstone Hall
2. Temples of Patience/
   Gingerbread Hall
3. The Cleft and Tunnel,
   1784-1799
4. The Grotto
5. Awful Precipice
6. Canopy and Indian Rock
   (exact location unknown)
7. Swiss Bridge

8. Hermitage
9. St Francis's Cave, 1784
10. Foxes Knob
11. Reynard's Walk
12. Tower Glen and Urn
13. The White Tower
14. Obelisk
15. Menagerie
16. Greenhouse
17. The Red Castle

18. The Giant's Well, 1784
19. The Lion's Den, 1784
20. Swiss Chalet
21. Neptune's Whim
22. Windmill
23. Boathouse
24. The Scene in Otaheite,
    1784-1799 (exact location
    unknown)
25. The Terrace, 1784

View from Terrace Hill (photograph by B. Kwast)

On the ledge of Terrace Hill, not far from Grotto Hill, was a hermitage inhabited by the 'venerable barefooted Father Francis', a genuine recluse equipped with the traditional *vanitas* symbols, who spoke a cautious *memento mori* to visitors. After 1800 he was replaced by a slot machine and later still by a guide who played the role of a recluse. In 1795 an obelisk was erected on Terrace Hill in memory of Sir Rowland Hill, the founder of the dynasty. The statue on the column looks north across the Shropshire Plain.

In 1832 new Pleasure Grounds were laid out with the help of William Gilpin. The scenic drives of the 2nd Viscount incorporated the landscape around the steep hills into the design of the landscape garden. In 1853 a new approach was made from Weston, through a ravine between Grotto Hill and Terrace Hill. Along the upper edge of the terrace and the southern steep edge an avenue was laid to Hodnet. Two wrought iron bridges spanning the Glade at the Vineyard and a ravine at Marchamley Hill were needed for this. The link with Weston on the south side of Hawk River was kept as a public road (this now runs via North Lodge and Hawkstone Abbey Farm on the north shore of the lake). On the south side was the route to Hodnet running along the Menagerie Pool, the obelisk at Terrace Hill and the citadel.

SEE AND SHIVER
The scenic walks at Hawkstone can be seen as the last phase of a development that started with the circuit walk around Home Park at Stowe and, via the classic trip around Stourhead Lake and Brown's belt, gradually became detached from its original social significance. The relatively small and elitist gatherings of the early 18th century, the heart of social life at the country estate, made way for hordes of urban tourists who visited Hawkstone from afar for a few days' guided tour: a foretaste of the mass recreation of the 19th-century metropolis.

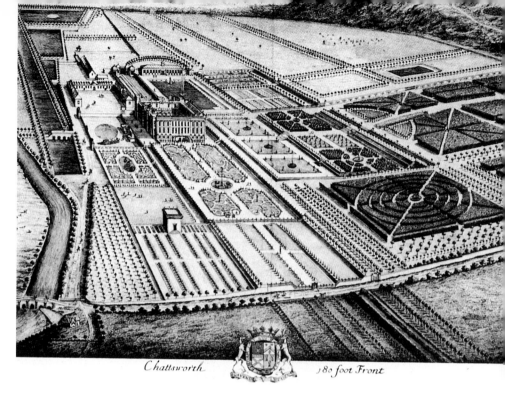

Chattsworth ꞏ *18o foot Front*

Bird's eye view from the south. Engraving by Leendert Knyff, 1699

Chatsworth

There is no one whose name will be so permanently associated with Chatsworth as Paxton.
     The 7th Earl on Paxton's death in 1865

Chatsworth lies along the River Derwent in the Peak District, 20 kilometres south-west of Sheffield. The garden covers some 42 hectares, while Chatsworth Park is now around 440 hectares. The garden became famous in the 19th century: Charles de Saint-Amant, director of the Tuileries in Paris, for instance, compared it to Versailles. In our own age Chatsworth is one of the most visited and popular gardens in England.

     The layout for Chatsworth dates back to the 17th century. The landscaping of Lancelot Brown from the 18th century did not play a decisive role in the ultimate form of the garden. Joseph Paxton succeeded in enlarging the 18th-century concept of the landscape garden while making use of the technical advances of the Victorian Age. How is this formal layering of the landscape made visible at Chatsworth?

HISTORY

Sir William Cavendish (1505-57) was one of the agents of Henry VIII during the Dissolution of the Monasteries and was married to Elizabeth Barley (c. 1527-1608), also known as 'Bess of Hardwick'. He purchased the Chatsworth estate in 1549 from the Leche family and began building a new house in 1552. In 1608 Chatsworth came into the possession of their son William, who became 1st Earl of Devonshire in 1618. William, the 4th Earl, who had been raised during the Protectorate under Cromwell, was later made the 1st Duke of Devonshire by King William III. The 4th Duke (1720-64), an influential Whig, married Charlotte Boyle in 1748, the heiress of the 3rd Earl of Burlington, so that her inheritance came into the possession of the Cavendish family.

William Spencer Cavendish (1790-1858), the 6th Duke, inherited Chatsworth in 1811. Within a few months he began working on new plans for the estate, together with Jeffry Wyatville (1766-1840) and Joseph Paxton (1803-65). Chatsworth became his life's work; the improvements were to preoccupy him for the next 47 years.

Joseph Paxton began as head gardener at Chatsworth in 1826 when he was 23 years old. He remained there for 35 years and from there developed into one of the most influential landscape architects of the Victorian Age, a worthy successor to Humphry Repton and John Claudius Loudon. Paxton possessed remarkable botanical knowledge and an exceptional imagination. He worked within the existing stylistic conventions, his greatest talents lying in combining design, science and technique. He was an innovator in constructing buildings, machines and waterworks, such as the Great Conservatory at Chatsworth, the forerunner of his world-famous Crystal Palace built at Sydenham for the 1851 World Exhibition.

MORPHOLOGY AND GEOGRAPHY

The Peak District consists of lime-deficient, igneous rock and slate dating from the Pre-Cambrian and Palaeozoic ages. The resulting landscape is bare and inhospitable with steep hills rising to 300 metres. The garden lies at the foot of Millstone Grit, a steep hill of impermeable rock which forms the basis of the spectacular waterworks at Chatsworth. The Derwent lies about 100 metres above sea level at Chatsworth, while the difference in height between the South Lawn and the Hunting Tower, at the top of the hill, is roughly 100 metres. On the plateau of East Moor are the peat moors and downs, the extensively used grasslands. Derwent valley has an irregular shape with a steep east hill (fig. 1).

The present road network follows the Derwent in a mainly south-north direction. Earlier on, Chatsworth was reached from the east side, via Chesterfield across East Moor. The road descended the hill and emerged at the rear of the cascade house, where one then had to circumscribe the south side of the garden along Holmes Lane. At the Derwent one turned right before the bridge into the approach drive that went up to the west forecourt. In 1761 Brown designed a new approach (Park Drive) through the village of Edensor along the western boundary of the estate (fig. 2).

The house of Sir William Cavendish and Bess of Hardwick had four corner towers and diagonally placed turrets at the central entrance gate, surrounded by a wall with roundels and square defence towers. In 1685 the 1st Duke commissioned William Talman, a new, relatively unknown architect, to design a new south front. Talman's pioneering design for an English country house consisted of two storeys on a rustic foundation. In 1687 the Tudor lodges in front of the west front were replaced by a classic courtyard. There was now a marked difference between the west front and the new south front and attempts were made to create a more unified whole, probably with the help of Thomas Archer. Under the 4th Duke, James Paine (c. 1716-89) demolished several smaller buildings on the north side of the house and made a new entrance with a triumphal arch on the axis of the north front.

In 1816, the 6th Duke had the east side rebuilt by Wyatville (then still Jeffry Wyatt). The service wing by Paine was not designed to be seen from the new northern access and detracted from the grandeur of the entrance court. Wyatville designed a new façade with a larger entrance screen consisting of a porch and lodges next to the existing gate by James Paine, which was pulled down. In 1827 the house, with an orangery added between the Theatre Tower and the Sculpture Gallery, took on its present-day outline.

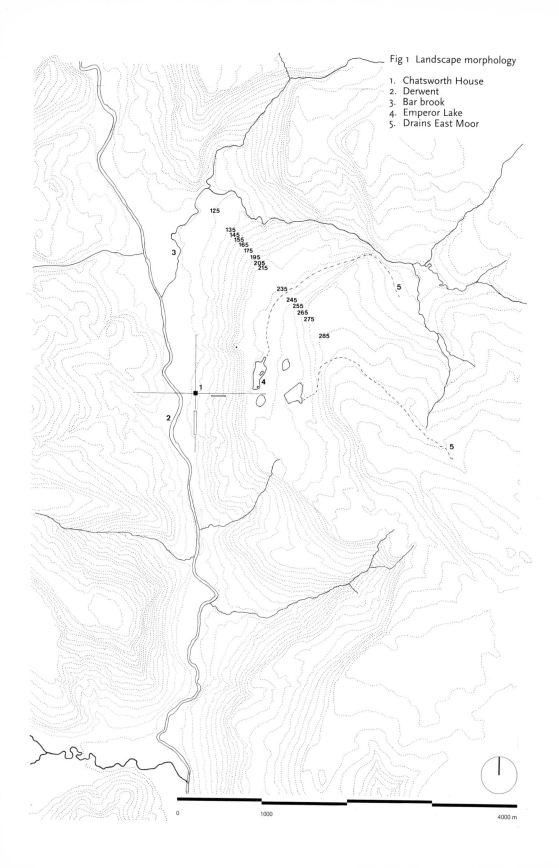

Fig 1 Landscape morphology

1. Chatsworth House
2. Derwent
3. Bar brook
4. Emperor Lake
5. Drains East Moor

125
135
145
155
165
175
195
205
215
235
245
255
265
275
285

3

5

1

2

4

5

0   1000   4000 m

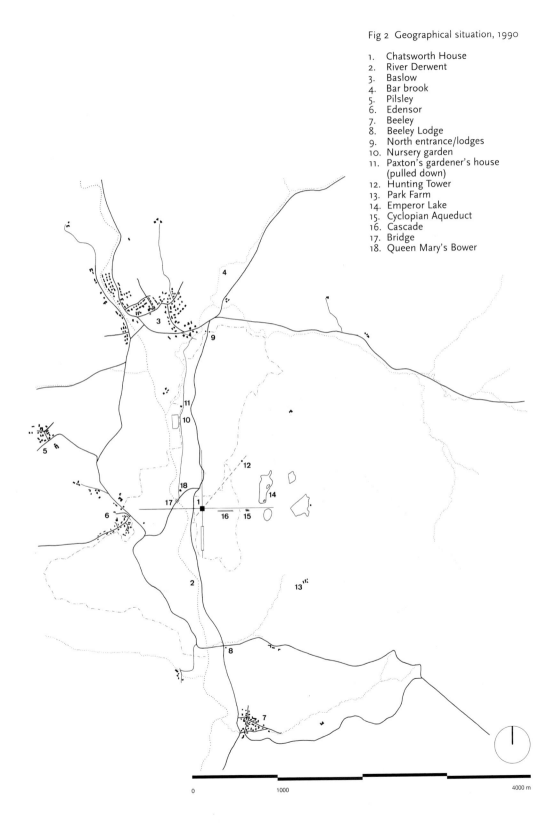

Fig 2 Geographical situation, 1990

1. Chatsworth House
2. River Derwent
3. Baslow
4. Bar brook
5. Pilsley
6. Edensor
7. Beeley
8. Beeley Lodge
9. North entrance/lodges
10. Nursery garden
11. Paxton's gardener's house
    (pulled down)
12. Hunting Tower
13. Park Farm
14. Emperor Lake
15. Cyclopian Aqueduct
16. Cascade
17. Bridge
18. Queen Mary's Bower

0   1000   4000 m

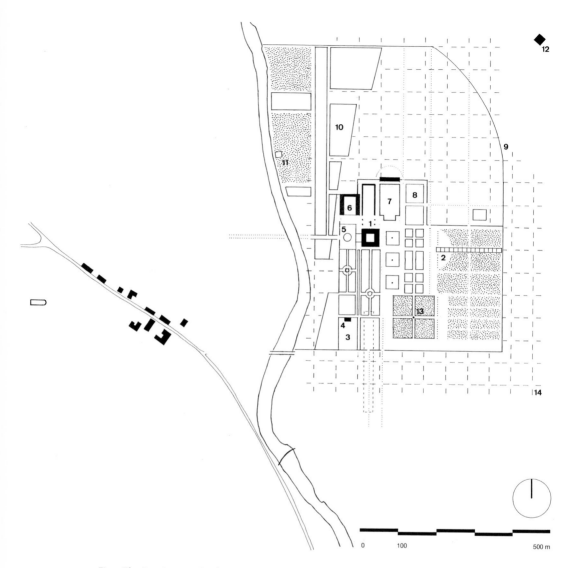

Fig 3 The Renaissance Garden, 1690

1. Chatsworth House
2. Cascade
3. Bowling Green
4. Bowling Green/Flora Temple
5. Forecourt
6. Stables
7. Reflecting pond
8. Kitchen Garden
9. Wall
10. Fish ponds
11. Queen Mary's Bower
12. The Stand/Hunting Tower
13. Probable place of Weeping Willow Fountain
14. Design matrix

0   100   500 m

Proposal for a cascade in Stand Wood by William Kent, 1740

THE RENAISSANCE GARDEN OF 1690

It was in 1560, eight years after the rebuilding of the house had begun, that there was first mention of a garden. Later in 1636 it was described in a poem by Thomas Hobbes, *De mirabilis pecci*, as 'the wonder of the Peak', so called because of the miraculous transformation of a desolate wilderness into a paradisiacal garden. There are no known drawings or illustrations from which the garden can be faithfully reconstructed, though the level terrace of the South Lawn and the retaining wall on the west side date from this time. The Hunting Tower was placed around 1580 on the highest point of the eastern steep edge of East Moor, at an angle to the Elizabethan house. In 1688 the 1st Duke commissioned George London and Henry Wise to design a formal parterre with a bowling green on the south front of the new forecourt, to which Talman added a bowling house (Flora's Temple, now at the north entrance of the garden) in 1695. In 1694 the Great Parterre followed, from which a few parts have been preserved.

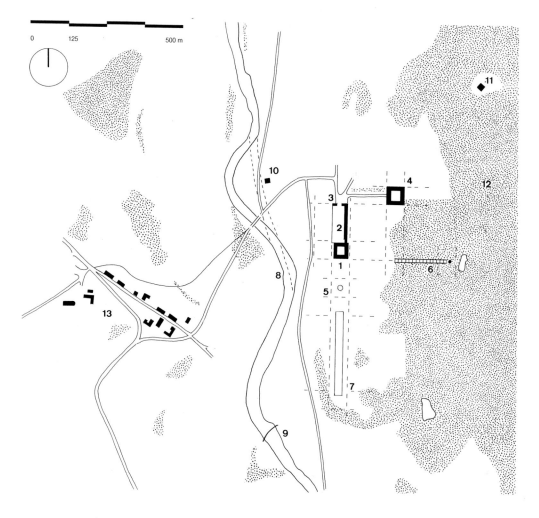

Fig 4 The landscape garden, 1756

1. Chatsworth House
2. North Wing by James Paine
3. Entrance by James Paine
4. Stables
5. Sea Horse Fountain
6. Cascade and Cascade House
7. Canal Pond, 1703
8. Repositioned Derwent River
9. Dam
10. Queen Mary's Bower
11. The Stand/Hunting Tower
12. Stand Wood
13. Edensor

The layout of Chatsworth was formed by a rational square grid, parallel to the course of the Derwent and the edge of the escarpment of East Moor, based on the size of the house. When compared with Blenheim estate, it would seem that the use of a design grid must have been mainly an idea of Henry Wise. The rational matrix, held up in Brown's landscape garden and in Paxton's Victorian design, was again the co-ordinating structure for the further extensions.

The arrangement of the garden and the avenues in the parkland outside the garden were designed on the lines of the matrix. The estate was enclosed by a wall which also incorporated a part of the parkland on its north side. The actual garden within this was bounded by a second wall and divided into three north to south areas of parterres, lawns with fountains and orchards, as well as a *bosco*. On the north side was an enclosed courtyard, flanked by a reflecting pool (fig. 3).

In 1696 the Frenchman Grillet, a pupil of Le Nôtre, designed the cascade, comprising 24 steps of irregular length, on one of the lines of the matrix. The cascade house, built by Thomas Archer (1668-1743) in 1703, contained an ingenious system of water jets and water games in the dome and the floor of its interior. The canal pond, some 100 metres long, was dug out in 1702 of a former hill, which had restricted the view from the house across the valley. The level of the pond is about 10 centimetres higher than the South Lawn, so that the house seen from the south side appears to rise out of the water.

THE LANDSCAPE GARDEN OF 1756

Around 1740 William Kent proposed a large cascade and various temples for Stand Hill but this was never carried out. In 1756 Lancelot 'Capability' Brown was commissioned to replan the garden. Paine designed new stables on the north side of the house in 1763, while the fish ponds on the west side were drained. The Derwent, which had hardly played a role from the viewpoint of the garden, was widened by building a dam and the bend in the river on the north-west side of the house was lengthened to improve the view.

Around 1761 Brown designed the new Park Drive along the western boundary of the estate. Arriving from Beeley, the visitor was led through the rolling landscape, across Paine's new bridge, to the north entrance, where there was a view of the house and garden against the backdrop of Stand Wood. The part of Edensor village which was in the direct line of vision of the house was pulled down, while the entrances at Beeley and Baslow had gates and lodges built. The parterre around the cascade was changed into the rolling Salisbury Lawns and clumps of plantings linked it with Stand Wood on the hill.

Brown added many tree plantings. He created a woodland area not only of Stand Hill, on the east side of the house, as a new backdrop but also of New Piece and Lindup Wood on the hills of the south-west side. Thus the desolate hills of East Moor on the east side disappeared from view. This panoramic design increased the visual unity of the parkland though at the expense of visual contrasts (fig. 4).

THE VICTORIAN GARDEN, 1826-50

Joseph Paxton, who came to work at Chatsworth later than Wyatville, took the existing garden, including the Broad Walk from 1820 (which according to the 6th Duke was 'Wyatville's first great hit out of doors'), as a starting point: neither the garden nor the parkland were redesigned (aside from Edensor, which was probably not Paxton's idea). Paxton placed the emphasis on newly acquired 19th century techniques and the sharply contrasting visual effects of the picturesque. At the same time, however, the garden became more firmly anchored in the original design matrix (fig. 5).

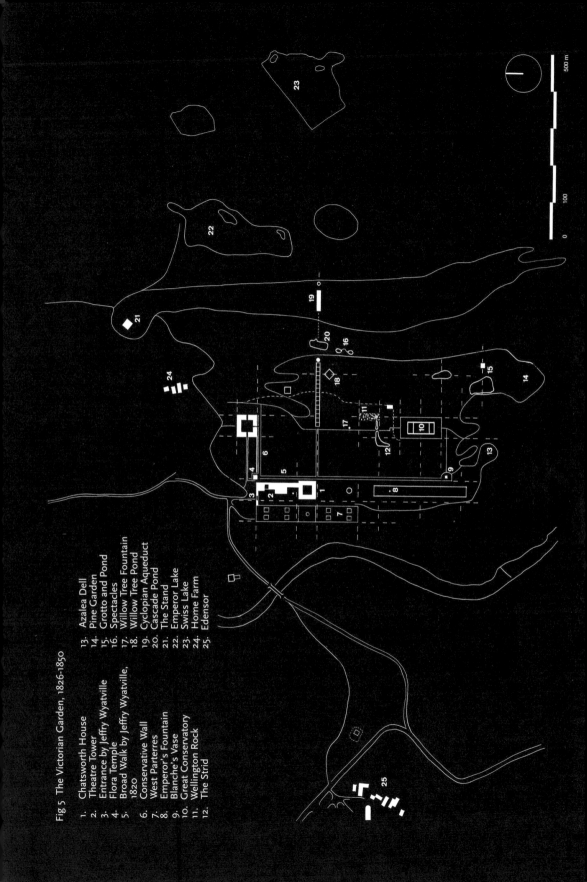

Fig 5 The Victorian Garden, 1826-1850

1. Chatsworth House
2. Theatre Tower
3. Entrance by Jeffry Wyatville
4. Flora Temple
5. Broad Walk by Jeffry Wyatville,
    1820
6. Conservative Wall
7. West Parterres
8. Emperor's Fountain
9. Blanche's Vase
10. Great Conservatory
11. Wellington Rock
12. The Strid

13. Azalea Dell
14. Pine Garden
15. Grotto and Pond
16. Spectacles
17. Willow Tree Fountain
18. Willow Tree Pond
19. Cyclopian Aqueduct
20. Cascade Pond
21. The Stand
22. Emperor Lake
23. Swiss Lake
24. Home Farm
25. Edensor

500 m

100

0

Joseph Paxton's Edensor with The Stand in the background

The Cyclopian Aqueduct is situated in line with the existing cascade, facing Stand Wood and is therefore in line with one of the most important lines of the design matrix. In this way Paxton introduced a much larger scale into the garden as well as achieving a new balance with the Derwent valley, the deer park and Edensor village on the other side. This went hand in hand with a stunning visual effect: when seen over the cascade, the aqueduct's column of water appears to tumble from the sky.

Paxton designed the Emperor Fountain in the canal pond to mark the visit of Tsar Nicholas II of Russia in 1843, but the visit never took place. Lake Emperor was made on East Moor, a dam covering two hectares and fed by drains in the moor. The natural water pressure was sufficient for a fountain that threw a water jet 80 metres high. The water was transported via a watercourse, 2.5 kilometres long, hewn out of the rocks and double acting valves set it at the correct pressure.

In 1842 there was still no trace of the rockery that today faces Stand Wood. The sheer size of Paxton's creation with its gigantic rocks is far removed from the rock garden that took hold of the landscape garden during the 18th century. Paxton's main concern was not the plants but the composition or picturesque assemblage of the natural rocks. An artificial waterfall, 15 metres high, tumbles from Wellington Rock and flows into Strid Pond, named after a small ravine at Bolton Abbey in Yorkshire. Thus a wild landscape was again represented *in* the garden.

Within a few years Paxton had turned Chatsworth House into a centre for botanical research. Expeditions were made to North and South Africa as well as to the Far East to collect specimens. Along the north garden wall Paxton made the Conservative Wall, a series of wooden wall cases for growing plants. The most spectacular was the design for the Great Conservatory (The Lily House), a huge greenhouse covering 3,000 square metres, built of glass, wood and cast iron between 1863-40 by Paxton

View from the Cyclopian Aqueduct of 'Capability' Brown's park landscape

Chatsworth from the west, 1993

and Decimus Burton (1800-81) after years of experimenting. In 1916 when Britain was at war, the authorities did not allow it to be stoked and thus it meant the end for the tropical plants. The greenhouse was torn down in 1920.

A small underground train delivered the coals to stoke the kettles used to heat the greenhouse, made visible in a grotto south of The Strid. The smoke was carried away by an underground chimney to Stand Wood. Paxton expanded on the duality between the utopian ideal of the greenhouse and the technology that lay behind it. The chimney was transformed into a monument and became part of the pine gardens.

In 1829, 3.5 hectares of parkland to the south of the garden was enclosed and Paxton began laying out a pine garden. In 1835 the arboretum was designed according to a botanical classification system. Paxton created a hermitage where a fish pond had earlier marked the boundary between the garden and the surrounding park, and left the skeletons of dying oak trees that had once been part of medieval Sherwood Forest.

Around 1840 ancient Edensor village, east of the Park Drive, was pulled down and replaced by a picturesque model village designed by Paxton. This was concealed between two transverse valleys of the Derwent and was linked via a gatehouse to the park landscape where cattle grazed. Paxton lies buried in Edensor.

The waterworks at Chatsworth suggest those of Villa Pratolino in its heyday. Paxton was a technical maestro employing various water forms, such as a spring, waterfall, mountain stream, cascade and fountain. The Mannerist tradition of his illustrious predecessors Isaac and Solomon de Caus and Stephen Switzer had an unexpected sequel.

The rainwater of East Moor was collected via drains in Emperor Lake and Swiss Lake and, by natural water pressure, fed the cascade and fountains at Chatsworth. There are three water sources that flow from the plateau to the Derwent: the cascade, the waterfall of Wellington Rock and The Strid and the stream from Grotto Pond. These three lines of water come together in the garden culminating in a play of fountains and reflecting pools.

THE APOTHEOSIS OF 300 YEARS OF GARDEN DESIGN

Chatsworth is the garden of all gardens, magnificently regular and, with an unrivalled wealth of detail and contrasts, it is the apotheosis of 300 years of landscape design. Paxton provided a definitive synopsis of the entire visual spectrum of the 18th-century landscape garden. Brown understood that the discrepancy between the low-lying garden and the surrounding hilly landscape (still partly wild at the time) was an essential feature of Chatsworth. Paxton took this as a starting point. By making this contrast more pronounced across the entire reach of the 18th-century park landscape, he created a visual synthesis which surpassed the dialectics of Brown's composition.

Paxton succeeded in accentuating Chatsworth's visual contrasts and in combining these with the planning and building technology of the 19th-century industrial city. His experiments, perhaps more than Repton's design technique, laid the foundation for controlling the landscape architecture of the urban design.

BIBLIOGRAPHY

• Ackerman, J.S., 'The Belvedere as a classical villa', in: *Journal of the Warburg and Courtauld Institutes*, 16/1951
• Ackerman, J.S., *The Cortile del Belvedere*, Vatican City 1954
• Ackerman, J.S., *Palladio's Villas*, New York 1967
• Acton, H., *Gamberaia*, Florence 1971
• Acton, H., *The Villas of Tuscany*, London 1984
• Adams, W.H., *The French garden*, New York 1979
• Alberti, L.B., *De re aedificatoria*, Firenze 1485, ed. Ticozzi, Milano 1883
• Aldrich, H., *Elementa Architecturae Civilis*, 1750
• Appleton, J., 'Some Thoughts on the Geology of the Picturesque', in: *Journal of Garden History*, nr 6/1986
• Argan G.C., *Sul concetto di tipologia architettonica, Progetto e destino*, Milano, 1965
• Argan, G.C., *The Renaissance city*, New York 1969
• Atkyns, J.T., *Iter Boreale*, 1732
• Bafile, M., *Villa Giulia, L'architettura, il giardino*, Istituto d'archeologia e storia dell'arte Opera d'arte, Fascicolo 14, Rome 1948
• Baltrusaitis, J., *Anamorphoses, ou magie artificielle des effets merveilleux*, Paris 1969
• Bargellini C. and P. de la Ruffinière du Prey, 'Sources for a reconstruction of the Villa Medici. Fiesole', in: *Burlington Magazine*, vol. CXI nr. 799, oct. 1969
• Batey, M. and Lambert D., *The English Garden Tour. A view into the Past*, London 1990
• Battisti, E., 'Natura Artificiosa to Natura Artificialis', in: D.R. Coffin (ed.), *The Italian Garden*. Washington, DC & Dumbarton Oaks 1972
• Beard, G., *The work of Sir John Vanbrugh*, London 1986
• Bell, E.T., *Les grands mathématiciens*, Paris 1950
• Belli Barsali, I. and M.G. Branchetti, *Ville della Campagna Romana*, Milano 1975
• Belli Barsali, I., *Ville di Roma*, Milano 1983
• Benedetti, S., *Giacomo Del Duca e l'architettura del Cinquecento*, Roma 1972
• Benevolo, L., *The Architecture of the Renaissance*, London 1978
• Bentmann R. and M. Müller, *Die Villa als Herrschaftsarchitektur*, Frankfurt a/M., 1970
• Bigot, P., *Rome Antique au IV Siècle*, Paris 1942

• Blunt, A., *Guide to Baroque Rome*, London/New York 1982
• Bold, J. and J. Reeves, *Wilton House and English Palladianism*, London 1988
• Boyceau, J., *Traité du jardinage selon les raisons de la nature et de l'art*, Paris 1638
• Braunfels, W., *Mittelalterliche Stadtbaukunst in der Toskana*, Berlin 1953
• Bredekamp, H., *Vicino Orsini und der heilige Wald von Bomarzo*, 2 vols., Worms 1985
• Brinckmann, A.E., *Stadtbaukunst in der Vergangenheit*, 2 Aufl. Frankfurt 1921
• Brockett, O.G., *History of the Theatre*, Boston/London 1991 (1968)
• Bruschi, A., *Bramante architetto*, Bari 1969
• Buckle, R., *Harewood. A New Guide Book to the Yorkshire Seat of the Earls of Harewood*, Derby 1972 (1959, 1962)
• Burke, E., *Philosophical Inquiry into the Origins of our Ideas of the Sublime and the Beautiful*, 1756
• Burke, J., *English Art 1714-1800*, Oxford 1976
• Bury, J.B., 'Review Essay: Bomarzo Revisited', in: *Journal of Garden History*, 1985, pp. 213-223
• Calvino, I., *Invisible cities*, New York 1974
• Campbell, C., *Vitruvius brittanicus*, vols. I, II, III (1715, 1717, 1725)
• Campos, D.R. de, *I palazzi Vaticani*, Bologna 1967
• Caneva, C., *Boboli Gardens*, Florence 1982
• Carli, E., *Pienza*, Basel/Stuttgart 1965
• Casotti, M.W., *Il Vignola*, 2 vols, Trieste 1960
• Castell, R., *The villas of the ancients illustrated*, London 1728. Reprinted London & New York 1982
• Castex, J. et al., *Lecture d'une ville: Versailles*, Paris 1980
• Cevese, R., *I modelli della mostra del Palladio*, Venezia 1976
• Chadwick, G.F., *The works of Sir Joseph Paxton 1803-1865*, London 1961
• Chambers, D.D.C., *The Planters of the English Landscape Garden*, New Haven/London 1993
• Charageat, M., 'André le Nôtre et l'optique de son temps', in: *Bulletin de la Société de l'Histoire de l'Art Français*, 1955
• Chatfield, J., *A Tour of Italian Gardens*, New York 1988
• Chiavo, A., *Pienza*, Milano 1942
• Clarke, G., 'Ancient and Medieval Stowe', in: *Stoic* XXII, March 1967

• Clarke, G., 'Sir Richard Temple's House and Gardens', in: *Stoic* XXIII, March 1968
• Clarke, G., 'Vanbrugh-Bridgeman Gardens', in: *Stoic* XXIII, July 1969
• Clarke, G., 'The Gardens of Stowe', in: *Apollo* Vol. 97 June 1973, pp. 558-565
• Clarke, G., 'Grecian Taste and Gothic Virtue: Lord Cobham's gardening programme and its iconography', in: *Apollo* Vol. 97 June 1973, pp. 566-571
• Clarke, G., P. Inskip, R. Wheeler, *English Arcadia. The Landscape and Buildings of Stowe*, Huntington Library, San Marino California 1992
• Cobham, R., 'Brown in Memoriam: Blenheim Park in Perpetuity', in: *Landscape Design*, 12/1983
• Coffin, D.R., *The Villa d'Este at Tivoli*, Princeton 1960
• Coffin, D.R., *The Villa in the Life of Renaissance Rome*, Princeton, New Jersey 1979
• Colonna, Fra. F. (attributed to), *Hypnerotomachia poliphili*, Venice 1499, Ed. Methuen. London 1904
• Comito, T., *The Idea of the Garden in the Renaissance*, New Brunswick, New Jersey 1978
• Conrad-Martius, H., *Der Raum*, Munich 1958
• Constant, C., *The Palladio Guide*, London 1987
• Cooper, A.A. 3rd Earl of Shaftesbury, *The Moralists. A Philosophical Rhapsody*, 1709
• Cooper, A.A. 3rd Earl of Shaftesbury, *Characteristics of Men, Manners, Opinions, Times*, 1711
• Cornforth, J., 'Chatsworth, Derbyshire V, VI and IX. A seat of the Duke of Devonshire', in: *Country Life*, April 1968, pp. 146-49, pp. 220-23 and pp. 552-55
• Corpechot, L., *Parcs et jardins de France*, Paris 1937
• Crandell, G., *Nature Pictorialized. The 'View' in Landscape History*, Baltimore/London 1993
• Cunningham, P. (ed.), *The letters of Horace Walpole*, Vol.3. London 1891
• D'Argenville, *La Théorie et la Pratique du Jardinage*, 1709
• De Caus, S., *La perspective avec la raison des ombres et miroirs*, Londres 1612
• De Caus, I., *Le Jardin de Wilton*, Paris 1645
• Defoe D., *A Tour through the Whole Island of Great Britain*, 3 vols., London 1738
• Desmond, R., *Bibliography of British Gardens*, Winchester (Hampshire) 1984

• Devonshire Duchess of, *The Garden at Chatsworth*, 1990
• Devonshire, the 6th Duke of, *Handbook of Chatsworth and Hardwick*, 1844
• Dijk, H. van and D. Lambert, 'Een vraaggesprek met Bernard Tschumi' ['An interview with Bernard Tschumi'], in: *Archis*, 9/1988
• Dixon Hunt, J., *Garden and Grove: The Italian Renaissance Garden in the English Imagination: 1600-1750*, London 1986
• Dixon Hunt, J., *William Kent. Landscape garden designer*, London 1987
• Dixon Hunt, J., *Gardens and the Picturesque. Studies in the History of Landscape Architecture*, Cambridge Massachusetts/London 1992
• Dixon Hunt, J. and De Jong, E. (eds.), *The Anglo-Dutch Garden in the Age of William and Mary*, (Journal of Garden History, no's 2 and 3 - special), 1988
• Dixon Hunt, J. and P. Willis (eds.) *The Genius of the Place. The English Landscape Garden 1620-1820*, London 1975
• Elliot, B., *Victorian Gardens*, London 1986
• Estienne, C., *Praedium Rusticum*, Lutetiae 1564 (L'Agriculture en maison rustique 1564 - From 1572 onward with additions by Jean Liébault)
• Evelyn, J., *Fumifugium, or the Inconvenience of the Aer and Smoke dissipated*, London 1660
• Faccini, M., *Guida ai giardini d'Italia*, Milano 1983
• Fagiolo, M. and A. Rinaldi, 'Artifex et/aut natura', in: *Lotus International* (1981), pp. 113-127
• Falk, T., 'Studien zur Topographie und Geschichte der Villa Giulia in Rom', in: *Römisches Jahrbuch für Kunstgeschichte*, XIII/1971
• Fanelli, G., *Firenze, Architettura e Citta*, Firenze 1973
• Fanelli, G., *Brunelleschi*, Firenze 1977
• Firth, I.J.W., 'Landscape Management: The Conservation of a Capability Brown Landscape - Harewood, Yorkshire', in: *Landscape Planning*, Vol. 7 no 2 May 1980, pp. 121-149
• Fleming, L. and A. Gore, *The English Garden*, London 1979
• Foster, P.E., *A study of Lorenzo de Medici's villa at Poggio a Caiano*, New York/London 1978
• Franck, C., *Die Barock-villen in Frascati*, Munich 1956
• Frankl, P., *Die Entwicklungsfasen der neueren Baukunst*, Leipzig/Berlin, 1914
• Furttenbach, *Architectura civilis*, 1628
• Gadol, J., *Leon Battista Alberti, Universal Man of the Early Renaissance*, Chicago 1969

• Gaehtgens, T., *Napoleons Arc de Triomphe*, Göttingen 1974
• Ganay, E. de, *André le Nostre*, Paris 1962
• Gebser, J., *Ursprung und Gegenwart*, vol. I: *Die Fundamente der aperspektivischen Welt*, Stuttgart 1949
• Giacomo, L., *The Architecture of A. Palladio*, Revis'd, Design'd and publish'd by Giacomo Leoni, a Venetian, Architect to his most Serene Highness the Elector Palatine, 1715-16, 2 vols.
• Gilpin, W., *Observations... on Several Parts of England: Particularly the Mountains, and Lakes of Cumberland and Westmoreland*, London 1786
• Gilpin, W., *Three Essays: On Picturesque Beauty; On Picturesque Travel; and On Sketching Landscape*, 1794
• Girouard, M., *Life in the English Country House. A Social and Architectural History*, New Haven/London 1978
• Gothein, M.L., *Geschichte der Gartenkunst*, 2 vols., Jena 1914
• Harris, J., *The Artist and the Country House*, London 1977
• Harris, J. and A. Tait, *Catalogue of the Drawings by Inigo Jones, John Webb and Isaac de Caus at Worcester College*, Worcester 1979
• Hautecoeur, L., *Histoire de l'architecture classique en France*, Paris 1948
• Hazlehurst, F.H., *Jacques Boyceau and the French Formal Garden*, Georgia 1966
• Hazlehurst, F.H., *Gardens of Illusion*, Nashville/Tennessee 1980
• Heydenrich, J., 'Pius II als Bauherr von Pienza', in: *Zeitschrift für Kunstgeschichte*, VI/1936
• Hillairet, J., *Dictionnaire Historique des Rues de Paris*, Paris 1963
• Hobbes, Th., *De mirabilis pecci; being the Wonders of the Peak*, London 1638
• Hogarth, W., *The Analysis of Beauty*, 1753
• Hoskins, W.G., *The Making of the English Landscape*, London 1970 (1955)
• Hume, D., *Treatise on Human Nature*, 1739
• Hume, D., *Enquiry Concerning Human Understanding*, 1758
• Hunter, J., 'The Pre-industrial Countryside of Lowland England. Its Appearance and Management', in: *Landscape Design* nr 126, May 1979
• Hussey, Ch., *The Picturesque: Studies in a Point of View*, Connecticut 1967 (1927)
• Hussey, Ch., 'A Georgian Arcady, II', in: *Country Life*, June 1946
• Hussey, Ch., 'Introduction' (1950) in: Dorothy Stroud, *Capability Brown*, London 1975 (1950)
• Hussey, Ch., 'Gardens of Wilton House, Wiltshire, I, II and III, in: *Country Life*, 7-8-9/1963

• Hussey, Ch., *English gardens and landscapes 1700 - 1750*, London 1967
• Ivins, W.M., *On the Rationalization of Sight, De Artificiali Perspectiva*, New York 1973
• Jackson-Stops, G., *Sharawadgi Rediscovered. The Chinese House at Stowe*, Apollo 1993
• Jacques, D., *Georgian Gardens. The Reign of Nature*, London 1983
• James, S., *Exploring the World of the Celts*, London 1993
• Jeannel, B., *Le Nôtre*, Paris 1985
• Jellicoe, G. et al., *Italian Gardens of the Renaissance*, London 1966
• Jellicoe, G. et al., *The Oxford Companion to Gardens*, Oxford/New York 1987
• Jonathan Richardson the Elder, *Two Discourses on the Art of Criticism in so far it [is] related to Painting, and the Science of a Connoisseur*, 1719
• Jong, E. de, *Natuur en Kunst. Nederlandse tuin- en landschapsarchitectuur 1650-1740* [Nature and Art. Dutch Garden- and Landscape Architecture 1650–1740], Amsterdam 1993
• Jourdain, M., *The Work of William Kent*, 1948
• Karling, S., *The French Formal Garden*, Washington 1974
• Kask, T., *Symmetrie und Regelmässigkeit, Französische Architektur im Grand Siècle*, Basel/Stuttgart 1971
• Kent, W., *Designs of Inigo Jones, with some Additional Designs*, 2 vols., 1727
• Kerber, B., *Andrea Pozzo*, New York 1971
• Knight Payne, R., *The Landscape*, London 1794
• Knight Payne, R., *An Analytical Enquiry into the Principles of Taste*, 1794
• Komrij, G., *Over de noodzaak van tuinieren* [About the Necessity of Gardening], Amsterdam 1991
• Kristeller, P.O., *Eight Philosophers of the Italian Renaissance*, Stanford, California 1964
• Lamb, C., *Die Villa d'Este in Tivoli*, Munich 1966
• Lang, S., 'Bomarzo', in: *The Architectural Review* (1957), pp. 427-430
• Lascelles, G., 7th Earl of Harewood, *Harewood House, Yorkshire. Home of the Earl and Countess of Harewood*, Oxford s.d.
• Laugier, M.A., *Essai sur l'Architecture*, Paris 1755
• Lavedan, P., *Histoire de l'urbanisme: Renaissance et temps modernes*, vol. 2, Paris 1952
• Lazzaro, C., *The Italian Renaissance Garden*, New Haven & London 1990
• Leeman, F. et al., *Anamorfosen*, Cologne 1975
• Lees-Milne, J., *Earls of Creation*, London 1962

• Lees-Milne, J., 'Chatsworth, Derbyshire I. A seat of the Duke of Devonshire', in: *Country Life*, April 1968, pp. 890-93
• Lemmon, K., *The Covered Garden*, London 1962
• Ligorio, P., *L'Antiquità*, Rome *c.* 1560
• Linnaeus, *Species plantarum*, 1753
• Lipsius, J., *De constantia in publicis malis*, 1584
• Locke, J., *Essay Concerning Human Understanding*, 1690
• Lord Burlington, *Fabbriche antiche disegnate da Andrea Palladio Vicentino*, 1730
• Loudon, J.C (ed.), *The Landscape Gardening and Landscape Architecture of the Late Humphrey Repton*, London 1840
• Loukomski, G., *Vignole*, Paris 1927
• Lurcat, A., *Formes, composition et lois d'harmonie*, t. 5, Paris 1954
• MacDougall, E., 'Ars Hortulorum: Sixteenth Century Garden Iconography and Literary Theory in Italy', in: D.R. Coffin (ed.), *The Italian Garden*, Washington, DC & Dumbarton Oaks 1972
• MacDougall, E., 'The Sleeping Nimph, Origins of a Humanist Fountain Type', in: *Art Bulletin* 57/1975, p. 365
• Malins, E., *English Landscaping and Literature, 1660-1840*, Oxford 1966
• Mariage, T., 'L'univers de le Nostre et les origines de l'aménagement du territoire', in: *Monuments Historiques*, no. 143, février/mars 1986
• Marie, A., *Jardins Francais Classiques des XVIIe et XVIIIe siècle*, Paris 1949
• Markham, V., *Paxton and the Bachelor Duke*, 1935
• Martin, P., *Pursuing Innocent Pleasures. The Gardening World of Alexander Pope*, Connecticut 1984
• Masson, G., *Italian Gardens*, London 1987
• Mauchline, M., *Harewood House*, Exeter 1974
• Mignani, D., *Le Ville Medicee di Giusto Utens*, Firenze 1982
• Mingay, G.E., *The Gentry. The Rise and Fall of a Ruling Class*, London/New York 1976
• Moggridge, H., 'Blenheim Park. The Restoration Plan', in: *Landscape Design* 12/1983
• Moggridge, H., 'Notes on Kent's Garden at Rousham', in: *Journal of Garden History* no 3, Sept. 1986
• Montaigne, M. de, *Giornale di Viaggio in Italia*, Milano 1956
• Montgomery-Massingberd, H., *Blenheim Revisited. The Spencer-Churchills and their palace*, London 1985
• Morini, M., *Atlante di Storia dell' Urbanistica*, Milano 1963

• Mosser M., 'The Impossible Quest for the Past: Thoughts on the Restoration of Gardens', in: M. Mosser and G. Teyssot, *The History of Garden Design*, London 1991
• Mosser, M. and Teyssot G., *The History of Garden Design. The Western Tradition from the Renaissance to the Present Day*, London 1991
• Murray, P., *The Architecture of the Italiano Renaissance*, London 1963
• Nobile, B.M., *I giardini d'Italia*, Bologna 1984
• Oswald, A., 'Hawkstone Hall, Shropshire I and II. Formerly the seat of the Hills', in: *Country Life* April 1958, pp. 640-43 and 698-701
• Oswald, A., 'Beauties and Wonders of Hawkstone. Nature and Artifice in a Shropshire Park' (2 vols.), *Country Life*, July 1958
• Ovidius Naso, P., *Metamorphoses*, ed. Hondius, J.J. a.o., Groningen 1959
• Palissy, B., *Récepte Véritable*, La Rochelle 1563
• Palladio, A., *I Quattro libri dell'architettura*, Venice 1570; English translation: *The Four Books of Architecture*, London 1965
• Panofsky, E., *Hercules am Scheidewege*, Leipzig 1930
• Pascal, B., *Pensées*, Dutch translation by J. Lenders, Utrecht-Antwerpen 1962
• Patzak, B., *Die Renaissance und Barockvilla in Italien*, Leipzig 1913
• Paul Lévy, P., *La ville en croix*, Paris 1984
• Paulson, R., *Emblem and Expression: Meaning in English Art of the Eighteenth Century*, London 1975
• Pawson, E., *Transport and Economy: The Turnpike Roads of Eighteenth Century Britain*, New York/San Francisco, 1977
• Paxton, J., 'Design for Forming Subscription Gardens in the vicinity of Large Commercial Towns', in: *The Horticultural Register and General Magazine* 1/1831, pp. 58-61
• Pearsall, D. and E. Salter, *Landscapes and seasons of the medieval world*, London 1973
• Pechere, R., *Jardins dessinés, grammaire des jardins*, Brussels 1987
• Pedretti, C., *Leonardo da Vinci on Painting, a Lost Book (libro A)*, Berkeley/Los Angeles 1964
• Peneira, A., *American Express Pocket Guide to Rome*, London 1983
• Pevsner, N., *The Englishness of English Art*, London 1956
• Pevsner, N., 'Genesis of the Picturesque', in: *Studies in Art, Architecture and Design*, London 1968 (*Architectural Review* XCVL/1944)
• Pevsner, N. (ed.), *The Picturesque Garden and its Influence outside the British Isles*, Dumbarton Oaks, Washington 1974

• Pfnor, R. et al., *Le Château de Vaux-le-Vicomte*, Paris 1888
• Pieper, J., 'Pienza', in: *Forum* 30/1, 1986, pp. 44 et seq.
• Piper, F.M., *Beskrifning öfwer Idéen och General-Plann till en Ångelsk Lustpark*, Stockholm 1799
• Piranesi, G.B., *Antichità Romane*, 1756
• Plantenga, J., *Versailles*, Amsterdam 1939
• Pliny the Younger (trans. W. Melmoth), *Letters*, Cambridge/London 1961
• Pope, A., *An Essay on Criticism, Written in the Year 1709*, 1711
• Pope, A., *An Epistel to Lord Burlington*, 1731
• Pope, A., *The Dunciad*, 1743
• Portoghesi, P., *Rome of the Renaissance*, London 1972
• Price, U., *Essays on the Picturesque, as Compared with the Sublime and the Beautiful, 1794*, 3 vols., (Reissued) Farnborough 1971
• Publications Elysées, *Vaux-le-Vicomte*, Maincy s.d.
• Puppi, L. 'The Villa Garden of the Veneto from the Fifteenth to the Eighteenth Century', in D.R. Coffin (ed.): *The Italian Garden*, Washington DC/Dumbarton Oaks 1972
• Puppi, L., *Andrea Palladio*, Venice 1973
• Puppi, L., *Andrea Palladio. Das Gesamtwerk*, Stuttgart 1977
• Redig, de Campos, Deoclecio, *I palazzi Vaticani*, Bologna 1967
• Ree, P. van der, Smienk, G., Steenbergen, C.M., *Italian Villas and Gardens, A corso di disegno*, Amsterdam/Munich/London 1991
• Reh, W., 'Voorbij de videoclip [Emulating the videoclip]. Een panorama van fragmenten, schijngestalten en herinneringen', in: *Nederlandse landschapsarchitectuur. Tussen traditie en experiment [Dutch Landscape Architecture. Between Tradition and Experiment]*), Amsterdam 1993
• Reh, W., Arcadia en Metropolis. Het landschapsexperiment van de Verlichting. ['Arcadia and Metropolis. The landscape experiment of the Enlightenment'], Delft 1996
• Repton, H., *Observations on the Theory and Practice of Landscape Gardening*, London 1803
• Robinson, J.M., *Temples of Delight. Stowe Landscape Gardens*, London 1990
• Rosenau, H., *The Ideal City in its Architectural Evolution*, London 1959
• Ross, J., *Lives of the Early Medici as told in their Correspondence*, Boston 1911
• Rousseau, J.-J., *Discours sur les arts et les sciences*, Geneva 1750
• Saalman, H., *Filippo Brunelleschi, the Cupola of S.M. del Fiore*, 1980

• Saint Sauveur, H., *Châteaux de France*, Paris 1948
• Saint-Amant, Ch. de, *Le Second Versailles*, Paris 1854
• Saumarez Smith, Ch., *The building of Castle Howard*, London 1990
• Saxl, F. and R. Wittkower, *British Art and the Mediterranean*, London 1948
• Schöne, G., 'Die Entwicklung der Perpektivbühne von Serlio bis Galli-Bibiena', in: *Theatergeschichtliche Forschungen* Heft 43. Leipzig 1977 (1933)
• Sciolla, G., *Ville Medicee*, Istituto Geografico de Agostini-novara 1982
• Serlio, S., *Libri d'Architettura*, Paris 1545
• Serres, Olivier de, *Agriculture ou mesnage des champs*, Paris 1600
• Shepherd, J.C. & G.A. Jellicoe, *Italian Gardens of the Renaissance*, London 1986
• Smith, A., *An Inquiry into the Nature and Causes of the Wealth of Nations*, 1776
• Speckter, H., *Paris, Städtebau von der Renaissance bis zur Neuzeit*, Munich 1964
• Steenbergen, C. M., *De stap over de horizon. Een ontleding van het formele ontwerp in de landschapsarchitectuur* [*The Step over the Horizon. An Analysis of the Formal Design in Landscape Architecture*], Delft 1990
• Steenbergen, C.M., 'Teatro Rustico. The formal strategy and grammar of landscape architecture', in: *Modern Park Design. Recent Trends*, Amsterdam 1993
• Steenbergen, C.M., De poëzie van de vlakte [The Poetics of the Dutch Landscape), in: *Nederlandse landschapsarchitectuur. Tussen traditie en experiment* [*Dutch Landscape Architecture. Between Tradition and Experiment*], Amsterdam 1993
• Stegman, C. & H. Geymüller, *Die Architectur der Renaissance in Toscana*, vol. 2, Munich 1885-93
• Stein, O., *Die Architecturtheoretiker der Italienischen Renaissance*, Karlsruhe 1914
• Sterne, L., *Life and Opinions of Tristram Shandy, Gentleman*, 9 vols., London 1760-67
• Strong, R., *The Renaissance Garden in England*, London 1979
• Stroud, D., *'Capability' Brown*, London 1975
• Stukeley, W., *Itinerarium curiosum*, 2 vols., London 1776
• Summerson, J., *Heavenly Mansions and Other Essays on Architecture IV. John Wood and the English Town Planning Tradition*, London 1949
• Summerson, J., 'The Classical Country House in 18th-Century England', in: *Journal of the Royal Society of Arts*, vol. CVII, July 1959

• Summerson, J., *Georgian London*, London 1988 (1962)
• Switzer, S., *Ichnographia Rustica* (3 vols.), London 1718
• Switzer, S., *Nobleman, Gentleman and Gardener's Recreation*, 1718
• Switzer, S., *An Introduction to a General System of Hydrostatics and Hydraulics*, 1729
• Tanzer, H., *The Villas of Pliny the Younger*, New York 1924
• Temple, Sir William, *Gardens of Epicure*, 1685
• Thomas, K., *Man and the Natural World. Changing Attitudes in England 1500-1800*, London 1983
• Thompson, F., *A History of Chatsworth*, Country Life, 1949
• Thompson, F., *Chatsworth, a Short History*, Country Life, 1951
• Tolsen, A.R. and M.E. Johnstone, *A Geography of Britain*, London 1970
• Trueman, A.E., *Geology and Scenery in England and Wales*, Pelican Books 1948
• Turner, R., *Capability Brown and the eighteenth-century English landscape*, London 1985
• Veltman, K.H., *Studies on Leonardo da Vinci I, Linear Perspective and the Visual Dimensions of Science and Art*, Munich 1986
• Venturini, *Le fontane del Giardino Estese in Tivoli*, Rome s.d.
• Vero, R, *Understanding perspective*, New York/Cincinnati 1980
• Vidler, A, The production of types, in: *Oppositions*, nr 8/1977
• Vidler, A, *The Third Typology. Rational/Rationelle Architecture*, Brussels 1978
• Vitruvius, *De architectura libri decem*, English translation: *The Ten Books on Architecture*, London 1960
• Walding Ass., *Hawkstone. A Short History and Guide*, Shrewsbury 1993
• Walpole, H., *Essay on Modern Gardening*, London 1785
• Walpole, H., *Correspondence*, Arranged by W.S. Lewis (48 vols.). Oxford/New Haven 1937-1983
• Ware, I., *The Four Books of Architecture of Andrea Palladio*, 1738
• Watkin, D., *The English Vision. The Picturesque in Architecture, Landscape & Garden Design*, London 1982
• Whatley, T., *Observations on Modern Gardening*, 1765 (?)
• Wheatly, J.B., *Diary of Samuel Pepys*, London 1899
• Wheeler, R., 'The Park and Garden Survey at Stowe: The Replanting and Restoration of the Historical Landscape, in: The Huntington Library, *English Arcadia. The Landscape and Buildings of Stowe*, San Marino California 1992
• Whistler, L., *The Imagination of Vanbrugh and his Fellow Artists*, London 1954

• Whistler, L., *Stowe, a Guide to the Gardens*, London 1956
• Willebrand, J., *Grundriss einer schönen Stadt*, Hamburg/Leipzig 1775
• Willis, P., *Charles Bridgeman and the English Landscape Garden*, London 1977
• Wittkower, R., *Architectural Principles in the Age of Humanism*, London 1949
• Woodbridge, K., *Landscape and Antiquity: Aspects of English Culture at Stourhead 1718 to 1838*, Oxford 1970
• Woodbridge, K., 'William Kent's Gardening. The Rousham Letters', in: *Apollo* 100/1974, pp. 282-291
• Woodbridge, K., *The Stourhead Landscape*, The National Trust, Hampshire 1982
• Woodbridge, K., *Princely Gardens*, 1986
• Wotton, Sir Henry, *The Elements of Architecture*, 1624
• Wundram, M. & T. Pape, *Andrea Palladio*, Cologne 1988

INDEX

The figure set in **bold** type refers to an illustration.